HENRY THE FOURTH, *PART I*

REVISED

An Authorized Text
Cultural Contexts
Extracts from the Major Sources
Essays in Criticism
Bibliography

NORTON CRITICAL EDITIONS

AUSTEN *Emma* edited by Stephen M. Parrish
AUSTEN *Pride and Prejudice* edited by Donald J. Gray
BRONTË, CHARLOTTE *Jane Eyre* edited by Richard J. Dunn
BRONTË, EMILY *Wuthering Heights*, Revised edited by William M. Sale, Jr.
CARROLL *Alice in Wonderland* edited by Donald J. Gray
CLEMENS *Adventures of Huckleberry Finn* edited by Sculley Bradley, Richmond Croom Beatty, and E. Hudson Long
CONRAD *Heart of Darkness*, Revised edited by Robert Kimbrough
CONRAD *Lord Jim* edited by Thomas Moser
CRANE *The Red Badge of Courage* edited by Sculley Bradley, Richmond Croom Beatty, and E. Hudson Long
Darwin edited by Philip Appleman
DEFOE *Moll Flanders* edited by Edward Kelly
DICKENS *Hard Times* edited by George Ford and Sylvère Monod
John Donne's Poetry selected and edited by A. L. Clements
DOSTOEVSKY *Crime and Punishment* (the Coulson translation) edited by George Gibian
DREISER *Sister Carrie* edited by Donald Pizer
FIELDING *Tom Jones* edited by Sheridan Baker
FLAUBERT *Madame Bovary* edited with a substantially new translation by Paul de Man
HARDY *The Return of the Native* edited by James Gindin
HARDY *Tess of the D'Urbervilles* edited by Scott Elledge
HAWTHORNE *The House of the Seven Gables* edited by Seymour L. Gross
HAWTHORNE *The Scarlet Letter* edited by Sculley Bradley, Richmond Croom Beatty, and E. Hudson Long
HOMER *The Odyssey* translated and edited by Albert Cook
IBSEN *The Wild Duck* translated and edited by Dounia B. Christiani
JAMES *The Ambassadors* edited by S. P. Rosenbaum
JAMES *The Turn of the Screw* edited by Robert Kimbrough
MELVILLE *The Confidence-Man* edited by Hershel Parker
MELVILLE *Moby-Dick* edited by Harrison Hayford and Hershel Parker
NEWMAN *Apologia Pro Vita Sua* edited by David J. DeLaura
The Writings of St. Paul edited by Wayne A. Meeks
SHAKESPEARE *Hamlet* edited by Cyrus Hoy
SHAKESPEARE *Henry IV, Part I*, Revised edited by James L. Sanderson
Bernard Shaw's Plays edited by Warren Sylvester Smith
SOPHOCLES *Oedipus Tyrannus* translated and edited by Luci Berkowitz and Theodore F. Brunner
Edmund Spenser's Poetry selected and edited by Hugh Maclean
STENDHAL *Red and Black* translated and edited by Robert M. Adams
SWIFT *Gulliver's Travels*, Revised edited by Robert A. Greenberg
The Writings of Jonathan Swift edited by Robert A. Greenberg and William B. Piper
TENNYSON *In Memoriam* edited by Robert Ross
Tennyson's Poetry selected and edited by Robert W. Hill, Jr.
THOREAU *Walden and Civil Disobedience* edited by Owen Thomas
TOLSTOY *Anna Karenina* (the Maude translation) edited by George Gibian
TOLSTOY *War and Peace* (the Maude translation) edited by George Gibian
TURGENEV *Fathers and Sons* edited with a substantially new translation by Ralph E. Matlaw
VOLTAIRE *Candide* translated and edited by Robert M. Adams
WHITMAN *Leaves of Grass* edited by Sculley Bradley and Harold W. Blodgett
A Norton Critical Edition of Modern Drama edited by Anthony Caputi
Restoration and Eighteenth-Century Comedy edited by Scott McMillin

A NORTON CRITICAL EDITION

Revised

WILLIAM SHAKESPEARE

HENRY THE FOURTH, *Part I*

AN AUTHORIZED TEXT

CULTURAL CONTEXTS

EXTRACTS FROM THE MAJOR SOURCES

ESSAYS IN CRITICISM

BIBLIOGRAPHY

Edited by

JAMES L. SANDERSON

RUTGERS UNIVERSITY

W · W · NORTON & COMPANY · INC · *New York*

W. W. NORTON & COMPANY, INC.
also publishes

THE NORTON ANTHOLOGY OF ENGLISH LITERATURE
edited by M. H. Abrams et al.

THE NORTON ANTHOLOGY OF MODERN POETRY
edited by Richard Ellmann and Robert O'Clair

THE NORTON ANTHOLOGY OF POETRY
edited by Arthur M. Eastman et al.

THE NORTON INTRODUCTION TO LITERATURE
edited by Carl E. Bain, Jerome Beaty, and J. Paul Hunter

WORLD MASTERPIECES
edited by Maynard Mack et al.

THE NORTON READER
edited by Arthur M. Eastman et al.

THE NORTON FACSIMILE OF
THE FIRST FOLIO OF SHAKESPEARE
prepared by Charlton Hinman

and the

NORTON CRITICAL EDITIONS

ISBN 0 393 04234 0 Cloth Edition
ISBN 0 393 09554 1 Paper Edition

Library of Congress Catalog Card No. 68-58749

PRINTED IN THE UNITED STATES OF AMERICA

5 6 7 8 9 0

CONTENTS

PREFACE TO THE SECOND EDITION

This revision offers something old and something new. The text of the play, the source materials, and the critical essays of the first edition have been retained; but a number of important additions have been made.

Among them are, first, selections from the first Quarto (1598) and the *Variorum* edition, which illustrate some of the editorial problems involved in a Shakespearean play and their solutions by a modern editor. Second, a new section, "Cultural Contexts," presents statements of ideas and attitudes representing important elements in the climate of opinion in which Shakespeare wrote the play. Third, eight essays have been added to "Essays in Criticism," most of them having appeared since the publication of the first edition. Wherever possible the essays have been reprinted in their entirety in the belief that students can profit from studying the authors' various critical approaches to the play and the development and support of their interpretations. Finally, the Bibliography has been revised and the annotated list of critical studies "refreshed" by new entries.

I gratefully acknowledge my debt to the writers and publishers who have permitted their work to be reprinted in this revision, to my wife, Rosamond, who has assisted me in proofreading it, and to those whose friendly reception of the first edition of this book has justified its second.

Camden, New Jersey
August 1968

James L. Sanderson

PREFACE

Since its first appearance on the stage in 1597 and in print in 1598, *Henry IV, Part I,* has been one of Shakespeare's most popular plays. The dramatization of the struggle for a kingdom, focused in the climactic and mortal competition of two attractive heroes, Prince Henry and Harry Percy ("Hotspur"), still commands our attention more than five hundred years after the historical event. To the contemplation of those sterner realities upon which the fates of kingdoms and individuals depend is added the inexhaustibly entertaining Falstaff, one of Shakespeare's most complex and most debated creations. With something of Cleopatra's "infinite variety," Falstaff eludes attempts to confine him in too narrow interpretational categories as nimbly as he carried himself away to safety one memorable night on Gad's Hill. As a result, his power to amuse and interest us remains fresh after more than three centuries. Whether he is in our minds a "sanguine coward" and a "villainous abominable misleader of youth" or "sweet," "kind," "true," and "valiant Jack Falstaff," or perhaps something of all of these, it is impossible not to like the source of so much fun. And it is equally impossible not to surrender, momentarily one hopes, to his timeless invitation, as Charles Lamb said in another context, "to take an airing from the diocese of the strict conscience."

The play's success on the stage has been equaled, perhaps surpassed, by its success in the quiet of the study. It has been reprinted many times and has received a large amount of scholarly and critical comment. The purpose of this edition of the play is to provide an annotated text and a generous sampling of this comment. Placing the text and the critical essays in the same volume suggests a mode of approach in studying the play. The student's own reading of the play is, of course, basic. The reading of secondary comment cannot be a satisfying substitute for a great literary work itself. But understanding a play and getting at its meaning involve also a consideration of what it has meant to other responsible readers. The scholarly and critical insights of those who have devoted a lifetime to the study of Shakespeare and critics who are graced with a special alertness to literary values can add that keener pleasure to the student's experience which comes from a more nearly complete understanding and appreciation of the play. Such insights are to be gained from the essays selected for this anthology.

The essays are divided into two parts: those in the first part discuss the theme, characters, structure, and style of the play; those in the second part illustrate the variety of interpretation that has befallen the character of Falstaff during the last two centuries. The works listed in the Bibliography offer opportunity for a further study of these matters. For those who wish to use these secondary materials in documented reports, publication data are included. Unless otherwise specified, the materials have been reprinted exactly as they appeared in the sources from which they were drawn.

In addition to the text and criticism of the play, extracts are included from three of the more important works generally believed to have been sources which Shakespeare drew upon in writing *Henry IV, Part I:* Holinshed's *Chronicles of England,* Samuel Daniel's *The Civil Wars,* and *The Famous Victories of Henry the Fifth.*

I am chiefly indebted to the writers whose work appears in the anthology, but I also wish to acknowledge the help derived from the splendid *Variorum* edition of the play by the late Professor S. B. Hemingway and its equally useful *Supplement* by Professor G. Blakemore Evans. Thanks are due Professor M. H. Abrams for suggestions that I have incorporated in the book and the Master and Fellows of Trinity College, Cambridge, for permission to reproduce the title-page from the Trinity College Library copy of the first quarto. My wife, Rosamond, assisted as needed, in the proofreading and, as needed, in the maintaining of a sympathetic silence, for both of which I here extend "a liberal thanks."

Camden, New Jersey James L. Sanderson
January 1962

A NOTE ON THE TEXT

The present text, with few departures, follows that of the first quarto (1598) edition of the play. Act and scene divisions are not indicated in the quarto; those of the first folio have been incorporated here with one exception: Scene ii of Act V has been divided into two scenes and the concluding scenes renumbered accordingly. Stage directions supplemental to those in the quarto have been placed in brackets. Aside from the adoption of modern conventions of spelling and punctuation, I have made only a few textual emendations. Words added have been placed in brackets; the other emendations are as follows:

I.ii.69. *similes:* smiles Q 137. *thou:* the Q 141. *Bardolph, Peto:* Haruey, Rossill Q 166. *to-night:* to morrow night Q I.iii.233. *I will:* ile Q II.ii.45. *Bardolph. What news?:* [Printed as part of Poins' preceding lines] Q 46–48. *assigned to Gadshill:* [assigned to Bard.] Q II.iii.3. *respect:* the respect Q II.iv.29. *precedent:* present Q 32. *Assigned to Poins:* [assigned to Prince] Q 157–60. *Parts assigned to Prince, Gadshill, Falstaff, Gadshill:* Gad, Ross., Falst., Ross. [respectively] Q 164–65. *Gadshill:* Ross Q 222. *eel-skin:* elsskin Q 272. *Tell:* Faith tell Q 303. *Owen:* O Q 350. *tristful:* trustfull Q 357. *yet:* so Q 404. *reverend:* reverent Q III.i.100. *cantle:* scantle Q 116. *I will:* Ile Q 192. *She will:* sheele Q III.iii.29. *that's:* that Q 48. *tithe:* tight Q 89. *lose:* loose Q 175. *Poins:* Peto Q 182. *they or we:* we or they Q IV.i.20. *bear:* beares Q; *lord:* mind Q 108. *dropped:* drop Q 126. *cannot:* can Q 127. *yet:* it Q IV.ii.29. *that* (1): *as* Q 66. *on:* in Q IV.iii.21. *horse:* horses Q 82. *country's:* Countrey Q V.i.2. *busky: bulky* Q V.ii.3. *undone:* vnder one Q 10. *ne'er:* neuer Q 70. *Upon:* On Q V.iv.33. *So:* and Q 67. *Nor:* Q 153. *ours:* our Q 154. *let's:* let us Q

ABBREVIATED GENEALOGY OF THE MORTIMERS AND THE HOUSE OF LANCASTER

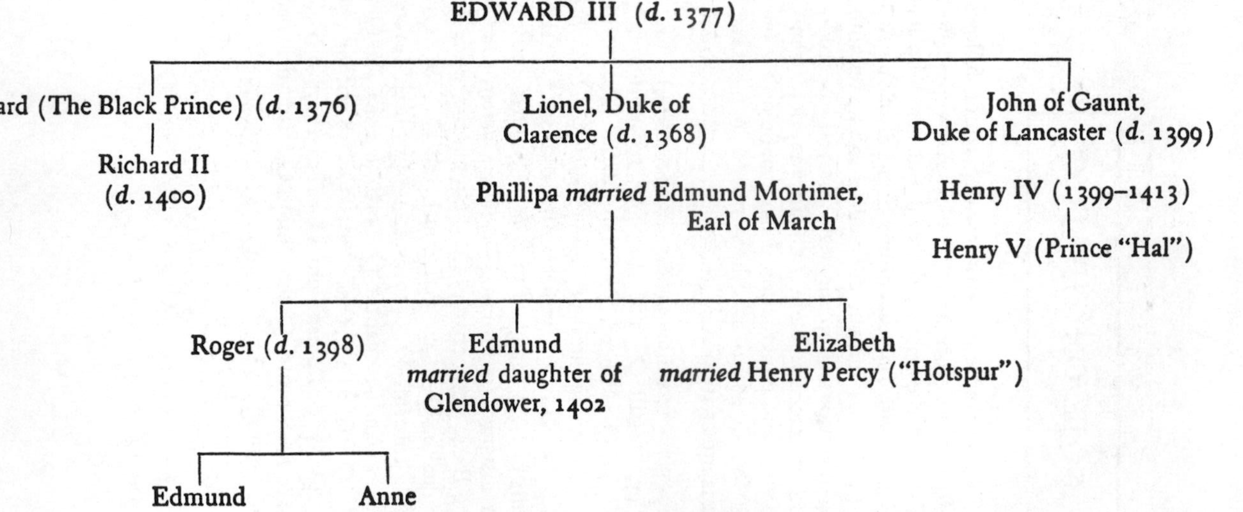

THE HISTORY OF HENRIE THE FOVRTH;

With the battell at Shrewsburie, *betweene the King and Lord* Henry Percy, surnamed Henrie Hotspur of the North.

With the humorous conceits of Sir Iohn Falstalffe.

AT LONDON,
Printed by *P. S.* for *Andrew Wise*, dwelling in Paules Churchyard, at the signe of the Angell. 1598.

[DRAMATIS PERSONÆ

KING HENRY THE FOURTH

HENRY ("HAL"), *Prince of Wales* } *sons of the* KING

PRINCE JOHN OF LANCASTER } *sons of the* KING

EARL OF WESTMORELAND

SIR WALTER BLUNT

THOMAS PERCY, *Earl of Worcester*

HENRY PERCY, *Earl of Northumberland*

HENRY PERCY ("HOTSPUR"), *his son*

EDMUND MORTIMER, *Earl of March*

ARCHIBALD, *Earl of Douglas*

OWEN GLENDOWER

SIR RICHARD VERNON

RICHARD SCROOP, *Archbishop of York*

SIR MICHAEL, *friend of the Archbishop of York*

} *enemies of the* KING

SIR JOHN FALSTAFF

POINS

GADSHILL

PETO

BARDOLPH

} *companions of* FALSTAFF

LADY PERCY ("KATE"), *wife of* HOTSPUR *and sister of* MORTIMER

LADY MORTIMER, *daughter of* GLENDOWER *and wife of* EDMUND

MISTRESS QUICKLY, *hostess of the Boar's Head Tavern*

Lords, Carriers, Ostler, Chamberlain, Travellers, Vintner, Drawers, Officers, Messengers, Sheriff, and Attendants

TIME: 1402–1403]

The First Part of
KING HENRY THE FOURTH

[ACT I. SCENE I. *London. The Palace.*]

Enter the KING, LORD JOHN OF LANCASTER, EARL OF WESTMORELAND, [SIR WALTER BLUNT], *with others.*

KING. So shaken as we are, so wan with care,
Find we a time for frighted peace to pant,
And breathe short-winded accents of new broils
To be commenced in stronds afar remote.
No more the thirsty entrance of this soil
Shall daub her lips with her own children's blood,
No more shall trenching war channel her fields,
Nor bruise her flow'rets with the armed hoofs
Of hostile paces; those opposed eyes
Which, like the meteors of a troubled heaven,
All of one nature, of one substance bred,
Did lately meet in the intestine shock
And furious close of civil butchery,
Shall now, in mutual well-beseeming ranks,
March all one way and be no more opposed
Against acquaintance, kindred, and allies.
The edge of war, like an ill-sheathed knife,
No more shall cut his master. Therefore, friends,
As far as to the sepulchre of Christ,
Whose soldier now, under whose blessed cross
We are impressed and engaged to fight,

2. **pant:** recover breath
3. **accents:** words
4. **stronds:** shores
7. **trenching:** cutting; **channel:** furrow
10. **meteors:** atmospheric conditions (hail, lightning, etc.)
12. **intestine:** internal
13. **close:** encounter
14. **mutual:** united
17. **edge:** sword
19. **sepulchre of Christ:** in Jerusalem
21. **impressed:** enlisted; **engaged:** pledged

Forthwith a power of English shall we levy,
Whose arms were moulded in their mother's womb
To chase these pagans in those holy fields
Over whose acres walked those blessed feet
Which fourteen hundred years ago were nailed
For our advantage on the bitter cross.
But this our purpose now is twelve month old,
And bootless 'tis to tell you we will go;
Therefore we meet not now. Then let me hear
Of you, my gentle cousin Westmoreland,
What yesternight our council did decree
In forwarding this dear expedience.

WESTMORELAND. My liege, this haste was hot in question
And many limits of the charge set down
But yesternight; when all athwart there came
A post from Wales, loaden with heavy news,
Whose worst was that the noble Mortimer,
Leading the men of Herefordshire to fight
Against the irregular and wild Glendower,
Was by the rude hands of that Welshman taken,
A thousand of his people butchered;
Upon whose dead corpse there was such misuse,
Such beastly shameless transformation,
By those Welshwomen done as may not be
Without much shame retold or spoken of.

KING. It seems then that the tidings of this broil
Brake off our business for the Holy Land.

WESTMORELAND. This matched with other did, my gracious lord;
For more uneven and unwelcome news
Came from the north, and thus it did import:

22. **power:** army
29. **bootless:** to no purpose
30. **Therefore . . . not:** we do not meet now concerning that matter
31. **cousin:** a friendly form of address
33. **dear expedience:** important enterprise
34. **hot in question:** being hotly discussed
35. **limits of the charge:** determination of responsibility
36. **athwart:** perversely
40. **irregular:** lawless
43. **corpse:** corpses
50. **uneven:** disconcerting

On Holy-rood Day the gallant Hotspur there,
Young Harry Percy, and Brave Archibald,
That ever-valiant and approved Scot,
At Holmedon met,
Where they did spend a sad and bloody hour;
As by discharge of their artillery
And shape of likelihood the news was told;
For he that brought them, in the very heat
And pride of their contention did take horse,
Uncertain of the issue any way.

KING. Here is [a] dear, a true industrious friend,
Sir Walter Blunt, new lighted from his horse,
Stained with the variation of each soil
Betwixt that Holmedon and this seat of ours,
And he hath brought us smooth and welcome news.
The Earl of Douglas is discomfited.
Ten thousand bold Scots, two and twenty knights,
Balked in their own blood, did Sir Walter see
On Holmedon's plains. Of prisoners, Hotspur took
Mordake Earl of Fife and eldest son
To beaten Douglas, and the Earl of Athol,
Of Murray, Angus, and Menteith.
And is not this an honorable spoil?
A gallant prize? Ha, cousin, is it not?

WESTMORELAND. In faith,
It is a conquest for a prince to boast of.

KING. Yea, there thou mak'st me sad, and mak'st me sin
In envy that my Lord Northumberland
Should be the father to so blest a son,
A son who is the theme of honor's tongue,
Amongst a grove the very straightest plant,
Who is sweet fortune's minion and her pride;
Whilst I, by looking on the praise of him,

52. **Holy-rood Day:** September 14
55. **Holmedon:** a town in Northumberland
58. **shape of likelihood:** probability
59. **them:** i.e., the news
60. **pride . . . contention:** height of their battle
61. **issue:** outcome
69. **Balked:** (1) heaped up in ridges (2) thwarted
83. **minion:** favorite

See riot and dishonor stain the brow
Of my young Harry. O that it could be proved
That some night-tripping fairy had exchanged
In cradle clothes our children where they lay,
And called mine Percy, his Plantagenet!
Then would I have his Harry, and he mine.
But let him from my thoughts. What think you, coz,
Of this young Percy's pride? The prisoners
Which he in this adventure hath surprised
To his own use he keeps, and sends me word
I shall have none but Mordake Earl of Fife.

WESTMORELAND. This is his uncle's teaching, this is Worcester,
Malevolent to you in all aspects,
Which makes him prune himself and bristle up
The crest of youth against your dignity.

KING. But I have sent for him to answer this;
And for this cause awhile we must neglect
Our holy purpose to Jerusalem.
Cousin, on Wednesday next our council we
Will hold at Windsor. So inform the lords;
But come yourself with speed to us again,
For more is to be said and to be done
Than out of anger can be uttered.

WESTMORELAND. I will, my liege. *Exeunt.*

[SCENE II. *London. An apartment of the* PRINCE'S.]

Enter PRINCE OF WALES *and* SIR JOHN FALSTAFF.

FALSTAFF. Now, Hal, what time of day is it, lad?

PRINCE. Thou art so fat-witted with drinking of old sack, and unbuttoning thee after supper, and sleeping upon benches after noon, that thou hast forgotten to demand that truly which thou wouldest truly know. What a devil hast thou to do with

89. **Plantagenet:** a dynasty of English kings founded by Geoffrey of Anjou
91. **coz:** cousin
93. **surprised:** captured
97. **Malevolent . . . aspects:** an astrological expression comparing Worcester to a star exerting an evil influence on the fortunes of Henry IV
98. **prune:** preen
2. **sack:** a white Spanish wine

the time of the day? Unless hours were cups of sack, and minutes capons, and clocks the tongues of bawds, and dials the signs of leaping houses, and the blessed sun himself a fair hot wench in flame-colored taffeta, I see no reason why thou shouldst be so superfluous to demand the time of the day.

FALSTAFF. Indeed, you come near me now, Hal; for we that take purses go by the moon and the seven stars, and not by Phoebus, he, that wand'ring knight so fair. And I prithee, sweet wag, when thou art a king, as, God save thy grace—majesty I should say, for grace thou wilt have none—

PRINCE. What, none?

FALSTAFF. No, by my troth, not so much as will serve to be prologue to an egg and butter.

PRINCE. Well, how then? Come, roundly, roundly.

FALSTAFF. Marry, then, sweet wag, when thou art king let not us that are squires of the night's body be called thieves of the day's beauty. Let us be Diana's foresters, gentlemen of the shade, minions of the moon; and let men say we be men of good government, being governed as the sea is, by our noble and chaste mistress the moon, under whose countenance we steal.

PRINCE. Thou sayest well, and it holds well too; for the fortune of us that are the moon's men doth ebb and flow like the sea, being governed, as the sea is, by the moon. As, for proof now: a purse of gold most resolutely snatched on Monday night and most dissolutely spent on Tuesday morning; got with swearing "Lay by," and spent with crying "Bring in"; now in as low an ebb as the foot of the ladder, and by and by in as high a flow as the ridge of the gallows.

8. **leaping houses**: brothels
9. **flame-colored taffeta**: the kind of garb worn by prostitutes
12. **go**: (1) walk (2) tell time; **seven stars**: the Pleiades
13. **wag**: fellow
17. **troth**: faith
18. **prologue . . . butter**: prayer before a light meal
19. **roundly**: get to the point
20. **Marry**: to be sure
22. **Diana**: goddess of the moon and the hunt
32. **Lay by**: an outlaw's command to his victim; **Bring in**: a tavern expression, bring in the drinks
33. **ladder**: used to mount the gallows

FALSTAFF. By the Lord, thou say'st true, lad. And is not my hostess of the tavern a most sweet wench?

PRINCE. As the honey of Hybla, my old lad of the castle. And is not a buff jerkin a most sweet robe of durance?

FALSTAFF. How now, how now, mad wag? What, in thy quips and thy quiddities? What a plague have I to do with a buff jerkin?

PRINCE. Why, what a pox have I to do with my hostess of the tavern?

FALSTAFF. Well, thou hast called her to a reckoning many a time and oft.

PRINCE. Did I ever call for thee to pay thy part?

FALSTAFF. No, I'll give thee thy due; thou hast paid all there.

PRINCE. Yea, and elsewhere, so far as my coin would stretch; and where it would not, I have used my credit.

FALSTAFF. Yea, and so used it that, were it not here apparent that thou art heir apparent—But I prithee, sweet wag, shall there be gallows standing in England when thou art king? and resolution thus fubbed as it is with the rusty curb of old father antic the law? Do not thou, when thou art king, hang a thief.

PRINCE. No; thou shalt.

FALSTAFF. Shall I? O rare! By the Lord, I'll be a brave judge.

PRINCE. Thou judgest false already. I mean, thou shalt have the hanging of the thieves and so become a rare hangman.

FALSTAFF. Well, Hal, well; and in some sort it jumps with my humor as well as waiting in the court, I can tell you.

PRINCE. For obtaining of suits?

37. **Hybla:** a town in Sicily famous for its honey; **old lad . . . castle:** (1) a roisterer (2) a pun on Falstaff's original name, Oldcastle. The Castle was also the name of a London brothel.

38. **buff jerkin:** a leather jacket worn by sheriffs' sergeants; **durance:** (1) durable material (2) imprisonment

40. **quiddities:** subtleties of wit

42. **a pox:** an expression of annoyance

44. **reckoning:** (1) totalling of a bill (2) giving an account of herself

52. **resolution:** courage

53. **fubbed:** cheated

54. **antic:** buffoon

56. **brave:** finely arrayed

59. **jumps:** agrees

61. **suits:** (1) petitions (2) clothes

FALSTAFF. Yea, for obtaining of suits, whereof the hangman hath no lean wardrobe. 'Sblood, I am as melancholy as a gib cat or a lugged bear.

PRINCE. Or an old lion, or a lover's lute.

FALSTAFF. Yea, or the drone of a Lincolnshire bagpipe.

PRINCE. What sayest thou to a hare, or the melancholy of Moor Ditch?

FALSTAFF. Thou hast the most unsavory similes, and art indeed the most comparative, rascalliest, sweet young prince. But, Hal, I prithee trouble me no more with vanity. I would to God thou and I knew where a commodity of good names were to be bought. An old lord of the council rated me the other day in the street about you, sir, but I marked him not; and yet he talked very wisely, but I regarded him not; and yet he talked wisely, and in the street too.

PRINCE. Thou didst well, for wisdom cries out in the streets, and no man regards it.

FALSTAFF. O, thou hast damnable iteration, and art indeed able to corrupt a saint. Thou hast done much harm upon me, Hal; God forgive thee for it! Before I knew thee, Hal, I knew nothing; and now am I, if a man should speak truly, little better than one of the wicked. I must give over this life, and I will give it over! By the Lord, an I do not, I am a villain! I'll be damned for never a king's son in Christendom.

PRINCE. Where shall we take a purse to-morrow, Jack?

FALSTAFF. 'Zounds, where thou wilt, lad! I'll make one. An I

62–63. **hangman . . . wardrobe**: The hangman retained the clothing of his victims.

63. **'Sblood**: an oath, by God's blood

63–64. **gib cat**: tomcat

64. **lugged**: baited

66. **drone**: bass pipe of a bagpipe

67. **hare**: considered a melancholy animal; **Moor Ditch**: an open drain age ditch in London cluttered with refuse

72. **commodity**: quantity

73. **rated**: chided

77–78. Cf. Proverbs I: 20–24: "Wisdom crieth without; she uttereth her voice in the streets . . . saying . . . 'I have stretched out my hand, and no man regarded.'"

79. **iteration**: repetition (of scripture)

84. **an**: if

87. **'Zounds**: an oath, by God's wounds

do not, call me villain and baffle me.

PRINCE. I see a good amendment of life in thee: from praying to purse-taking.

FALSTAFF. Why, Hal, 'tis my vocation, Hal. 'Tis no sin for a man to labor in his vocation.

Enter POINS.

Poins! Now shall we know if Gadshill have set a match. O, if men were to be saved by merit, what hole in hell were hot enough for him? This is the most omnipotent villain that ever cried "Stand!" to a true man.

PRINCE. Good morrow, Ned.

POINS. Good morrow, sweet Hal. What says Monsieur Remorse? What says Sir John Sack and Sugar? Jack, how agrees the devil and thee about thy soul, that thou soldest him on Good Friday last for a cup of Madeira and a cold capon's leg?

PRINCE. Sir John stands to his word, the devil shall have his bargain; for he was never yet a breaker of proverbs. He will give the devil his due.

POINS. Then art thou damned for keeping thy word with the devil.

PRINCE. Else he had been damned for cozening the devil.

POINS. But, my lads, my lads, to-morrow morning, by four o'clock early at Gad's Hill, there are pilgrims going to Canterbury with rich offerings, and traders riding to London with fat purses. I have vizards for you all; you have horses for yourselves. Gadshill lies to-night in Rochester. I have bespoke supper to-morrow night in Eastcheap. We may do it as secure as sleep. If you will go, I will stuff your purses full of crowns; if you

88. **baffle:** disgrace
93. **set a match:** appoint a meeting (for the robbery)
96. **stand:** an outlaw's command, "Hands up!"
101. **Madeira:** a white wine
107. **cozening:** cheating
109. **pilgrims:** The pilgrims are taking gifts to the famous shrine of St. Thomas à Becket at Canterbury.
111. **vizards:** masks
112. **Gadshill:** Gadshill is the name of one of the thieves and also the site (on the road from London to Rochester) of the robbery. **Rochester:** a town thirty-three miles east of London
113. **Eastcheap:** a street in London

will not, tarry at home and be hanged!

FALSTAFF. Hear ye, Yedward; if I tarry at home and go not I'll hang you for going.

PRINCE. You will, chops?

FALSTAFF. Hal, wilt thou make one?

PRINCE. Who, I rob? I a thief? Not I, by my faith.

FALSTAFF. There's neither honesty, manhood, nor good fellowship in thee, nor thou cam'st not of the blood royal if thou darest not stand for ten shillings.

PRINCE. Well then, once in my days I'll be a madcap.

FALSTAFF. Why, that's well said.

PRINCE. Well, come what will, I'll tarry at home.

FALSTAFF. By the Lord, I'll be a traitor then, when thou art king.

PRINCE. I care not.

POINS. Sir John, I prithee, leave the prince and me alone; I will lay him down such reasons for this adventure that he shall go.

FALSTAFF. Well, God give thee the spirit of persuasion and him the ears of profiting, that what thou speakest may move and what he hears may be believed, that the true prince may (for recreation sake) prove a false thief; for the poor abuses of the time want countenance. Farewell; you shall find me in Eastcheap.

PRINCE. Farewell, thou latter spring! farewell, All-hallown summer! [*Exit* FALSTAFF.]

POINS. Now, my good sweet honey lord, ride with us to-morrow. I have a jest to execute that I cannot manage alone. Falstaff, Bardolph, Peto, and Gadshill shall rob those men that we have already waylaid; yourself and I will not be there, and when they have the booty, if you and I do not rob them, cut this head off from my shoulders.

PRINCE. How shall we part with them in setting forth?

POINS. Why, we will set forth before or after them and appoint them a place of meeting, wherein it is at our pleasure to fail; and then will they adventure upon the exploit themselves,

116. **Yedward:** Edward
118. **chops:** one with fat cheeks
122. **royal:** a play on the name of a coin worth 10 shillings
123. **stand:** fiight for
135. **want countenance:** lack encouragement
137. **All-hallown summer:** late autumn

which they shall have no sooner achieved, but we'll set upon them.

PRINCE. Yea, but 'tis like that they will know us by our horses, by our habits, and by every other appointment to be ourselves.

POINS. Tut, our horses they shall not see—I'll tie them in the wood; our vizards we will change after we leave them; and, sirrah, I have cases of buckram for the nonce, to immask our noted outward garments.

PRINCE. Yea, but I doubt they will be too hard for us.

POINS. Well, for two of them, I know them to be as true-bred cowards as ever turned back; and for the third, if he fight longer than he sees reason, I'll forswear arms. The virtue of this jest will be the incomprehensible lies that this same fat rogue will tell us when we meet at supper: how thirty, at least, he fought with; what wards, what blows, what extremities he endured; and in the reproof of this lives the jest.

PRINCE. Well, I'll go with thee. Provide us all things necessary and meet me to-night in Eastcheap; there I'll sup. Farewell.

POINS. Farewell, my lord. *Exit* POINS.

PRINCE. I know you all, and will awhile uphold
The unyoked humor of your idleness.
Yet herein will I imitate the sun,
Who doth permit the base contagious clouds
To smother up his beauty from the world,
That, when he please again to be himself,
Being wanted, he may be more wondered at
By breaking through the foul and ugly mists
Of vapors that did seem to strangle him.
If all the year were playing holidays,
To sport would be as tedious as to work;
But when they seldom come, they wished-for come,
And nothing pleaseth but rare accidents.

152. **habits**: clothing; **appointment**: equipment
155. **sirrah**: a form of address usually applied to inferiors; **cases of buckram**: clothing of coarse linen; **for the nonce**: for the purpose
157. **doubt**: fear
163. **wards**: defensive postures
164. **reproof**: confutation
169. **unyoked**: undisciplined
171. **base**: low-lying; **contagious**: poisonous
180. **accidents**: incidents

So, when this loose behavior I throw off
And pay the debt I never promised,
By how much better than my word I am,
By so much shall I falsify men's hopes;
And like bright metal on a sullen ground,
My reformation, glitt'ring o'er my fault,
Shall show more goodly and attract more eyes
Than that which hath no foil to set it off.
I'll so offend to make offense a skill,
Redeeming time when men think least I will. *Exit.*

[SCENE III. *London. The Palace.*]

Enter the KING, NORTHUMBERLAND, WORCESTER, HOTSPUR, SIR WALTER BLUNT, *with others.*

KING. My blood hath been too cold and temperate,
Unapt to stir at these indignities,
And you have found me, for accordingly
You tread upon my patience; but be sure
I will from henceforth rather be myself,
Mighty and to be feared, than my condition,
Which hath been smooth as oil, soft as young down,
And therefore lost that title of respect
Which the proud soul ne'er pays but to the proud.
WORCESTER. Our house, my sovereign liege, little deserves
The scourge of greatness to be used on it;
And that same greatness, too, which our own hands
Have holp to make so portly.
NORTHUMBERLAND. My lord,—
KING. Worcester, get thee gone; for I do see
Danger and disobedience in thine eye.
O, sir, your presence is too bold and peremptory,
And majesty might never yet endure

185. **sullen:** dark
188. **foil:** contrasting background
189. **skill:** good strategy
100. **Redeeming time:** saving time from being wasted
3. **found me:** found me out
6. **condition:** disposition
13. **holp:** helped
16. **danger:** ungracious conduct

The moody frontier of a servant brow.
You have good leave to leave us; when we need
Your use and counsel, we shall send for you.
Exit WORCESTER.
You were about to speak. [*to* NORTHUMBERLAND]
NORTHUMBERLAND. Yea, my good lord.
Those prisoners in your highness' name demanded
Which Harry Percy here at Holmedon took,
Were, as he says, not with such strength denied
As is delivered to your majesty.
Either envy, therefore, or misprision
Is guilty of this fault, and not my son.
HOTSPUR. My liege, I did deny no prisoners.
But I remember, when the fight was done,
When I was dry with rage and extreme toil,
Breathless and faint, leaning upon my sword,
Came there a certain lord, neat and trimly dressed,
Fresh as a bridegroom, and his chin new reaped
Showed like a stubble land at harvest home.
He was perfumed like a milliner,
And 'twixt his finger and his thumb he held
A pouncet box, which ever and anon
He gave his nose, and took't away again;
Who therewith angry, when it next came there,
Took it in snuff; and still he smiled and talked;
And as the soldiers bore dead bodies by,
He called them untaught knaves, unmannerly,
To bring a slovenly unhandsome corse
Betwixt the wind and his nobility.
With many holiday and lady terms
He questioned me, amongst the rest demanded
My prisoners in your majesty's behalf.

19. **frontier:** forehead
27. **envy:** malice; **misprision:** misunderstanding
35. **harvest-home:** the close of harvesting
38. **pouncet box:** small container for perfumes
40. **Who:** i.e., the nose
41. **Took . . . snuff:** a play on the proverbial expression meaning to take offense
46. **holiday . . . terms:** terms appropriate to a festive or sportive occasion

I then, all smarting with my wounds being cold,
To be so pestered with a popingay,
Out of my grief and my impatience
Answered neglectingly—I know not what—
He should, or he should not; for he made me mad
To see him shine so brisk, and smell so sweet,
And talk so like a waiting gentlewoman
Of guns and drums and wounds,—God save the mark!—
And telling me the sovereignest thing on earth
Was parmaceti for an inward bruise,
And that it was great pity, so it was,
This villainous saltpetre should be digged
Out of the bowels of the harmless earth,
Which many a good tall fellow had destroyed
So cowardly, and but for these vile guns,
He would himself have been a soldier.
This bald unjointed chat of his, my lord,
I answered indirectly, as I said,
And I beseech you, let not his report
Come current for an accusation
Betwixt my love and your high majesty.

BLUNT. The circumstance considered, good my lord,
Whate'er Lord Harry Percy then had said
To such a person, and in such a place,
At such a time, with all the rest retold,
May reasonably die, and never rise
To do him wrong, or any way impeach
What then he said, so he unsay it now.

KING. Why, yet he doth deny his prisoners,

50. **popingay:** parrot
51. **grief:** pain
54. **brisk:** smartly dressed
57. **sovereignest:** most excellent
58. **parmaceti:** spermaceti, a fatty substance found in the head of the sperm-whale and used in various medicinal preparations
62. **tall:** brave
65. **bald:** trivial; **unjointed:** incoherent
66. **indirectly:** negligently
68. **come current:** be accepted as genuine
75. **impeach:** disparage
77. **yet:** still

But with proviso and exception,
That we at our own charge shall ransom straight
His brother-in-law, the foolish Mortimer,
Who, on my soul, hath willfully betrayed
The lives of those that he did lead to fight
Against that great magician, damned Glendower,
Whose daughter, as we hear, that Earl of March
Hath lately married. Shall our coffers, then,
Be emptied to redeem a traitor home?
Shall we buy treason? and indent with fears
When they have lost and forfeited themselves?
No, on the barren mountains let him starve!
For I shall never hold that man my friend
Whose tongue shall ask me for one penny cost
To ransom home revolted Mortimer.

HOTSPUR. Revolted Mortimer!
He never did fall off, my sovereign liege,
But by the chance of war. To prove that true
Needs no more but one tongue for all those wounds,
Those mouthèd wounds, which valiantly he took
When on the gentle Severn's sedgy bank,
In single opposition hand to hand,
He did confound the best part of an hour
In changing hardiment with great Glendower.
Three times they breathed, and three times did they drink,
Upon agreement, of swift Severn's flood,
Who then, affrighted with their bloody looks,
Ran fearfully among the trembling reeds
And hid his crisp head in the hollow bank,
Bloodstained with these valiant combatants.
Never did bare and rotten policy
Color her working with such deadly wounds,

87. **indent:** enter into a compact
94. **fall off:** withdraw his allegiance
100. **confound:** consume
101. **changing hardiment:** exchanging blows
102. **breathed:** rested in their fighting
106. **crisp:** rippled
108. **policy:** dissimulation
109. **Color:** disguise

Nor never could the noble Mortimer
Receive so many, and all willingly.
Then let not him be slandered with revolt.

KING. Thou dost belie him, Percy, thou dost belie him!
He never did encounter with Glendower.
I tell thee,
He durst as well have met the devil alone
As Owen Glendower for an enemy.
Art thou not ashamed? But, sirrah, henceforth
Let me not hear you speak of Mortimer.
Send me your prisoners with the speediest means,
Or you shall hear in such a kind from me
As will displease you. My Lord Northumberland,
We license your departure with your son.
Send us your prisoners, or you will hear of it.

Exeunt KING, [BLUNT, *and* TRAIN].

HOTSPUR. An if the devil come and roar for them,
I will not send them. I will after straight
And tell him so, for I will ease my heart,
Albeit I make a hazard of my head.

NORTHUMBERLAND. What, drunk with choler? Stay, and pause awhile.
Here comes your uncle.

Enter WORCESTER.

HOTSPUR. Speak of Mortimer?
'Zounds, I will speak of him, and let my soul
Want mercy if I do not join with him!
Yea, on his part I'll empty all these veins,
And shed my dear blood drop by drop in the dust,
But I will lift the downtrod Mortimer
As high in the air as this unthankful king,
As this ingrate and cankered Bolingbroke.

NORTHUMBERLAND. Brother, the king hath made your nephew mad.

113. **belie:** lie about
128. **make . . . of:** gamble
129. **choler:** wrath
137. **cankered:** venomous; **Bolingbroke:** i.e., Henry IV

WORCESTER. Who struck this heat up after I was gone?
HOTSPUR. He will, forsooth, have all my prisoners;
And when I urged the ransom once again
Of my wife's brother, then his cheek looked pale,
And on my face he turned an eye of death,
Trembling even at the name of Mortimer.
WORCESTER. I cannot blame him. Was not he proclaimed
By Richard that dead is, the next of blood?
NORTHUMBERLAND. He was; I heard the proclamation.
And then it was when the unhappy king
(Whose wrongs in us God pardon!) did set forth
Upon his Irish expedition;
From whence he intercepted did return
To be deposed, and shortly murdered.
WORCESTER. And for whose death we in the world's wide mouth
Live scandalized and foully spoken of.
HOTSPUR. But soft, I pray you. Did King Richard then
Proclaim my brother Edmund Mortimer
Heir to the crown?
NORTHUMBERLAND. He did; myself did hear it.
HOTSPUR. Nay, then I cannot blame his cousin king,
That wished him on the barren mountains starve.
But shall it be that you, that set the crown
Upon the head of this forgetful man,
And for his sake wear the detested blot
Of murtherous subornation—shall it be
That you a world of curses undergo,
Being the agents or base second means,
The cords, the ladder, or the hangman rather?
O, pardon me that I descend so low
To show the line and the predicament
Wherein you range under this subtle king!
Shall it for shame be spoken in these days,

140. **forsooth:** in truth
145–46. **proclaimed . . . blood:** specified as the successor to the throne
156. **brother:** brother-in-law
163. **murtherous subornation:** encouraging one to commit murder
165. **second:** subordinate
168. **line:** degree; **predicament:** situation, position
169. **range:** occupy a position

Or fill up chronicles in time to come,
That men of your nobility and power
Did gage them both in an unjust behalf
(As both of you, God pardon it! have done)
To put down Richard, that sweet lovely rose,
And plant this thorn, this canker, Bolingbroke?
And shall it in more shame be further spoken
That you are fooled, discarded, and shook off
By him for whom these shames ye underwent?
No! yet time serves wherein you may redeem
Your banished honors and restore yourselves
Into the good thoughts of the world again;
Revenge the jeering and disdained contempt
Of this proud king, who studies day and night
To answer all the debt he owes to you
Even with the bloody payment of your deaths.
Therefore, I say—

WORCESTER. Peace, cousin, say no more;
And now I will unclasp a secret book,
And to your quick-conceiving discontents
I'll read you matter deep and dangerous,
As full of peril and adventurous spirit
As to o'erwalk a current roaring loud
On the unsteadfast footing of a spear.

HOTSPUR. If he fall in, good night, or sink or swim!
Send danger from the east unto the west,
So honor cross it from the north to south,
And let them grapple. O, the blood more stirs
To rouse a lion than to start a hare!

NORTHUMBERLAND. Imagination of some great exploit
Drives him beyond the bounds of patience.

[HOTSPUR.] By heaven, methinks it were an easy leap
To pluck bright honor from the pale-faced moon,
Or dive into the bottom of the deep,
Where fathom-line could never touch the ground,
And pluck up drowned honor by the locks,

173. **gage:** pledge
187. **Peace:** calm down
196. **So:** so long as
198. **start:** startle

So he that doth redeem her thence might wear
Without corrival all her dignities;
But out upon this half-faced fellowship!
WORCESTER. He apprehends a world of figures here,
But not the form of what he should attend.
Good cousin, give me audience for a while.
HOTSPUR. I cry you mercy.
WORCESTER. Those same noble Scots
That are your prisoners—
HOTSPUR. I'll keep them all!
By God, he shall not have a Scot of them!
No, if a Scot would save his soul, he shall not.
I'll keep them, by this hand!
WORCESTER. You start away
And lend no ear unto my purposes.
Those prisoners you shall keep.
HOTSPUR. Nay, I will! That's flat!
He said he would not ransom Mortimer,
Forbade my tongue to speak of Mortimer,
But I will find him when he lies asleep,
And in his ear I'll holla "Mortimer!"
Nay, I'll have a starling shall be taught to speak
Nothing but "Mortimer," and give it him
To keep his anger still in motion.
WORCESTER. Hear you, cousin, a word.
HOTSPUR. All studies here I solemnly defy,
Save how to gall and pinch this Bolingbroke;
And that same sword-and-buckler Prince of Wales,
But that I think his father loves him not
And would be glad he met with some mischance,
I would have him poisoned with a pot of ale.
WORCESTER. Farewell, kinsman. I will talk to you
When you are better tempered to attend.
NORTHUMBERLAND. Why, what a wasp-stung and impatient fool
Art thou to break into this woman's mood,

208. **out upon**: an expression of indignation; **half-faced fellowship**: imperfect partnership
212. **cry you mercy**: beg your pardon
227. **studies**: interests or pleasures; **defy**: reject
229. **sword-and-buckler**: roughneck

Tying thine ear to no tongue but thine own!
HOTSPUR. Why, look you, I am whipped and scourged with rods,
Nettled, and stung with pismires when I hear
Of this vile politician, Bolingbroke.
In Richard's time—what do you call the place?—
A plague upon it! it is in Gloucestershire;
'Twas where the madcap duke his uncle kept,
His uncle York—where I first bowed my knee
Unto this king of smiles, this Bolingbroke—
'Sblood!—when you and he came back from Ravenspurgh—
NORTHUMBERLAND. At Berkeley Castle.
HOTSPUR. You say true.
Why, what a candy deal of courtesy
This fawning greyhound then did proffer me!
Look, "when his infant fortune came to age,"
And "gentle Harry Percy," and "kind cousin"—
O, the devil take such cozeners! God forgive me!
Good uncle, tell your tale, [for] I have done.
WORCESTER. Nay, if you have not, to it again.
We will stay your leisure.
HOTSPUR. I have done, i' faith.
WORCESTER. Then once more to your Scottish prisoners.
Deliver them up without their ransom straight,
And make the Douglas' son your only mean
For powers in Scotland—which, for divers reasons
Which I shall send you written, be assured
Will easily be granted. You, my lord, [*to* NORTHUMBERLAND]
Your son in Scotland being thus employed,
Shall secretly into the bosom creep
Of that same noble prelate well-beloved,
The archbishop.
HOTSPUR. Of York, is it not?
WORCESTER. True; who bears hard
His brother's death at Bristow, the Lord Scroop.

239. **pismires:** ants
243. **kept:** lived
249. **candy deal:** sweet bit
253. **cozeners:** impostors
256. **stay:** wait for
268. **Lord Scroop:** William Scrope, Earl of Wiltshire, executed by Henry IV in 1399

I speak not this in estimation,
As what I think might be, but what I know
Is ruminated, plotted, and set down,
And only stays but to behold the face
Of that occasion that shall bring it on.

HOTSPUR. I smell it. Upon my life, it will do well.

NORTHUMBERLAND. Before the game is afoot thou still let'st slip.

HOTSPUR. Why, it cannot choose but be a noble plot.
And then the power of Scotland and of York
To join with Mortimer, ha?

WORCESTER. And so they shall.

HOTSPUR. In faith, it is exceedingly well aimed.

WORCESTER. And 'tis no little reason bids us speed
To save our heads by raising of a head;
For, bear ourselves as even as we can,
The king will always think him in our debt,
And think we think ourselves unsatisfied,
Till he hath found a time to pay us home.
And see already how he doth begin
To make us strangers to his looks of love.

HOTSPUR. He does, he does! We'll be revenged on him!

WORCESTER. Cousin, farewell. No further go in this
Than I by letters shall direct your course.
When time is ripe, which will be suddenly,
I'll steal to Glendower and Lord Mortimer,
Where you and Douglas, and our pow'rs at once,
As I will fashion it, shall happily meet,
To bear our fortunes in our own strong arms,
Which now we hold at much uncertainty.

NORTHUMBERLAND. Farewell, good brother. We shall thrive, I trust.

HOTSPUR. Uncle, adieu. O, let the hours be short
Till fields and blows and groans applaud our sport!

Exeunt.

274. **smell**: discern or discover
275. **Before . . . slip**: An expression from hunting: the dogs are loosed before the game is afoot.
281. **head**: armed force
282. **even**: equably
285. **pay us home**: punish us severely
291. **suddenly**: very soon

[ACT II, SCENE I. *Rochester. An inn yard.*]

Enter a CARRIER *with a lantern in his hand.*

1 CARRIER. Heigh-ho! an it be not four by the day, I'll be hanged. Charles' wain is over the new chimney, and yet our horse not packed.—What, ostler!

OSTLER. [*within*] Anon, anon.

1 CARRIER. I prithee, Tom, beat Cut's saddle, put a few flocks in the point. [The] poor jade is wrung in the withers out of all cess.

Enter another CARRIER.

2 CARRIER. Peas and beans are as dank here as a dog, and that is the next way to give poor jades the bots. This house is turned upside down since Robin Ostler died.

1 CARRIER. Poor fellow never joyed since the price of oats rose. It was the death of him.

2 CARRIER. I think this be the most villainous house in all London road for fleas. I am stung like a tench.

1 CARRIER. Like a tench? By the mass, there is ne'er a king christen could be better bit than I have been since the first cock.

2 CARRIER. Why, they will allow us ne'er a jordan, and then we leak in your chimney, and your chamber-lye breeds fleas like a loach.

1 CARRIER. What, ostler! come away and be hanged! come away!

S.D. **Carrier:** a transporter of goods
1. **four by the day:** four A. M.
2. **Charles' wain:** the constellation *Ursa Major*
3. **ostler:** groom
4. **Anon:** right away
5. **flocks:** tufts of wool (for padding)
6. **point:** part of the saddle; **jade:** worn-out horse; **wrung:** galled; **withers:** the juncture of the shoulder-bones and neck
6–7. **out . . . cess:** beyond measure
9. **next:** nearest; **bots:** worms
14. **tench:** a fish with red spots
15. **By the mass:** an oath
16. **first cock:** midnight
17. **jordan:** chamberpot
18. **chamber-lye:** urine
19. **loach:** a prolific fish

2 CARRIER. I have a gammon of bacon and two razes of ginger, to be delivered as far as Charing Cross.

1 CARRIER. God's body! the turkeys in my pannier are quite starved. What, ostler! A plague on thee! hast thou never an eye in thy head? Canst not hear? An 'twere not as good deed as drink to break the pate on thee, I am a very villain. Come, and be hanged! Hast no faith in thee?

Enter GADSHILL.

GADSHILL. Good morrow, carriers. What's o'clock?

1 CARRIER. I think it be two o'clock.

GADSHILL. I prithee lend me thy lantern to see my gelding in the stable.

1 CARRIER. Nay, by God, soft! I know a trick worth two of that, i' faith.

GADSHILL. I pray thee lend me thine.

2 CARRIER. Ay, when? canst tell? Lend me thy lantern, quoth he? Marry, I'll see thee hanged first!

GADSHILL. Sirrah carrier, what time do you mean to come to London?

2 CARRIER. Time enough to go to bed with a candle, I warrant thee. Come, neighbor Mugs, we'll call up the gentlemen. They will along with company, for they have great charge.

Exeunt [CARRIERS].

Enter CHAMBERLAIN.

GADSHILL. What, ho! chamberlain!

CHAMBERLAIN. At hand, quoth pickpurse.

GADSHILL. That's even as fair as "at hand, quoth the chamberlain"; for thou variest no more from picking of purses than giving direction doth from laboring; thou layest the plot how.

21. **gammon**: haunch; **razes**: roots
22. **Charing Cross**: i.e., the village of Charing, between London and Westminster
23. **pannier**: basket
26. **pate**: head
41. **charge**: baggage
42. **chamberlain**: room attendant at an inn
43. **At hand . . . pickpurse**: a proverbial expression, "near at hand"
44. **even**: just; **fair**: plausible

CHAMBERLAIN. Good morrow, Master Gadshill. It holds current that I told you yesternight. There's a franklin in the Wild of Kent hath brought three hundred marks with him in gold. I heard him tell it to one of his company last night at supper; a kind of auditor, one that hath abundance of charge too, God knows what. They are up already and call for eggs and butter. They will away presently.

GADSHILL. Sirrah, if they meet not with Saint Nicholas' clerks, I'll give thee this neck.

CHAMBERLAIN. No, I'll none of it. I pray thee keep that for the hangman; for I know thou worshippest Saint Nicholas as truly as a man of falsehood may.

GADSHILL. What talkest thou to me of the hangman? If I hang, I'll make a fat pair of gallows; for if I hang, old Sir John hangs with me, and thou knowest he is no starveling. Tut! there are other Trojans that thou dream'st not of, the which for sport sake are content to do the profession some grace; that would, if matters should be looked into, for their own credit sake make all whole. I am joined with no foot land-rakers, no long-staff six-penny strikers, none of these mad mustachio purple-hued maltworms; but with nobility and tranquillity, burgomasters and great oneyers, such as can hold in, such as will strike sooner than speak, and speak sooner than drink, and drink sooner than pray; and yet, 'zounds, I lie; for they pray continually to their saint, the commonwealth, or rather, not pray to her, but prey on her, for they ride up and down on her and make her their boots.

CHAMBERLAIN. What, the commonwealth their boots? Will she hold out water in foul way?

47. **holds current:** remains true
48. **franklin:** a landowner; **Wild:** weald, open country
49. **mark:** the equivalent of 13 shillings 4 pence
53. **presently:** right away
54. **Saint Nicholas' clerks:** highwaymen
62. **Trojans:** good fellows
65. **foot land-rakers:** highwaymen
66. **sixpenny strikers:** petty thieves
67. **maltworms:** topers
68. **oneyers:** ones; **hold in:** keep counsel
73. **boots:** spoils
75. **foul way:** muddy roads

GADSHILL. She will, she will! Justice hath liquored her. We steal as in a castle, cocksure; we have the receipt of fernseed, we walk invisible.

CHAMBERLAIN. Nay, by my faith, I think you are more beholding to the night than to fernseed for your walking invisible.

GADSHILL. Give me thy hand. Thou shalt have a share in our purchase, as I am a true man.

CHAMBERLAIN. Nay, rather let me have it, as you are a false thief.

GADSHILL. Go to; *homo* is a common name to all men. Bid the ostler bring my gelding out of the stable. Farewell, you muddy knave. [*Exeunt.*]

[SCENE II. *The Highway, near Gadshill.*]

Enter PRINCE, POINS, PETO, *and* [BARDOLPH].

POINS. Come, shelter, shelter! I have removed Falstaff's horse, and he frets like a gummed velvet.

PRINCE. Stand close. [*They step back.*]

Enter FALSTAFF.

FALSTAFF. Poins! Poins, and be hanged! Poins!

PRINCE. [*coming forward*] Peace, ye fat-kidneyed rascal! What a brawling dost thou keep!

FALSTAFF. Where's Poins, Hal?

PRINCE. He is walked up to the top of the hill; I'll go seek him. [*Steps aside.*]

FALSTAFF. I am accursed to rob in that thief's company. The rascal hath removed my horse and tied him I know not where. If I travel but four foot by the squire further afoot, I shall break my wind. Well, I doubt not but to die a fair death for all this, if I 'scape hanging for killing that rogue. I have forsworn his company hourly any time this two and twenty years, and yet I am bewitched with the rogue's company. If the rascal have not

76. **liquored:** water-proofed

77. **in a castle:** i.e., in safety; **receipt:** recipe; **fernseed:** It was popularly believed that fernseed could render one invisible.

81. **purchase:** booty

85. **muddy:** dull

2. **frets . . . velvet:** Gum used to stiffen velvet peeled off ("fretted") when it became hardened.

11. **squire:** rule

given me medicines to make me love him, I'll be hanged. It could not be else; I have drunk medicines. Poins! Hal! A plague upon you both! Bardolph! Peto! I'll starve ere I'll rob a foot further. An 'twere not as good a deed as drink to turn true man and to leave these rogues, I am the veriest varlet that ever chewed with a tooth. Eight yards of uneven ground is threescore and ten miles afoot with me, and the stony-hearted villains know it well enough. A plague upon it when thieves cannot be true one to another! (*They whistle.*) Whew! A plague upon you all! Give me my horse, you rogues! give me my horse and be hanged!

PRINCE. [*coming forward*] Peace, ye fat-guts! Lie down, lay thine ear close to the ground, and list if thou canst hear the tread of travellers.

FALSTAFF. Have you any levers to lift me up again, being down? 'Sblood, I'll not bear mine own flesh so far afoot again for all the coin in thy father's exchequer. What a plague mean ye to colt me thus?

PRINCE. Thou liest; thou art not colted, thou art uncolted.

FALSTAFF. I prithee, good Prince Hal, help me to my horse, good king's son.

PRINCE. Out, ye rogue! Shall I be your ostler?

FALSTAFF. Hang thyself in thine own heir-apparent garters! If I be ta'en, I'll peach for this. An I have not ballads made on you all, and sung to filthy tunes, let a cup of sack be my poison. When a jest is so forward, and afoot too, I hate it.

Enter GADSHILL.

GADSHILL. Stand!

FALSTAFF. So I do, against my will.

POINS. [*coming forward*] O, 'tis our setter; I know his voice.

BARDOLPH. What news?

GADSHILL. Case ye, case ye! On with your vizards! There's money

16. **medicines:** love potions
20. **veriest:** in the most extreme degree; **varlet:** rascal
33. **colt:** trick
38. **Hang . . . garters:** an adaptation of a proverbial expression
39. **peach:** turn king's evidence
44. **setter:** one who decoys persons to be robbed
46. **Case ye:** put on your disguises

of the king's coming down the hill; 'tis going to the king's exchequer.

FALSTAFF. You lie, ye rogue! 'Tis going to the king's tavern.

GADSHILL. There's enough to make us all.

FALSTAFF. To be hanged.

PRINCE. Sirs, you four shall front them in the narrow lane; Ned Poins and I will walk lower. If they 'scape from your encounter, then they light on us.

PETO. How many be there of them?

GADSHILL. Some eight or ten.

FALSTAFF. 'Zounds! will they not rob us?

PRINCE. What, a coward, Sir John Paunch?

FALSTAFF. Indeed, I am not John of Gaunt, your grandfather, but yet no coward, Hal.

PRINCE. Well, we leave that to the proof.

POINS. Sirrah Jack, thy horse stands behind the hedge; when thou need'st him, there thou shalt find him. Farewell and stand fast.

FALSTAFF. Now cannot I strike him, if I should be hanged.

PRINCE. [*aside to* POINS] Ned, where are our disguises?

POINS. [*aside to* PRINCE] Here, hard by. Stand close.

[*Exeunt* PRINCE *and* POINS.]

FALSTAFF. Now, my masters, happy man be his dole, say I. Every man to his business.

Enter the TRAVELLERS.

TRAVELLER. Come, neighbor. The boy shall lead our horses down the hill; we'll walk afoot awhile and ease our legs.

THIEVES. Stand!

TRAVELLER. Jesus bless us!

FALSTAFF. Strike! down with them! cut the villains' throats! Ah, whoreson caterpillars! bacon-fed knaves! they hate us youth. Down with them! Fleece them!

TRAVELLER. O, we are undone, both we and ours for ever!

FALSTAFF. Hang ye, gorbellied knaves, are ye undone? No, ye fat chuffs; I would your store were here! On, bacons, on! What,

66. **hard:** near
67. **happy . . . dole:** good luck
74. **whoreson:** bastard; **caterpillars:** parasites
77. **gorbellied:** fat-paunched
78. **chuffs:** churls; **store:** possessions; **bacons:** fat men

ye knaves! young men must live. You are grandjurors, are ye? We'll jure ye, 'faith!

Here they rob them and bind them. Exeunt.

Enter the PRINCE *and* POINS [*in buckram*].

PRINCE. The thieves have bound the true men. Now could thou and I rob the thieves and go merrily to London, it would be argument for a week, laughter for a month, and a good jest for ever.

POINS. Stand close! I hear them coming.

Enter the THIEVES *again.*

FALSTAFF. Come, my masters, let us share, and then to horse before day. An the prince and Poins be not two arrant cowards, there's no equity stirring. There's no more valor in that Poins than in a wild duck.

PRINCE. Your money!
POINS. Villains!

As they are sharing, the PRINCE *and* POINS *set upon them. They all run away, and* FALSTAFF, *after a blow or two, runs away too, leaving the booty behind them.*

PRINCE. Got with much ease. Now merrily to horse. The thieves are all scattered, and possessed with fear so strongly that they dare not meet each other; each takes his fellow for an officer. Away, good Ned. Falstaff sweats to death and lards the lean earth as he walks along. Were't not for laughing, I should pity him.

POINS. How the [fat] rogue roared! *Exeunt.*

[SCENE III. *Warkworth Castle.*]

Enter HOTSPUR *solus, reading a letter.*

HOTSPUR. "But, for mine own part, my lord, I could be well contented to be there, in respect of the love I bear your house."

79. **grandjurors:** people of sufficient importance to be selected as jurors
83. **argument:** subject for conversation
87. **arrant:** out-and-out
88. **equity:** impartiality
S.D. ***solus:*** alone
2. **house:** family

He could be contented: why is he not then? In respect of the love he bears our house! He shows in this he loves his own barn better than he loves our house. Let me see some more. "The purpose you undertake is dangerous"—why, that's certain! 'Tis dangerous to take a cold, to sleep, to drink; but I tell you, my lord fool, out of this nettle, danger, we pluck this flower, safety. "The purpose you undertake is dangerous, the friends you have named uncertain, the time itself unsorted, and your whole plot too light for the counterpoise of so great an opposition." Say you so, say you so? I say unto you again, you are a shallow, cowardly hind, and you lie. What a lack-brain is this! By the Lord, our plot is a good plot as ever was laid; our friends true and constant: a good plot, good friends, and full of expectation; an excellent plot, very good friends. What a frosty-spirited rogue is this! Why, my Lord of York commends the plot and the general course of the action. 'Zounds, an I were now by this rascal, I could brain him with his lady's fan! Is there not my father, my uncle, and myself; Lord Edmund Mortimer, my Lord of York, and Owen Glendower? Is there not, besides, the Douglas? Have I not all their letters to meet me in arms by the ninth of the next month, and are they not some of them set forward already? What a pagan rascal is this! an infidel! Ha! you shall see now, in very sincerity of fear and cold heart, will he to the king and lay open all our proceedings. O, I could divide myself and go to buffets for moving such a dish of skim milk with so honorable an action! Hang him, let him tell the king! We are prepared. I will set forward to-night.

Enter his LADY.

How now, Kate? I must leave you within these two hours.

LADY. O my good lord, why are you thus alone?
For what offense have I this fortnight been
A banished woman from my Harry's bed?
Tell me, sweet lord, what is't that takes from thee

10. **unsorted:** ill-chosen
13. **hind:** rustic
17. **Lord of York:** Archbishop of York
27–28. **divide . . . buffets:** strike myself

Thy stomach, pleasure, and thy golden sleep?
Why dost thou bend thine eyes upon the earth,
And start so often when thou sit'st alone?
Why hast thou lost the fresh blood in thy cheeks
And given my treasures and my rights of thee
To thick-eyed musing and cursed melancholy?
In thy faint slumbers I by thee have watched,
And heard thee murmur tales of iron wars,
Speak terms of manage to thy bounding steed,
Cry "Courage! to the field!" And thou hast talked
Of sallies and retires, of trenches, tents,
Of palisadoes, frontiers, parapets,
Of basilisks, of cannon, culverin,
Of prisoners' ransom, and of soldiers slain,
And all the currents of a heady fight.
Thy spirit within thee hath been so at war,
And thus hath so bestirred thee in thy sleep,
That beads of sweat have stood upon thy brow
Like bubbles in a late-disturbed stream,
And in thy face strange motions have appeared,
Such as we see when men restrain their breath
On some great sudden hest. O, what portents are these?
Some heavy business hath my lord in hand,
And I must know it, else he loves me not.

HOTSPUR. What, ho!

[*Enter a* SERVANT.]

Is Gilliams with the packet gone?

SERVANT. He is, my lord, an hour ago.

HOTSPUR. Hath Butler brought those horses from the sheriff?

SERVANT. One horse, my lord, he brought even now.

36. **stomach:** appetite
41. **thick-eyed:** dim-sighted
42. **faint:** light
47. **palisadoes:** fences made of stakes; **frontiers:** outlying defenses; **parapets:** walls
48. **basilisks . . . culverin:** cannons
50. **currents:** tides; **heady:** violent
57. **hest:** determination
58. **heavy:** serious
60. **packet:** parcel of letters

HOTSPUR. What horse? [A] roan, a crop-ear, is it not?
SERVANT. It is, my lord.
HOTSPUR. That roan shall be my throne.
Well, I will back him straight. O esperance!
Bid Butler lead him forth into the park.
[*Exit* SERVANT.]
LADY. But hear you, my lord.
HOTSPUR. What say'st thou, my lady?
LADY. What is it carries you away?
HOTSPUR. Why, my horse, my love, my horse!
LADY. Out, you mad-headed ape!
A weasel hath not such a deal of spleen
As you are tossed with. In faith,
I'll know your business, Harry; that I will!
I fear my brother Mortimer doth stir
About his title and hath sent for you
To line his enterprise; but if you go—
HOTSPUR. So far afoot, I shall be weary, love.
LADY. Come, come, you paraquito, answer me
Directly unto this question that I ask.
In faith, I'll break thy little finger, Harry,
An if thou wilt not tell me all things true.
HOTSPUR. Away, away, you trifler! Love? I love thee not;
I care not for thee, Kate. This is no world
To play with mammets and to tilt with lips.
We must have bloody noses and cracked crowns,
And pass them current too. God's me, my horse!
What say'st thou, Kate? What wouldst thou have with me?
LADY. Do you not love me? do you not indeed?
Well, do not then, for since you love me not,

66. **esperance:** hope (part of the Percy family motto: ***Espérance en dieu***)
73. **spleen:** caprice
74. **tossed with:** agitated by
76. **stir:** cause commotion
78. **line:** strengthen
80. **paraquito:** small parrot
86. **mammets:** puppets
87. **crowns:** (1) heads (2) gold coins worth 5 shillings
88. **pass them current:** place them in circulation; **God's me:** God save me

I will not love myself. Do you not love me?
Nay, tell me if you speak in jest or no.

HOTSPUR. Come, wilt thou see me ride?
And when I am a-horseback, I will swear
I love thee infinitely. But hark you, Kate:
I must not have you henceforth question me
Whither I go, nor reason whereabout.
Whither I must, I must, and to conclude,
This evening must I leave you, gentle Kate.
I know you wise, but yet no farther wise
Than Harry Percy's wife; constant you are,
But yet a woman; and for secrecy,
No lady closer, for I well believe
Thou wilt not utter what thou dost not know,
And so far will I trust thee, gentle Kate.

LADY. How! so far?

HOTSPUR. Not an inch further. But hark you, Kate:
Whither I go, thither shall you go too;
To-day will I set forth, to-morrow you.
Will this content you, Kate?

LADY. It must of force. *Exeunt.*

[SCENE IV. *The Boar's Head Tavern in Eastcheap.*]

Enter PRINCE *and* POINS.

PRINCE. Ned, prithee, come out of that fat room and lend me thy hand to laugh a little.

POINS. Where hast been, Hal?

PRINCE. With three or four loggerheads amongst three or four-score hogsheads. I have sounded the very bass-string of humility. Sirrah, I am sworn brother to a leash of drawers and can call them all by their christen names, as Tom, Dick, and Francis. They take it already upon their salvation that, though I be but Prince of Wales, yet I am the king of courtesy, and

111. **of force:** of necessity
1. **fat:** stuffy
4. **loggerheads:** blockheads
5. **bass-string:** i.e., the lowest degree
6. **leash:** three (the usual number of hounds coupled to one leash); **drawers:** tapsters

tell me flatly I am no proud Jack like Falstaff, but a Corinthian, a lad of mettle, a good boy (by the Lord, so they call me!), and when I am King of England I shall command all the good lads in Eastcheap. They call drinking deep, dyeing scarlet; and when you breathe in your watering, they cry "hem!" and bid you play it off. To conclude, I am so good a proficient in one quarter of an hour that I can drink with any tinker in his own language during my life. I tell thee, Ned, thou hast lost much honor that thou wert not with me in this action. But, sweet Ned—to sweeten which name of Ned, I give thee this pennyworth of sugar, clapped even now into my hand by an under-skinker, one that never spake other English in his life than "Eight shillings and sixpence," and "You are welcome," with this shrill addition, "Anon, anon, sir! Score a pint of bastard in the Half-moon," or so. But, Ned to drive away the time till Falstaff come, I prithee do thou stand in some by-room while I question my puny drawer to what end he gave me the sugar; and do thou never leave calling "Francis!" that his tale to me may be nothing but "Anon!" Step aside, and I'll show thee a precedent.

POINS. Francis!

PRINCE. Thou art perfect.

POINS. Francis! [*Exit* POINS.]

Enter [FRANCIS, *the*] DRAWER.

FRANCIS. Anon, anon, sir. Look down into the Pomgarnet, Ralph.

PRINCE. Come hither, Francis.

FRANCIS. My lord?

PRINCE. How long hast thou to serve, Francis?

10. **Corinthian:** gay fellow

13–14. **drinking . . . scarlet:** J. Dover Wilson (ed. 1946) notes that the urine of topers was used in making scarlet dyes.

14. **breathe . . . watering:** take a breath while drinking

15. **play it off:** drink up

21. **under-skinker:** tapster

24. **Score:** charge; **bastard:** sweet Spanish wine; **Half-moon:** the name of a room in the inn

26. **by-room:** private room; **puny:** novice

29. **precedent:** illustration

33. **Pomgarnet:** the Pomegranate, the name of another room

36. **serve:** i.e., as an apprentice

FRANCIS. Forsooth, five years, and as much as to—

POINS. [*within*] Francis!

FRANCIS. Anon, anon, sir.

PRINCE. Five year! by'r Lady, a long lease for the clinking of pewter. But, Francis, darest thou be so valiant as to play the coward with thy indenture and show it a fair pair of heels and run from it?

FRANCIS. O Lord, sir, I'll be sworn upon all the books in England I could find in my heart—

POINS. [*within*] Francis!

FRANCIS. Anon, sir.

PRINCE. How old art thou, Francis?

FRANCIS. Let me see—about Michaelmas next I shall be—

POINS. [*within*] Francis!

FRANCIS. Anon, sir. Pray stay a little, my lord.

PRINCE. Nay, but hark you, Francis: for the sugar thou gavest me—'twas a pennyworth, was't not?

FRANCIS. O Lord, I would it had been two!

PRINCE. I will give thee for it a thousand pound. Ask me when thou wilt, and thou shalt have it.

POINS. [*within*] Francis!

FRANCIS. Anon, anon.

PRINCE. Anon, Francis? No, Francis; but to-morrow, Francis; or, Francis, a Thursday; or indeed, Francis, when thou wilt. But, Francis—

FRANCIS. My lord?

PRINCE. Wilt thou rob this leathern-jerkin, crystal-button, not-pated, agate-ring, puke-stocking, caddis-garter, smooth-tongue, Spanish-pouch—

FRANCIS. O Lord, sir, who do you mean?

PRINCE. Why then, your brown bastard is your only drink; for look you, Francis, your white canvas doublet will sully. In Barbary, sir, it cannot come to so much.

42. **indenture:** a contract between an apprentice and his master
49. **Michaelmas:** September 29
63–64. **not-pated:** short-haired
64. **puke:** woolen; **caddis:** worsted tape
64. **caddis:** worsted tape
65. **Spanish-pouch:** a pouch made of Spanish leather
67–69. The obscurity of these lines was probably intended by Hal further to confuse Francis.

FRANCIS. What, sir?

POINS. [*within*] Francis!

PRINCE. Away, you rogue! Dost thou not hear them call?

Here they both call him. The DRAWER *stands amazed, not knowing which way to go.*

Enter VINTNER.

VINTNER. What! stand'st thou still, and hear'st such a calling? [Lo]ok to the guests within. [*Exit* FRANCIS.] My lord, old Sir John, with half-a-dozen more, are at the door. Shall I let them in?

PRINCE. Let them alone awhile, and then open the door. [*Exit* VINTNER.] Poins!

POINS. [*within*] Anon, anon, sir.

Enter POINS.

PRINCE. Sirrah, Falstaff and the rest of the thieves are at the door. Shall we be merry?

POINS. As merry as crickets, my lad. But hark ye; what cunning match have you made with this jest of the drawer? Come, what's the issue?

PRINCE. I am now of all humors that have showed themselves humors since the old days of goodman Adam to the pupil age of this present twelve o'clock at midnight.

[*Enter* FRANCIS.]

What's o'clock, Francis?

FRANCIS. Anon, anon, sir. [*Exit.*]

PRINCE. That ever this fellow should have fewer words than a parrot, and yet the son of a woman! His industry is upstairs and and downstairs, his eloquence the parcel of a reckoning. I am not yet of Percy's mind, the Hotspur of the North, he that kills me some six or seven dozen of Scots at a breakfast, washes his hands, and says to his wife, "Fie upon this quiet life! I want work." "O my sweet Harry," says she, "how many

85–87. **I am now . . . midnight:** "I am willing to indulge myself in gayety and frolick, and try all the varieties of human life" (Johnson).

86. **pupil age:** youth

hast thou killed to-day?" "Give my roan horse a drench," says he, and answers, "Some fourteen," an hour after; "a trifle, a trifle." I prithee call in Falstaff. I'll play Percy, and that damned brawn shall play Dame Mortimer his wife. "Rivo!" says the drunkard. Call in ribs, call in tallow.

Enter FALSTAFF, [GADSHILL, BARDOLPH, *and* PETO; *followed by* FRANCIS *with wine*].

POINS. Welcome, Jack! Where hast thou been?

FALSTAFF. A plague of all cowards, I say, and a vengeance too! Marry and amen! Give me a cup of sack, boy. Ere I lead this life long, I'll sew netherstocks, and mend them and foot them too. A plague of all cowards! Give me a cup of sack, rogue. Is there no virtue extant? *He drinketh*

PRINCE. Didst thou never see Titan kiss a dish of butter, pitiful-hearted Titan, that melted at the sweet tale of the sun's? If thou didst, then behold that compound.

FALSTAFF. You rogue, here's lime in this sack too! There is nothing but roguery to be found in villainous man; yet a coward is worse than a cup of sack with lime in it—a villainous coward! Go thy ways, old Jack, die when thou wilt; if manhood, good manhood, be not forgot upon the fact of the earth, then am I a shotten herring. There lives not three good men unhanged in England; and one of them is fat and grows old. God help the while! A bad world, I say. I would I were a weaver; I could sing psalms or anything. A plague of all cowards, I say still!

PRINCE. How now, wool-sack? What mutter you?

FALSTAFF. A king's son! If I do not beat thee out of thy kingdom with a dagger of lath and drive all thy subjects afore thee

97. **drench:** dose of medicine
100. **brawn:** boar; **Rivo:** probably a drinker's exclamation
103. **of:** on
105. **netherstocks:** stockings
108. **Titan:** the sun
110. **compound:** mass
111. **lime:** added to clarify the wine
116. **shotten herring:** a herring that has shed its roe (and is thus thin)
118. **the while:** the present time
119. **weaver . . . psalms:** Weavers were noted for their singing while working at their looms.
123. **dagger of lath:** an imitation weapon

like a flock of wild geese, I'll never wear hair on my face more. You Prince of Wales!

PRINCE. Why, you whoreson round man, what's the matter?

FALSTAFF. Are not you a coward? Answer me to that, and Poins there?

POINS. 'Zounds, ye fat paunch, an ye call me coward, by the Lord, I'll stab thee.

FALSTAFF. I call thee coward? I'll see thee damned ere I call thee coward, but I would give a thousand pound I could run as fast as thou canst. You are straight enough in the shoulders; you care not who sees your back. Call you that backing of your friends? A plague upon such backing! Give me them that will face me. Give me a cup of sack. I am a rogue if I drunk to-day.

PRINCE. O villain! thy lips are scarce wiped since thou drunk'st last.

FALSTAFF. All is one for that. (*He drinketh.*) A plague of all cowards, still say I.

PRINCE. What's the matter?

FALSTAFF. What's the matter? There be four of us here have ta'en a thousand pound this day morning.

PRINCE. Where is it, Jack? where is it?

FALSTAFF. Where is it? Taken from us it is. A hundred upon poor four of us!

PRINCE. What, a hundred, man?

FALSTAFF. I am a rogue if I were not at half-sword with a dozen of them two hours together. I have 'scaped by miracle. I am eight times thrust through the doublet, four through the hose; my buckler cut through and through, my sword hacked like a handsaw—*ecce signum!* [*Shows his sword.*] I never dealt better since I was a man. All would not do. A plague of all cowards! Let them speak. If they speak more or less than truth, they are villains and the sons of darkness.

PRINCE. Speak, sirs. How was it?

GADSHILL. We four set upon some dozen—

149. **at half-sword:** at close quarters
151. **doublet:** close-fitting body garment
152. **hose:** breeches; **buckler:** shield
153. ***ecce signum:*** behold the sign
154. **dealt:** fought

FALSTAFF. Sixteen at least, my lord.

GADSHILL. And bound them.

PETO. No, no, they were not bound.

FALSTAFF. You rogue, they were bound, every man of them, or I am a Jew else, an Ebrew Jew.

GADSHILL. As we were sharing, some six or seven fresh men set upon us—

FALSTAFF. And unbound the rest, and then come in the other.

PRINCE. What, fought you with them all?

FALSTAFF. All? I know not what you call all, but if I fought not with fifty of them, I am a bunch of radish! If there were not two or three and fifty upon poor old Jack, then am I no two-legged creature.

PRINCE. Pray God you have not murdered some of them.

FALSTAFF. Nay, that's past praying for. I have peppered two of them. Two I am sure I have paid, two rogues in buckram suits. I tell thee what, Hal, if I tell thee a lie, spit in my face, call me horse. Thou knowest my old ward. Here I lay, and thus I bore my boint. Four rogues in buckram let drive at me.

PRINCE. What, four? Thou saidst but two even now.

FALSTAFF. Four, Hal. I told thee four.

POINS. Ay, ay, he said four.

FALSTAFF. These four came all afront and mainly thrust at me. I made me no more ado but took all their seven points in my target, thus.

PRINCE. Seven? Why, there were but four even now.

FALSTAFF. In buckram?

POINS. Ay, four, in buckram suits.

FALSTAFF. Seven, by these hilts, or I am a villain else.

PRINCE. [*aside to* POINS] Prithee let him alone. We shall have more anon.

FALSTAFF. Dost thou hear me, Hal?

170. **three and fifty:** G. R. Stewart has noted that fifty-three was the number of Spanish ships against which the *Revenge* heroically fought in 1591.

173. **peppered:** made it hot for

174. **paid:** killed

176. **horse:** a term of abuse; **ward:** fighting posture

183. **target:** shield

187. **by these hilts:** Falstaff swears by the cross-like shape made by the handle and blade of his sword

PRINCE. Ay, and mark thee too, Jack.

FALSTAFF. Do so, for it is worth the listening to. These nine in buckram that I told thee of—

PRINCE. So, two more already.

FALSTAFF. Their points being broken—

POINS. Down fell their hose.

FALSTAFF. Began to give me ground; but I followed me close, came in, foot and hand, and with a thought seven of the eleven I paid.

PRINCE. O monstrous! Eleven buckram men grown out of two!

FALSTAFF. But, as the devil would have it, three misbegotten knaves in Kendal green came at my back and let drive at me, for it was so dark, Hal, that thou couldst not see thy hand.

PRINCE. These lies are like their father that begets them—gross as a mountain, open, palpable. Why, thou clay-brained guts, thou knotty-pated fool, thou whoreson, obscene, greasy tallow-catch—

FALSTAFF. What, art thou mad? art thou mad? Is not the truth the truth?

PRINCE. Why, how couldst thou know these men in Kendal green when it was so dark thou couldst not see thy hand? Come, tell us your reason. What sayest thou to this?

POINS. Come, your reason, Jack, your reason.

FALSTAFF. What, upon compulsion? 'Zounds, an I were at the strappado or all the racks in the world, I would not tell you on compulsion. Give you a reason on compulsion? If reasons were as plentiful as blackberries, I would give no man a reason upon compulsion, I.

PRINCE. I'll be no longer guilty of this sin. This sanguine coward, this bed-presser, this horseback-breaker, this huge hill of flesh—

FALSTAFF. 'Sblood, you starveling, you eel-skin, you dried neat's-tongue, you bull's pizzle, you stockfish! O for breath to utter what is like thee! you tailor's yard, you sheath, you bowcase,

195. **points**: (1) sword-points (2) laces supporting the hose
206. **knotty-pated**: thick headed; **tallow-catch**: tub of tallow
212. **reason**: explanation
215. **strappado**: a torture machine
219. **sanguine**: red-faced
220. **bed-presser**: lazy fellow
223. **stockfish**: dried cod

you vile standing tuck!

PRINCE. Well, breathe awhile, and then to it again; and when thou hast tired thyself in base comparisons, hear me speak but this.

POINS. Mark, Jack.

PRINCE. We two saw you four set on four, and bound them and were masters of their wealth. Mark now, how a plain tale shall put you down. Then did we two set on you four and, with a word, outfaced you from your prize, and have it; yea, and can show it you here in the house. And, Falstaff, you carried your guts away as nimbly, with as quick dexterity, and roared for mercy, and still run and roared, as ever I heard bullcalf. What a slave art thou to hack thy sword as thou hast done, and then say it was in fight! What trick, what device, what starting hole canst thou now find out to hide thee from this open and apparent shame?

POINS. Come, let's hear, Jack. What trick hast thou now?

FALSTAFF. By the Lord, I knew ye as well as he that made ye. Why, hear you, my masters: Was it for me to kill the heir apparent? Should I turn upon the true prince? Why, thou knowest I am as valiant as Hercules, but beware instinct. The lion will not touch the true prince. Instinct is a great matter. I was now a coward on instinct. I shall think the better of myself, and thee, during my life; I for a valiant lion, and thou for a true prince. But, by the Lord, lads, I am glad you have the money. Hostess, clap to the doors. Watch to-night, pray to-morrow. Gallants, lads, boys, hearts of gold, all the titles of good fellowship come to you! What, shall we be merry? Shall we have a play extempore?

PRINCE. Content—and the argument shall be thy running away.

FALSTAFF. Ah, no more of that, Hal, an thou lovest me!

Enter HOSTESS.

HOSTESS. O Jesu, my lord the Prince!

PRINCE. How now, my lady the hostess! What say'st thou to me?

225. **tuck:** rapier
233. **outfaced:** frightened
238. **starting hole:** loophole, escape
250–51. **watch . . . to-morrow:** Cf. Matthew 26:41: "Watch and pray, that ye enter not into temptation. . . ."
254. **argument:** subject

HOSTESS. Marry, my lord, there is a noble man of the court at door would speak with you. He says he comes from your father.

PRINCE. Give him as much as will make him a royal man, and send him back again to my mother.

FALSTAFF. What manner of man is he?

HOSTESS. An old man.

FALSTAFF. What doth gravity out of his bed at midnight? Shall I give him his answer?

PRINCE. Prithee do, Jack.

FALSTAFF. Faith, and I'll send him packing. *Exit.*

PRINCE. Now, sirs, by'r Lady, you fought fair; so did you, Peto; so did you, Bardolph. You are lions too: you ran away upon instinct, you will not touch the true prince; no, fie!

BARDOLPH. Faith, I ran when I saw others run.

PRINCE. Tell me now in earnest, how came Falstaff's sword so hacked?

PETO. Why, he hacked it with his dagger, and said he would swear truth out of England but he would make you believe it was done in fight, and persuaded us to do the like.

BARDOLPH. Yea, and to tickle our noses with speargrass to make them bleed, and then to beslubber our garments with it and swear it was the blood of true men. I did that I did not this seven year before. I blushed to hear his monstrous devices.

PRINCE. O villain! thou stolest a cup of sack eighteen years ago and wert taken with the manner, and ever since thou hast blushed extempore. Thou hadst fire and sword on thy side, and yet thou ran'st away. What instinct hadst thou for it?

BARDOLPH. My lord, do you see these meteors? [*pointing to his own face*] Do you behold these exhalations?

PRINCE. I do.

BARDOLPH. What think you they portend?

PRINCE. Hot livers and cold purses.

BARDOLPH. Choler, my lord, if rightly taken.

Enter FALSTAFF.

258–260. **noble . . . royal:** puns on court terms and names of coins: noble (6s.8d) and royal (10s)

282. **wert . . . manner:** caught in the act

285–86. Bardolph is describing the eruptions on his face.

289. **Hot . . . purses:** drunkenness and poverty

290. **Choler:** anger

PRINCE. No, if rightly taken, halter. Here comes lean Jack; here comes bare-bone. How now, my sweet creature of bombast? How long is't ago, Jack, since thou sawest thine own knee?

FALSTAFF. My own knee? When I was about thy years, Hal, I was not an eagle's talon in the waist; I could have crept into any alderman's thumb-ring. A plague of sighing and grief! It blows a man up like a bladder. There's villainous news abroad. Here was Sir John Bracy from your father. You must to the court in the morning. That same mad fellow of the north, Percy, and he of Wales that gave Amamon the bastinado, and made Lucifer cuckold, and swore the devil his true liegeman upon the cross of a Welsh hook—what a plague call you him?

POINS. Owen Glendower.

FALSTAFF. Owen, Owen, the same; and his son-in-law Mortimer, and old Northumberland, and that sprightly Scot of Scots, Douglas, that runs a-horseback up a hill perpendicular—

PRINCE. He that rides at high speed and with his pistol kills a sparrow flying.

FALSTAFF. You have hit it.

PRINCE. So did he never the sparrow.

FALSTAFF. Well, that rascal hath good metal in him; he will not run.

PRINCE. Why, what a rascal art thou then, to praise him so for running!

FALSTAFF. A-horseback, ye cuckoo! but afoot he will not budge a foot.

PRINCE. Yes, Jack, upon instinct.

FALSTAFF. I grant ye, upon instinct. Well, he is there too, and one Mordake, and a thousand bluecaps more. Worcester is stolen away to-night; thy father's beard is turned white with the news; you may buy land now as cheap as stinking mackerel.

PRINCE. Why then, it is like, if there come a hot June, and this

291. **taken:** (1) construed (2) apprehended; **halter:** the hangman's noose, i.e., a "collar" with a pun on "choler" above

292. **bombast:** cotton padding

300. **Amamon:** the name of a devil; **bastinado:** beating

301. **made . . . cuckhold:** i.e., caused horns to grow on Lucifer's head; **liegeman:** vassal sworn to the service of his lord

302. **Welsh hook:** a pike with a curved blade ending in a hook

319. **bluecaps:** Scots

civil buffeting hold, we shall buy maidenheads as they buy hobnails, by the hundreds.

FALSTAFF. By the mass, lad, thou sayest true; it is like we shall have good trading that way. But tell me, Hal, art not thou horrible afeared? Thou being heir apparent, could the world pick thee out three such enemies again as that fiend Douglas, that spirit Percy, and that devil Glendower? Art thou not horribly afraid? Doth not thy blood thrill at it?

PRINCE. Not a whit, i' faith. I lack some of thy instinct.

FALSTAFF. Well, thou wilt be horribly chid to-morrow when thou comest to thy father. If thou love me, practice an answer.

PRINCE. Do thou stand for my father and examine me upon the particulars of my life.

FALSTAFF. Shall I? Content. This chair shall be my state, this dagger my sceptre, and this cushion my crown.

PRINCE. Thy state is taken for a joined-stool, thy golden sceptre for a leaden dagger, and thy precious rich crown for a pitiful bald crown.

FALSTAFF. Well, an the fire of grace be not quite out of thee, now shalt thou be moved. Give me a cup of sack to make my eyes look red, that it may be thought I have wept; for I must speak in passion, and I will do it in King Cambyses' vein.

PRINCE. Well, here is my leg.

FALSTAFF. And here is my speech. Stand aside, nobility.

HOSTESS. O Jesu, this is excellent sport, i' faith!

FALSTAFF. Weep not, sweet queen, for trickling tears are vain.

HOSTESS. O, the Father, how he holds his countenance!

FALSTAFF. For God's sake, lords, convey my tristful queen! For tears do stop the floodgates of her eyes.

HOSTESS. O Jesu, he doth it as like one of these harlotry players as ever I see!

330. **thrill**: tingle (with fear)
336. **state**: chair of state
338. **joined-stool**: a common piece of furniture
344. **King Cambyses**: a character in *Cambyses, King of Persia* (1570), an old play noted for its bombast
345. **leg**: obeisance
349. **holds his countenance**: maintains a dignified appearance or, perhaps, strikes a pose
350. **convey**: escort; **tristful**: sad
352. **harlotry**: worthless

FALSTAFF. Peace, good pintpot. Peace, good tickle-brain. Harry, I do not only marvel where thou spendest thy time, but also how thou art accompanied. For though the camomile, the more it is trodden on, the faster it grows, yet youth, the more it is wasted, the sooner it wears. That thou art my son I have partly thy mother's word, partly my own opinion, but chiefly a villainous trick of thine eye and a foolish hanging of thy nether lip that doth warrant me. If then thou be son to me, here lies the point: why, being son to me, art thou so pointed at? Shall the blessed sun of heaven prove a micher and eat blackberries? A question not to be asked. Shall the son of England prove a thief and take purses? A question to be asked. There is a thing, Harry, which thou hast often heard of, and it is known to many in our land by the name of pitch. This pitch, as ancient writers do report, doth defile; so doth the company thou keepest. For, Harry, now I do not speak to thee in drink, but in tears; not in pleasure, but in passion; not in words only, but in woes also; and yet there is a virtuous man whom I have often noted in thy company, but I know not his name.

PRINCE. What manner of man, an it like your majesty?

FALSTAFF. A goodly portly man i' faith, and a corpulent; of a cheerful look, a pleasing eye, and a most noble carriage; and, as I think, his age some fifty, or, by'r Lady, inclining to threescore; and now I remember me, his name is Falstaff. If that man should be lewdly given, he deceiveth me; for, Harry, I see virtue in his looks. If then the tree may be known by the fruit, as the fruit by the tree, then, peremptorily I speak it, there is virtue in that Falstaff. Him keep with, the rest banish. And tell me now, thou naughty varlet, tell me where hast thou

354. **pintpot:** a nickname for a seller of beer; **tickle-brain:** strong liquor

360. **trick:** characteristic expression

361. **warrant:** assure

363. **micher:** truant

363–64. **eat blackberries:** i.e., wander here and there

369–71. **now . . . also:** a parody of the style of *Euphues* (1578), a popular novel by John Lyly

379. **lewdly given:** accustomed to vile practices

380–81. **the tree . . . fruit:** Cf. Matthew 12:33.

381. **peremptorily:** positively

been this month?

PRINCE. Dost thou speak like a king? Do thou stand for me, and I'll play my father.

FALSTAFF. Depose me? If thou dost it half so gravely, so majestically, both in word and matter, hang me up by the heels for a rabbit-sucker or a poulter's hare.

PRINCE. Well, here I am set.

FALSTAFF. And here I stand. Judge, my masters.

PRINCE. Now, Harry, whence come you?

FALSTAFF. My noble lord, from Eastcheap.

PRINCE. The complaints I hear of thee are grievous.

FALSTAFF. 'Sblood, my lord, they are false! Nay, I'll tickle ye for a young prince, i' faith.

PRINCE. Swearest thou, ungracious boy? Henceforth ne'er look on me. Thou art violently carried away from grace. There is a devil haunts thee in the likeness of an old fat man; a tun of man is thy companion. Why dost thou converse with that trunk of humors, that bolting hutch of beastliness, that swollen parcel of dropsies, that huge bombard of sack, that stuffed cloakbag of guts, that roasted Manningtree ox with the pudding in his belly, that reverend vice, that grey iniquity, that father ruffian, that vanity in years? Wherein is he good, but to taste sack and drink it? wherein neat and cleanly, but to carve a capon and eat it? wherein cunning, but in craft? wherein crafty, but in villainy? wherein villainous, but in all things? wherein worthy, but in nothing?

FALSTAFF. I would your grace would take me with you. Whom means your grace?

PRINCE. That villainous abominable misleader of youth, Falstaff, that old white-bearded Satan.

FALSTAFF. My lord, the man I know.

389. **rabbit-sucker:** suckling rabbit

395–96. **I'll tickle . . . prince:** Falstaff offers to amuse Hal by acting the part of a young prince.

401. **humors:** body fluids; **bolting hutch:** sifting bin

402. **bombard:** leather jug for liquor

403. **Manningtree:** a town in Essex at whose annual fairs oxen, famous for their size, were roasted.

404. **vice:** a mischievous character in the morality play

407. **cunning:** knowing

410. **take . . . you:** let me understand you

PRINCE. I know thou dost.

FALSTAFF. But to say I know more harm in him than in myself were to say more than I know. That he is old, the more the pity, his white hairs do witness it; but that he is, saving your reverence, a whoremaster, that I utterly deny. If sack and sugar be a fault, God help the wicked! If to be old and merry be a sin, then many an old host that I know is damned. If to be fat be to be hated, then Pharaoh's lean kine are to be loved. No, my good lord: banish Peto, banish Bardolph, banish Poins; but for sweet Jack Falstaff, kind Jack Falstaff, true Jack Falstaff, valiant Jack Falstaff, and therefore more valiant being, as he is, old Jack Falstaff, banish not him thy Harry's company, banish not him thy Harry's company. Banish plump Jack, and banish all the world!

PRINCE. I do, I will.

[*A great knocking heard. Exeunt* HOSTESS, FRANCIS, *and* BARDOLPH.]

Enter BARDOLPH, *running.*

BARDOLPH. O, my lord, my lord! the sheriff with a most monstrous watch is at the door.

FALSTAFF. Out, ye rogue! Play out the play. I have much to say in the behalf of that Falstaff.

Enter the HOSTESS.

HOSTESS. O Jesu, my lord, my lord!

PRINCE. Heigh, heigh, the devil rides upon a fiddlestick! What's the matter?

HOSTESS. The sheriff and all the watch are at the door. They are come to search the house. Shall I let them in?

FALSTAFF. Dost thou hear, Hal? Never call a true piece of gold a counterfeit. Thou art essentially mad without seeming so.

PRINCE. And thou a natural coward without instinct.

FALSTAFF. I deny your major. If you will deny the sheriff, so; if not, let him enter. If I become not a cart as well as another

418. **saving:** with all respect to
422. **Pharaoh's lean kine:** see Genesis 41:19–21
435. **the devil . . . fiddlestick:** proverbial, much ado about nothing
440. **essentially made:** made of genuine substance
442. **major:** major premise
443. **cart:** used to transport prisoners to their execution

man, a plague on my bringing up! I hope I shall as soon be strangled with a halter as another.

PRINCE. Go hide thee behind the arras. The rest walk up above. Now, my masters, for a true face and good conscience.

FALSTAFF. Both which I have had; but their date is out, and therefore I'll hide me. [*Exit.*]

PRINCE. Call in the sheriff.

[*Exeunt all but the* PRINCE *and* PETO.]

Enter SHERIFF *and the* CARRIER.

Now, master sheriff, what is your will with me?
SHERIFF. First, pardon me, my lord. A hue and cry
Hath followed certain men into this house.
PRINCE. What men?
SHERIFF. One of them is well known, my gracious lord,
A gross fat man.
CARRIER. As fat as butter.
PRINCE. The man, I do assure you, is not here,
For I myself at this time have employed him.
And, Sheriff, I will engage my word to thee
That I will by to-morrow dinner time
Send him to answer thee, or any man,
For anything he shall be charged withal;
And so let me entreat you leave the house.
SHERIFF. I will, my lord. There are two gentlemen
Have in this robbery lost three hundred marks.
PRINCE. It may be so. If he have robbed these men,
He shall be answerable; and so farewell.
SHERIFF. Good night, my noble lord.
PRINCE. I think it is good morrow, is it not?
SHERIFF. Indeed, my lord, I think it be two o'clock.

Exeunt [SHERIFF *and* CARRIER].

PRINCE. This oily rascal is known as well as Paul's. Go call him forth.

PETO. Falstaff! Fast asleep behind the arras, and snorting like a

446. **arras:** tapestry
447. **true:** honest-looking
448. **date is out:** term has expired
459. **engage:** pledge
471. **Paul's:** St. Paul's Cathedral, London

horse.

PRINCE. Hark how hard he fetches breath. Search his pockets.

He searcheth his pocket[s] and findeth certain papers.

What hast thou found?

PETO. Nothing but papers, my lord.

PRINCE. Let's see what they be. Read them.

[PETO.] [*reads*]

"Item, A capon .... 2s. 2d.
Item, Sauce .... 4d.
Item, Sack two gallons .... 5s. 8d.
Item, Anchovies and sack after supper 2s. 6d.
Item, Bread .... ob."

[PRINCE.] O monstrous! but one halfpennyworth of bread to this intolerable deal of sack! What there is else, keep close; we'll read it at more advantage. There let him sleep till day. I'll to the court in the morning. We must all to the wars, and thy place shall be honorable. I'll procure this fat rogue a charge of foot, and I know his death will be a march of twelve score. The money shall be paid back again with advantage. Be with me betimes in the morning, and so good morrow, Peto.

PETO. Good morrow, good my lord. *Exeunt.*

[ACT III. SCENE I. *Wales.* GLENDOWER'S *Castle.*]

Enter HOTSPUR, WORCESTER, LORD MORTIMER, OWEN GLENDOWER.

MORTIMER. These promises are fair, the parties sure,
And our induction full of prosperous hope.

HOTSPUR. Lord Mortimer, and cousin Glendower,
Will you sit down?
And uncle Worcester,—a plague upon it!
I have forgot the map.

GLENDOWER. No, here it is.
Sit, cousin Percy; sit, good cousin Hotspur,

483. **ob.:** halfpenny
485. **deal:** large quantity
488–89. **charge of foot:** infantry command
489. **twelve score:** twelve score yards
490. **advantage:** interest
491. **betimes:** early
2. **induction:** initial step

For by that name as oft as Lancaster
Doth speak of you, his cheek looks pale and with
A rising sigh he wisheth you in heaven.

HOTSPUR. And you in hell, as oft as he hears Owen
Glendower spoke of.

GLENDOWER. I cannot blame him. At my nativity
The front of heaven was full of fiery shapes
Of burning cressets, and at my birth
The frame and huge foundation of the earth
Shaked like a coward.

HOTSPUR. Why, so it would have done at the same season if your mother's cat had but kittened, though yourself had never been born.

GLENDOWER. I say the earth did shake when I was born.

HOTSPUR. And I say the earth was not of my mind,
If you suppose as fearing you it shook.

GLENDOWER. The heavens were all on fire, the earth did tremble.

HOTSPUR. O, then the earth shook to see the heavens on fire,
And not in fear of your nativity.
Diseased nature oftentimes breaks forth
In strange eruptions; oft the teeming earth
Is with a kind of colic pinched and vexed
By the imprisoning of unruly wind
Within her womb, which, for enlargement striving,
Shakes the old beldame earth and topples down
Steeples and mossgrown towers. At your birth
Our grandam earth, having this distemp'rature
In passion shook.

GLENDOWER. Cousin, of many men
I do not bear these crossings. Give me leave
To tell you once again that at my birth
The front of heaven was full of fiery shapes,
The goats ran from the mountains, and the herds
Were strangely clamorous to the frighted fields.

8. **Lancaster:** i.e., Henry IV
14. **front:** forehead
15. **cressets:** fire baskets used as beacons
31. **enlargement:** release from confinement
32. **beldame:** grandmother
34. **distemp'rature:** disease
36. **bear . . . crossings:** tolerate these contradictions

These signs have marked me extraordinary;
And all the courses of my life do show
I am not in the roll of common men.
Where is he living, clipped in with the sea
That chides the banks of England, Scotland, Wales,
Which calls me pupil or hath read to me?
And bring him out that is but woman's son
Can trace me in the tedious ways of art
And hold me pace in deep experiments.

HOTSPUR. I think there's no man speaks better Welsh.
I'll to dinner.

MORTIMER. Peace, cousin Percy; you will make him mad.

GLENDOWER. I can call spirits from the vasty deep.

HOTSPUR. Why, so can I, or so can any man;
But will they come when you do call for them?

GLENDOWER. Why, I can teach you, cousin, to command
The devil.

HOTSPUR. And I can teach thee, coz, to shame the devil
By telling truth. Tell truth and shame the devil.
If thou have power to raise him, bring him hither,
And I'll be sworn I have power to shame him hence.
O, while you live, tell truth and shame the devil!

MORTIMER. Come, come, no more of this unprofitable chat.

GLENDOWER. Three times hath Henry Bolingbroke made head
Against my power; thrice from the banks of Wye
And sandy-bottomed Severn have I sent him
Bootless home and weather beaten back.

HOTSPUR. Home without boots, and in foul weather too?
How 'scapes he agues, in the devil's name?

GLENDOWER. Come, here is the map. Shall we divide our right
According to our threefold order ta'en?

MORTIMER. The archdeacon hath divided it
Into three limits very equally:

44. **clipped in with:** encircled by
45. **chides:** lashes
46. **read to:** taught
48. **art:** magic
49. **hold me pace:** keep up with me
64. **made head:** raised an army
67. **Booteless:** profitless
69. **agues:** fevers and chills

England, from Trent and Severn hitherto,
By south and east is to my part assigned;
All westward, Wales beyond the Severn shore,
And all the fertile land within that bound,
To Owen Glendower; and, dear coz, to you
The remnant northward lying off from Trent.
And our indentures tripartite are drawn,
Which being sealed interchangeably
(A business that this night may execute),
To-morrow, cousin Percy, you and I
And my good Lord of Worcester will set forth
To meet your father and the Scottish power,
As is appointed us, at Shrewsbury.
My father Glendower is not ready yet,
Nor shall we need his help these fourteen days.
Within that space you may have drawn together
Your tenants, friends, and neighboring gentlemen.

GLENDOWER. A shorter time shall send me to you, lords;
And in my conduct shall your ladies come,
From whom you now must steal and take no leave,
For there will be a world of water shed
Upon the parting of your wives and you.

HOTSPUR. Methinks my moiety, north from Burton here,
In quantity equals not one of yours.
See how this river comes me cranking in
And cuts me from the best of all my land
A huge half-moon, a monstrous cantle out.
I'll have the current in this place dammed up,
And here the smug and silver Trent shall run
In a new channel fair and evenly.
It shall not wind with such a deep indent
To rob me of so rich a bottom here.

GLENDOWER. Not wind? It shall, it must! You see it doth.

80. **indentures tripartite:** three-party compact
87. **father:** father-in-law
96. **moiety:** share
98. **cranking:** winding
100. **cantle:** piece
102. **smug:** smooth

MORTIMER. Yea, but
Mark how he bears his course, and runs me up
With like advantage on the other side,
Gelding the opposed continent as much
As on the other side it takes from you.
WORCESTER. Yea, but a little charge will trench him here
And on this north side win this cape of land;
And then he runs straight and even.
HOTSPUR. I'll have it so. A little charge will do it.
GLENDOWER. I will not have it altered.
HOTSPUR. Will not you?
GLENDOWER. No, nor you shall not.
HOTSPUR. Who shall say me nay?
GLENDOWER. Why, that will I.
HOTSPUR. Let me not understand you then; speak it in Welsh.
GLENDOWER. I can speak English, lord, as well as you;
For I was trained up in the English court,
Where, being but young, I framed to the harp
Many an English ditty lovely well,
And gave the tongue a helpful ornament,
A virtue that was never seen in you.
HOTSPUR. Marry, and I am glad of it with all my heart!
I had rather be a kitten and cry mew
Than one of these same metre ballet-mongers.
I had rather hear a brazen canstick turned
Or a dry wheel grate on the axletree,
And that would set my teeth nothing on edge,
Nothing so much as mincing poetry.
'Tis like the forced gait of a shuffling nag.
GLENDOWER. Come, you shall have Trent turned.
HOTSPUR. I do not care. I'll give thrice so much land
To any well-deserving friend;
But in the way of bargain, mark ye me,
I'll cavil on the ninth part of a hair.
Are the indentures drawn? Shall we be gone?

110. **opposed continent:** opposite shore
112. **charge:** cost
128. **ballet-mongers:** those who sang and sold ballads in the streets
129. **canstick:** candlestick; **turned:** shaped on a lathe

GLENDOWER. The moon shines fair; you may away by night.
I'll haste the writer, and withal
Break with your wives of your departure hence.
I am afraid my daughter will run mad,
So much she doteth on her Mortimer. *Exit.*

MORTIMER. Fie, cousin Percy! how you cross my father!

HOTSPUR. I cannot choose. Sometimes he angers me
With telling me of the moldwarp and the ant,
Of the dreamer Merlin and his prophecies,
And of a dragon and a finless fish,
A clip-winged griffin and a moulten raven,
A couching lion and a ramping cat,
And such a deal of skimble-skamble stuff
As puts me from my faith. I tell you what:
He held me last night at least nine hours
In reckoning up the several devils' names
That were his lackeys. I cried "hum," and "Well, go to!"
But marked him not a word. O, he is as tedious
As a tired horse, a railing wife;
Worse than a smoky house. I had rather live
With cheese and garlic in a windmill far
Than feed on cates and have him talk to me
In any summer house in Christendom.

MORTIMER. In faith, he is a worthy gentleman,
Exceedingly well read, and profited
In strange concealments, valiant as a lion,
And wondrous affable, and as bountiful
As mines of India. Shall I tell you, cousin?
He holds your temper in a high respect
And curbs himself even of his natural scope

141. **withal**: at the same time
142. **Break with**: tell
147. **moldwarp**: mole
148. **Merlin**: famous magician of Celtic legend
150. **griffin**: fabulous animal half lion, half eagle
151. **ramping**: rearing
152. **skimble-skamble**: nonsensical
153. **puts . . . faith**: makes me forget I am a Christian
156. **go to**: an expression of derisive disbelief
161. **cates**: dainties
164–65. **profited . . . concealments**: skilled in magic
169. **natural scope**: disposition

When you come 'cross his humor. Faith, he does.
I warrant you that man is not alive
Might so have tempted him as you have done
Without the taste of danger and reproof;
But do not use it oft, let me entreat you.

WORCESTER. In faith, my lord, you are too willful-blame,
And since your coming hither have done enough
To put him quite besides his patience.
You must needs learn, lord, to amend this fault.
Though sometimes it show greatness, courage, blood—
And that's the dearest grace it renders you—
Yet oftentimes it doth present harsh rage,
Defect of manners, want of government,
Pride, haughtiness, opinion, and disdain;
The least of which haunting a nobleman
Loseth men's hearts, and leaves behind a stain
Upon the beauty of all parts besides,
Beguiling them of commendation.

HOTSPUR. Well, I am schooled. Good manners be your speed!
Here come our wives, and let us take our leave.

Enter GLENDOWER *with the* LADIES..

MORTIMER. This is the deadly spite that angers me:
My wife can speak no English, I no Welsh.

GLENDOWER. My daughter weeps; she will not part with you;
She'll be a soldier too, she'll to the wars.

MORTIMER. Good father, tell her that she and my aunt Percy
Shall follow in your conduct speedily.

GLENDOWER *speaks to her in Welsh, and she answers him in the same.*

GLENDOWER. She is desperate here. A peevish self-willed harlotry,
One that no persuasion can do good upon.

172. **tempted:** defied
175. **willful-blame:** obstinately blamable
179. **blood:** mettle
182. **government:** becoming conduct
183. **opinion:** arrogance
187. **Beguiling:** depriving
188. **be your speed:** give you success
190. **spite:** vexation
196. **peevish:** obstinate; **harlotry:** silly wench

The LADY *speaks in Welsh.*

MORTIMER. I understand thy looks. That pretty Welsh
Which thou pourest down from these swelling heavens
I am too perfect in; and, but for shame,
In such a parley should I answer thee.

The LADY *again in Welsh.*

I understand thy kisses, and thou mine,
And that's a feeling disputation.
But I will never be a truant, love,
Till I have learnt thy language; for thy tongue
Makes Welsh as sweet as ditties highly penned,
Sung by a fair queen in a summer's bow'r,
With ravishing division, to her lute.

GLENDOWER. Nay, if you melt, then will she run mad.

The LADY *speaks again in Welsh.*

MORTIMER. O, I am ignorance itself in this!

GLENDOWER. She bids you on the wanton rushes lay you down
And rest your gentle head upon her lap,
And she will sing the song that pleaseth you
And on your eyelids crown the god of sleep,
Charming your blood with pleasing heaviness,
Making such difference 'twixt wake and sleep
As is the difference betwixt day and night
The hour before the heavenly-harnessed team
Begins his golden progress in the east.

MORTIMER. With all my heart I'll sit and hear her sing.
By that time will our book, I think, be drawn.

GLENDOWER. Do so,
And those musicians that shall play to you
Hang in the air a thousand leagues from hence,
And straight they shall be here. Sit, and attend.

HOTSPUR. Come, Kate, thou art perfect in lying down.

201. **such a parley:** i.e., language of tears
203. **disputation:** conversation
206. **highly penned:** written in a lofty style
208. **division:** melody
211. **wanton:** luxuriant; **rushes:** used for floor covering
215. **blood:** disposition
221. **book:** i.e., the rebel compact
224. **attend:** listen
225. **perfect:** well-instructed

Come, quick, quick, that I may lay my head in thy lap.
LADY PERCY. Go, ye giddy goose. *The music plays.*
HOTSPUR. Now I perceive the devil understands Welsh.
And 'tis no marvel he is so humorous,
By'r Lady, he is a good musician.
LADY PERCY. Then should you be nothing but musical, for you are altogether governed by humors. Lie still ye thief, and hear the lady sing in Welsh.
HOTSPUR. I had rather hear Lady, my brach, howl in Irish.
LADY PERCY. Wouldst thou have thy head broken?
HOTSPUR. No.
LADY PERCY. Then be still.
HOTSPUR. Neither! 'Tis a woman's fault.
LADY PERCY. Now God help thee!
HOTSPUR. To the Welsh lady's bed.
LADY PERCY. What's that?
HOTSPUR. Peace! she sings.

Here the LADY *sings a Welsh song.*

Come, Kate, I'll have your song too.
LADY PERCY. Not mine, in good sooth.
HOTSPUR. Not yours in good sooth? Heart, you swear like a comfit-maker's wife. "Not you in good sooth!" and "as true as I live!" and "as God shall mend me!" and "as sure as day!"
And givest such sarcenet surety for thy oaths
As if thou never walk'st further than Finsbury.
Swear me, Kate, like a lady as thou art,
A good mouth-filling oath, and leave "in sooth"
And such protest of pepper gingerbread
To velvet guards and Sunday citizens.
Come, sing.
LADY PERCY. I will not sing.

229. **humorous:** capricious
232. **humors:** whims
234. **brach:** bitch-hound
244. **sooth:** truth
246. **comfit-maker's:** confectioner's
248. **sarcenet:** a finely-woven silk
249. **Finsbury:** a popular place of recreation near London
253. **velvet guards:** wearers of clothing trimmed with velvet; **Sunday citizens:** citizens in their Sunday finery (and perhaps on their Sunday behavior)

HOTSPUR. 'Tis the next way to turn tailor or be redbreast–teacher. An the indentures be drawn, I'll away within these two hours; and so come in when ye will. *Exit.*

GLENDOWER. Come, come, Lord Mortimer. You are as slow
As hot Lord Percy is on fire to go.
By this our book is drawn; we'll but seal,
And then to horse immediately.

MORTIMER. With all my heart.

Exeunt.

[SCENE II. *London. The Palace.*]

Enter the KING, PRINCE OF WALES, *and others.*

KING. Lords, give us leave: the Prince of Wales and I
Must have some private conference; but be near at hand,
For we shall presently have need of you. *Exeunt* LORDS.
I know not whether God will have it so
For some displeasing service I have done,
That, in his secret doom, out of my blood
He'll breed revengement and a scourge for me;
But thou dost in thy passages of life
Make me believe that thou art only marked
For the hot vengeance and the rod of heaven
To punish my mistreadings. Tell me else,
Could such inordinate and low desires,
Such poor, such bare, such lewd, such mean attempts,
Such barren pleasures, rude society,
As thou art matched withal and grafted to,
Accompany the greatness of thy blood
And hold their level with thy princely heart?

PRINCE. So please your majesty, I would I could

256. **tailor:** tailors were noted for their singing
261. **this:** this time
6. **doom:** judgment
8. **passages:** actions
9–10. **marked for:** appointed as an instrument of
13. **bare:** wretched; **lewd:** base

Quit all offenses with as clear excuse
As well as I am doubtless I can purge
Myself of many I am charged withal.
Yet such extenuation let me beg
As, in reproof of many tales devised,
Which oft the ear of greatness needs must hear
By smiling pickthanks and base newsmongers,
I may, for some things true wherein my youth
Hath faulty wandered and irregular,
Find pardon on my true submission.

KING. God pardon thee! Yet let me wonder, Harry,
At thy affections, which do hold a wing
Quite from the flight of all thy ancestors.
Thy place in council thou hast rudely lost,
Which by thy younger brother is supplied,
And art almost an alien to the hearts
Of all the court and princes of my blood.
The hope and expectation of thy time
Is ruined, and the soul of every man
Prophetically do forethink thy fall.
Had I so lavish of my presence been,
So common-hackneyed in the eyes of men,
So stale and cheap to vulgar company,
Opinion, that did help me to the crown,
Had still kept loyal to possession
And left me in reputeless banishment,
A fellow of no mark nor likelihood.
By being seldom seen, I could not stir
But like a comet I was wondered at;
That men would tell their children, "This is he!"
Others would say, "Where? Which is Bolingbroke?"

19. **Quit**: acquit
23. **reproof**: refutation
25. **pickthanks**: flatterers
30. **affections**: inclinations
32. **rudely**: by violent behavior
36. **time**: youth
38. **forethink**: predict
40. **common-hackneyed**: vulgarized
42. **Opinion**: public opinion
43. **Had . . . possession**: i.e., remained loyal to Richard II

And then I stole all courtesy from heaven,
And dressed myself in such humility
That I did pluck allegiance from men's hearts,
Loud shouts and salutations from their mouths
Even in the presence of the crownéd king.
Thus did I keep my person fresh and new,
My presence like a robe pontifical,
Ne'er seen but wondered at; and so my state,
Seldom but sumptuous, showed like a feast
And won by rareness such solemnity.
The skipping king, he ambled up and down
With shallow jesters and rash bavin wits,
Soon kindled and soon burnt; carded his state;
Mingled his royalty with cap'ring fools;
Had his great name profanéd with their scorns
And gave his countenance, against his name,
To laugh at gibing boys and stand the push
Of every beardless vain comparative;
Grew a companion to the common streets,
Enfeoffed himself to popularity;
That, being daily swallowed by men's eyes,
They surfeited with honey and began
To loathe the taste of sweetness, whereof a little
More than a little is by much too much.
So, when he had occasion to be seen,
He was but as the cuckoo is in June,
Heard, not regarded; seen, but with such eyes
As, sick and blunted with community,
Afford no extraordinary gaze
Such as is bent on sunlike majesty
When it shines seldom in admiring eyes;
But rather drowsed and hung their eyelids down,

60. **skipping:** flighty; **king:** i.e., Richard II
61. **bavin:** brushwood
62. **carded:** mixed with something base
66. **stand the push:** tolerate the (verbal) jostling
67. **vain comparative:** foolish scoffer
69. **Enfeoffed:** surrendered; **popularity:** common people
77. **community:** commonness

Slept in his face, and rendered such aspect
As cloudy men use to their adversaries,
Being with his presence glutted, gorged, and full.
And in that very line, Harry, standest thou;
For thou hast lost thy princely privilege
With vile participation. Not an eye
But is a-weary of thy common sight,
Save mine, which hath desired to see thee more,
Which now doth that I would not have it do:
Make blind itself with foolish tenderness. [*Weeping*]

PRINCE. I shall hereafter, my thrice gracious lord,
Be more myself.

KING. For all the world,
As thou art to this hour was Richard then
When I from France set foot at Ravenspurgh;
And even as I was then is Percy now.
Now, by my sceptre, and my soul to boot,
He hath more worthy interest to the state
Than thou, the shadow of succession;
For of no right, nor color like to right,
He doth fill fields with harness in the realm,
Turns head against the lion's armed jaws,
And, being no more in debt to years than thou,
Leads ancient lords and reverend bishops on
To bloody battles and to bruising arms.
What never-dying honor hath he got
Against renowned Douglas! whose high deeds,
Whose hot incursions, and great name in arms
Holds from all soldiers chief majority

82. **Slept . . . face:** insulted him by going to sleep in his presence; **aspect:** look
83. **cloudy:** sullen
85. **line:** i.e., line of descent
87. **vile participation:** fellowship with the low in rank
98. **interest:** title
99. **shadow:** mere name without a man to correspond to it
100. **color:** semblance
101. **harness:** men in armor
103. Historically, Hal was actually twenty-three years Hotspur's junior.
109. **majority:** superiority

And military title capital
Through all the kingdoms that acknowledge Christ.
Thrice hath this Hotspur, Mars in swathling clothes,
This infant warrior, in his enterprises
Discomfited great Douglas; ta'en him once,
Enlarged him, and made a friend of him,
To fill the mouth of deep defiance up
And shake the peace and safety of our throne.
And what say you to this? Percy, Northumberland,
The Archbishop's grace of York, Douglas, Mortimer
Capitulate against us and are up.
But wherefore do I tell these news to thee?
Why, Harry, do I tell thee of my foes
Which art my nearest and dearest enemy?
Thou that art like enough, through vassal fear,
Base inclination, and the start of spleen,
To fight against me under Percy's pay,
To dog his heels and curtsy at his frowns,
To show how much thou art degenerate.

PRINCE. Do not think so. You shall not find it so.
And God forgive them that so much have swayed
Your majesty's good thoughts away from me.
I will redeem all this on Percy's head,
And in the closing of some glorious day
Be bold to tell you that I am your son,
When I will wear a garment all of blood,
And stain my favors in a bloody mask,
Which, washed away, shall scour my shame with it.
And that shall be the day, whene'er it lights,
That this same child of honor and renown,
This gallant Hotspur, this all-praised knight,
And your unthought-of Harry chance to meet.

110. **capital:** chief
115. **Enlarged:** set at liberty
116. **To . . . up:** make defiance more vociferous
120. **Capitulate:** draw up articles of agreement; **up:** in arms
123. **dearest:** most beloved (with a possible play on "direst")
125. **start of spleen:** impulse
132. **redeem:** make up for
136. **favors:** facial features
138. **lights:** (1) dawns (2) happens

For every honor sitting on his helm,
Would they were multitudes, and on my head
My shames redoubled! For the time will come
That I shall make this northern youth exchange
His glorious deeds for my indignities.
Percy is but my factor, good my lord,
To engross up glorious deeds on my behalf;
And I will call him to so strict account
That he shall render every glory up,
Yea, even the slightest worship of his time;
Or I will tear the reckoning from his heart.
This in the name of God I promise here;
The which if He be pleased I shall perform,
I do beseech your majesty, may salve
The long-grown wounds of my intemperance.
If not, the end of life cancels all bands,
And I will die a hundred thousand deaths
Ere break the smallest parcel of this vow.

KING. A hundred thousand rebels die in this!
Thou shalt have charge and sovereign trust herein.

Enter BLUNT [*hastily*].

How now, good Blunt? Thy looks are full of speed.

BLUNT. So hath the business that I come to speak of.
Lord Mortimer of Scotland hath sent word
That Douglas and the English rebels met
The eleventh of this month at Shrewsbury.
A mighty and a fearful head they are,
If promises be kept on every hand,
As ever offered foul play in a state.

KING. The Earl of Westmoreland set forth to-day,
With him my son, Lord John of Lancaster,
For this advertisement is five days old.

146. **indignities**: unworthy traits
147. **factor**: agent
148. **engross**: buy up
151. **worship**: honor; **time**: lifetime
156. **intemperance**: intemperateness
159. **parcel**: portion
167. **head**: armed force
172. **advertisement**: information

On Wednesday next, Harry, you shall set forward;
On Thursday we ourselves will march. Our meeting
Is Bridgenorth; and, Harry, you shall march
Through Gloucestershire; by which account,
Our business valued, some twelve days hence
Our general forces at Bridgenorth shall meet.
Our hands are full of business. Let's away;
Advantage feeds him fat while men delay. *Exeunt.*

[SCENE III. *Eastcheap. The Boar's Head Tavern.*]

Enter FALSTAFF *and* BARDOLPH.

FALSTAFF. Bardolph, am I not fallen away vilely since this last action? Do I not bate? Do I not dwindle? Why, my skin hangs about me like an old lady's loose gown. I am withered like an old apple-john. Well, I'll repent, and that suddenly, while I am in some liking. I shall be out of heart shortly, and then I shall have no strength to repent. An I have not forgotten what the inside of a church is made of, I am a peppercorn, a brewer's horse. The inside of a church! Company, villainous company, hath been the spoil of me.

BARDOLPH. Sir John, you are so fretful you cannot live long.

FALSTAFF. Why, there is it; come, sing me a bawdy song; make me merry. I was as virtuously given as a gentleman need to be, virtuous enough: swore little, diced not above seven times a week, went to a bawdy house not above once in a quarter of an hour, paid money that I borrowed three or four times, lived well, and in good compass; and now I live out of all order, out of all compass.

BARDOLPH. Why, you are so fat, Sir John, that you must needs be out of all compass, out of all reasonable compass, Sir John.

FALSTAFF. Do thou amend thy face, and I'll amend my life; thou

174. **meeting:** meeting-place
175. **Bridgenorth:** a market town twenty miles from Shrewsbury.
177. **Our . . . valued:** considering how long our business will take
1–2. **last action:** i.e., the robbery at Gad's Hill
2. **bate:** shrink, decrease
4. **apple-john:** a shrivelled and withered apple
7–8. **brewer's horse:** an emaciated nag
16. **in good compass:** orderly
19. **compass:** circumference

art our admiral: thou bearest the lantern in the poop, but 'tis in the nose of thee. Thou art the Knight of the Burning Lamp.

BARDOLPH. Why, Sir John, my face does you no harm.

FALSTAFF. No, I'll be sworn; I make as good use of it as many a man doth of a death's-head or a *memento mori*. I never see thy face but I think upon hellfire and Dives that lived in purple, for there he is in his robes, burning, burning. If thou wert any way given to virtue, I would swear by thy face; my oath should be "By this fire, that's God's angel." But thou art altogether given over, and wert indeed, but for the light in thy face, the son of utter darkness. When thou ran'st up Gad's Hill in the night to catch my horse, if I did not think thou hadst been an *ignis fatuus* or a ball of wildfire, there's no purchase in money. O, thou art a perpetual triumph, an everlasting bonfire-light! Thou hast saved me a thousand marks in links and torches, walking with thee in the night betwixt tavern and tavern; but the sack that thou has drunk me would have bought me lights as good cheap at the dearest chandler's in Europe. I have maintained that salamander of yours with fire any time this two and thirty years. God reward me for it!

BARDOLPH. 'Sblood, I would my face were in your belly!

FALSTAFF. God-a-mercy! so should I be sure to be heartburned.

Enter HOST[ESS].

How now, Dame Partlet the hen? Have you inquired yet who picked my pocket?

HOSTESS. Why, Sir John; what do you think, Sir John? Do you think I keep thieves in my house? I have searched, I have in-

21. **admiral:** flagship; **poop:** stern
25. **death's head:** skull; ***memento mori:*** reminder of death
26. **Dives:** for the parable of Dives and Lazarus, see Luke 16:19–31
29. **By . . . angel:** Cf. Exodus 3:2: "And the Angel of the Lord appeared to him in a flame of fire out of the midst of a bush. . . ."
30. **given over:** abandoned
33. ***ignis fatuus:*** will-o'-the-wisp; **wildfire:** fireworks; **purchase:** advantage
34. **triumph:** public festivity
35. **links:** torches
38. **good cheap:** cheaply; **chandler:** seller of candles
39. **salamander:** a kind of lizard believed able to live in fire
43. **Dame Partlet:** a talkative, advice-giving hen in Chaucer's ***Nun's Priest's Tale***

quired, so has my husband, man by man, boy by boy, servant by servant. The tithe of a hair was never lost in my house before.

FALSTAFF. Ye lie, hostess. Bardolph was shaved and lost many a hair, and I'll be sworn my pocket was picked. Go to, you are a woman, go!

HOSTESS. Who, I? No; I defy thee! God's light, I was never called so in mine own house before!

FALSTAFF. Go to, I know you well enough.

HOSTESS. No, Sir John; you do not know me, Sir John. I know you, Sir John; you owe me money, Sir John, and now you pick a quarrel to beguile me of it. I bought you a dozen of shirts to your back.

FALSTAFF. Dowlas, filthy dowlas. I have given them away to bakers' wives; they have made bolters of them.

HOSTESS. Now, as I am a true woman, holland of eight shillings an ell. You owe money here besides, Sir John, for your diet and by-drinkings, and money lent you, four and twenty pound.

FALSTAFF. He had his part of it; let him pay.

HOSTESS. He? Alas, he is poor; he hath nothing.

FALSTAFF. How? Poor? Look upon his face. What call you rich? Let them coin his nose; let them coin his cheeks. I'll not pay a denier. What, will you make a younker of me? Shall I not take mine ease in mine inn but I shall have my pocket picked? I have lost a seal-ring of my grandfather's worth forty mark.

HOSTESS. O Jesu, I have heard the prince tell him, I know not how oft, that that ring was copper!

FALSTAFF. How? the prince is a Jack, a sneak-up.

48. **tithe**: tenth part
50. **shaved**: contracted venereal disease
50–51. **lost . . . hair**: baldness was considered a symptom of venereal disease
52. **woman**: mistress
60. **Dowlas**: a coarse linen
61. **bolters**: flour-sieves
62. **holland**: a linen fabric
63. **ell**: a cloth measure of forty-five inches
64. **by-drinkings**: drinks at odd times
69. **denier**: a French coin worth one-twelfth of a sou; **younker**: youngster
74. **Jack**: knave; **sneak-up**: servile person

'Sblood, an he were here, I would cudgel him like a dog if he would say so.

Enter the PRINCE *[and* POINS*], marching, and* FALSTAFF *meets [them], playing upon his truncheon like a fife.*

How now, lad? Is the wind in that door, i' faith? Must we all march?

BARDOLPH. Yea, two and two, Newgate fashion.

HOSTESS. My lord, I pray you hear me.

PRINCE. What sayest thou, Mistress Quickly? How doth thy husband? I love him well; he is an honest man.

HOSTESS. Good my lord, hear me.

FALSTAFF. Prithee let her alone and list to me.

PRINCE. What sayest thou, Jack?

FALSTAFF. The other night I fell asleep here behind the arras and had my pocket picked. This house is turned bawdy house; they pick pockets.

PRINCE. What didst thou lose, Jack?

FALSTAFF. Wilt thou believe me, Hal, three or four bonds of forty pound apiece and a seal-ring of my grandfather's.

PRINCE. A trifle, some eight-penny matter.

HOSTESS. So I told him, my lord, and I said I heard your grace say so; and, my lord, he speaks most vilely of you, like a foul-mouthed man as he is, and said he would cudgel you.

PRINCE. What? he did not.

HOSTESS. There's neither faith, truth, nor womanhood in me else.

FALSTAFF. There's no more faith in thee than in a stewed prune, nor no more truth in thee than in a drawn fox; and for womanhood, Maid Marian may be the deputy's wife of the ward to thee. Go, you thing, go!

HOSTESS. Say, what thing? what thing?

S.D. **truncheon**: cudgel

79. **Newgate fashion**: as prisoners shackled together; **Newgate**: a prison in London

98. **stewed prune**: bawd

99. **drawn fox**: a fox lured (i.e., "drawn") by hunters from his lair would exercise his proverbial cunning to escape his pursuers; hence, a cunning creature; **womanhood**: womanly qualities

100. **Maid Marian**: A female companion of Robin Hood in the legends of that outlaw; hence a light, not very respectable woman; **Maid Marian . . . thee**: even Maid Marian would be a model matron compared to you

FALSTAFF. What thing? Why, a thing to thank God on.

HOSTESS. I am no thing to thank God on, I would thou shouldst know it! I am an honest man's wife, and, setting thy knighthood aside, thou art a knave to call me so.

FALSTAFF. Setting thy womanhood aside, thou art a beast to say otherwise.

HOSTESS. Say, what beast, thou knave, thou?

FALSTAFF. What beast? Why, an otter.

PRINCE. An otter, Sir John? Why an otter?

FALSTAFF. Why, she's neither fish nor flesh; a man knows not where to have her.

HOSTESS. Thou art an unjust man in saying so. Thou or any man knows where to have me, thou knave, thou!

PRINCE. Thou say'st true, hostess, and he slanders thee most grossly.

HOSTESS. So he doth you, my lord, and said this other day you ought him a thousand pound.

PRINCE. Sirrah, do I owe you a thousand pound?

FALSTAFF. A thousand pound, Hal? A million! Thy love is worth a million; thou owest me thy love.

HOSTESS. Nay, my lord, he called you Jack and said he would cudgel you.

FALSTAFF. Did I, Bardolph?

BARDOLPH. Indeed, Sir John, you said so.

FALSTAFF. Yea, if he said my ring was copper.

PRINCE. I say 'tis copper. Darest thou be as good as thy word now?

FALSTAFF. Why, Hal, thou knowest, as thou art but man, I dare; but as thou art prince, I fear thee as I fear the roaring of the lion's whelp.

PRINCE. And why not as the lion?

FALSTAFF. The king himself is to be feared as the lion. Dost thou think I'll fear thee as I fear thy father? Nay, an I do, I pray God my girdle break.

PRINCE. O, if it should, how would thy guts fall about thy knees! But, sirrah, there's no room for faith, truth, nor honesty in this bosom of thine. It is all filled up with guts and midriff. Charge an honest woman with picking thy pocket! Why, thou whore-

130–31. Cf. Proverbs, 20:2: "The fear of a king is as the roaring of a lion."

135. girdle: belt

son, impudent, embossed rascal, if there were anything in thy pocket but tavern reckonings, memorandums of bawdy houses, and one poor pennyworth of sugar candy to make thee long-winded, if thy pocket were enriched with any other injuries but these, I am a villain. And yet you will stand to it; you will not pocket up wrong. Art thou not ashamed?

FALSTAFF. Dost thou hear, Hal? Thou knowest in the state of innocency Adam fell, and what should poor Jack Falstaff do in the days of villainy? Thou seest I have more flesh than another man, and therefore more frailty. You confess then, you picked my pocket?

PRINCE. It appears so by the story.

FALSTAFF. Hostess, I forgive thee. Go make ready breakfast, love thy husband, look to thy servants, cherish thy guests. Thou shalt find me tractable to any honest reason. Thou seest I am pacified still. Nay, prithee be gone.

Exit HOSTESS.

Now, Hal, to the news at court: for the robbery, lad—how is that answered?

PRINCE. O my sweet beef, I must still be good angel to thee; the money is paid back again.

FALSTAFF. O, I do not like that paying back; 'tis a double labor.

PRINCE. I am good friends with my father and may do anything.

FALSTAFF. Rob me the exchequer the first thing thou doest and do it with unwashed hands too.

BARDOLPH. Do, my lord.

PRINCE. I have procured thee, Jack, a charge of foot.

FALSTAFF. I would it had been of horse. Where shall I find one that can steal well? O for a fine thief of the age of two and twenty or thereabouts! I am heinously unprovided. Well, God be thanked for these rebels. They offend none but the virtuous. I laud them, I praise them.

PRINCE. Bardolph!

140. **embossed:** swollen

144. **stand to it:** i.e., maintain this deception

144–45. **you . . . wrong:** Proverbial: you will not accept it without protest.

153. **cherish:** entertain kindly

163. **with unwashed hands:** quickly, without taking time to wash your hands

165. **charge of foot:** an infantry command

BARDOLPH. My lord?
PRINCE. Go bear this letter to Lord John of Lancaster,
To my brother John; this to my Lord of Westmoreland.
[*Exit* BARDOLPH.]
Go Poins, to horse, to horse; for thou and I
Have thirty miles to ride yet ere dinner time.
[*Exit* POINS.]
Jack, meet me to-morrow in the Temple Hall
At two o'clock in the afternoon.
There shalt thou know thy charge, and there receive
Money and order for their furniture.
The land is burning; Percy stands on high;
And either they or we must lower lie. [*Exit.*]
FALSTAFF. Rare words! brave world! Hostess, my breakfast, come.
O, I could wish this tavern were my drum! [*Exit.*]

[ACT IV, SCENE I. *The Rebel camp near Shrewsbury.*]

[*Enter* HOTSPUR, WORCESTER, *and* DOUGLAS.]

HOTSPUR. Well said, my noble Scot. If speaking truth
In this fine age were not thought flattery,
Such attribution should the Douglas have
As not a soldier of this season's stamp
Should go so general current through the world.
By God, I cannot flatter; I do defy
The tongues of soothers; but a braver place
In my heart's love hath no man than yourself.
Nay, task me to my word; approve me, lord.
DOUGLAS. Thou art the king of honor.
No man so potent breathes upon the ground
But I will beard him.

180. **furniture:** equipment
183. **brave:** excellent
4. **stamp:** coinage
5. **go . . . current:** be widely circulated
6. **defy:** despise
7. **soothers:** flatterers; **braver:** better
9. **task . . . word:** challenge me to be as good as my word; **approve:** try
12. **beard:** oppose with boldness

Enter one with letters.

HOTSPUR. Do so and 'tis well.—
What letters hast thou there?—I can but thank you.
MESSENGER. These letters come from your father.
HOTSPUR. Letters from him? Why comes he not himself?
MESSENGER. He cannot come, my lord; he is grievous sick.
HOTSPUR. 'Zounds! how has he the leisure to be sick
In such a justling time? Who leads his power?
Under whose government come they along?
MESSENGER. His letters bear his mind, not I, my lord.
WORCESTER. I prithee tell me, doth he keep his bed?
MESSENGER. He did, my lord, four days ere I set forth,
And at the time of my departure thence
He was much feared by his physicians.
WORCESTER. I would the state of time had first been whole
Ere he by sickness had been visited.
His health was never better worth than now.
HOTSPUR. Sick now? droop now? This sickness doth infect
The very life blood of our enterprise.
'Tis catching hither, even to our camp.
He writes me here that inward sickness—
And that his friends by deputation could not
So soon be drawn; nor did he think it meet
To lay so dangerous and dear a trust
On any soul removed but on his own.
Yet doth he give us bold advertisement
That with our small conjunction we should on
To see how fortune is disposed to us;
For, as he writes, there is no quailing now,
Because the king is certainly possessed
Of all our purposes. What say you to it?
WORCESTER. Your father's sickness is a maim to us.

18. **justling:** contentious
25. **time:** the present state of affairs
33. **drawn:** brought together; **meet:** suitable
35. **removed:** not immediately concerned
36. **advertisement:** advice
37. **conjunction:** united force; **on:** go ahead
40. **possessed:** informed

HOTSPUR. A perilous gash, a very limb lopped off.
And yet, in faith, it is not! His present want
Seems more than we shall find it. Were it good
To set the exact wealth of all our states
All at one cast? to set so rich a main
On the nice hazard of one doubtful hour?
It were not good, for therein should we read
The very bottom and the soul of hope,
The very list, the very utmost bound
Of all our fortunes.

DOUGLAS. Faith, and so we should.
Where now remains a sweet reversion,
We may boldly spend upon the hope
Of what is to come in.
A comfort of retirement lives in this.

HOTSPUR. A rendezvous, a home to fly unto,
If that the devil and mischance look big
Upon the maidenhead of our affairs.

WORCESTER. But yet I would your father had been here.
The quality and hair of our attempt
Brooks no division. It will be thought
By some that know not why he is away,
That wisdom, loyalty, and mere dislike
Of our proceedings kept the earl from hence.
And think how such an apprehension
May turn the tide of fearful faction
And breed a kind of question in our cause.
For well you know we of the off'ring side
Must keep aloof from strict arbitrement,

44. **His present want:** our present lack of him
46. **set:** stake; **exact:** entire
47. **main:** stake
48. **nice:** doubtful; **hazard:** (1) risk (2) a game of chance
51. **list:** limit
53. **reversion:** hope of future possession
58. **big:** haughtily, boastfully
61. **hair:** nature
62. **Brooks:** tolerates, permits
64. **mere:** downright
67. **faction:** conspiracy
69. **off'ring:** attacking
70. **strict:** accurately determined; **arbitrement:** investigation

And stop all sight-holes, every loop from whence
The eye of reason may pry in upon us.
This absence of your father's draws a curtain
That shows the ignorant a kind of fear
Before not dreamt of.

HOTSPUR. You strain too far.
I rather of his absence make this use:
It lends a lustre and more great opinion,
A larger dare to our great enterprise,
Than if the earl were here; for men must think,
If we, without his help, can make a head
To push against a kingdom, with his help
We shall o'erturn it topsy-turvy down.
Yet all goes well; yet all our joints are whole.

DOUGLAS. As heart can think. There is not such a word
Spoke of in Scotland as this term of fear.

Enter SIR RI[CHARD] VERNON.

HOTSPUR. My cousin Vernon! welcome, by my soul.

VERNON. Pray God my news be worth a welcome, lord.
The Earl of Westmoreland, seven thousand strong,
Is marching hitherwards; with him Prince John.

HOTSPUR. No harm. What more?

VERNON. And further, I have learned,
The king himself in person is set forth,
Or hitherwards intended speedily,
With strong and mighty preparation.

HOTSPUR. He shall be welcome too. Where is his son,
The nimble-footed madcap Prince of Wales,
And his comrades, that daffed the world aside
And bid it pass?

VERNON. All furnished, all in arms;
All plumed like estridges that with the wind
Bated like eagles having lately bathed;

75. **strain:** exaggerate
77. **opinion:** reputation
92. **intended:** purposed to come
96. **daffed:** thrust
98. **estridges:** ostriches
99. **Bated:** fluttered their wings

Glittering in golden coats like images;
As full of spirit as the month of May
And gorgeous as the sun at midsummer;
Wanton as youthful goats, wild as young bulls.
I saw young Harry with his beaver on,
His cushes on his thighs, gallantly armed,
Rise from the ground like feathered Mercury,
And vaulted with such ease into his seat
As if an angel dropped down from the clouds
To turn and wind a fiery Pegasus
And witch the world with noble horsemanship.

HOTSPUR. No more, no more! Worse than the sun in March
This praise doth nourish agues. Let them come.
They come like sacrifices in their trim,
And to the fire-eyed maid of smoky war
All hot and bleeding will we offer them.
The mailed Mars shall on his altar sit
Up to the ears in blood. I am on fire
To hear this rich reprisal is so nigh,
And yet not ours. Come, let me taste my horse,
Who is to bear me like a thunderbolt
Against the bosom of the Prince of Wales.
Harry to Harry shall, hot horse to horse,
Meet, and ne'er part till one drop down a corse.
O that Glendower were come!

VERNON. There is more news.
I learned in Worcester, as I rode along,
He cannot draw his power this fourteen days.

DOUGLAS. That's the worst tidings that I hear of yet.

100. **images:** statues
103. **Wanton:** frolicsome
104. **beaver:** face-guard of a helmet
105. **cushes:** armor for the thighs
106. **Mercury:** the speedy messenger of the gods
109. **wind:** wheel; **Pegasus:** the winged horse of Greek mythology
112. **agues:** fevers
113. **trim:** fine trappings
114. **maid:** Bellona, Roman goddess of war
116. **mailed:** in armor; **Mars:** Roman god of war
118. **reprisal:** prize
126. **draw:** bring together

WORCESTER. Ay, by my faith, that bears a frosty sound.
HOTSPUR. What may the king's whole battle reach unto?
VERNON. To thirty thousand.
HOTSPUR. Forty let it be.
My father and Glendower being both away,
The powers of us may serve so great a day.
Come, let us take a muster speedily.
Doomsday is near. Die all, die merrily.
DOUGLAS. Talk not of dying. I am out of fear
Of death or death's hand for this one half-year.

Exeunt.

[SCENE II. *A public road near Coventry.*]

Enter FALSTAFF [*and*] BARDOLPH.

FALSTAFF. Bardolph, get thee before to Coventry; fill me a bottle of sack. Our soldiers shall march through. We'll to Sutton Cophill to-night.

BARDOLPH. Will you give me money, captain?

FALSTAFF. Lay out, lay out.

BARDOLPH. This bottle makes an angel.

FALSTAFF. An if it do, take it for thy labor; and if it make twenty, take them all; I'll answer the coinage. Bid my lieutenant Peto meet me at town's end.

BARDOLPH. I will, captain. Farewell. *Exit.*

FALSTAFF. If I be not ashamed of my soldiers, I am a soused gurnet. I have misused the king's press damnably. I have got, in exchange of a hundred and fifty soldiers, three hundred and odd pounds. I press me none but good householders, yeomen's

129. **battle:** army

2–3. **Sutton Cophill:** Sutton-Coldfield, a town in northern Warwickshire on the road to Shrewsbury

5. **Lay out:** i.e., you pay for it

6. **makes an angel:** this purchase makes an angel (10 shillings) I have spent

7. **An . . . labor:** Falstaff puns on "make," saying if the bottle can be made into an angel Bardolph may keep the money for his labor.

8. **answer:** be responsible for

11. **soused gurnet:** pickled fish

12. **press:** conscription of soldiers; Falstaff has accepted money from the hundred and fifty *not* to draft them.

sons; inquire me out contracted bachelors, such as had been asked twice on the banns, such a commodity of warm slaves as had as lieve hear the devil as a drum, such as fear the report of a caliver worse than a struck fowl or a hurt wild duck. I pressed me none but such toasts-and-butter, with hearts in their bellies no bigger than pins' heads, and they have bought out their services; and now my whole charge consists of ancients, corporals, lieutenants, gentlemen of companies—slaves as ragged as Lazarus in the painted cloth, where the glutton's dogs licked his sores; and such as, indeed, were never soldiers, but discarded unjust serving-men, younger sons to younger brothers, revolted tapsters, and ostlers trade-fallen; the cankers of a calm world and a long peace; ten times more dishonorable ragged than an old fazed ancient; and such have I to fill up the rooms of them that have bought out their services that you would think that I had a hundred and fifty tattered prodigals lately come from swine-keeping, from eating draff and husks. A mad fellow met me on the way, and told me I had unloaded all the gibbets and pressed the dead bodies. No eye hath seen such scarecrows. I'll not march through Coventry with them, that's flat. Nay, and the villains march wide betwixt the legs, as if they had gyves on, for indeed I had the most of them out of prison. There's not a shirt and a half in all my company, and the half-shirt is two napkins tacked together and thrown over the shoulders like a herald's coat without sleeves; and the shirt, to say the truth, stolen from my host at Saint Alban's, or the

15–16. **contracted . . . banns**: i.e., those on the very verge of matrimony
16. **commodity**: parcel; **warm**: well-off
18. **caliver**: musket; **struck**: wounded
19. **toasts-and-butter**: delicate fellows
21. **ancients**: standard bearers
22. **gentlemen of companies**: soldiers above the rank of regular enlisted men
23. **Lazarus**: see Luke 16:19–31; **painted cloth**: a decorative hanging for a room
26. **revolted**: faithless; **trade-fallen**: unemployed
28. **fazed ancient**: ragged flag
31. **draff**: swill
33. **gibbets**: gallows
36. **gyves**: shackles
40–41. **Saint Albans . . . Daventry**: towns on the road from London to Coventry

red-nose innkeeper of Daventry. But that's all one; they'll find linen enough on every hedge.

Enter the PRINCE [*and the*] LORD OF WESTMORELAND.

PRINCE. How now, blown Jack? How now, quilt?

FALSTAFF. What, Hal? How now, mad wag? What a devil dost thou in Warwickshire? My good Lord of Westmoreland, I cry you mercy. I thought your honor had already been at Shrewsbury.

WESTMORELAND. Faith, Sir John, 'tis more than time that I were there, and you too, but my powers are there already. The king, I can tell you, looks for us all. We must away all night.

FALSTAFF. Tut, never fear me; I am as vigilant as a cat to steal cream.

PRINCE. I think, to steal cream indeed, for thy theft hath already made thee butter. But tell me, Jack, whose fellows are these that come after?

FALSTAFF. Mine, Hal, mine.

PRINCE. I did never see such pitiful rascals.

FALSTAFF. Tut, tut! good enough to toss; food for powder, food for powder. They'll fill a pit as well as better. Tush, man, mortal men, mortal men.

WESTMORELAND. Ay, but, Sir John, methinks they are exceeding poor and bare, too beggarly.

FALSTAFF. Faith, for their poverty, I know not where they had that, and for their bareness, I am sure they never learned that of me.

PRINCE. No, I'll be sworn, unless you call three fingers on the ribs bare. But, sirrah, make haste. Percy is already in the field.

Exit.

FALSTAFF. What, is the king encamped?

WESTMORELAND. He is, Sir John. I fear we shall stay too long.

FALSTAFF. Well, to the latter end of a fray and the beginning of a feast fits a dull fighter and a keen guest. *Exeunt.*

41–42. **they'll . . . hedge**: i.e., they will steal laundry placed on the hedges to dry

43. **blown**: inflated

50. **away**: march

58. **to toss**: to carry aloft on the point of a pike

[SCENE III. *The rebel camp near Shrewsbury.*]

Enter HOTSPUR, WORCESTER, DOUGLAS, VERNON.

HOTSPUR. We'll fight with him to-night.
WORCESTER. It may not be.
DOUGLAS. You give him then advantage.
VERNON. Not a whit.
HOTSPUR. Why say you so? Looks he not for supply?
VERNON. So do we.
HOTSPUR. His is certain, ours is doubtful.
WORCESTER. Good cousin, be advised; stir not to-night.
VERNON. Do not, my lord.
DOUGLAS. You do not counsel well.
You speak it out of fear and cold heart.
VERNON. Do me no slander, Douglas. By my life,
And I dare well maintain it with my life,
If well-respected honor bid me on,
I hold as little counsel with weak fear
As you, my lord, or any Scot that this day lives.
Let it be seen to-morrow in the battle
Which of us fears.
DOUGLAS. Yea, or to-night.
VERNON. Content.
HOTSPUR. To-night, say I.
VERNON. Come, come, it may not be. I wonder much,
Being men of such great leading as you are,
That you foresee not what impediments
Drag back our expedition. Certain horse
Of my cousin Vernon's are not yet come up.
Your uncle Worcester's horse came but to-day;
And now their pride and mettle is asleep,
Their courage with hard labor tame and dull,
That not a horse is half the half of himself.
HOTSPUR. So are the horses of the enemy
In general journey-bated and brought low.

3. **supply**: reinforcements
10. **well-respected**: well-considered
19. **expedition**: haste; **horse**: cavalry
26. **journey-bated**: travel-wearied

The better part of ours are full of rest.
WORCESTER. The number of the king exceedeth ours.
For God's sake, cousin, stay till all come in.

The trumpet sounds a parley. Enter SIR WALTER BLUNT.

BLUNT. I come with gracious offers from the king,
If you vouchsafe me hearing and respect.
HOTSPUR. Welcome, Sir Walter Blunt; and would to God
You were of our determination.
Some of us love you well; and even those some
Envy your great deservings and good name,
Because you are not of our quality,
But stand against us like an enemy.
BLUNT. And God defend but still I should stand so.
So long as out of limit and true rule
You stand against anointed majesty.
But to my charge. The king hath sent to know
The nature of your griefs, and whereupon
You conjure from the breast of civil peace
Such bold hostility, teaching his duteous land
Audacious cruelty. If that the king
Have any way your good deserts forgot,
Which he confesseth to be manifold,
He bids you name your griefs, and with all speed
You shall have your desires with interest,
And pardon absolute for yourself and these
Herein misled by your suggestion.
HOTSPUR. The king is kind, and well we know the king
Knows at what time to promise, when to pay.
My father and my uncle and myself
Did give him that same royalty he wears;
And when he was not six and twenty strong,
Sick in the world's regard, wretched and low,
A poor unminded outlaw sneaking home,
My father gave him welcome to the shore;
And when he heard him swear and vow to God

31. **respect:** attention
33. **determination:** way of thinking
36. **quality:** party
38. **defend:** forbid

He came but to be Duke of Lancaster,
To sue his livery and beg his peace,
With tears of innocency and terms of zeal,
My father, in kind heart and pity moved,
Swore him assistance, and performed it too.
Now when the lords and barons of the realm
Perceived Northumberland did lean to him,
The more and less came in with cap and knee,
Met him in boroughs, cities, villages,
Attended him on bridges, stood in lanes,
Laid gifts before him, proffered him their oaths,
Gave him their heirs as pages, followed him
Even at the heels in golden multitudes.
He presently, as greatness knows itself,
Steps me a little higher than his vow
Made to my father, while his blood was poor,
Upon the naked shore at Ravenspurgh;
And now, forsooth, takes on him to reform
Some certain edicts and some strait decrees
That lie too heavy on the commonwealth;
Cries out upon abuses, seems to weep
Over his country's wrongs; and by this face,
This seeming brow of justice, did he win
The hearts of all that he did angle for;
Proceeded further, cut me off the heads
Of all the favorites that the absent king
In deputation left behind him here
When he was personal in the Irish war.

BLUNT. Tut! I came not to hear this.

HOTSPUR. Then to the point.
In short time after, he deposed the king,

62. **sue his livery:** seek possession of his inheritance
63. **zeal:** ardent affection
72. **pages:** court attendants
73. **golden:** well-dressed
74. **as greatness knows itself:** i.e., as greatness becomes aware of its own greatness
79. **strait:** strict
82. **face:** pretence
87. **In deputation:** as his deputies
88. **personal:** in person

Soon after that deprived him of his life,
And in the neck of that tasked the whole state;
To make that worse, suffered his kinsman March
(Who is, if every owner were well placed,
Indeed his king) to be engaged in Wales,
There without ransom to lie forfeited,
Disgraced me in my happy victories,
Sought to entrap me by intelligence,
Rated mine uncle from the council board,
In rage dismissed my father from the court,
Broke oath on oath, committed wrong on wrong,
And in conclusion drove us to seek out
This head of safety, and withal to pry
Into his title, the which we find
Too indirect for long continuance.

BLUNT. Shall I return this answer to the king?

HOTSPUR. Not so, Sir Walter. We'll withdraw awhile.
Go to the king; and let there be impawned
Some surety for a safe return again,
And in the morning early shall mine uncle
Bring him our purposes; and so farewell.

BLUNT. I would you would accept of grace and love.

HOTSPUR. And may be so we shall.

BLUNT. Pray God you do. [*Exeunt.*]

[SCENE IV. *York, The Archbishop's palace.*]

Enter ARCHBISHOP OF YORK [*and*] SIR MICHAEL.

ARCHBISHOP. Hie, good Sir Michael; bear this sealed brief
With winged haste to the lord marshal;
This to my cousin Scroop; and all the rest
To whom they are directed. If you knew
How much they do import, you would make haste.

92. **in . . . that:** immediately after; **tasked:** taxed
95. **engaged:** held as hostage
98. **intelligence:** espionage
99. **Rated:** scolded
103. **withal:** at the same time
108. **impawned:** pledged
1. **brief:** letter

SIR MICHAEL. My good lord,
I guess their tenor.
ARCHBISHOP. Like enough you do.
To-morrow, good Sir Michael, is a day
Wherein the fortune of ten thousand men
Must bide the touch; for, sir, at Shrewsbury,
As I am truly given to understand,
The king with mighty and quick-raised power
Meets with Lord Harry; and I fear, Sir Michael,
What with the sickness of Northumberland,
Whose power was in the first proportion,
And what with Owen Glendower's absence thence,
Who with them was a rated sinew too
And comes not in, overruled by prophecies—
I fear the power of Percy is too weak
To wage an instant trial with the king.
SIR MICHAEL. Why, my good lord, you need not fear;
There is Douglas and Lord Mortimer.
ARCHBISHOP. No, Mortimer is not there.
SIR MICHAEL. But there is Mordake, Vernon, Lord Harry Percy,
And there is my Lord of Worcester, and a head
Of gallant warriors, noble gentlemen.
ARCHBISHOP. And so there is; but yet the king hath drawn
The special head of all the land together:
The Prince of Wales, Lord John of Lancaster,
The noble Westmoreland and warlike Blunt,
And many mo corrivals and dear men
Of estimation and command in arms.
SIR MICHAEL. Doubt not, my lord, they shall be well opposed.
ARCHBISHOP. I hope no less, yet needful 'tis to fear;
And, to prevent the worst, Sir Michael, speed.
For if Lord Percy thrive not, ere the king
Dismiss his power, he means to visit us,
For he hath heard of our confederacy,

7. **tenor:** import
10. **Must . . . touch:** must be put to the test
15. **proportion:** magnitude
17. **rated sinew:** esteemed strength
31. **mo:** more; **corrivals:** companions; **dear:** worthy
36. **thrive:** succeed

And 'tis but wisdom to make strong against him.
Therefore make haste. I must go write again
To other friends; and so farewell, Sir Michael. *Exeunt.*

[ACT V, SCENE I. *The King's camp near Shrewsbury.*]

Enter the KING, PRINCE OF WALES, LORD JOHN OF LANCASTER, SIR WALTER BLUNT, FALSTAFF.

KING. How bloodily the sun begins to peer
Above yon busky hill! The day looks pale
At his distemp'rature.
PRINCE. The southern wind
Doth play the trumpet to his purposes
And by his hollow whistling in the leaves
Foretells a tempest and a blust'ring day.
KING. Then with the losers let it sympathize,
For nothing can seem foul to those that win.

The trumpet sounds. Enter WORCESTER [*and* VERNON].

How now, my Lord of Worcester! 'Tis not well
That you and I should meet upon such terms
As now we meet. You have deceived our trust
And made us doff our easy robes of peace
To crush our old limbs in ungentle steel.
This is not well, my lord; this is not well.
What say you to it? Will you again unknit
This churlish knot of all-abhorred war,
And move in that obedient orb again
Where you did give a fair and natural light,
And be no more an exhaled meteor,
A prodigy of fear, and a portent
Of broached mischief to the unborn times?

2. **busky:** bushy, wooded
3. **his:** the sun's; **distemp'rature:** discomposure
4. **trumpet:** trumpeter; **his purposes:** what the sun portends by its unusual appearance
16. **churlish:** hard
17. **orb:** sphere of action
19. **exhaled:** evaporated
20. **prodigy of fear:** fearful omen
21. **broached:** set running

WORCESTER. Hear me, my liege.
For mine own part, I could be well content
To entertain the lag-end of my life
With quiet hours, for I [do] protest
I have not sought the day of this dislike.
KING. You have not sought it! How comes it then?
FALSTAFF. Rebellion lay in his way, and he found it.
PRINCE. Peace, chewet, peace!
WORCESTER. It pleased your majesty to turn your looks
Of favor from myself and all our house;
And yet I must remember you, my lord,
We were the first and dearest of your friends.
For you my staff of office did I break
In Richard's time, and posted day and night
To meet you on the way and kiss your hand
When yet you were in place and in account
Nothing so strong and fortunate as I,
It was myself, my brother, and his son
That brought you home and boldly did outdare
The dangers of the time. You swore to us,
And you did swear that oath at Doncaster,
That you did nothing purpose 'gainst the state,
Nor claim no further than your new-fall'n right,
The seat of Gaunt, dukedom of Lancaster.
To this we swore our aid. But in short space
It rained down fortune show'ring on your head,
And such a flood of greatness fell on you,
What with our help, what with the absent king,
What with the injuries of a wanton time,
The seeming sufferances that you had borne,
And the contrarious winds that held the king
So long in his unlucky Irish wars
That all in England did repute him dead;
And from this swarm of fair advantages

24. **lag-end:** latter part
29. **chewet:** chatterer
32. **remember:** remind
35. **posted:** rode fast
40. **outdare:** defy
51. **sufferances:** distresses
52. **contrarious:** adverse

You took occasion to be quickly wooed
To gripe the general sway into your hand;
Forgot your oath to us at Doncaster;
And, being fed by us, you used us so
As that ungentle gull, the cuckoo's bird,
Useth the sparrow, did oppress our nest;
Grew by our feeding to so great a bulk
That even our love durst not come near your sight
For fear of swallowing; but with nimble wing
We were enforced for safety sake to fly
Out of your sight and raise this present head;
Whereby we stand opposed by such means
As you yourself have forged against yourself
By unkind usage, dangerous countenance,
And violation of all faith and troth
Sworn to us in your younger enterprise.

KING. These things, indeed, you have articulate,
Proclaimed at market crosses, read in churches,
To face the garment of rebellion
With some fine color that may please the eye
Of fickle changelings and poor discontents,
Which gape and rub the elbow at the news
Of hurlyburly innovation.
And never yet did insurrection want
Such water colors to impaint his cause,
Nor moody beggars, starving for a time
Of pell-mell havoc and confusion.

PRINCE. In both your armies there is many a soul
Shall pay full dearly for this encounter,
If once they join in trial. Tell your nephew
The Prince of Wales doth join with all the world

57. **gripe:** grasp firmly
60–61. The cuckoo lays its eggs in the nest of another bird.
69. **dangerous:** threatening
70. **troth:** truth
72. **articulate:** spelled out
73. **market crosses:** places of prominence at the markets
74. **face:** trim
76. **changelings:** inconstant persons
77. **rub the elbow:** show oneself pleased
78. **hurlyburly:** tumultuous; **innovation:** revolution

In praise of Henry Percy. By my hopes,
This present enterprise set off his head,
I do not think a braver gentleman,
More active-valiant or more valiant-young,
More daring or more bold, is now alive
To grace this latter age with noble deeds.
For my part, I may speak it to my shame,
I have a truant been to chivalry;
And so I hear he doth account me too.
Yet this before my father's majesty—
I am content that he shall take the odds
Of his great name and estimation,
And will, to save the blood on either side,
Try fortune with him in a single fight.

KING. And, Prince of Wales, so dare we venture thee,
Albeit considerations infinite
Do make against it. No, good Worcester, no!
We love our people well; even those we love
That are misled upon your cousin's part;
And, will they take the offer of our grace,
Both he, and they, and you, yea, every man
Shall be my friend again, and I'll be his.
So tell your cousin, and bring me word
What he will do. But if he will not yield,
Rebuke and dread correction wait on us,
And they shall do their office. So be gone.
We will not now be troubled with reply.
We offer fair; take it advisedly.

Exit WORCESTER [*and* VERNON].

PRINCE. It will not be accepted, on my life.
The Douglas and the Hotspur both together
Are confident against the world in arms.

KING. Hence, therefore, every leader to his charge;

88. **set . . . head:** not laid to his charge
94. **chivalry:** the duties of knighthood
98. **estimation:** reputation
111. **wait on us:** are in our service

For, on their answer, will we set on them,
And God befriend us as our cause is just!

Exeunt. Manent PRINCE, FALSTAFF.

FALSTAFF. Hal, if thou see me down in the battle and bestride me, so! 'Tis a point of friendship.

PRINCE. Nothing but a colossus can do thee that friendship. Say thy prayers, and farewell.

FALSTAFF. I would 'twere bedtime, Hal, and all well.

PRINCE. Why, thou owest God a death. [*Exit.*]

FALSTAFF. 'Tis not due yet: I would be loath to pay him before his day. What need I be so forward with him that calls not on me? Well, 'tis no matter; honor pricks me on. Yea, but how if honor prick me off when I come on? How then? Can honor set to a leg? No. Or an arm? No. Or take away the grief of a wound? No. Honor hath no skill in surgery then? No. What is honor? A word. What is in that word honor? What is that honor? Air. A trim reckoning! Who hath it? He that died a Wednesday. Doth he feel it? No. Doth he hear it? No. 'Tis insensible then? Yea, to the dead. But will [it] not live with the living? No. Why? Detraction will not suffer it. Therefore I'll none of it. Honor is a mere scutcheon—and so ends my catechism. *Exit.*

[SCENE II. *The rebel camp.*]

Enter WORCESTER [*and*] SIR RICHARD VERNON.

WORCESTER. O no, my nephew must not know, Sir Richard,
The liberal and kind offer of the king.

VERNON. 'Twere best he did.

S.D. ***Manent:*** remain
122. **so:** good
130. **prick:** select a name (i.e., check his name off as a casualty)
130–31. **set to:** mend
131. **grief:** pain
134. **trim:** fine
136. **insensible:** not perceptible to the senses
137. **Detraction:** slander
138. **scutcheon:** escutcheon, a painted representation of a shield bearing a coat of arms

WORCESTER. Then are we all undone.
It is not possible, it cannot be,
The king should keep his word in loving us.
He will suspect us still and find a time
To punish this offense in other faults.
Supposition all our lives shall be stuck full of eyes;
For treason is but trusted like the fox,
Who, ne'er so tame, so cherished and locked up,
Will have a wild trick of his ancestors.
Look how we can, or sad or merrily,
Interpretation will misquote our looks,
And we shall feed like oxen at a stall,
The better cherished still the nearer death.
My nephew's trespass may be well forgot;
It hath the excuse of youth and heat of blood
And an adopted name of privilege,
A hare-brained Hotspur, governed by a spleen.
All his offenses live upon my head
And on his father's. We did train him on;
And, his corruption being ta'en from us,
We, as the spring of all, shall pay for all.
Therefore, good cousin, let not Harry know,
In any case, the offer of the king.

Enter HOTSPUR [*and* DOUGLAS].

VERNON. Deliver what you will, I'll say 'tis so.
Here comes your cousin.
HOTSPUR. My uncle is returned.
Deliver up my Lord of Westmoreland.
Uncle, what news?
WORCESTER. The king will bid you battle presently.
DOUGLAS. Defy him by the Lord of Westmoreland.
HOTSPUR. Lord Douglas, go you and tell him so.

8. **Supposition:** suspicion
12. **or (1):** either
19. **spleen:** fiery temper
21. **train:** lure
23. **spring:** source
28. **Westmoreland:** the hostage given by the king
30. **presently:** immediately

DOUGLAS. Marry, and shall, and very willingly. *Exit.*
WORCESTER. There is no seeming mercy in the king.
HOTSPUR. Did you beg any? God forbid!
WORCESTER. I told him gently of our grievances,
Of his oath-breaking, which he mended thus,
By now forswearing that he is forsworn.
He calls us rebels, traitors, and will scourge
With haughty arms this hateful name in us.

Enter DOUGLAS.

DOUGLAS. Arm, gentlemen, to arms! for I have thrown
A brave defiance in King Henry's teeth,
And Westmoreland, that was engaged, did bear it;
Which cannot choose but bring him quickly on.
WORCESTER. The Prince of Wales stepped forth before the king
And, nephew, challenged you to single fight.
HOTSPUR. O, would the quarrel lay upon our heads,
And that no man might draw short breath to-day
But I and Harry Monmouth! Tell me, tell me,
How showed his tasking? Seemed it in contempt?
VERNON. No, by my soul. I never in my life
Did hear a challenge urged more modestly,
Unless a brother should a brother dare
To gentle exercise and proof of arms.
He gave you all the duties of a man;
Trimmed up your praises with a princely tongue;
Spoke your deservings like a chronicle;
Making you ever better than his praise
By still dispraising praise valued with you;
And, which became him like a prince indeed,
He made a blushing cital of himself,

37. **mended:** atoned for
38. **forswearing . . . forsworn:** falsely denying that he has broken his word
43. **engaged:** pledged as a hostage
49. **Harry Monmouth:** i.e., Hal
50. **tasking:** challenge
54. **proof:** trial
55. **duties of:** respects pertaining to
59. **valued . . . you:** compared with you in respect of worth
61. **cital:** citation

And chid his truant youth with such a grace
As if he mastered there a double spirit
Of teaching and of learning instantly.
There did he pause; but let me tell the world,
If he outlive the envy of this day,
England did never owe so sweet a hope,
So much misconstrued in his wantonness.

HOTSPUR. Cousin, I think thou art enamored
Upon his follies. Never did I hear
Of any prince so wild a liberty.
But be he as he will, yet once ere night
I will embrace him with a soldier's arm,
That he shall shrink under my courtesy.
Arm, arm with speed! and, fellows, soldiers, friends,
Better consider what you have to do
Than I, that have not well the gift of tongue,
Can lift your blood up with persuasion.

Enter a MESSENGER.

MESSENGER. My lord, here are letters for you.

HOTSPUR. I cannot read them now.
O gentlemen, the time of life is short!
To spend that shortness basely were too long
If life did ride upon a dial's point,
Still ending at the arrival of an hour.
An if we live, we live to tread on kings;
If die, brave death, when princes die with us!
Now for our consciences, the arms are fair,
When the intent of bearing them is just.

Enter another [MESSENGER].

MESSENGER. My lord, prepare. The king comes on apace.

HOTSPUR. I thank him that he cuts me from my tale,
For I profess not talking. Only this—
Let each man do his best; and here draw I

66. **envy:** malice
67. **owe:** own
83. **dial's point:** hand of a clock
84. **Still:** always
86. **brave:** excellent
89. **apace:** speedily

A sword whose temper I intend to stain
With the best blood that I can meet withal
In the adventure of this perilous day.
Now, Esperance! Percy! and set on.
Sound all the lofty instruments of war,
And by that music let us all embrace;
For, heaven to earth, some of us never shall
A second time do such a courtesy.

Here they embrace. The trumpets sound. [*Exeunt.*]

[SCENE III. *A Plain between the camps.*]

The KING *enters with his power* [*and passes over*]. *Alarum to the battle. Then enter* DOUGLAS *and* SIR WALTER BLUNT.

BLUNT. What is thy name, that in battle thus
Thou crossest me? What honor dost thou seek
Upon my head?
DOUGLAS. Know then my name is Douglas,
And I do haunt thee in the battle thus
Because some tell me that thou art a king.
BLUNT. They tell thee true.
DOUGLAS. The Lord of Stafford dear to-day hath bought
Thy likeness, for instead of thee, King Harry,
This sword hath ended him. So shall it thee,
Unless thou yield thee as my prisoner.
BLUNT. I was not born a yielder, thou proud Scot;
And thou shalt find a king that will revenge
Lord Stafford's death.

They fight. DOUGLAS *kills* BLUNT. *Then enter* HOTSPUR.

HOTSPUR. O Douglas, hadst thou fought at Holmedon thus,
I never had triumphed upon a Scot.
DOUGLAS. All's done, all's won. Here breathless lies the king.
HOTSPUR. Where?
DOUGLAS. Here.

95. **adventure:** chance
96. **Esperance:** motto of the Percy family used here as a battle cry
97. **lofty instruments:** drums and trumpets
S.D. ***Alarum:*** call to arms

HOTSPUR. This, Douglas? No. I know this face full well.
A gallant knight he was, his name was Blunt;
Semblably furnished like the king himself.
DOUGLAS. Ah fool, go with thy soul, whither it goes!
A borrowed title hast thou bought too dear:
Why didst thou tell me that thou wert a king?
HOTSPUR. The king hath many marching in his coats.
DOUGLAS. Now, by my sword, I will kill all his coats;
I'll murder all his wardrobe, piece by piece,
Until I meet the king.
HOTSPUR. Up and away!
Our soldiers stand full fairly for the day. [*Exeunt.*]

Alarum. Enter FALSTAFF *solus.*

FALSTAFF. Though I could 'scape shot-free at London, I fear the shot here. Here's no scoring but upon the pate. Soft! who are you? Sir Walter Blunt. There's honor for you! Here's no vanity! I am as hot as molten lead, and as heavy too. God keep lead out of me. I need no more weight than mine own bowels. I have led my ragamuffins where they are peppered. There's not three of my hundred and fifty left alive, and they are for the town's end, to beg during life. But who comes here?

Enter the PRINCE.

PRINCE. What, stand'st thou idle here? Lend me thy sword.
Many a nobleman lies stark and stiff
Under the hoofs of vaunting enemies,
Whose deaths are yet unrevenged. I prithee
Lend me thy sword.
FALSTAFF. O Hal, I prithee give me leave to breathe awhile. Turk Gregory never did such deeds in arms as I have done this day. I have paid Percy; I have made him sure.

21. **Semblably furnished:** similarly dressed
29. **fairly:** favorable
30. **shot-free:** without having to pay the bill
31. **scoring:** (1) making a reckoning of a bill (2) cutting
35. **peppered:** done for
43–44. **Turk Gregory:** Possibly Pope Gregory XIII, a supporter of Philip II and the Irish insurrectionists, is intended. "Turk" was synonymous with cruelty and savagery.
45. **paid:** killed; **made him sure:** rendered him harmless

PRINCE. He is indeed, and living to kill thee.
I prithee lend me thy sword.

FALSTAFF. Nay, before God, Hal, if Percy be alive, thou get'st not my sword; but take my pistol, if thou wilt.

PRINCE. Give it me. What, is it in the case?

FALSTAFF. Ay, Hal. 'Tis hot, 'tis hot. There's that will sack a city.

The PRINCE *draws it out and finds it to be a bottle of sack.*

PRINCE. What, is it a time to jest and dally now?

He throws the bottle at him. Exit.

FALSTAFF. Well, if Percy be alive, I'll pierce him. If he do come in my way, so; if he do not, if I come in his willingly, let him make a carbonado of me. I like not such grinning honor as Sir Walter hath. Give me life; which if I can save, so; if not, honor comcs unlooked for, and there's an end. [*Exit.*]

[SCENE IV. *Another part of the field.*]

Alarum. Excursions. Enter the KING, *the* PRINCE, LORD JOHN OF LANCASTER, EARL OF WESTMORELAND.

KING. I prithee, Harry, withdraw thyself; thou bleedest too much.
Lord John of Lancaster, go you with him.

JOHN. Not I, my lord, unless I did bleed too.

PRINCE. I [do] beseech your majesty make up,
Lest your retirement do amaze your friends.

KING. I will do so.
My Lord of Westmoreland, lead him to his tent.

WESTMORELAND. Come, my lord, I'll lead you to your tent.

PRINCE. Lead me, my lord? I do not need your help;
And Cod forbid a shallow scratch should drive
The Prince of Wales from such a field as this,
Where stained nobility lies trodden on,
And rebels' arms triumph in massacres!

JOHN. We breathe too long. Come, cousin Westmoreland,
Our duty this way lies. For God's sake, come!

[*Exeunt* PRINCE JOHN *and* WESTMORELAND.]

56. **carbonado:** meat cut crosswise and broiled
S.D. ***Excursions:*** sorties
4. **make up:** bring up your forces
5. **amaze:** bewilder

PRINCE. By God, thou has deceived me, Lancaster!
I did not think thee lord of such a spirit.
Before, I loved thee as a brother, John;
But now, I do respect thee as my soul.

KING. I saw him hold Lord Percy at the point
With lustier maintenance than I did look for
Of such an ungrown warrior.

PRINCE. O, this boy
Lends mettle to us all! *Exit.*

[*Enter* DOUGLAS.]

DOUGLAS. Another king? They grow like Hydra's heads.
I am the Douglas, fatal to all those
That wear those colors on them. What art thou
That counterfeit'st the person of a king?

KING. The king himself, who, Douglas, grieves at heart
So many of his shadows thou hast met,
And not the very king. I have two boys
Seek Percy and thyself about the field;
But seeing thou fall'st on me so luckily,
I will assay thee. So defend thyself.

DOUGLAS. I fear thou art another counterfeit;
And yet, in faith, thou bearest thee like a king.
But mine I am sure thou art, whoe'er thou be,
And thus I win thee.

They fight. The KING *being in danger, enter* PRINCE OF WALES.

PRINCE. Hold up thy head, vile Scot, or thou art like
Never to hold it up again. The spirits
Of valiant Shirley, Stafford, Blunt are in my arms.
It is the Prince of Wales that threatens thee,
Who never promiseth but he means to pay.
They fight. DOUGLAS *flieth.*
Cheerly, my lord, how fares your grace?

21. **lustier maintenance:** more vigorous conduct
24. **Hydra:** the nine-headed monster of Greek mythology which grew two new heads for each one cut off
29. **shadows:** likenesses
33. **assay:** challenge
43. **Cheerly:** a cry of encouragement

Sir Nicholas Gawsey hath for succor sent,
And so hath Clifton. I'll to Clifton straight.

KING. Stay and breathe awhile.
Thou hast redeemed thy lost opinion,
And showed thou mak'st some tender of my life
In this fair rescue thou hast brought to me.

PRINCE. O God, they did me too much injury
That ever said I hearkened for your death.
If it were so, I might have let alone
The insulting hand of Douglas over you,
Which would have been as speedy in your end
As all the poisonous potions in the world,
And saved the treacherous labor of your son.

KING. Make up to Clifton; I'll to Sir Nicholas Gawsey.

Exit.

Enter HOTSPUR.

HOTSPUR. If I mistake not, thou art Harry Monmouth.

PRINCE. Thou speak'st as if I would deny my name.

HOTSPUR. My name is Harry Percy.

PRINCE. Why, then I see
A very valiant rebel of the name.
I am the Prince of Wales, and think not, Percy,
To share with me in glory any more.
Two stars keep not their motion in one sphere,
Nor can one England brook a double reign
Of Harry Percy and the Prince of Wales.

HOTSPUR. Nor shall it, Harry, for the hour is come
To end the one of us; and would to God
Thy name in arms were now as great as mine!

PRINCE. I'll make it greater ere I part from thee,
And all the budding honors on thy crest
I'll crop to make a garland for my head.

HOTSPUR. I can no longer brook thy vanities. *They fight.*

47. **redeemed:** recovered; **opinion:** reputation
48. **tender:** regard
51. **hearkened for:** desired
53. **insulting:** scornfully triumphing
71. **budding . . . crest:** the plumes on his helmet
73. **vanities:** idle statements

Enter FALSTAFF.

FALSTAFF. Well said, Hal! to it, Hal! Nay, you shall find no boy's play here, I can tell you.

Enter DOUGLAS. *He fighteth with* FALSTAFF, [*who*] *falls down as if he were dead.* [*Exit* DOUGLAS.] *The* PRINCE *killeth* PERCY.

HOTSPUR. O Harry, thou hast robbed me of my youth!
I better brook the loss of brittle life
Than those proud titles thou hast won of me.
They wound my thoughts worse than thy sword my flesh.
But thoughts the slaves of life, and life time's fool,
And time, that takes survey of all the world,
Must have a stop. O, I could prophesy,
But that the earthy and cold hand of death
Lies on my tongue. No, Percy, thou art dust,
And food for— [*Dies.*]

PRINCE. For worms, brave Percy. Fare thee well, great heart;
Ill-weaved ambition, how much art thou shrunk!
When that this body did contain a spirit,
A kingdom for it was too small a bound;
But now two paces of the vilest earth
Is room enough. This earth that bears thee dead
Bears not alive so stout a gentleman.
If thou wert sensible of courtesy,
I should not make so dear a show of zeal.
But let my favors hide thy mangled face;
And, even in thy behalf, I'll thank myself
For doing these fair rites of tenderness.
Adieu, and take thy praise with thee to heaven.
Thy ignominy sleep with thee in the grave,
But not remember'd in thy epitaph.
He spieth FALSTAFF *on the ground.*
What, old acquaintance? Could not all this flesh

80. **fool:** dupe
92. **stout:** valiant
94. **dear:** heartfelt
95. **favors:** plumes (see note to l. 71 above)

Keep in a little life? Poor Jack, farewell!
I could have better spared a better man.
O, I should have a heavy miss of thee
If I were much in love with vanity.
Death hath not struck so fat a deer to-day,
Though many dearer, in this bloody fray.
Embowelled will I see thee by and by;
Till then in blood by noble Percy lie. *Exit.*

FALSTAFF *riseth up.*

FALSTAFF. Embowelled? If thou embowel me to-day, I'll give you leave to powder me and eat me too to-morrow. 'Sblood, 'twas time to counterfeit, or that hot termagant Scot had paid me scot and lot too. Counterfeit? I lie; I am no counterfeit. To die is to be a counterfeit, for he is but the counterfeit of a man who hath not the life of a man; but to counterfeit dying when a man thereby liveth is to be no counterfeit, but the true and perfect image of life indeed. The better part of valor is discretion, in the which better part I have saved my life. 'Zounds, I am afraid of this gunpowder Percy, though he be dead. How if he should counterfeit too and rise? By my faith, I am afraid he would prove the better counterfeit. Therefore I'll make him sure; yea, and I'll swear I killed him. Why may not he rise as well as I? Nothing confutes me but eyes, and nobody sees me. Therefore, sirrah [*stabbing him*], with a new wound in your thigh, come you along with me.

He takes up HOTSPUR *on his back. Enter* PRINCE [*and*] JOHN OF LANCASTER.

PRINCE. Come, brother John; full bravely hast thou fleshed
Thy maiden sword.
JOHN. But, soft! whom have we here?

104. **have . . . miss:** disadvantaged by Falstaff's loss (with a pun on Sir John's heaviness)
105. **vanity:** foolishness
108. **Embowelled:** disembowelled
111. **powder:** salt
112. **termagant:** violent
113. **scot and lot:** thoroughly
126–27. **fleshed . . . sword:** used it for the first time in battle

Did you not tell me this fat man was dead?

PRINCE. I did; I saw him dead,
Breathless and bleeding on the ground. Art thou alive?
Or is it fantasy that plays upon our eyesight?
I prithee speak. We will not trust our eyes
Without our ears. Thou art not what thou seem'st.

FALSTAFF. No, that's certain, I am not a double man; but if I be not Jack Falstaff, then am I a Jack. There is Percy [*throwing the body down*]. If your father will do me any honor, so; if not, let him kill the next Percy himself. I look to be either earl or duke, I can assure you.

PRINCE. Why, Percy I killed myself, and saw thee dead!

FALSTAFF. Didst thou? Lord, Lord, how this world is given to lying. I grant you I was down, and out of breath, and so was he; but we rose both at an instant and fought a long hour by Shrewsbury clock. If I may be believed, so; if not, let them that should reward valor bear the sin upon their own heads. I'll take it upon my death, I gave him this wound in the thigh. If the man were alive and would deny it, 'zounds! I would make him eat a piece of my sword.

JOHN. This is the strangest tale that ever I heard.

PRINCE. This is the strangest fellow, brother John.
Come, bring your luggage nobly on your back.
For my part, if a lie may do thee grace,
I'll gild it with the happiest terms I have.

A retreat is sounded.

The trumpet sounds retreat; the day is ours.
Come, brother, let's to the highest of the field,
To see what friends are living, who are dead.

Exeunt [PRINCE HENRY *and* PRINCE JOHN].

FALSTAFF. I'll follow, as they say, for reward. He that rewards me, God reward him. If I do grow great, I'll grow less; for I'll purge, and leave sack, and live cleanly, as a nobleman should do.

Exit [*dragging off the body*].

134. **double man:** (1) an apparition (2) two men (i.e., with Hotspur on his shoulder)
135. **Jack:** knave
151. **do . . . grace:** reflect credit on you

[SCENE V. *Another part of the field.*]

The trumpets sound. Enter the KING, PRINCE OF WALES, LORD JOHN OF LANCASTER, EARL OF WESTMORELAND, *with* WORCESTER *and* VERNON *prisoners.*

KING. Thus ever did rebellion find rebuke.
Ill-spirited Worcester, did not we send grace,
Pardon, and terms of love to all of you?
And wouldst thou turn our offers contrary?
Misuse the tenor of thy kinsman's trust?
Three knights upon our party slain to-day,
A noble earl, and many a creature else
Had been alive this hour,
If like a Christian thou hadst truly borne
Betwixt our armies true intelligence.
WORCESTER. What I have done my safety urged me to;
And I embrace this fortune patiently,
Since not to be avoided it falls on me.
KING. Bear Worcester to the death, and Vernon too;
Other offenders we will pause upon.
[*Exeunt* WORCESTER *and* VERNON, *guarded.*]
How goes the field?
PRINCE. The noble Scot, Lord Douglas, when he saw
The fortune of the day quite turned from him,
The noble Percy slain, and all his men
Upon the foot of fear, fled with the rest;
And falling from a hill, he was so bruised
That the pursuers took him. At my tent
The Douglas is, and I beseech your grace
I may dispose of him.
KING. With all my heart.
PRINCE. Then, brother John of Lancaster, to you
This honorable bounty shall belong.
Go to the Douglas and deliver him
Up to his pleasure, ransomless and free.

2. **grace:** good will
5. **tenor:** tenure
15. **pause upon:** delay action on
26. **bounty:** act of generosity

His valors shown upon our crests to-day
Have taught us how to cherish such high deeds,
Even in the bosom of our adversaries.

JOHN. I thank your grace for this high courtesy,
Which I shall give away immediately.

KING. Then this remains, that we divide our power.
You, son John, and my cousin Westmoreland,
Towards York shall bend you with your dearest speed
To meet Northumberland and the prelate Scroop,
Who, as we hear, are busily in arms.
Myself and you, son Harry, will towards Wales
To fight with Glendower and the Earl of March.
Rebellion in this land shall lose his sway,
Meeting the check of such another day;
And since this business so fair is done,
Let us not leave till all our own be won. *Exeunt.*

36. bend you: proceed

A TEXTUAL SUPPLEMENT

"The business of him that republishes an ancient book," wrote Dr. Johnson, in many ways a very gifted editor of Shakespeare, "is to correct what is corrupt and to explain what is obscure." These responsibilities and a great many more have been assumed by the editors of the New Variorum Editions of Shakespeare. Regarded as one of the major contributions by American scholars to the study of Shakespeare, the New Variorum was begun in 1871 by H. H. Furness, continued by his son, and, with increasing sophistication in method and exhaustive treatment, is still in progress under the sponsorship of the Modern Language Association of America. Each volume includes a text of the play, collation with other texts, a compendium of all significant comments on all aspects of the play, extracts from the sources, and so on. The task of preparing such an edition, given the great proliferation of scholarly studies of Shakespeare, has become so enormous that it is now more often undertaken by a group of scholars.

The two selections which follow are intended to give some idea of the task of a modern scholarly editor. Both are concerned chiefly with Hal's famous soliloquy at the end of Act I, Scene ii. The first is the largely unadorned text of the first Quarto (1598), and the second is the elaborate version of S. B. Hemingway's *Variorum* edition (to which should be added the appropriate pages in G. Blakemore Evans' *Supplement*).

Prin. How shall we part with them in setting forth?

Po. Why, we wil set forth before or after them, and appoint them a place of meeting, wherein it is at our pleasure to faile: and then wil they aduenture vpõ the exploit themselues, which they shal haue no sooner atchieued but weele set vpon them.

Prin. Yea but tis like that they wil know vs by our horses, by our habits, and by euery other appointment to be our selues.

Po. Tut, our horses they shal not see, ile tie them in the wood, our vizards wee wil change after wee leaue them: and sirrha, I haue cases of Buckrom for the nonce, to immaske our noted outward garments.

Prin. Yea, but I doubt they wil be too hard for vs.

Po. Wel, for two of them, I know them to bee as true bred cowards as euer turnd backe: and for the third, if he fight longer then he sees reason, ile forsweare armes. The vertue of this ieast wil be the incomprehensible lies, that this same fat rogue wil tel vs when we meet at supper, how thirtie at least he fought with, what wardes, what blowes, what extremities he indured, and in the reproofe of this liues the iest.

Prin. Well, ile goe with thee, prouide vs all thinges necessarie, and meete me to morrow night in Eastcheape, there ile sup: farewell.

Po. Farewel my Lord. *Exit Poines.*

Prin. I know you all, and wil a while vphold
The vnyokt humour of your idlenes,
Yet herein wil I imitate the sunne,
Who doth permit the base contagious clouds
To smother vp his beautie from the world,
That when he please againe to be himselfe,
Being wanted he may be more wondred at
By breaking through the foule and ougly mists
Of vapours that did seeme to strangle him.
If all the yeere were playing holly-dayes,
To sport would be as tedious as to worke;
But when they seldome come, they wisht for come,
And nothing pleaseth but rare accidents:
So when this loose behauiour I throw off,
And pay the debt I neuer promised,

By how much better then my word I am,
By so much shall I falsifie mens hopes,
And like bright mettal on a sullein ground,
My reformation glittring ore my fault,
Shal shew more goodly, and attract more eyes
Then that which hath no soile to set it off.
Ile so offend, to make offence a skill,
Redeeming time when men thinke least I wil. *Exit.*

Enter the King, Northumberland, Worcester, Hotspur, sir Walter blunt, with others.

King. My blood hath bin too colde and temperate,
Vnapt to stir at these indignities,
And you haue found me, for accordingly
You tread vpon my patience, but be sure
I will from henceforth rather be my selfe
Mightie, and to be fearde, then my condition
Which hath bin smooth as oile, soft as yong downe,
And therefore lost that title of respect,
Which the proud soule neare payes but to the proud.

Wor. Our house (my soueraigne liege) little deserues
The scourge of greatnes to be vsd on it,
And that same greatnesse to, which our owne hands
Haue holpe to make so portly. *Nor.* My Lord.

King. Worcester get thee gone, for I do see
Danger, and disobedience in thine eie:
O sir, your presence is too bold and peremptorie,
And Maiestie might neuer yet endure
The moodie frontier of a seruant browe,
You haue good leaue to leaue vs, when we need
Your vse and counsel we shall send for you. *Exit Wor.*
You were about to speake.

North. Yea my good Lord.
Those prisoners in your highnes name demanded,
Which Harry Percy here at Holmedon tooke,
Were as he saies, not with such strength denied
As is deliuered to your maiestie.
Either enuie therefore, or misprision,
Is guiltie of this fault, and not my sonne.

there ile ſup : farewell.
Po. Farewel my Lord. *Exit Poines.*
Prin. I know you all, and wil a while vphold

185. Poines.] Om. Dyce, Cam., Glo., Huds. ii, Wh. ii, Rlf., Tud., Ox., Ard.

186. *a while*] *a-while* F_1F_2.

---

183. **to morrow night**] STEEVENS (Var. ed. 1778): I think we should read to-night. The disguises were to be provided for the purposes of the robbery which was to be committed at *four o'clock in the morning;* and they would come too late if the prince was not to receive them 'till the night after the day of the exploit. This is another instance to prove that Shakespeare could forget in the end of a scene what he had said in the beginning.—KNIGHT (ed. 1839): [See Knight's reading in Textual Notes, which he here explains.—ED.] The prince is here thinking less of the exploit at Gadshill than of "the virtue of the jest" after the robbery. Perhaps some intermediate place of meeting was thought of by the prince; but he breaks off exultingly, with his head full of the supper to-morrow night.—COWL (ed. 1914): Change is unnecessary. The prince's appointment with Poins is for the evening after the robbery. [But is not this, then, a very strange farewell to Poins: "provide things necessary and meet me"? This surely implies that the meeting is to be before the robbery. Steevens's point is well taken.—ED.]

186 ff.] THEOBALD (ed. 1733, *Pref.*, p. xx): The prince's reformation is not so sudden as not to be prepar'd and expected by the audience. . . . Our poet has so well and artfully guarded him from the suspicions of habitual profligateness that even from the first showing him upon the stage . . . he has taken care not to carry him off the scene without the intimation that "he knows them all, &c."—JOHNSON (ed. 1765): This speech is very artfully introduced to keep the prince from appearing vile in the opinion of the audience; it prepares them for his future reformation, and, what is yet more valuable, exhibits a natural picture of a great mind offering excuses to itself, and palliating those follies which it can neither justify nor forsake.—GENTLEMAN (*Introd.* to Bell's ed., 1773): This is not a very allowable apology.—HORN (*Shs. Schauspiele erlautert*, 1826, ii, 260): Shakespeare leaves us no doubt as to the inner thoughts of the prince. Even in the second scene, as soon as the prose portion is over, the poetry begins in truly royal manner. Readers have often admired this passage; and, no doubt, justly; yet they would have enjoyed it more if they had considered it in its fullest significance. Of course, Prince Henry is a favorite of the author; but does that mean that the poet must refrain from clever irony in his treatment of him? And is it not clear that there is irony here? . . . Even in the second line of his speech the prince ignores the fact that he takes part in this cheerful idleness with real enjoyment. . . . The comparison with the sun, itself so commonplace, . . . is yet much too lofty, too pompous, and the reader cannot forbear smiling a little. We ask with justice, what has this charming and clever young prince done that he should praise himself as the counterpart of the sun? Is it not almost a Bolingbroke attitude?—LLOYD (*Essays on Sh.*, 1858): We are at liberty to think as we please of the prince's deliberate scheme of politic stage-effect in a sudden reformation.—MEZIÈRES (*Sh., ses Œuvres,*

[186 ff.]

&c., 1860, p. 287): At this point Henry is less appealing and less natural. His careful calculation is too wise for a young débauché. . . . There is clumsiness here. The poet, who must present the conversion of a hero and who must conduct him through youthful wanderings to strong manhood, finds only one way of explaining the change: namely, that at the time when the prince is committing most of his faults, he has decided to reform. . . . Racine would have been more skilful.—ELTON (ed. 1889): There is something sophistical in this fine speech. The prince enjoys Falstaff, and rather pays himself off with fine metaphors to excuse his enjoyment. . . . Perhaps, however, these are modern refinements of feeling; Shakespeare wrote for the stage, and his effect is broad, natural, and simple.—RANSOME (*Short Stud. of Sh. Plots*, 1890, p. 198): Shakespeare was careful to differentiate between Richard II and Henry V. Richard could never have made this speech. . . . After this speech the audience would enjoy the Falstaff scenes; which would have been quite impossible had they believed themselves to be looking on the creation of another ruined character like Richard.—BOAS (*Sh. and his Predecessors*, 1896, p. 270): This Pharisaical declaration need not be taken too literally, as it is probably meant for little more than a dramatic "aside" to the audience, assuring them that Henry is not in reality what he appears.—BRANDES (*Wm. Sh., a Crit. Study*, 1896, p. 200): The son is not so unlike the father as the father believes. Shakespeare has made him, in his way, adopt a scarcely less diplomatic policy. . . . This self-consciousness of Henry's was to some extent imposed upon Shakespeare. Without it he could scarcely have brought upon the stage in such questionable company a prince who had become a national hero. Yet if the prince had acted with the cut-and-dried deliberation of purpose which he here attributes to himself, we should have had to write him down an unmitigated charlatan. . . . We must allow for Shakespeare's use of soliloquy. He frequently regards it as an indispensable stage-convention, which does not really reveal the thoughts of the speaker, but only serves . . . to give the hearer information he requires. Such a soliloquy ought to be spoken with a good deal of sophisticated self-justification, or else in a tone of gay raillery.—ARNOLD (*Soliloquies of Sh.*, 1911, p. 30): Excluding the villain's soliloquy, there is only one flagrant case of the self-characterizing monologue in Shakespeare, that of Prince Hal. This speech exists for the sake of the exposition.—AX (*Rel. of Sh. to Hol.*, 1912, pp. 20–22): We deem this monologue unnâtural, the speaker's explanations strange, and the motives he states hateful. . . . How easy would it have been for the author to give Harry's behavior a natural explanation. Could he not have made him say that his escapades were but tricks of youth, and that if God should ever give him the crown, He would also give him the power to bear it? . . . If we wish to enjoy this play, we must try to forget these words of the prince. But Shakespeare comes to our aid by forgetting them himself, and whenever we see Harry in Falstaff's company, he is delighting in it heartily and we have nowhere the impression of seeing before us a player within a play, but an ingenuous youth who is anything but a hypocrite. —TOLMAN (*P.M.L.A.*, 1919): I have sometimes wished that Shakespeare had given Hal at this point merely a few broken phrases that should suggest the stirrings of a better purpose. [SCHÜCKING (*Char. Prob. in Sh. Plays*, 1922,

The vnyokt humour of your idlenes,
Yet herein wil I imitate the ſunne,
Who doth permit the baſe contagious clouds
To ſmother vp his beautie from the world,
That when he pleaſe againe to be himſelfe,
Being wanted he may be more wondred at
By breaking through the foule and ougly miſts
Of vapours that did ſeeme to ſtrangle him.
If all the yeere were playing holly-dayes,
To ſport would be as tedious as to worke ;
But when they ſeldome come, they wiſht for come,
And nothing pleaſeth but rare accidents :
So when this looſe behauiour I throw off,
And pay the debt I neuer promiſed,
By how much better then my word I am,
By ſo much ſhall I falſifie mens hopes,

192. *wondred*] *wondered* Var. '85, Sing.
193. *ougly*] *vgly* Q_2, et seq.
194. *Of*] *And* Huds. ii.
vapours] *vapour* Dyce ii, iii.
202. *hopes*] *fears* Warb.

p. 221) and STOLL (*Poets and Playwrights*, 1930, p. 48) stress the fact that this speech must not be taken psychologically but as mere exposition by the playwright to the audience. See also Appendix: Characters: Prince Hal; especially QUILLER-COUCH (*Notes on Sh.'s Workmanship*, 1917).—ED.]

188–194.] HALLIWELL (ed. 1859): Elmham, a contemporary chronicler, after noticing the youthful follies of the prince, proceeds: " . . . Such cloudy passages may well be buried in obscurity. But the author's reason for alluding to them is to afford matter of rejoicing . . . by presenting the sudden change from night into day, of cloud into clear sky, of an eclipse into perfect splendour, of darkness into light. Lo, the time is at hand when upon the vanishing of a cloud, the solar rays will dart forth."—MALONE (*Second Appendix to Suppl.*, 1783): So, in our author's 33rd Sonnet: "Full many a glorious morning have I seen Flatter the mountain-tops with sovereign eye,—Anon permit the basest clouds to ride With ugly rack on his celestial face."

195–197.] MALONE (*Second Supplement*, 1783): So, in our author's 52nd Sonnet: "Therefore are feasts so solemn and so rare, Since, seldom coming in the long year set, Like stones of price they thinly placed are."

198. **accidents**] COWL (ed. 1914): For accidents in the sense of incidents, cf. *Tempest*, V, i, 250.

202. **falsifie . . . hopes**] JOHNSON (ed. 1765): To falsify hope is to exceed hope.—FARMER (Var. ed. 1773, Appendix ii, vol. x): Hopes is used for expectations, whether good or bad. This is still common in the Midland counties. "Such manner of uncouth speech," says Puttenham, "did the tanner of Tamworth use to King Edward IV; which tanner having mistaken him and used very broad talk, at length perceiving that it was the king, was afraid, and said

And like bright mettal on a ſullein ground,
My reformation glittring ore my fault,
Shal ſhew more goodly, and attract more eyes
Then that which hath no foile to ſet it off.
Ile ſo offend, to make offence a skill,
Redeeming time when men thinke leaſt I wil. *Exit.*

[*Scœna Tertia.*]

Enter the King, Northumberland, Worceſter, Hotſpur, ſir Walter blunt, with others.

King. My blood hath bin too colde and temperate,
Vnapt to ſtir at theſe indignities,

206. *foile*] *soile* Q_{4-6}. *soyle* Q_7Q_8, Ff. *Soil* Rowe, T. J. (1710).

208. Exit] Omit Ff.

Scœna Tertia.] Ff. Om. Qq. SCENE III. Rowe. SCENE IV. Pope. Scene changes to an Apartment in the Palace. Theob. SCENE IV. An Apartment in the Palace. Han. SCENE IV. Changes to an Apartment in the Palace. Warb., Johns. SCENE III. The Same. Another Room. Cap. SCENE III. An Apartment in the Palace. Varr., Ran., et seq. with some variations (*e. g.*, SCENE III. Room of State in the Palace. Wh. i. SCENE III. Windsor. A Room in the Palace. Hal. i.)

sir Walter] Om. Huds. i.

blunt] Blunt Q_2, et seq.

with] Qq, Cam., Glo., Wh. ii, Rlf., Tud., Ard. and Ff, et cet.

. . . 'I *hope* I shall be hanged,' whereat the king laughed, not only to see the tanner's vain *fear*, but also to hear his mis-shapen terms."—N. E. D. (1901): Hope: 3. (*Obsolete*) Expectation, without implication of desire.

203–206. **sullein . . . foile**] STEEVENS (ed. 1793): So, in *Richard II*, I, iii, 265: "The sullen passage of thy weary steps Esteem a foil, wherein thou art to set The precious jewel of thy home-return."—COWL (ed. 1914): Sullen ground; dark background; foil; a leaf of dull metal that "sets off" a brighter metal or jewel.

207. **skill**] ONIONS (1911): Piece of good policy.—COWL (ed. 1914): Art. —N. E. D. (1919): An art, a science.

I, iii.] DAVIES (*Dram. Misc.*, 1785): The action of this scene is very animating and important. The jealousy, suspicion and distrust of the king are finely contrasted with the high spirit and impetuosity of Hotspur: Agamemnon and Achilles are not more strongly delineated, nor their passions more highly coloured. The conduct of the scene is truly dramatic.

Scene-heading.] ANDERS (*Sh.'s Books*, 1904, p. 253): The scene is Windsor; cf. Holinshed, and I, i, 104.

1–124.] LLOYD (*Essays on Sh.*, 1858): Hotspur professes to have denied no prisoners, and yet still sticks for a consideration for surrendering them. He repudiates the charge of revolt made against Mortimer, supports his repudiation by a lively declaration of Mortimer's bloody contest with Glendower, and

CULTURAL CONTEXTS

. . . the purpose of playing, whose end, both at the first and now, was and is to hold as 'twere the mirror up to Nature—to show Virtue her own feature, scorn her own image, and the very age and body of the time his form and pressure.

—*Hamlet*, III, ii

* * * * *

There is a history in all men's lives,
Figuring the nature of the times deceased.
The which observed, a man may prophesy,
With a near aim, of the main chance of things
As yet not come to life, which in their seeds
And weak beginnings lie intreasured.

—*Henry the Fourth, Part II*, III, i

According to Ben Jonson Shakespeare "was not of an age, but for all time." But modern scholarship has increasingly made clear that however unique and unbounded Shakespeare's genius might have been, he and his work were also very much "of an age," responding to and reflecting the multiple impulses of a complex historical period. The plays were not the creations of a solitary and sequestered talent; they carry the form and pressure of the age and time in which they were fashioned, a form and pressure which owe much to the dramatic traditions from which they emerged and to the theater, actors, and audience for which they were written—indeed, to the whole cultural milieu in which they were conceived.

The selections that follow suggest some of the intellectual climate relevant to Shakespeare's history plays and to *Henry the Fourth, Part I* in particular. They are not presented as statements of abstract ideas which Shakespeare dutifully and deliberately set about illustrating in the play, nor are they offered as "sources," although it is most likely that Shakespeare was familiar with all of them. They suggest a contemporary context of received opinion and attitude against which it is profitable to consider the play.

The Homilies, authorized for delivery in the Church of England, represent "official" state-church views. The passage from *Troilus and Cressida* is one of the best-known statements of the imperatives of an ordered, stratified society. Elyot's *Governour*, Castiglione's *Courtier*, and *A Myrrovr for Magistrates* were highly esteemed and influential works in sixteenth-century England. Finally, Lord Berners' preface to his popular translation of Froissart offers a useful compendium of Tudor attitudes toward the recorded past and the benefits to be derived from its study; and Hall and Daniel provide interpretations of the Lancaster-York conflict with its resolution in the providential accession of Henry VII, aspects of what E. M. W. Tillyard has termed "the Tudor myth," which are relevant to the vision of the past which Shakespeare dramatizes in his Histories.

ORDER IN THE UNIVERSE, STATE, AND INDIVIDUAL

An exhortacion, concernyng good ordre and obedience, to rulers and magistrates

Almightie God hath created & appointed al thynges, in heauẽ, yearth, and waters, in a moste excellent and perfect order. In heauẽ, he hath appoynted distinct orders and states of Archangelles and Angels. In yearth he hath assigned kynges, princes, with other gouernors vnder them, all in good & necessarie ordre. The water aboue is kept and raineth doune in due time and ceason. The sunne, mone, sterres, rainbow, thũder, lightning, cloudes, and al birdes of the aire, do kepe their ordre. The yearth, trees, seedes, plantes, herbes, corne, grasse, and al maner of beastes kepe thẽ in their ordre. All the partes of ye whole yere as winter, somer, monethes, nightes, & dayes, continue in their ordre. All kyndes of fishes in the sea, riuers and waters, with all fountaynes, sprynges, yea, the seas themselfes, kepe their comely course and ordre. And mã hymself also, hath al his partes, both within & without: as soule, harte, mynd, memory, vnderstandyng, reason, speache, withall and synguler corporall mẽbres of his body, in a profitable, necessary and pleasaunt ordre. Euery degre of people, in their vocacion, callyng, & office, hath appoynted to them, their duetie & ordre. Some are in high degre, some in lowe, some kynges & princes, some inferiors and subiectes, priestes, and laimen, masters & seruauntes, fathers & children, husbandes & wifes, riche and poore, and euery one haue nede of other: so that in all things, is to be laude[d] & praised the goodly ordre of God, without the whiche, no house, no citie, no cōmon wealth can continue & endure. For where there is no right ordre, there reigneth all abuse, carnall libertie, enormitie, syn, &

From Sermon X, *Certeyne Sermons, or Homelies appoynted by the Kynges Maiestie to bee declared and redd* (1547), Sig. Ri^r-Rii^r. Marginal glosses have been omitted.

babilonicall cõfusion. Take awaye kynges, princes, rulers, magistrates, iudges, and such states of Gods ordre, no man shall ride or go by the high waie vnrobbed, no man shall slepe in his awne house or bed vnkilled, no mã shall kepe his wife, children, & possessions in quietnes, all thyngse shalbe cōmon, and there must nedes folow all mischief and vtter destructiō, both of soules, bodies, goodes, and common wealthes. But blessed be God, that we in this realme of England, fele not the horrible calamities, miseries, & wretchednes, which all thei vndoubtedly fele & suffre, y[t] lacke this godly ordre. And praised be God, that we knowe the great excellēt benefite of god, shewed towardes vs in this behalfe. God hath sente vs his high gifte, our moste dere souereigne lord king Edward y[e] sixt, with godly, wise, and honorable coũsail, with other superiors and inferiors, in a beautifull ordre. Wherefore, let vs subiectes do our bounden duties, geuing hartie thankes to God, and praiyng for the preseruaciō of this Godly ordre. Let vs al obey euen from the botome of our hartes, al their Godly procedynges, lawes, statutes, proclamacions, and iniunctiōs, with al other Godly orders. Let vs considre the scriptures of the holy ghost, whiche perswade & cōmaunde vs al, obediently to be subiect: first & chiefly, to the kynges maiestie, supreme hed ouer all, & next, to his honorable counsail, and to all other noble men, magistrates, and officers, whiche by Gods goodnes be placed and ordred; for almightie God, is the onely aucthor and prouider of thys forenamed state and ordre, as it is written of God, in the boke of the prouerbes: through me, kynges do reigne, through me counsailors make iust lawes, through me, doo princes beare rule, and all iudges of the yearth execute iudgement: I am louyng to them, that loue me.

Here let vs marke wel, & remembre, that the high power & aucthoritie of kynges, with theyr makyng of lawes, iudgemētes, & officers, are the ordinaunces, not of man, but of God: & therefore is this word (through me) so many tymes repeted. Here is also well to be cōsidred and remembred, that this good ordre is appoynted of Gods wisedom, fauor, & loue, specially for them that loue God, & therefore he saith: I loue them, y[t] loue me. Also, in the boke of wisedom we may euidently learne, that a kynges power, aucthoritie, & strength, is a greate benefite of God, geuen of his great mercy, to the comfort of our greate misery. For thus wee rede there spoken to kynges. Here o ye kinges & vnderstand: learne ye y[t] be iudges of thendes [sic] of the yearth: geue eare ye, that rule the multitudes:

for ye power is geuen you of ye lord, and the strength frõ the highest. Let vs learne also here by the infallible word of God, that kinges and other supreme & higher officers, are ordeined of god who is most highest, & therfore they are here diligẽtely taught, to apply thẽselfes, to knowledge & wisedom, necessary for the orderynge of Gods people, to their gouernaũce committed. And thei be here also taught by almighty God, that thei should reknowledge thẽselfes, to haue al their power and strength, not frõ Rome, but immediatly of God most highest. . . .

WILLIAM SHAKESPEARE

The Spectre of Disorder

Ulysses. . . . Degree being vizarded,
The unworthiest shows as fairly in the mask.
The heavens themselves, the planets and this centre
Observe degree, priority and place,
Insisture, course, proportion, season, form,
Office and custom, in all line of order;
And therefore is the glorious planet Sol
In noble eminence enthroned and sphered
Amidst the other; whose medicinable eye
Corrects the ill aspects of planets evil,
And posts, like the commandment of a king,
Sans check to good and bad: but when the planets
In evil mixture to disorder wander,
What plagues and what portents! what mutiny!
What raging of the sea! shaking of earth!
Commotion in the winds! frights, changes, horrors,
Divert and crack, rend and deracinate
The unity and married calm of states
Quite from their fixure! O, when degree is shaked,
Which is the ladder to all high designs,
The enterprise is sick! How could communities

Degrees in schools and brotherhoods in cities,
Peaceful commerce from dividable shores,
The primogenitive and due of birth,
Prerogative of age, crowns, sceptres, laurels,
But by degree, stand in authentic place?
Take but degree away, untune that string,
And, hark, what discord follows! each thing meets
In mere oppugnancy: the bounded waters
Should lift their bosoms higher than the shores
And make a sop of all this solid globe:
Strength should be lord of imbecility,
And the rude son should strike his father dead:
Force should be right; or rather, right and wrong,
Between whose endless jar justice resides,
Should lose their names, and so should justice too.
Then every thing includes itself in power,
Power into will, will into appetite;
And appetite, an universal wolf,
So doubly seconded with will and power,
Must make perforce an universal prey,
And last eat up himself.

(*Troilus and Cressida* Act I, Scene iii)

An Homilee agaynst disobedience and wylful rebellion

. . . Thus you do see, that neyther heauen nor paradise coulde suffer anye rebellion in them, neyther be places for any rebels to remayne in. Thus became rebellion, as you see, both the first and greatest, and the verye roote of all other sinnes, and the first and principall cause both of all worldlye and bodyly miseries, sorowes, diseases, sicknesses, and deathes, and whiche is infinitely worse then all these, as is sayde, the very cause of death and dampnation eternall also. After this breache of obedience to God, and rebellion agaynst his maiestie, all mischeefes and miseries breaking in there-

From *The Second Tome of Homilies* (1571), Sermon XXI, pp. 546–547, 549–551, 552–555, 573–574, 594–595. Marginal glosses have been omitted. This homily was added in 1571 to those authorized for use in the English church in connection with the unsuccessful uprising in the North in 1569 and ends with a "thanksgiving for the suppression of the last rebellion."

with, and ouerflowing the worlde, lest all thinges shoulde come vnto confusion and vtter ruine, GOD forthwith by lawes geuen vnto mankynde, repayred agayne the rule and order of obedience thus by rebellion ouerthrowen, and besides the obedience due vnto his maiestie, he not onlye ordayned that in families and housholdes, the wyfe should be obedient vnto her husbande, the chyldren vnto their parentes, the seruauntes vnto their maisters: but also when mankynde increased, and spread it selfe more largely ouer the worlde, he, by his holye worde did constitute and or[d]ayne in Cities and Countreys seuerall and speciall gouernours and rulers, vnto whom the residue of his people shoulde be obedient.

As in readyng of the holye scriptures, we shall finde in very many and almost infinite places, as well of the olde Testament, as the newe, that kynges and princes, as well the euill as the good, do raigne by Gods ordinaunce, and that subiectes are bounden to obey them: that God doth geue princes wysdome, great power, and aucthoritie: that God defendeth them agaynst their enemies, and destroyeth their enemies horribly: that the anger and displeasure of the prince is as the roaring of a Lion, and the very messenger of death: and that the subiect, that prouoketh hym to displeasure, sinneth agaynst his owne soule: With many other thinges, concernyng both the aucthoritie of princes, and the duetie of subiectes.

* * * * *

. . . It commeth therfore neyther of chaunc and fortune (as they tearme it) nor of thambition [sic] of mortal men and women, climing vp of theyr owne accorde to dominion, that there be Kynges, Queenes, Princes, and other gouernors ouer men beyng theyr subiectes: but al Kinges, Queenes, and other gouernours are specially appoynted by the ordinaunce of GOD. And as GOD him selfe, beyng of an infinite maiestie, power, and wysdome, ruleth and gouerneth all thynges in heauen and in earth, as the vniuersal Monarche & onlye Kyng and Emperour ouer all, as beyng onlye able to take and beare the charge of all: so hath he constituted, ordayned, and set earthly princes ouer particuler kyngdomes and dominions in earth, both for the auoydyng of all confusion, whiche els woulde be in the worlde if it should be without gouernours, and for the great quiet and benefite of earthly men theyr subiectes, and also that the princes them selues in aucthoritie, power, wysdome, prouidence, and ryghteousnes in gouernment of people and countreys, committed to their charge, shoulde resemble his heauenly gouernance, as the maiestie of heauenly thinges may by the bacenes of earthly thinges be shadowed and resembled: And for that similitude that is betweene the heauenly Monarchie and earthly kyngdomes wel gouerned, our sauiour Christe in sundry parables, sayth that the kyngdome of heauen is resembled vnto a man a kyng, and as the name of the kyng is very often attributed and geuen vnto GOD in the holy scriptures, so doth GOD hym selfe in the same scriptures sometyme vouchsafe to communicate his name with earthly princes, tearming them gods: Doubtles for that similitude of gouernment which they haue or should haue not vnlike vnto GOD their king. Unto the which similitude of heauenly gouernment, the nearer and nearer that an earthly prince doth come in his regiment, the greater blessing of Gods mercie is he vnto that countrey and people ouer whom he raigneth: and the further and further that an earthlye prince doth swarue from the example of the heauenly gouernment, the greater plague he is of Gods wrath, and punishment by Gods iustice, vnto that countrey & people, ouer whom God for their sins hath placed suche a prince and gouernour.

* * * * *

. . . What shall suiectes do then? shall they obeye valiaunt, stout, wyse, and good Princes, and contempne, disobey, and rebel agaynst chyldren being theyr Princes, or against vndiscrete and euill gouernours: GOD forbid. For fyrst what a perilous thing were it to commit vnto the subiectes the iudgement whiche Prince is wyse and godly, and his gouernmẽt good, and which is otherwyse: as though the foote must iudge of the head: an enterprise very haynous, and must needes breede rebellion. For who els be they that are moste enclined to rebellion, but suche hautie spirites? From whom springeth suche foule ruine of Realmes? Is not rebellion the greatest of all mischiefs? And who are most readye to the greatest mischeefes, but the worste men? Rebelles therefore the worst of all subiectes are most redye to rebellion, as beyng the worst of all vices, and furthest from the duetie of a good subiect: as on the contrary part, the best subiectes are moste firme and constant in obedience, as in the speciall and peculier vertue of good subiectes. . . .

But what yf the prince be vndiscrete, and euil in deede, and it also euident to all mens eyes, that he so is? I aske agayne, what yf it be long of the wickedness of the subiectes, that the prince is vndiscrete and euyll? Shall the subiectes both by their wickednesse prouoke God for their deserued punishment to geue them an vndiscrete or euyll prince, and also rebell agaynst hym, and withall agaynst God, who for the punishment of their sinnes dyd geue them suche a prince? Wyll you heare the scriptures concernyng this poynt? God (say the holy scriptures) maketh a wicked man to raigne for the sinnes of the people. Agayne, God geueth a prince in his anger (meanyng an euill one) and taketh away a prince in his displeasure, meaning speciallye when he taketh away a good prince, for the sinnes of the people: as in our memorie he toke away our good Iosias kyng Edwarde in his young and good yeres for our wickednesse. And contrarilye the scriptures do teache that God geueth wysdome vnto princes, and maketh a wyse and good kyng to raigne ouer that people whom he loueth, and who loueth hym. Agayne, yf the people obey God, both they and theyr kyng shall prosper and be safe, els both shall perishe, sayth God by the mouth of Samuel.

Here you see, that GOD placeth as well euyll princes as good, and for what cause he doth both. If we therefore wyll haue a good prince, eyther to be geuen vs, or to continue, nowe we haue suche a one, let vs by our obedience to God and to our prince, moue God thereunto. If we wyll haue an euyll prince (when God shall sende such a one) taken away, and a good one in his place, let vs take away our wickednesse whiche prouoketh God to place such a one ouer vs, & God wyll eyther displace hym, or if an euyll prince, make hym a good prince: so that we first wyll chaunge our euyll into good.

* * * * *

. . . How horrible a sinne agaynst God and man rebellion is, cannot possible be expressed accordyng vnto the greatnesse thereof. For he that nameth rebellion, nameth not a singuler or one onely sinne, as is theft, robbery, murther, & such lyke: but he nameth the whole puddle and sinke of all sinnes agaynst God and man, agaynst his prince, his countrey, his countreymen, his parentes, his children, his kinsfolkes, his frendes, and agaynst all men vniuersally, all sinnes, I say agaynst God and al men heaped together nameth he, that nameth rebellion.

* * * * *

. . . Wherefore to conclude, let all good subiectes considering how horrible a sinne agaynst God, theyr prince, their countrey, and countreymen, agaynst all Gods and mans lawes rebellion is, beyng in deede not one seuerall sinne, but all sinnes agaynst God and man heaped together, consydering the mischeuous life and deedes, and the shamefull endes and deathes of all rebels hitherto, and the pitifull vndoyng of their wyues, chyldren, and families, and disheriting of theyr heyres for euer, and aboue all thinges consydering the eternall dampnation, that is prepared for all impenitent rebels in hell with Satan the first founder of rebellion, and graunde captayne of all rebels, let all good subiectes I say, consyderyng these thinges, auoide and flee all rebellion, as the greatest of all mischeefes, and embrace due obedience to God and our prince, as the greatest of all vertues, that we may both escape all euils and miseries that do folowe rebellion in this worlde, and eternall dampnation in the world to come and enioye peace, quietnesse, and securitie, with all other Gods benefites and blessinges, which folowe obedience in this life, and finally may enioy the kyngdome of heauen the peculier place of all obedient subiectes to God and their prince, in the world to come: which I beseche God the kyng of all kynges, graunt vnto vs for the obedience of his sonne our Sauiour Jesus Christe, vnto whom with the father and the holy ghost, one God and kyng immortall, all honour, seruice, and obedience of all his creatures is due for euer and euer. Amen.

THE EDUCATION OF A PRINCE

SIR THOMAS ELYOT

The Experience or practise necessary in the persone of a gouernour of a publike weale

. . . experience whiche is in our propre persones and is of some men called practise, is of no small moment or efficacie in the acquiringe of sapience, in so moche that it semeth that no operation or affaire may be perfecte, nor no science or arte may be complete, except experience be there unto added, whereby knowledge is ratified, and (as I mought saye) consolidate.

It is written that the great kynge Alexander on a tyme beinge (as it hapned) unoccupyed, came to the shoppe of Apelles, the excellent paynter, and standyng by hym whyles he paynted, the kynge raisoned with hym of lines, adumbrations, proportions, or other like thinges pertainyng to imagery, whiche the paynter a litle whyles sufferynge, at the last said to the kynge with the countenance all smylyng, Seest thou, noble prince, howe the boye that gryndeth my colours dothe laughe the to scorne? whiche wordes the kynge toke in good parte and helde hym therwith iustly corrected, considering by his owne office in martial affaires that he than had in hande, how great a portion of knowledge faileth, where lacketh experience. And therin gouernours shall nat disdayne to be resembled unto phisitions, consideryng their offices in curynge and preseruynge be moste lyke of any other. That parte of phisike called rationall, wherby is declared the faculties or powers of the body, the causis,

From Book III of *The Boke Named The Gouernour* (1531), reprinted from the edition of H. H. S. Croft (London, 1883), II, 402–417 [footnotes omitted].

accidentes, and tokens of sikenessis, can nat alwayes be sure without some experience in the temperature or distemperature of the regions, in the disposition of the patient in diete, concoction, quietnesse, exercise, and slepe.

And Galene, prince of phisitions, exhorteth them to knowe exactly the accustomed diete of their patientes, whiche can nat happen without moche resorte in to their companies, seriousely notyng their usage in diete. Semblably, the uniuersall state of a contray or citie may be well lykened to the body of man. Wherfore the gouernours, in the stede of phisitions attending on their cure, ought to knowe the causes of the decaye of their publike weale, whiche is the helthe of their countraye or cytie, and thanne with expedition to procede to the mooste spedy and sure remedy. But certes the very cause of decay, ne the true meane to cure it, may neuer be sufficiently knowen of gouernours, except they them selfes wyll personally resorte and peruse all partes of the countrayes under their gouernaunce, and inserche diligently as well what be the customes and maners of people good and badde, as also the commodities and discommodities, howe the one may be preserued, the other suppressed, or at the leste wayes amended. Also amonge them that haue ministration or execution of iustice, (whiche I may liken unto the membres), to taste and fele howe euery of them do practise their offices, that is to say, whether they do it febly or unprofitably, and whether it happen by negligence, discourage, corruption, or affection.

But nowe may the reder with good reason demaunde of me by what maner experience the gouernours may come to the true knowledge herof. That shall I nowe declare. Fyrst the gouernours them selfes adourned with vertue, being in suche wise an example of liuing to their inferiors, and making the people iudges of them and their domesticall seruauntes and adherentes, shulde sondry tymes duringe their gouernaunce, either purposely or by way of solace, repaire in to diuers partes of their iurisdiction or prouince, and making their abode, they shall partly them selfes attentifly here what is commonly or priuatly spoken concerning the astate of the contray or persones, partely they shall cause their seruauntes or frendes, of whose honestie and trouth they haue good assuraunce, to resorte in disporting them selfes in diuers townes and villages; and as they happen to be in company with the inhabitauntes priuyly and with some maner of circumstaunce, enquire what men of hauour dwell nighe unto them, what is the forme of their liuing, of what estimation they be in iustice, liberalitie, diligence in executing the lawes, and other semblable vertues; contrary wise whether they be oppressours, couetous men, maintenours of offendours, remisse or negligent, if they be officers; and what the examiners do here the gretter nombre of people reporte that they interly and truely denounce it to the sayde gouernour. By the whiche intimation and their owne prudent endeuour, they shall haue infallible knowlege who among the inhabitauntes be men towarde the publike weale best disposed. Them shall they calle for and mooste courtaisely entretaine, and (as it were) louingly embrace, with thankes for their good will and endeuour towarde the publike weale; commending them openly for their vertue and diligence, offring to them their assistence in their semblable doinges, and also their furtheraunce towarde the due recompence of their trauailes. On the contrary parte, whan they see any of them who amonge their inferiors obserue nat iustice, and likewise officers whiche be remisse or fauourable to commune offendours and brekers of lawes, and negligent in the execution of their auctorities, to them shall they gyue condigne reprehentions, manifestyng their defautes in omitting their dueties, and in giuing euil example to their companions, also boldnes to transgresse, to contemne the lawes, declaringe also that the ministring such occasion deserue nat onely a sharpe rebuke but also right greuous punisshement. And if he that thus admonesteth be a soueraigne gouernour or prince, if, I saye, he shortely here upon doth ratifie his wordes by expellyng some of them whiche I nowe rehersed from their offices, or otherwyse sharpely correctynge them, and contrarye wise aduaunce higher some good man and whom he hath proued to be diligent in the execution of iustice, undoubtedly he shall inflame the appetite and zele of good ministers, and also suscitate or raise the courage of all men inclined to vertue, so that there shal neuer lacke men apte and propise to be set in auctoritie. Where the merites of men beinge hidde and unknowen to the soueraigne gouernour, and the negligent ministers or inferior gouernours hauing nat only equal thanke or rewarde but perchaunce moche more than they which be diligent, or wolde be if they moughte haue assistence, there undoubtedly is grieuouse discourage and perill of conscience; for as moche as they omitte often tymes their dueties and offices, reputyng it great foly and madnes to acquire by the executyng of iustice nat only an opinion of tyrannye amonge the people, and consequently haterede, but also malignitie amonge his equalles and superiours, with a note of ambition.

This reuolued and considered by a circumspecte gouernour, lorde god, howe shortly and with litle difficultie shall he dispose the publike weale that is greued to receyue medicine, wherby it shulde be soone healed and reduced to his perfection.

WILLIAM BALDWIN

A Myrrovr for Magistrates

. . . the goodnes or badnes of any realme lyeth in the goodnes or badnes of ye rulers. And ther fore not without great cause do the holy Apostles so earnestly charge vs to pray for the magistrates: For in dede the welth and quiet of everye cõmon weale, the disorder also & miseries of the same, cum specially through them. I nede not go eyther to the Romans or Grekes for the proofe hereof, neyther yet to ye Iewes, or other nacions: whose cõmon weales have alway florished while their officers wer good, and decayed & ranne to ruyne, when noughtye men had the regiment[.] Our owne countrey stories (if we reade & marke them) will shewe vs examples ynow, would God we had not sene mo then ynowe. I purpose not to stand here vpon the particulers, because they be in part set furth in the tragedies. Yet by the waye this i note (wishing all other to do the like) namely, that as good governers have never lacked their deserved renowne, so have not the bad escaped infamy, besides such plages as are horrible to heare of[.] For God (the ordeyner of Offices) although he suffer them for punishmẽt of the people to be often occupied of such, as are rather spoylers & Iudasses, than toylers or Iustices (whõ the Scripture therfore calleth Hippocrites) yet suffreth he thẽ not to skape vnpunished, because they dishonour

From the Dedication of *A Myrrovr For Magistrates* (London, 1563), addressed "To the Nobilitie and all other in office."

him: For it is Gods owne office, yea his chiefe office, whyche they bear & abuse. For as Iustice is the chiefe vertue, so is the ministracion thereof, [t]he chiefest office: & therfore hath God established it with the chiefest name, honoring & calling kinges, & all officers vnder thẽ by his owne name: Gods. Ye be all Gods, as manye as have in your charge any ministracion of Iustice: What a fowle shame were it, for any nowe to take vpon thẽ the name & office of God, and in theyr doynges to shew them selves devils? God can not of Iustice, but plague suche shameles presumpc[i]on and hipocrisie, and that wyth shamefull death, diseases, or infamye. Howe he hath plagued euell rulers from time to time, in other nacions, you may see gathered in Boccas booke intituled the Fall of Princes, translated into Englyshe by Lydgate: Howe he hath delte with sume of our countreymen your auncestors, for sundrye vyces not yet left, thys booke named, *A Mirrour for Magistrates*, can shewe: which therfore I humbly offre vnto your honors, beseching you to accept it fauorably. For here as in a loking glas, you shall se (if any vice be in you) how the like hath bene punished in other heretofore, whereby admonished, I trust it wyl be a good occasion to move [you] to the sooner amendement. This is the chiefest ende, whye it is set furth, whych God graunt it may attayne.

BALDASSARE CASTIGLIONE

The Courtier

Then saide the L. Gaspar: In what manner wise be they [*i.e.*, princes] then to be commaunded that be discreete and vertuous and not by nature bonde?

The L. Octavian answeared: With that tractable commaundement kinglye and civill. And to such it is well done otherwhile to committe the bearing of suche offices as be meete for them, that

From Book IV of *The Courtyer of Count Baldessar Castilio,* as translated by Sir Thomas Hoby in 1561 and reprinted in *The Book of the Courtier,* Tudor Translations (London, 1900), pp. 313–315.

they maye likewise beare swey and rule over others of lesse with then they bee, yet so that the principal governement may full and wholy depend uppon the cheef Prince. And bicause you have said, that it is an easier matter to corrupt the minde of one, then of a great sort, I saye, that it is also an easier matter to finde one good and wise, then a great sorte. Both good and wise ought a man to suppose a kinge maye be, of a noble progenie, inclined to vertue of hys owne naturall motion, and throughe the famous memorye of his auncestoures, and brought up in good condicions. And though he be not of an other kinde then man . . . yet yf he be helped forwarde with the instructions, bringinge up, and arte of the Courtier, whom these Lordes have facioned so wise and good, he shall be moste wise, most continent, moste temperate, moste manlye, and moste juste, full of liberalitie, majestie, holynesse, and mercye: finallye, he shall be moste glorious and moste deerely beloved both to God and manne: throughe whose grace he shall atteine unto that heroicall and noble vertue, that shall make him passe the boundes of the nature of manne, and shall rather be called a Demy God, then a manne mortall. For God deliteth in and is the defendour not of those Princis that will folowe and counterfeit him in showinge great poure, and make themselves to be woorshipped of menne, but of such as beeside poure, whereby they are mightye, endevour themselves to resemble him also in goodnesse and wisedome, wherby they maye have a will and a knowleadge to doe well and to be his ministers, distributinge for the beehouf of manne the benifittes and giftes that they receive of him. Therfore even as in the firmamente the sonne and the moone and the other sterres show to the world (as it were) in a glasse, a certeine likenesse of God: so uppon the earth a muche more liker image of God are those good Princis that love and woorshippe him, and showe unto the people the cleere light of his justice, accompanied with a shadowe of the heavenlye reason and understandinge: and suche as these be doeth God make partners of his true dealing, rightuousnesse, justice and goodnesse, and of these other happy benefittes which I can not name, that disclose unto the worlde a much more evident proof of the Godhead, then doeth the light of the sonne, or the continuall tourninge of the firmamente with the sundrye course of the sterres. It is God therfore that hath appointed the people under the custodie of Princis, which ought to have a diligent care over them, that they may make him accompt of it, as good stewardes do their Lord, and love them and thinke their owne, all the profit and losse that happeneth to them, and principally above all thing provide for their good astate and welfare. Therfore ought the prince not only to be good, but also to make others good, like the Carpenters square, that is not only straight and just it self, but also maketh straight and just whatsoever it is occupied about. And the greatest proofe that the Prince is good, is whan the people are good: because the lief of the Prince is a lawe and ringleader of Citizins, and upon the condicions of him must needes al others depende: neyther is it meete for one that is ignorant, to teach: nor for him that is out of order, to give order: nor for him that falleth, to help up an other.

Therfore if the Prince will execute these offices aright, it is requisit that he apply all his studie and diligence to get knowleage, afterward to facion within him selfe and observe unchangeably in everye thinge the law of reason, not written in papers, or in mettall, but graven in his owne minde, that it maye be to him alwayes not onelie familier, but inwarde, and live with him, as a percell of him: to the intent it may night and day, in everye time and place admonish him and speake to him within his hart, riddinge him of those troublous affections that untemperate mindes feele, whiche bycause on the one side they be (as it were) cast into a moste deepe sleepe of ignorance, on the other overwhelmed with the unquietnesse which they feele through their weyward and blind desires, they are stirred with an unquiet rage, as he that sleepeth otherwhile with straunge and horrible visions: heaping then a greater powre upon their noughtie desire, there is heaped also a greater trouble withall.

USES OF THE PAST

LORD BERNERS, SIR JOHN BOURCHIER

Preface to The Chronicles of Froissart

What condign graces and thanks ought men to give to the writers of histories, who with their great labours have done so much profit to the human life. They shew, open, manifest and declare to the reader by example of old antiquity, what we should enquire, desire and follow, and also what we should eschew, avoid and utterly fly; for when we (being unexpert of chances) see, behold and read the ancient acts, gests and deeds, how and with what labours, dangers and perils they were gested and done, they right greatly admonish, ensign and teach us how we may lead forth our lives: and farther, he that hath the perfect knowledge of others' joy, wealth and high prosperity, and also trouble, sorrow and great adversity, hath the expert doctrine of all perils. And albeit that mortal folk are marvellously separated both by land and water, and right wondrously situate, yet are they and their acts (done peradventure by the space of a thousand year) compact together by the histographier, as it were the deeds of one self city and in one man's life: wherefore I say that history may well be called a divine providence; for as the celestial bodies above complect all and at every time the universal world, the creatures therein contained and all their deeds, semblably so doth history. Is it not a right noble thing for us, by the faults and errors of other to amend and erect our life into better? We should not seek and acquire that other did; but what thing was most best, most laudable and worthily done, we should put before our eyes to follow. Be not the sage counsels of two or three old fathers in a city, town or country, whom long age hath made wise,

From the Preface to Lord Berners' translation of *The Chronicles of Froissart* (1523), reprinted from the edition of G. C. Macaulay (London, 1899), pp. xxviii–xxx.

discreet and prudent, far more praised, lauded and dearly loved than of the young men? How much more then ought histories to be commended, praised and loved, in whom is included so many sage counsels, great reasons and high wisdoms of so innumerable persons of sundry nations and of every age, and that in so long space as four or five hundred year. The most profitable thing in this world for the institution of the human life is history. Once the continual reading thereof maketh young men equal in prudence to old men, and to old fathers stricken in age it ministereth experience of things. More, it yieldeth private persons worthy of dignity, rule and governance: it compelleth the emperors, high rulers and governours to do noble deeds, to the end they may obtain immortal glory: it exciteth, moveth and stirreth the strong, hardy warriors, for the great laud that they have after they ben dead, promptly to go in hand with great and hard perils in defence of their country: and it prohibiteth reprovable persons to do mischievous deeds, for fear of infamy and shame. So thus through the monuments of writing, which is the testimony unto virtue many men have been moved, some to build cities, some to devise and establish laws right profitable, necessary and behoveful for the human life, some other to find new arts, crafts and sciences, very requisite to the use of mankind. But above all things, whereby man's wealth riseth, special laud and cause ought to be given to history: it is the keeper of such things as have been virtuously done, and the witness of evil deeds, and by the benefit of history all noble, high and virtuous acts be immortal. What moved the strong and fierce Hercules to enterprise in his life so many great incomparable labours and perils? Certainly nought else but that for his merit immortality might be given to him of all folk. In som blable wise did his imitator, noble duke Theseus, and many other innumerable worthy princes and famous men, whose virtues ben redeemed from oblivion and shine by history. And whereas other monuments in process of time by variable chances are confused and lost, the virtue of history, diffused and spread through the universal world, hath to her custos and keeper it (that is to say, time) which consumeth the other writings. And albeit that those men are right worthy of great laud and praise, who by their writings shew and lead us the way to virtue, yet nevertheless the poems, laws and other acts that they found, devised and writ ben mixed with some damage, and sometime for the truth they ensign a man to lie; but only history, truly with words representing the acts, gests and deeds done, complecteth all profit: it moveth, stirreth and compelleth to honesty; detesteth, irketh and abhorreth vices; it extolleth, enhanceth and lifteth up such as ben noble and virtuous; depresseth, poistereth and thrusteth down such as ben wicked, evil and reprovable. What knowledge should we have of ancient things past, an history were not, which is the testimony thereof, the light of truth, the mistress of the life human, the president of remembrance and the messenger of antiquity? Why moved and stirred Phalerius the king Ptolemy oft and diligently to read books? Forsooth for none other cause, but that those things are found written in books that the friends dare not shew to the prince. Much more I would fain write of the incomparable profit of history, but I fear me that I should too sore torment the reader of this my preface; and also I doubt not but that the great utility thereof is better known than I could declare; wherefore I shall briefly come to a point. Thus, when I advertised and remembered the manifold commodities of history, how beneficial it is to mortal folk, and eke how laudable and meritorious a deed it is to write histories, fixed my mind to do something therein: and ever when this imagination came to me, I volved, turned and read many volumes and books containing famous histories; and among all other I read diligently the four volumes or books of sir John Froissart of the country of Hainault, written in the French tongue, which I judged commodious, necessary and profitable to be had in English, sith they treat of the famous acts done in our parts, that is to say, in England, France, Spain, Portugal, Scotland, Bretayne, Flanders and other places adjoining; and specially they redound to the honour of Englishmen. What pleasure shall it be to the noble gentlemen of England to see, behold and read the high enterprises, famous acts and glorious deeds done and achieved by their valiant ancestors? Forsooth and God, this hath moved me at the high commandment of my most redoubted sovereign lord king Henry the VIII., king of England and of France, and high defender of the Christian faith, etc., under his gracious supportation, to do my devoir to translate out of French into our maternal English tongue the said volumes of sir John Froissart; which chronicle beginneth at the reign of the most noble and valiant king Edward the third, the year of our Lord a thousand three hundred and twenty-six, and continueth to the beginning of the reign of king Henry the fourth, the year of our Lord God a thousand and four hundred. . . . AMEN.

EDWARD HALL

An Introduccion into the History of Kyng Henry the Fourthe

What mischiefe hath insurged in realmes by intestine deuision, what depopulacion hath ensued in countries by ciuill discenciõ, what detestable murder hath been cõmitted in citees by separate faccions, and what calamitee hath ensued in famous regiõs by domestical discord & vnnaturall controuersy: Rome hath felt, Italy can testifie, Fraunce can bere witnes, Beame can tell, Scotlande maie write, Denmarke can shewe, and especially this noble realme of Englande can apparently declare and make demonstracion. For who abhorreth not to expresse the heynous factes comitted in Rome, by the ciuill war betwene Julius Cesar and hardy Põpey by whose discorde the bright glory of the triũphant Rome was eclipsed & shadowed? Who can reherce what mischefes and what plages the pleasant countree of Italy hath tasted and suffered by the sedicious faccions of the Guelphes and Gebelynes? Who can reporte the misery that daiely hath ensued in Fraunce, by the discorde of the houses of Burgoyne and Orliens: Or in Scotland betwene the brother and brother, the vncle and the nephew? Who can curiously endite the manifolde battailles that were fought in the realme of Beame, betwene the catholikes and the pestiferous sectes of the Adamites and others? What damage discencion hath dooen in Germany and Denmarke, all christians at this daie can well declare.

From Hall's *The Vnion of the Two Noble and Illustre Famelies of Lancastre and Yorke, Beyng Long in Continual Discension for the Crowne of this Noble Realme, with all the Actes done in bothe the tymes of the Princes, bothe of the One Linage and of the Other, beginning at the Tyme of Kyng Henry the Fowerth, the First Aucthor of this deuison and so successiuely Proceadyng to the Reigne of the High and Prudent Prince: Kyng Henry the Eight, the vndubitate flower and very heire of both the sayd Linages* (1548), reprinted from the edition of Sir Henry Ellis (London, 1809), pp. 1–2.

And the Turke can bere good testimony, whiche by the discord of christen princes hath amplified greatly his seigniory and dominion. But what miserie, what murder, and what execrable plagues this famous region hath suffered by the deuision and discencion of the renoumed houses of Lancastre and Yorke, my witte cannot comprehende nor my toung declare nether yet my penne fully set furthe.

For what noble man liueth at this daie, or what gentleman of any auncient stocke or progeny is clere, whose linage hath not ben infested and plaged with this vnnaturall deuision. All the other discordes, sectes and faccions almoste liuely florishe and continue at this presente tyme, to the greate displesure and preiudice of all the christian publike welth. But the olde deuided controuersie betwene the fornamed families of Lãcastre and Yorke, by the vnion of Matrimony celebrate and consummate betwene the high and mighty Prince Kyng Henry the seuenth and the lady Elizabeth his moste worthy Quene, the one beeyng indubitate heire of the hous of Lancastre, and the other of Yorke was suspended and appalled in the person of their moste noble, puissãt and mighty heire kyng Henry the eight, and by hym clerely buried and perpetually extinct. So that all men (more clerer then the sonne) maie apparantly perceiue, that as by discord greate thynges decaie and fall to ruine, so the same by concord be reuiued and erected. In likewise also all regions whiche by deuisiõ and discencion be vexed, molested and troubled, bee by vnoin and agrement releued pacified and enriched.

By vnion of the Godhed to the manhod, manne was ioyned to God whiche before by the temptacion of the subtle serpente, was from hym segregate and deuided. By the vnion of the catholike churche and the outworne sinagoge, not only the hard ceremonies and dedly peines of the Mosaicall law wer clerely abholished and made frustrate, but also christian libertie is inferred and Christes religion stablished & erected. By the vnion of man & woman in the holy Sacrament of Matrimony the generacion is blessed, and the synne of the body clene extincte & put awaie. By the vnion of mariage, peace betwene realme and realme is exalted, and loue betwene countree and countree is norished. By coniunciõ of matrimony, malice is extinct, amitie is embraced, and indissoluble aliance and consanguinite is procured. What profite, what cõmfort, what ioy succeded in the realme of England by the vnion of the fornamed two noble families, you shall apparantly perceiue by the sequele of this rude and vnlearned history. And because there can be no vnion or agrement but in respect of a diuision, it is consequent to resō that I manifest to you not onely the originall cause and fōutain of the same, but also declare the calamities, trobles & miseries whiche happened and chaunced duryng the tyme of the said contencious discencion.

SAMUEL DANIEL

The Ciuile Wars

. . . And, whereas this Argument [the strife between the houses of Lancaster and York] was long since vndertaken (in a time which was not so well secur'd of the future, as God be blessed now it is) with a purpose, to shewe the deformities of Ciuile Dissension, and the miserable euents of Rebellions, Conspiracies, and bloudy Reuengements, which followed (as in a circle) vpon that breach of the due course of Succession, by the Vsurpation of Hen. 4; and thereby to make the blessings of Peace, and the happinesse of an established Gouernment (in a direct line) the better to appeare: I trust I shall doo a gratefull worke to my Countrie, to continue the same, vnto the glorious Vnion of Hen. 7: from whence is descended our present Happinesse.

* * * * *

<1>

I Sing the ciuill Warres, tumultuous Broyles
And bloody factions of a mightie Land:
Whose people hautie, proud with forraine spoyles,
Vpon themselues turn-backe their conquering hand;

From the Dedication and Book I of *The First Fowre Bookes of the Ciuile Wars Between the Two Houses of Lancaster and Yorke* (London, 1595).

Whilst Kin their Kin, Brother the Brother foyles;
Like Ensignes all against like Ensignes band;
Bowes against Bowes, the Crowne against Crowne;
Whil'st all pretending right, all right's throwne downe.

<2>

What furie, ô what madnes held thee so,
Deare *England* (too too prodigal of blood)
To waste so much, and warre without a foe,
Whilst *Fraunce,* to see thy spoyles, at pleasure stood!
How much might'st thou haue purchast with lesse woe,
T'haue done thee h[o]nour and thy people good?
Thine might haue beene what-euer lies betweene
The *Alps* and vs, the *Pyrenei* and *Rhene.*

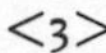
<3>

Yet now what reason haue we to complaine?
Since hereby came the calme we did inioy;
The blisse of thee *Eliza;* happie gaine
For all our losse: when-as no other way
The Heauens could finde, but to vnite againe
The fatall sev'red Families, that they
Might bring foorth thee: that in thy peace might growe
That glorie, which few Times could euer showe.

EXTRACTS FROM THE MAJOR SOURCES

This section contains selections from three of the works Shakespeare probably drew upon in writing *Henry IV, Part 1*. The first, Raphael Holinshed's *Chronicles of England*, provided the historical matter; the second, Samuel Daniel's *The Ciuile Wars*, a lengthy historical poem concerning the strife between the houses of Lancaster and York, suggested important elements in the characterization of the Prince and Hotspur; and the third, *The Famous Victories of Henry the Fifth*, a play entered in the *Stationers' Register* May 14, 1594, demonstrated the possibilities of the addition of certain comic scenes to the historical material.

Scholars have differed in their opinions, however, concerning the precise relationship between this last work and *Henry IV, Part 1*. Although some have maintained that Shakespeare actually used this play as a source, J. Dover Wilson and A. W. Pollard have argued that *The Famous Victories* is in reality an abridgment of two earlier plays, now lost, which Shakespeare made use of in writing *Henry IV, Part 1*. In their view, Shakespeare's play and *The Famous Victories* are related in that they derive from a common source.

RAPHAEL HOLINSHED

The Chronicles of England

[Anno 1402]: . . . Owen Glendouer, according to his accustomed manner, robbing and spoiling within the English borders, caused all the forces of the shire of Hereford to assemble togither against them, vnder the conduct of Edmund Mortimer earle of March. But com̃ing to trie the matter by battell, whether by treason or otherwise, so it fortuned, that the English power was discomfited, the earle taken prisoner, and aboue a thousand of his people slaine in the place. The shamefull villainie vsed by the Welshwomen towards the dead carcasses, was such, as honest eares would be ashamed to heare, and continent toongs to speake thereof. The dead bodies might not be buried, without great summes of monie giuen for libertie to conueie them awaie.

The king was not hastie to purchase the deliuerance of the earle March, bicause his title to the crowne was well inough knowen, and therefore suffered him to remaine in miserable prison, wishing both the said earle, and all other of his linage out of this life, with God and his saincts in heauen, so they had beene out of the waie, for then all had beene well inough as he thought. . . . About mid of August, the king to chastise the presumptuous attempts of the Welshmen, went with a great power of men into Wales, to pursue the capteine of the Welsh rebell Owen Glendouer, but in effect he lost his labor; for Owen conueied himselfe out of the waie, into his knowen lurking places, and (as was thought) through art magike, he caused such foule weather of winds, tempest, raine, snow, and haile to be raised, for the annoiance of the kings armie, that the like had

From *The Chronicles of England, from William the Conqueror . . . Faithfullie gathered and compiled by Raphaell Holinshed* (Second edition, 1587), III, 520–524, 539. Reprinted from the copy in the Furness Memorial Library, University of Pennsylvania.

not beene heard of; in such sort, that the king was constreined to returne home, hauing caused his people yet to spoile and burne first a great part of the countrie. . . . The Scots vnder the leding of Patrike Hepborne, of the Hales the yoonger, entring into England, were ouerthrowen at Nesbit, in the marches, as in the Scotish chronicle ye may find more at large. This battell was fought the two and twentith of Iune, in this yeare of our Lord 1402.

Archembald earle Dowglas sore displeased in his mind for this ouerthrow, procured a commission to inuade England, and that to his cost, as ye may likewise read in the Scotish histories. For at a place called Homildon, they were so fiercelie assailed by the Englishmen, vnder the leading of the lord Persie, surnamed Henrie Hotspur, and George earle of March, that with violence of the English shot they were quite vanquished and put to flight, on the Rood daie in haruest, with a great slaughter made by the Englishmen. . . . There were slaine of men of estimation, sir Iohn Swinton, sir Adam Gordon, sir Iohn Leuiston, sir Alexander Ramsie of Dalehousie, and three and twentie knights, besides ten thousand of the commons: and of prisoners among other were these, Mordacke earle of Fife, son to the gouernour Archembald earle Dowglas, which in the fight lost one of his eies, Thomas erle of Murrey, Robert earle of Angus, and (as some writers haue) the earles of Atholl & Menteith, with fiue hundred other of meaner degrees.

• • • • •

[Anno 1403] Edmund Mortimer earle of March, prisoner with Owen Glendouer, whether for irkesomnesse of cruell captiuitie, or feare of death, or for what other cause, it is vncerteine, agreed to take part with Owen, against the king of England, and tooke to wife the daughter of the said Owen.

Strange wonders happened (as men reported) at the natiuitie of this man, for the same night he was borne, all his fathers horsses in the stable were found to stand in bloud vp to the bellies. . . .

Henrie earle of Northumberland, with his brother Thomas earle of Worcester, and his sonne the lord Henrie Persie, surnamed Hotspur, which were to king Henrie in the beginning of his reigne, both faithfull freends, and earnest aiders, began now to enuie his wealth and felicitie; and especiallie they were greeued, bicause the king demanded of the earle and his sonne such Scotish prisoners as were taken at Homeldon and Nesbit: for of all the captiues which were taken in the conflicts foughten in those two places, there was deliuered to the kings possession onelie Mordake earle of Fife, the duke of Albanies sonne, though the king did diuers and sundrie times require deliuerance of the residue, and that with great threatnings: wherewith the Persies being sore offended, for that they claimed them as their owne proper prisoners, and their peculiar preies, by the counsell of the lord Thomas Persie earle of Worcester, whose studie was euer (as some write) to procure malice, and set things in a broile, came to the king vnto Windsore (vpon a purpose to prooue him) and there required of him, that either by ransome or otherwise, he would cause to be deliuered out of prison Edmund Mortimer earle of March, their cousine germane, whome (as they reported) Owen Glendouer kept in filthie prison, shakled with irons, onelie for that he tooke his part, and was to him faithfull and true.

The king began not a little to muse at the request, and not without cause: for in deed it touched him somewhat neere, sith this Edmund was sonne to Roger earle of March, sonne to the ladie Philip, daughter of Lionell duke of Clarence, the third sonne of king Edward the third; which Edmund at king Richards going into Ireland, was proclamed heire apparant to the crowne and realme, whose aunt called Elianor, the lord Henrie Persie had married; and therefore king Henrie could not well heare, that anie man should be earnest about the aduancement of that linage. The king when he had studied on the matter, made answer, that the earle of March was not taken prisoner for his cause, nor in his seruice, but willinglie suffered himselfe to be taken, bicause he would not withstand the attempts of Owen Glendouer, and his complices, & therefore he would neither ransome him, nor releeue him.

The Persies with this answer and fraudulent excuse were not a little fumed, insomuch that Henrie Hotspur said openlie: Behold, the heire of the relme is robbed of his right, and yet the robber with his owne will not redeeme him. So in this furie the Persies departed, minding nothing more than to depose king Henrie from the high type of his roialtie, and to place in his seat their cousine Edmund earle of March, whom they did not onlie deliuer out of captiuitie, but also (to the high displeasure of king Henrie) entered in league with the foresaid Owen Glendouer. Heerewith, they by their deputies in the house of the archdeacon of Bangor, diuided the realme amongst them, causing a tripartite indenture to be made and sealed with their seales, by the couenants whereof, all England from Seuerne and Trent, south and eastward, was assigned to the earle of March: all Wales, & the lands beyond Seuerne westward, were appointed to Owen Glendouer: and all the remnant from Trent northward, to the lord Persie.

This was doone (as some haue said) through a foolish credit giuen to a vaine prophesie, as though king Henrie was the moldwarpe, curssed of Gods owne mouth, and they three were the dragon, the lion, and the woolfe, which should diuide this realme betweene them. Such is the deuiation (saith Hall) and not diuination of those blind and fantasticall dreames of the Welsh prophesiers. King Henrie not knowing of this new confederacie, and nothing lesse minding than that which after happened, gathered a great armie to go againe into Wales, whereof the earle of Northumberland and his sonne were aduertised by the earle of Worcester, and with all diligence raised all the power they could make, and sent to the Scots which before were taken prisoners at Homeldon, for aid of men, promising to the earle of Dowglas the towne of Berwike, and a part of Northumberland, and to other Scotish lords, great lordships and seigniories, if they obteined the vpper hand. The Scots in hope of gaine, and desirous to be reuenged of their old greefes, came to the earle with a great companie well appointed.

The Persies to make their part seeme good, deuised certeine articles, by the aduise of Richard Scroope, archbishop of Yorke, brother to the lord Scroope, whome king Henrie had caused to be beheaded at Bristow. These articles being shewed to diuerse noblemen, and other states of the realme, mooued them to fauour their purpose, in so much that manie of them did not onelie promise to the Persies aid and succour by words, but also by their writings and seales confirmed the same. Howbeit when the matter came to triall, the most part of the confederates abandoned them, and at the daie of the conflict left them alone. Thus after that the conspirators had discouered themselues, the lord Henrie Persie desirous to proceed in the enterprise, vpon trust to be assisted by Owen Glendouer, the earle of March, & other, assembled an armie of men of armes and archers foorth of Cheshire and Wales. Incontinentlie his vncle Thomas Persie earle of Worcester, that had the gouernement of the prince of Wales, who as then laie at London in secret manner, conueied himselfe out of the princes house, and comming to Stafford (where he met his nephue) they increased their power by all waies and meanes they could deuise. The earle of Northumberland himselfe was not with them, but being sicke, had promised vpon his amendement to repaire vnto them (as some write) with all conuenient speed.

These noble men, to make their conspiracie to seeme excusable, besides the articles aboue mentioned, sent letters abroad, wherein was conteined, that their gathering of an armie tended to none other end, but onlie for the safegard of their owne persons, and to put some better gouernment in the commonwealth. For whereas taxes and tallages were dailie leuied, vnder pretense to be imploied in defense of the realme, the same were vainlie wasted, and vnprofitablie consumed: and where through the slanderous reports of their enimies, the king had taken a greeuous displeasure with them, they durst not appeare personallie in the kings presence, vntill the prelats and barons of the realme had obteined of the king licence for them to come and purge themselues before him, by lawfull triall of their peeres, whose iudgement (as they pretended) they would in no wise refuse. Manie that saw and heard these letters, did commend their diligence, and highlie praised their assured fidelitie and trustinesse towards the commonwealth.

But the king vnderstanding their cloaked drift, deuised (by what meanes he might) to quiet and appease the commons, and deface their contriued forgeries; and therefore he wrote an answer to their libels, that he maruelled much, sith the earle of Northumberland, and the lord Henrie Persie his sonne, had receiued the most part of the summes of monie granted to him by the cleargie and communaltie, for defense of the marches, as he could euidentlie prooue what should mooue them to complaine and raise such manifest slanders. And whereas he vnderstood, that the earles of Northumberland and Worcester, and the lord Persie had by their letters signified to their freends abroad, that by reason of the slanderous reports of their enimies, they durst not appeare in his presence, without the mediation of the prelats and nobles of the realme, so as they required pledges, whereby they might safelie come afore him, to declare and alledge what they had to saie in proofe of their innocencie, he protested by letters sent foorth vnder his seale, that they might safelie come and go, without all danger, or anie manner of indamagement to be offered to their persons.

But this could not satisfie those men, but that resolued to go forwards with their enterprise, they marched towards Shrewesburie, vpon hope to be aided (as men thought) by Owen Glendouer, and his Welshmen, publishing abroad throughout the countries on each side, that king Richard was aliue, whome if they wished to see, they willed them to repaire in armour vnto the castell of Chester, where (without all doubt) he was at that present, and redie to come forward. This tale being raised, though it were most vntrue, yet it bred variable motions in mens minds, causing them to wauer, so as they knew not to which part they should sticke; and verelie, diuers were well affected towards king Richard, speciallie such as had tasted of his princelie bountifulnes, of which there was no small number. And to speake a truth, no maruell it was, if manie enuied the prosperous state of king Henrie, sith it was euident inough to the world, that he had with wrong vsurped the crowne, and not onelie violentlie deposed king Richard, but also cruellie procured his death, for the which vndoubtedlie, both he and his posteritie tasted such troubles, as put them still in danger of their states, till their direct succeeding line was quite rooted out by the contrarie faction, as in Henrie the sixt and Edward the fourth it may appeare.

But now to returne where we left King Henrie aduertised of the proceedings of the Persies, foorthwith gathered about him such power as he might make, and being earnestlie called vpon by the Scot, the earle of March, to make hast and giue battell to his enimies, before their power by delaieng of time should still too much increase, he passed forward with such speed, that he was in sight of his enimies, lieng in campe neere to Shrewesburie, before they were in doubt of anie such thing, for the Persies thought that he would haue staied at Burton vpon Trent, till his councell had come thither to him to giue their aduise what he were best to doo. But herein the enimie was deceiued of his expectation, sith the king had great regard of expedition and making speed for the safetie of his owne person, wherevnto the earle of March incited him, considering that in delaie is danger, & losse in lingering. . . .

By reason of the kings sudden cōming in this sort, they staied from assaulting the towne of Shrewesburie, which enterprise they were readie at that instant to haue taken in hand, and foorthwith the lord Persie (as a capteine of high courage) began to exhort the capteines and souldiers to prepare themselues to battell, sith the matter was growen to that point, that by no meanes it could be auoided, so that (said he) this daie shall either bring vs all to aduancement & honor, or else if it shall chance vs to be ouercome, shall delieuer vs from the kings spitefull malice and cruell disdaine: for plaieng the men (as we ought to doo) better it is to die in battell for the commonwealths cause, than through cowardlike feare to prolong life, which after shall be taken from vs, by sentence of the enimie.

Herevpon, the whole armie being in number about fourteene thousand chosen men, promised to stand with him so long as life lasted. There were with the Persies as chiefteines of this armie, the earle of Dowglas a Scotish man, the baron of Kinderton, sir Hugh Browne, and sir Richard Vernon knights, with diuerse other stout and right valiant capteins. Now when the two armies were incamped, the one against the other, the earle of Worcester and the lord Persie with their complices sent the articles (whereof I spake before) by Thomas Caiton, and Thomas Saluain esquiers to king Henrie, vnder their hands and seales, which articles in effect charged him with manifest periurie, in that (contrarie to his oth receiued vpon the euangelists at Doncaster, when he first entred the realme after his exile) he had taken vpon him the crowne and roiall dignitie, imprisoned king Richard, caused him to resigne his title, and finallie to be murthered. Diuerse other matters they laid to his charge, as leuieng of taxes and tallages, contrarie to his promise, infringing of lawes & customes of the realme, and suffering the earle of March to remaine in prison, without trauelling to haue him delieuered. All which things they as procurors & protectors of the common-wealth, tooke vpon them to prooue against him, as they protested vnto the whole world.

King Henrie after he had read their articles, with the defiance which they annexed to the same, answered the esquiers, that he was readie with dint of sword and fierce battell to prooue their quarrell false, and nothing else than a forged matter, not doubting, but that God would aid and assist him in his righteous cause, against the disloiall and false forsworne traitors. The next daie in the morning earlie, being the euen of Marie Magdalene, they set their battels in order on both sides, and now whilest the warriors looked when the token of battell should be giuen, the abbat of Shrewesburie, and one of the clearks of the priuie seale, were sent from the king vnto the Persies, to offer them pardon, if they would come to any reasonable agreement. By their persuasions, the lord Henrie Persie began to giue eare vnto the kings offers, & so sent with them his vncle the earle of Worcester, to declare vnto the king the causes of those troubles, and to require some effectuall reformation in the same.

It was reported for a truth, that now when the king had condescended vnto all that was resonable at his hands to be required, and seemed to humble himselfe more than was meet for his estate, the earle of Worcester (vpon his returne to his nephue) made relation cleane contrarie to that the king had said, in such sort that he set his nephues hart more in displeasure towards the king, than euer it was before, driuing him by that meanes to fight whether he would or not: then suddenlie blew the trumpets, the kings part crieng S. George vpon them, the aduersaries cried *Esperance Persie,* and so the two armies furiouslie ioned. The archers on both sides shot for the best game, laieng on such load with arrowes, that manie died, and were driuen downe that neuer rose againe.

The Scots (as some write) which had the fore ward on the Persies side, intending to be reuenged of their old displeasures doone to them by the English nation, set so fiercelie on the kings fore ward, led by the earle of Stafford, that they made the same draw backe, and had almost broken their aduersaries arraie. The Welshmen also which before had laine lurking in the woods, mounteines, and marishes, hearing of this battell toward, came to the aid of the Persies, and refreshed the wearied people with new succours. The king perceiuing that his men were thus put to distresse, what with the violent impression of the Scots, and the tempestuous stormes of arrowes, that his aduersaries discharged freely against him and his people, it was no need to will him to stirre: for suddenlie with his fresh battell, he approched and relieued his men; so that the battell began more fierce than before. Here the lord Henrie Persie, and the earle Dowglas, a right stout and hardie capteine, not regarding the shot of the kings battell, nor the close order of the ranks, pressing forward togither bent their whole forces towards the kings person, comming vpon him with speares and swords so fiercelie, that the earle of March the Scot, perceiuing their purpose, withdrew the king from that side of the field (as some write) for his great benefit and safegard (as it appeared) for they gaue such a violent onset vpon them that stood about the kings standard, that slaieng his standard-bearer sir Walter Blunt, and ouerthrowing the standard, they made slaughter of all those that stood about it, as the earle of Stafford, that daie made by the king constable of the realme, and diuerse other.

The prince that daie holpe his father like a lustie yoong gentleman: for although he was hurt in the face with an arrow, so that diuerse noble men that were about him, would haue conueied him foorth of the field, yet he would not suffer them so to doo, least his departure from amongst his men might happilie haue striken some feare into their harts: and so without regard of his hurt, he continued with his men, & neuer ceassed, either to fight where the battell was most hot, or to incourage his men where it seemed most need. This battell lasted three long houres, with indifferent fortune on both parts, till at length, the king crieng saint George victorie, brake the arraie of his enimies, and aduentured so farre, that (as some write) the earle Dowglas strake him downe, & at that instant slue sir Walter Blunt, and three other, apparelled in the kings sute and clothing, saieng: I maruell to see so many kings thus suddenlie arise one in the necke of an other. The king in deed was raised, & did that daie manie a noble feat of armes, for as it is written, he slue that daie with his owne hands six and thirtie persons of his enimies. The other on his part incouraged by his doings, fought valiantlie, and slue the lord Persie, called sir Henrie Hotspurre. To conclude, the kings enimies were vanquished, and put to flight, in which flight, the earle of Dowglas, for hast, falling from the crag of an hie mounteine, brake one of his cullions, and was taken, and for his valiantnesse, of the king frankelie and freelie deliuered.

There was also taken the earle of Worcester, the procurer and setter foorth of all this mischeefe, sir Richard Vernon, and the baron of Kinderton, with diuerse other. There were slaine vpon the kings part, beside the earle of Stafford, to the number of ten knights, sir Hugh Shorlie, sir Iohn Clifton, sir Iohn Cokaine, sir Nicholas Gausell, sir Walter Blunt, sir Iohn Caluerleie, sir Iohn Massie of Podington, sir Hugh Mortimer, and sir Robert Gausell, all the which receiued the same morning the order of knighthood: sir Thomas Wendesleie was wounded to death, and so passed out of this life shortlie after. There died in all vpon the kings side sixteene hundred, and foure thousand were greeuouslie wounded. On the contrarie side were slaine, besides the lord Persie, the most part of the knights and esquiers of the countie of Chester, to the number of two hundred, besides yeomen and footmen, in all there died of those that fought on the Persies side, about fiue thousand. This battell was fought on Marie Magdalene euen, being saturdaie. Vpon the mondaie folowing, the earle of Worcester, the baron of Kinderton, and sir Richard Vernon knights, were condemned and beheaded. The earles head was sent to London, there to be set on the bridge.

* * * * *

[Anno 1412] . . . lord Henrie prince of Wales, eldest sonne to king Henrie, got knowledge that certeine of his fathers seruants were busie to giue informations against him, whereby discord might arise betwixt him and his father: for they put into the kings head, not onelie what euill rule (according to the course of youth) the prince kept to the offense of manie: but also what great resort of people came to his house, so that the court was nothing furnished with such a traine as dailie followed the prince. These tales brought no small suspicion into the kings head, least his sonne would presume to vsurpe the crowne, he being yet aliue, through which suspicious gelousie, it was perceiued that he fauoured not his sonne, as in times past he had doone.

The Prince sore offended with such persons, as by slanderous reports, sought not onelie to spot his good name abrode in the realme, but to sowe discord also betwixt him and his father, wrote his letters into euerie part of the realme, to reprooue all such slanderous deuises of those that sought his discredit. And to cleare himselfe the better, that the world might vnderstand what wrong he had to be slandered in such wise: about the feast of Peter and Paule, to wit, the nine and twentith daie of Iune, he came to the court with such a number of noble men and other his freends that wished him well, as the like traine had beene sildome seene repairing to the court at any one time in those daies. He was apparelled in a gowne of blew satten, full of small oilet holes, at euerie hole the needle hanging by a silke thred with which it was sewed. About his arme he ware an hounds collar set full of SS of gold, and the tirets likewise being of the same metall.

The court was then at Westminster, where he being entred into the hall, not one of his companie durst once aduance himselfe further than the fire in the same hall, notwithstanding they were earnestlie requested by the lords to come higher: but they regarding what they had in commandement of the prince, would not presume to doo in any thing contrarie therevnto. He himselfe onelie accompanied with those of the kings house, was streight admitted to the presence of the king his father, who being at that time greeuouslie diseased, yet caused himselfe in his chaire to be borne into his priuie chamber, where in the presence of three or foure persons, in whome he had most confidence, he commanded the prince to shew what he had to saie concerning the cause of his comming.

The prince kneeling downe before his father said: "Most redoubted and souereigne lord and father, I am at this time come to your presence as your liege man, and as your naturall sonne, in all things to be at your commandement. And where I vnderstand you haue in suspicion my demeanour against your grace, you know verie well, that if I knew any man within this realme, of whome you should stand in feare, my duetie were to punish that person, thereby to remooue that greefe from your heart. Then how much more ought I to suffer death, to ease your grace of that greefe which you haue of me, being your naturall sonne and liege man: and to that end I haue this daie made my selfe readie by confession and receiuing of the sacrament. And therefore I beseech you most redoubted lord and deare father, for the honour of God, to ease your heart of all such suspicion as you haue of me, and to dispatch me heere before your knees, with this same dagger [and withall he deliuered vnto the king his dagger, in all humble reuerence; adding further, that his life was not so deare to him, that he wished to liue one daie with his displeasure] and therefore in thus ridding me out of life, and your selfe from all suspicion, here in presence of these lords, and before God at the daie of the generall iudgement, I faithfullie protest clearlie to forgiue you."

The king mooued herewith, cast from him the dagger, and imbracing the prince kissed him, and with shedding teares confessed, that in deed he had him partlie in suspicion, though now (as he perceiued) not with iust cause, and therefore from thencefoorth no misreport should cause him to haue him in mistrust, and this he promised of his honour. So by his great wisedome was the wrongfull suspicion which his father had conceiued against him remooued, and he restored to his fauour. And further, where he could not but greeuouslie complaine of them that had slandered him so greatlie, to the defacing not onelie of his honor, but also putting him in danger of his life, he humblie besought the king that they might answer their vniust accusation; and in case they were found to haue forged such matters vpon a malicious purpose, that then they might suffer some punishment for their faults, though not to the full of that they had deserued. The king seeming to grant his resonable desire, yet told him that he must tarrie a parlement, that such offendors might be punished by iudgement of their peeres: and so for that time he was dismissed, with great loue and signes of fatherlie affection.

Thus were the father and the sonne reconciled, betwixt whom the said pickthanks had sowne diuision, insomuch that the sonne vpon a vehement conceit of vnkindnesse sproong in the father, was in the waie to be worne out of fauour. Which was the more likelie to come to passe, by their informations that priuilie charged him with riot and other vnciuill demeanor vnseemelie for a prince. Indeed he was youthfullie giuen, growne to audacitie, and had chosen him companions agreeable to his age; with whome he spent the time in such recreations, exercises, and delights as he fansied. But yet (it should seeme by the report of some writers) that his behauiour was not offensiue or at least tending to the damage of anie bodie; sith he had a care to auoid dooing of wrong, and to tedder his affections within the tract of vertue, whereby he opened vnto himselfe a redie passage of good liking among the prudent sort, and was beloued of such as could discerne his disposition, which was in no degree so excessiue, as that he deserued in such vehement maner to be suspected. In whose dispraise I find little, but to his praise verie much. . . .

SAMUEL DANIEL

The Ciuile Wars

<BOOK III>

<86>

And yet new *Hydraes* lo, new heades appeare
T'afflict that peace reputed then so sure,
And gaue him much to do, and much to feare,
And long and daungerous tumults did procure,
And those euen of his chiefest followers were
Of whom he might presume him most secure,
Who whether not so grac'd or so preferd
As they expected, these new factions stird.

<87>

The *Percyes* were the men, men of great might,
Strong in alliance, and in courage strong
That thus conspire, vnder pretence to right
The crooked courses they had suffered long:
Whether their conscience vrgd them or despight,
Or that they saw the part they tooke was wrong,
Or that ambition hereto did them call,
Or others enuide grace, or rather all.

<88>

What cause soeuer were, strong was their plot,
Their parties great, meanes good, th'occasion fit:
Their practice close, their faith suspected not,
Their states far off and they of wary wit:

From *The First Fowre Bookes of the Ciuile Wars Between the Two Houses of Lancaster and Yorke* (1595) as reprinted by Samuel B. Hemingway in the Variorum edition of *Henry IV, Part 1* (Philadelphia, 1936), pp. 365–371.

Who with large promises draw in the Scot
To ayde their cause, he likes, and yeeldes to it,
Not for the loue of them or for their good,
But glad hereby of meanes to shed our bloud.

<89>

Then ioyne they with the *Welsh*, who fitly traind
And all in armes vnder a mightie head
Great *Glendowr*, who long warr'd, and much attaind,
Sharp conflicts made, and many vanquished:
With whom was *Edmond Earle* of *March* retaind
Being first his prisoner, now confedered,
A man the king much fear'd, and well he might
Least he should looke whether his Crown stood right.

<90>

For *Richard*, for the quiet of the state,
Before he tooke those *Irish* warres in hand
About succession doth deliberate,
And finding how the certaine right did stand,
With full consent this man did ordinate
The heyre apparent in the crowne and land:
Then iudge if this the king might nerely touch,
Although his might were smal, his right being much.

<91>

With these the *Percyes* them confederate,
And as three heades they league in one intent,
And instituting a Triumuirate
Do part the land in triple gouerment:
Deuiding thus among themselues the state,
The *Percyes* should rule all the *North* from *Trent*
And *Glendowr Wales*: the *Earle* of *March* should bee
Lord of the *South* from *Trent*; and thus they gree.

<92>

Then those two helpes which still such actors find
Pretence of common good, the kings disgrace
Doth fit their course, and draw the vulgar mind
To further them and aide them in this case:

The king they accusd for cruell, and vnkind
That did the state, and crowne, and all deface;
A periurde man that held all faith in skorne,
Whose trusted othes had others made forsworne.

<93>

Besides the odious detestable act
Of that late murdered king they aggrauate,
Making it his that so had will'd the fact
That he the doers did remunerate:
And then such taxes daily doth exact
That were against the orders of the state,
And with all these or worse they him assaild
Who late of others with the like preuaild.

<94>

Thus doth contentious proud mortality
Afflict each other and itselfe torment:
And thus o thou mind-tortring misery
Restles ambition, borne in discontent,
Turn'st and retossest with iniquity
The vnconstant courses frailty did inuent:
And fowlst faire order and defilst the earth
Fostring vp warre, father of bloud and dearth.

<95>

Great seemd the cause, and greatly to, did ad
The peoples loue thereto these crimes rehearst,
That manie gathered to the troupes they had
And many more do flocke from costs disperst:
But when the king had heard these newes so bad,
Th'vnlookt for dangerous toyle more nearly perst;
For bēt t'wards *Wales* t'appease those tumults there,
H'is forst diuert his course, and them forbeare.

<96>

Not to giue time vnto th'increasing rage
And gathering fury, forth he hastes with speed,
Lest more delay or giuing longer age
To th'euill growne, it might the cure exceed:

All his best men at armes, and leaders sage
All he prepard he could, and all did need;
For to a mighty worke thou goest ô king,
To such a field that power to power shall bring.

<97>

There shall young *Hotespur* with a fury lead
Meete with thy forward sonne as fierce as he:
There warlike *Worster* long experienced
In forraine armes, shall come t'incounter thee:
There *Dowglas* to thy *Stafford* shall make head:
There *Vernon* for thy valiant *Blunt* shalbe:
There shalt thou find a doubtfull bloudy day,
Though sicknesse keepe *Northumberland* away.

<98>

Who yet reseru'd, though after quit for this,
Another tempest on thy head to raise,
As if still wrong reuenging *Nemesis*
Did meane t'afflict all thy continuall dayes:
And yet this field he happely might misse
For thy great good, and therefore well he staies:
What might his force haue done being ioynd thereto
When that already gaue so much to do?

<99>

The swift approch and vnexpected speed
The king had made vpon this new-raisd force
In th' vnconfirmed troupes much feare did breed,
Vntimely hindring their intended course;
The ioyning with the *Welsh* they had decreed
Was hereby stopt, which made their part the worse,
Northumberland with forces from the *North*
Expected to be there, was not set forth.

<100>

And yet vndaunted *Hotspur* seeing the king
So nere approch'd, leauing the worke in hand
With forward speed his forces marshalling,
Sets forth his farther comming to withstand:

And with a cheerfull voice incouraging
By his great spirit his well imboldened band,
Bringes a strong host of firme resolued might,
And plac'd his troupes before the king in sight.

<101>

This day (saith he) ô faithfull valiaunt frendes,
What euer it doth giue, shall glorie giue:
This day with honor frees our state, or endes
Our misery with fame, that still shall liue,
And do but thinke how well this day he spendes
That spendes his bloud his countrey to relieue:
Our holie cause, our freedome, and our right,
Sufficient are to moue good mindes to fight.

<102>

Besides th' assured hope of victory
That wee may euen promise on our side
Against this weake-constrained companie,
Whom force & feare, not will, and loue doth guide
Against a prince whose foule impiety
The heauens do hate, the earth cannot abide,
Our number being no lesse, our courage more,
What need we doubt if we but worke therefore.

<103>

This said, and thus resolu'd euen bent to charge
Vpon the king, who well their order viewd
And carefull noted all the forme at large
Of their proceeding, and their multitude:
And deeming better if he could discharge
The day with safetie, and some peace conclude,
Great proffers sendes of pardon, and of grace
If they would yeeld, and quietnes imbrace.

<104>

But this refusd, the king with wrath incensd
Rage against fury doth with speed prepare:
And ô saith he, though I could haue dispensd
With this daies bloud, which I haue sought to spare

That greater glory might haue recompensd
The forward worth of these that so much dare,
That we might honor had by th' ouerthrown
That th' wounds we make, might not haue bin our own.

<105>

Yet since that other mens iniquity
Calles on the sword of wrath against my will,
And that themselues exact this cruelty,
And I constrained am this bloud to spill:
Then on my maisters, on couragiously
True-harted subiects against traitors ill,
And spare them not who seeke to spoile vs all,
Whose fowle confused end soone see you shall.

<106>

Straight moues with equall motion equall rage
The like incensed armies vnto bloud,
One to defend, another side to wage
Foule ciuill war, both vowes their quarrell good:
Ah too much heate to bloud doth nowe inrage
Both who the deed prouokes and who withstood,
That valor here is vice, here manhood sin,
The forward'st hands doth ô least honor win.

<107>

But now begin these fury-mouing soundes
The notes of wrath that musicke brought from hell,
The ratling drums which trumpets voice cōfounds,
The cryes, th' incouragements, the shouting shrell:
That all about the beaten ayre reboundes,
Thundring confused, murmurs horrible,
To rob all sence except the sence to fight,
Well handes may worke, the mind hath lost his sight.

<108>

O war! begot in pride and luxury,
The child of wrath and of dissention,
Horrible good; mischiefe necessarie,
The fowle reformer of confusion,

Vniust-iust scourge of our iniquitie,
Cruell recurer of corruption:
O that these sin-sicke states in need should stand
To be let bloud with such a boystrous hand!

<109>

And ô how well thou hadst been spar'd this day
Had not wrong counsaild *Percy* bene peruers,
Whose yong vndanger'd hand now rash makes way
Vpon the sharpest fronts of the most fierce:
Where now an equall fury thrusts to stay
And rebeat-backe that force and his disperse,
Then these assaile, then those chace backe againe,
Till staid with new-made hils of bodies slaine.

<110>

There lo that new-appearing glorious starre
Wonder of Armes, the terror of the field
Young *Henrie*, laboring where the stoutest are,
And euen the stoutest forces backe to yeild,
There is that hand boldned to bloud and warre
That must the sword in woundrous actions weild:
But better hadst thou learnd with others bloud
A lesse expence to vs, to thee more good.

<111>

Hadst thou not there lent present speedy ayd
To thy indaungerde father nerely tyrde,
Whom fierce incountring *Dowglas* ouerlaid,
That day had there his troublous life expirde:
Heroycall Couragious *Blunt* araid
In habite like as was the king attirde
And deemd for him, excusd that fate with his,
For he had what his Lord did hardly misse.

<112>

For thought a king he would not now disgrace
The person then supposd, but princelike shewes
Glorious effects of worth that fit his place,
And fighting dyes, and dying ouerthrowes:

Another of that forward name and race
In that hotte worke his valiant life bestowes,
Who bare the standard of the king that day,
Whose colours ouerthrowne did much dismaie.

<113>

And deare it cost, and ô much bloud is shed
To purchase thee this loosing victory
O trauayld king: yet hast thou conquered
A doubtfull day, a mightie enemy:
But ô what woundes, what famous worth lyes dead!
That makes the winner looke with sorrowing eye,
Magnanimous *Stafford* lost that much had wrought,
And valiant *Shorly* who great glory gote.

<114>

Such wracke of others bloud thou didst behold
O furious *Hotspur*, ere thou lost thine owne!
Which now once lost that heate in thine waxt cold,
And soone became thy Armie ouerthrowne;
And ô that this great spirit, this courage bold,
Had in some good cause bene rightly showne!
So had not we thus violently then
Haue termd that rage, which valor should haue ben.

The Famous Victories of Henry the Fifth

Enter the yoong PRINCE, NED, *and* TOM.

HENRY THE FIFTH.

Come away *Ned* and *Tom.*

BOTH. Here my Lord.

HENR. 5. Come away my Lads:
Tell me sirs, how much gold haue you got?

NED. Faith my Lord, I hauc got fiue hundred pound.

HEN. 5. But tell me *Tom,* how much hast thou got?

TOM. Faith my Lord, some foure hundred pound.

HEN. 5. Foure hundred pounds, brauely spoken Lads.
But tell me sirs, thinke you not that it was a villainous part of me to rob my fathers Receiuers?

NED. Why no my Lord, it was but a tricke of youth.

HEN. 5. Faith *Ned* thou sayest true.
But tell me sirs, whereabouts are we?

TOM. My Lord, we are now about a mile off *London.*

HEN. 5. But sirs, I maruell that sir *Iohn Old-castle*
Comes not away: Sounds see where he comes.

Enters IOCKEY.

How now *Iockey,* what newes with thee?

IOCKEY. Faith my Lord, such newes as passeth,
For the Towne of *Detfort* is risen,
With hue and crie after your man,
Which parted from vs the last night,
And has set vpon, and hath robd a poore Carrier.

HEN. 5. Sownes, the vilaine that was wont to spie
Out our booties.

IOCK. I my Lord, euen the very same.

HEN. 5. Now base minded rascal to rob a poore carrier,
Wel it skils not, ile saue the base vilaines life:

From *The Famous Victories of Henry the fifth: Containing the Honourable Battell of Agin-court: As it was plaide by the Queenes Maiesties Players* (1598). Reprinted from the Bodleian Library copy of the 1598 quarto edition as reproduced in the facsimile published by C. Praetorius (Shakespere Quarto Facsimiles, No. 39, ed. P. A. Daniel, 1887).

I, I may: but tel me *Iockey*, whereabout be the Receiuers?

IOC. Faith my Lord, they are hard by,
But the best is, we are a horse backe and they be a foote,
So we may escape them.

HEN. 5. Wel, I[f] the vilaines come, let me alone with them.
But tel me *Iockey*, how much gots thou from the knaues?
For I am sure I got something, for one of the vilaines
So belamd me about the shoulders,
As I shal feele it this moneth.

IOCK. Faith my Lord, I haue got a hundred pound.

HEN. 5. A hundred pound, now brauely spoken *Iockey:*
But come sirs, laie al your money before me,
Now by heauen here is a braue shewe:
But as I am true Gentleman, I wil haue the halfe
Of this spent to nıght, but sirs take vp your bags,
Here comes the Receiuers, let me alone.

Enters two Receiuers.

ONE. Alas good fellow, what shal we do?
I dare neuer go home to the Court, for I shall be hangd.
But looke, here is the yong Prince, what shal we doo?

HEN. 5. How now you vilaines, what are you?

ONE RECEI. Speake you to him.

OTHER. No I pray, speake you to him.

HEN. 5. Why how now you rascals, why speak you not?

ONE. Forsooth we be. Pray speake you to him.

HEN. 5. Sowns, vilains speak, or ile cut off your heads.

OTHER. Forsooth he can tel the tale better then I.

ONE. Forsooth we be your fathers Receiuers.

HEN. 5. Are you my fathers Receiuers?
Then I hope ye haue brought me some money.

ONE. Money, Alas sir we be robd.

HEN. 5. Robd, how many were there of them?

ONE. Marry sir, there were foure of them:
And one of them had sir *Iohn Old-Castles* bay Hobbie,
And your blacke Nag.

HEN. 5. Gogs wounds how like you this *Iockey*?
Blood you vilaines: my father robd of his money abroad,
And we robd in our stables.
But tell me, how many were of them?

ONE RECEI. If it please you, there were foure of them,
And there was one about the bignesse of you:
But I am sure I so belambd him about the shoulders,
That he wil feele it this month.
HEN. 5. Gogs wounds you lamd them faierly,
So that they haue carried away your money.
But come sirs, what shall we do with the vilaines?
BOTH RECEI. I beseech your grace, be good to vs.
NED. I pray you my Lord forgiue them this once.
[HEN. 5.] Well stand vp and get you gone,
And looke that you speake not a word of it,
For if there be, sownes ile hang you and all your kin.
Exit Purseuant[*s*].
HEN. 5. Now sirs, how like you this?
Was not this brauely done?
For now the vilaines dare not speake a word of it,
I haue so feared them with words.
Now whither shall we goe?
ALL. Why my Lord, you know our old hostes
At *Feuersham*.
HEN. 5. Our hostes at *Feuersham*, blood what shal we do there?
We haue a thousand pound about vs,
And we shall go to a pettie Ale-house.
No, no: you know the olde Tauerne in Eastcheape,
There is good wine: besides, there is a pretie wench
That can talke well, for I delight as much in their toongs,
As any part about them.
ALL. We are readie to waite vpon your grace.
HEN. 5. Gogs wounds wait, we will go altogither,
We are all fellowes, I tell you sirs, and the King
My father were dead, we would be all Kings,
Therefore come away.
NED. Gogs wounds, brauely spoken *Harry*.

[*Exeunt omnes.*]

[In the scene which follows, the night-watch, John Cobler, Robin Pewterer, and Lawrence Costermonger, assisted by Dericke, a clown, apprehend a "Theefe" (Gadshill), who had taken part in the robbery of the carriers. A "Vintners boy" closes the scene with a report on a tavern escapade of the Prince.]

BOY. How now good man Cobler?

COB. How now *Robin*, what makes thou abroad
At this time of night?

BOY. Marrie I haue beene at the Counter,
I can tell such newes as neuer you haue heard the like.

COBLER. What is that *Robin*, what is the matter?

BOY. Why this night about two houres ago, there came the young Prince, and three or foure more of his companions, and called for wine good store, and then they sent for a noyse of Musitians, and were very merry for the space of an houre, then whether their Musicke liked them not, or whether they had drunke too much Wine or no, I cannot tell, but our pots flue against the wals, and then they drew their swordes, and went into the streete and fought, and some tooke one part, & some tooke another, but for the space of halfe an houre, there was such a bloodie fray as passeth, and none coulde part them vntill such time as the Maior and Sheriffe were sent for, and then at the last with much adoo, they tooke them, and so the yong Prince was carried to the Counter, and then about one houre after, there came a Messenger from the Court in all haste from the King, for my Lord Maior and the Sheriffe, but for what cause I know not.

[Gadshill is then taken to Newgate Prison to await his appearance before the Lord Chief Justice. In the following scene Henry IV receives an account from the Lord Mayor of London of his imprisoning the young Prince. Henry IV replies:]

HEN. 4. Stand aside vntill we haue further deliberated on your answere.

Exit Maior.

HEN. 4. Ah *Harry*, *Harry*, now thrice accursed *Harry*,
That hath gotten a sonne, which with greefe
Will end his fathers dayes.
Oh my sonne, a Prince thou art, I a Prince indeed,
And to deserue imprisonment,
And well haue they done, and like faithfull subiects:
Discharge them and let them go.

[The next episode is the trial of Gadshill before the Lord Chief Justice. The Prince appears and demands custody of Gadshill. When the Chief Justice refuses, the Prince "giueth him a boxe on the eare." The Chief Justice then commits the Prince to the Fleet. There follows a "play extempore" between Dericke and John Cobler.]

DER. Sownds maisters, heres adoo,
When Princes must go to prison:
Why *Iohn*, didst euer see the like?
IOHN. O *Dericke*, trust me, I neuer saw the like.
DER. Why *Iohn* thou maist see what princes be in choller,
A Iudge a boxe on the eare, Ile tel thee *Iohn, O Iohn,*
I would not haue done it for twentie shillings.
IOHN. No nor I, there had bene no way but one with vs,
We should haue bene hangde.
DER. Faith *Iohn*, Ile tel thee what, thou shalt be my
Lord chiefe Iustice, and thou shalt sit in the chaire,
And ile be the yong prince, and hit thee a boxe on the eare,
And then thou shalt say, to teach you what prerogatiues
Meane, I commit you to the Fleete.
IOHN. Come on, Ile be your iudge,
But thou shalt not hit me hard.
DER. No, no.
IOHN. What hath he done?
DER. Marry he hath robd *Dericke*.
IOHN. Why then I cannot let him go.
DER. I must needs haue my man.
IOHN. You shall not haue him.
DER. Shall I not haue my man, say no and you dare:
How say you, shall I not haue my man?
IOHN. No marry shall you not.
DER. Shall I not *Iohn?*
IOHN. No *Dericke*.
DER. Why then take you that till more come,
Sownes, shall I not haue him?
IOHN. Well I am content to take this at your hand,
But I pray you, who am I?
DER. Who art thou, Sownds, doost not know thy self?
IOHN. No.
DER. Now away simple fellow,
Why man, thou art *Iohn* the Cobler.
IOHN. No, I am my Lord chiefe Iustice of England.

DER. Oh *Iohn,* Masse thou saist true, thou art indeed.
IOHN. Why then to teach you what prerogatiues mean
I commit you to the Fleete.
DER. Wel I will go, but yfaith you gray beard knaue,
Ile course you.

• • • • •

Enter the yoong PRINCE, *with* NED *and* TOM.

HEN. 5. Come away sirs, Gogs wounds *Ned,*
Didst thou not see what a boxe on the eare
I tooke my Lord chiefe Iustice?
TOM. By gogs blood it did me good to see it,
It made his teeth iarre in his head.

Enter sir Iohn Old-Castle.

HEN. 5. How now sir *Iohn Old-Castle,*
What newes with you?
IOH. OLD. I am glad to see your grace at libertie,
I was come I, to visit you in prison.
HEN. 5. To visit me, didst thou not know that I am a Princes son, why tis inough for me to looke into a prison, though I come not in my selfe, but heres such adoo now adayes, heres prisoning, heres hanging, whipping, and the diuel and all: but I tel you sirs, when I am King, we will haue no such things, but my lads, if the old king my father were dead, we would be all kings.
IOH. OLD. Hee is a good olde man, God take him to his mercy the sooner.
HEN. 5. But *Ned,* so soone as I am King, the first thing
I wil do, shal be to put my Lord chief Iustice out of office,
And thou shalt be my Lord chiefe Iustice of England.
NED. Shall I be Lord chiefe Iustice?
By gogs wounds, ile be the brauest Lord chiefe Iustice
That euer was in England.
HEN. 5. Then *Ned,* ile turne all these prisons into fence Schooles, and I will endue thee with them, with landes to maintaine them withall: then I wil haue a bout with my Lord chiefe Iustice, thou shalt hang none but picke purses and horse stealers, and such base binded villaines, but that fellow that will stand by the high

way side couragiously with his sword and buckler and take a purse, that fellow giue him commendations, beside that, send him to me and I will giue him an anuall pension out of my Exchequer, to maintaine him all the dayes of his life.

IOH. Nobly spoken *Harry*, we shall neuer haue a mery world til the old king be dead.

NED. But whither are ye going now?

HEN. 5. To the Court, for I heare say, my father lies verie sicke.

TOM. But I doubt he wil not die.

HEN. 5. Yet will I goe thither, for the breath shal be no sooner out of his mouth, but I wil clap the Crowne on my head.

IOCKEY. Wil you goe to the Court with that cloake so full of needles?

HEN. 5. Cloake, ilat-holes, needles, and all was of mine owne deuising, and therefore I wil weare it.

TOM. I pray you my Lord, what may be the meaning thereof?

HEN. 5. Why man, tis a signe that I stand vpon thorns, til the Crowne be on my head.

IOC. Or that euery needle might be a prick to their harts that repine at your doings.

HEN. 5. Thou saist true *Iockey*, but thers some wil say, the yoong Prince will be a well toward yoong man and all this geare, that I had as leeue they would breake my head with a pot, as to say any such thing, but we stand prating here too long, I must needs speake with my father, therefore come away.

* * * * *

Enter the KING, *with the* LORD OF EXETER.

HEN. 4. And is it true my Lord, that my sonne is alreadie sent to the Fleete? now truly that man is more fitter to rule the Realme then I, for by no meanes could I rule my sonne, and he by one word hath caused him to be ruled. Oh my sonne, my sonne, no sooner out of one prison, but into an other, I had thought once whiles I had liued, to haue seene this noble Realme of England flourish by thee my sonne, but now I see it goes to ruine and decaie.

He wepeth.

Enters LORD OF OXFORD

OX. And please your grace, here is my Lord your sonne,
That commeth to speake with you,
He saith, he must and wil speake with you.

HEN. 4. Who my sonne *Harry?*

OXF. I and please your Maiestie.

HEN. 4. I know wherefore he commeth,
But looke that none come with him.

OXF. A verie disordered company, and such as make
Verie ill rule in your Maiesties house.

HEN. 4. Well let him come,
But looke that none come with him.

He goeth.

• • • • •

Enters the PRINCE *with a dagger in his hand.*

HEN. 4. Come my sonne, come on a Gods name,
I know wherefore thy comming is,
Oh my sonne, my sonne, what cause hath euer bene,
That thou shouldst forsake me, and follow this vilde and
Reprobate company, which abuseth youth so manifestly:
Oh my sonne, thou knowest that these thy doings
Wil end thy fathers dayes.

He weepes.

I so, so, my sonne, thou fearest not to approach the presence of thy sick father, in that disguised sort, I tel thee my sonne, that there is neuer a needle in thy cloke, but it is a prick to my heart, & neuer an ilat-hole, but it is a hole to my soule: and wherefore thou bringest that dagger in thy hande I know not, but by coniecture.

He weepes.

HEN. 5. My cōscience accuseth me, most soueraign Lord, and welbeloued father, to answere first to the last point, That is, whereas you coniecture that this hand and this dagger shall be armde against your life: no, know my beloued father, far be the thoughts of your sonne, sonne said I, an vnworthie sonne for so good a father: but farre be the thoughts of any such pretended mischiefe: and I most humbly render it to your Maiesties hand, and liue my Lord and soueraigne for euer: and with your dagger arme show like vengeance vpon the bodie of that your sonne, I was about [to] say and dare not, ah woe is me therefore, that your wilde slaue, tis not the Crowne that I come for, sweete father, because I am vnworthie, and those vilde & reprobate company I abandon, & vtterly abolish their company for euer. Pardon sweete father, pardon: the least thing and most desire: and this ruffianly cloake, I here teare from my backe, and sacrifice it to the diuel, which is maister of al mischiefe: Pardō me, sweet father, pardon me: good my Lord of *Exeter* speak for me: pardon me, pardō good father, not a word: ah he wil not speak one word: A *Harry*, now thrice vnhappie *Harry*. But what shal I do? I wil go take me into some solitarie place, and there lament my sinfull life, and when I haue done, I wil laie me downe and die.

Exit.

HEN. 4. Call him againe, call my sonne againe.
HEN. 5. And doth my father call me again? now *Harry*,
Happie be the time that thy father calleth thee againe.
HEN. 4. Stand vp my son, and do not think thy father,
But at the request of thee my sonne I wil pardon thee,
And God blesse thee, and make thee his seruant.
HEN. 5. Thanks good my Lord, & no doubt but this day,
Euen this day, I am borne new againe.
HEN. 4. Come my son and Lords, take me by the hands.

Exeunt omnes.

[The remaining two-thirds of the play is chiefly concerned with Henry the Fifth's victory at Agincourt and his winning the hand of Katharine, daughter of Charles VI of France.]

ESSAYS IN CRITICISM

The greatest success in "history" that Shakespeare attained was in *I Henry IV*. Here is to be found his liveliest and most richly-colored picture of tavern and country; here is to be found Falstaff, and Falstaff at his best; and here, in Hotspur, and in young Harry roused to emulation, are to be found a pair of Shakespeare's most radiant figures of English youth and chivalry.

E. E. Stoll, *Poets and Playwrights.*

FALSTAFF. . . . . I am not only witty in myself, but the cause that wit is in other men.

2 *Henry IV, I.ii.*

The essays which follow are divided into two parts. In Part I, following Harold E. Toliver's discussion of the dramatic type to which the play belongs and Gareth Lloyd Evans' study of the dramatic technique employed in the *Henry IV* plays, the remaining essays focus more specifically on *Henry the Fourth, Part I,* and treat its structure, characters, themes, and language. Concluding Part I is Arthur C. Sprague's account of the stage history of the play. Part II is composed of excerpts which in a kind of historical survey in brief illustrate significant interpretations of Falstaff and modes of critical approach in studying this figure.

Line-number citations, wherever pertinent in these essays, have been made to agree with the text of the play as given in the present volume.

I

HAROLD E. TOLIVER

Falstaff, the Prince, and the History Play

<1>

A rational eighteenth-century man of letters such as Maurice Morgann would undoubtedly bristle a little at our abandon in destroying his premises. He would have difficulty recognizing our portraits of Henry IV, for example, whom, in his simplicity, he had thought to be a rather impressive king despite a certain weakness at first for another man's crown. And he would be even more mystified by Henry V as Machiavellian strong-man and confused war-maker. Ignorant of Frazer and Freud, he would not think to look for the key to the complexity and interest of Falstaff, the "whoreson, obscene, greasy tallow-catch," in ritualistic and magical analogues;[1] he would probably want to ask whether critics ought to be getting into such things in the first place, and if so, how the a-rational elements of motivation, imagery, and symbolic action, if they exist, can be made intelligible. For when we consider these elements, the discussion of "character" in the sense of certain definite traits appears extremely limited; questions such as whether or not Falstaff is a coward are not important in themselves, and the facts were never really facts anyway. And concepts of form naturally grow more uncertain as response to character shifts. Hence, the question of

From *Shakespeare Quarterly,* XVI (Winter 1965), 63–80. Reprinted by permission of the author and the Shakespeare Association of America. With minor revisions by the author.

[1] See C. L. Barber's essay, "Saturnalia in the Henriad," which is printed in *Shakespeare: Modern Essays in Criticism,* ed. Leonard F. Dean (New York, 1957), pp. 169–191, and in *Shakespeare's Festive Comedy.* Cf. J. I. M. Stewart, *Character and Motive in Shakespeare* (Bristol, 1949), p. 127; Northrop Frye, "The Argument of Comedy," *English Institute Essays* (1949), p. 71; and Philip Williams, "The Birth and Death of Falstaff Reconsidered," *SQ,* VIII (1957), 359–365.

what *kind* the history play belongs to can no longer be answered in strictly Aristotelian terms.[2] Once over the initial shock, however, the traditional raltionalist might discover certain fruitful interactions between his approach to the history play and modern approaches. In the matter of the relative place of comic and heroic figures in the history play, for example, the neoclassicist's sense of "decorum" —of a form following certain laws of plot, character, and language —might be made to engage more profoundly the raw stuff of the human psyche and its institutions and rituals imitated in the form. In return, we might have to admit that while it may not be necessary for all purposes to read history plays under the auspices of a category, we gain from being aware that they are not simply studies in isolated problems of motivation, or fragments of primitive ritual. They do indeed have "form," as some kings have "character." Approaching the history play through either perspective by

[2] The most complete attempts to arrive at a working concept of the history play *sui generis* are Irving Ribner's "The Tudor History Play: An Essay in Definition." *PMLA,* LXIX (1954), 591–609 and *The English History Play in the Age of Shakespeare* (Princeton University Press, 1957), pp. 1–32; H. B. Charlton's *Shakespeare: Politics and Politicians,* The English Association Pamphlet no. 72 (1929), pp. 7, 11, 13; Una Ellis-Fermor, *The Frontiers of Drama* (London, 1945), pp. 5–14, 34–55; Felix Schelling, *The English Chronicle Play* (New York, 1902); G. K. Hunter, "Shakespeare's Politics and the Rejection of Falstaff," *Critical Quarterly,* I (1959), 229–236. See also Coleridge's *Literary Remains,* H. N. Coleridge, ed. (London, 1836), VI, 160 ff.; A. C. Bradley, *Oxford Lectures on Poetry* (London, 1909), pp. 247–275; John Palmer, *Political Characters of Shakespeare* (London, 1945), pp. 184 ff.; W. H. Auden, "The Fallen City: Some Reflections on Shakespeare's *Henry IV,*" *Encounter,* XIII, no. 5 (1959), 25 and, of course, Maurice Morgann, *An Essay on the Dramatic Character of Sir John Falstaff,* first published in 1777. Northrop Frye's *Anatomy of Criticism* is stimulating as usual, especially the following remarks: "The History merges so gradually into tragedy that we often cannot be sure when communion has turned into catharsis," and "The central theme of Elizabethan history is the unifying of the nation and the binding of the audience into the myth as the inheritors of that unity, set over against the disasters of civil war and weak leadership" (pp. 283–284). Finally, A. P. Rossiter's brief book *English Drama from Early Times to the Elizabethans* (London, 1950) illuminates the "mungrell" forms brilliantly, from an inclusive perspective. I have not attempted to make allowances for the discontinuity and structural separateness of the Henry plays; nothing in the common concerns that I discuss presupposes more continuity of action and character than the plays have been shown to have.

itself is likely to leave us unsatisfied, as though we had gone hunting kudu and flushed jerboa.

For the history play at its best attempts to do more than evoke purely chauvinistic emotion through heroic pageantry and spectacle, as it was once assumed; and it is not totally incapable of containing its Saturnalian kings of misrule and its Oedipal overtones in a form that transcends and orders them. Shakespeare, at least, appears to have sought in the history play a fresh artistic form capable of integrating providential order, pragmatic political concerns, and timeless human impulses.[3] One of the primary effects of that integration is an adjustment between inner and outer worlds, both in the hero and, since the history play is more nationalistic and "rhetorical" than other dramatic forms, through the hero in the audience, didactically. In ethical matters, the adjustment is between the inner conscience and the amoral demands of political life; in economic motives, between personal and collective "property"; and in broadly social and religious matters, between the old Adam who rushes impulsively to Eastcheap and the redeemed Adam who takes his fixed place in the ranks or at Whitehall.

These adjustments involve the audience in a communal "rhythm" through a language generally more openly incantational than the language of Shakespearean tragedy and ritualistic in a different sense. For more than one kind of ritual and one kind of magic is involved in dramatic action. In a broad sense, "ritual" means any closely patterned visual ceremony or rhythmic language that engages the emotions of its participants and fuses them into a harmonious community. Both spectacle and rhythm work by raising like emotions throughout an audience and providing a common symbolic or "pulsing" medium for their transmission. Some rituals depend upon primitive forms of magic, and Falstaff, as J. I. M. Stewart, C. L. Barber, and Philip Williams believe, reflects certain fragments of them. But others become assimilated into sophisticated art and are consciously manipulated as one of its dimensions. In less primitive forms, they work not only through contact with highly charged cur-

[3] Shakespeare's experimentation with the form is clear from the varieties he tried and from devices such as Rumour's induction to *2 Henry IV* (which suggests the uncertainty of historical events as experienced and yet offers the broader vision of the chronicler who sees everything with accuracy) and the chorus in *Henry V*, which moves the play toward dramatized epic.

rents from the subconscious, which criticism, as Morgann conceived of it, is ill-equipped to deal with, but also through a complex assortment of powers released by formal art. In the rejection scene, for example, the ritual of the new king depends upon the total of thematic, imagistic, and formal pressures brought to bear by the whole play or series of plays—and their social and political context. If tragic ritual reconciles the audience to a higher density of some sort, perhaps to the power of the gods or to a world of suffering beyond the protagonist's control, the ritual of the history play aims somewhat lower, at adjustment to political life—which may be thought to reveal destiny also, but destiny at least *filtered through* a social medium.

Social and political context is thus especially important in the history play, which in England developed under special historical conditions that caused it to rise and decline rapidly as literary types go. Though other dramatists experimented with it, Shakespeare (with the possible exception of the anonymous author of *Woodstock*) was the only one to see its full potential as a separate form. In his variation, it appealed strongly to an audience prepared to see it in a certain way, or in Mr. Barber's term, to "participate" in its special kind of ritualized nationalistic emotion. Like English tragedy, it arose partly out of the old morality and mystery plays; but onto these it grafted chronicle accounts of past events, folk-lore, native myth, and a new spirit of nationalism, all of which it shaped into moral patterns designed to bring out the providential guidance, the "meaning," of history. Since an audience removed from the original context cannot "participate" in historical ritual with the same intensity as an Elizabethan royalist who believed in the king's divine prerogatives, the historical context and content create problems that are less obtrusive in other dramatic forms, if present at all. But despite its inherent shortcomings, the history play at its best (in the series of plays from *Richard II* to *Henry V*) achieves an essentially new structure and dramatic rhythm, both peculiar to itself and effective.

Some aspects of that structure are borrowed from comedy and tragedy, and here again the neoclassicist, if put to the test, might be quick to see some aspects of the blend that others would overlook. Aristotle's concept of *anagnorisis* and *catharsis* would seem relevant for example, in describing Falstaff's role as tragic victim—only one role among several, needless to say, but involved and crucial.[4] In one aspect the "plot" of *2 Henry IV* can be taken as a *mixed variation* of comic and tragic action, culminating in a sacrificial act with the new king acting as personal vicegerent for destiny. The effectiveness of the rejection speech as incantation depends upon our seeing the accumulated evidence as to the way of a world that Falstaff has affronted and does not fit, a world *requiring* a certain political order that cannot tolerate Falstaff as Chief Justice. The evidences of tragic form are clear enough before that, once we set aside the oversimplified notion that a figure must be either comic or tragic and not both. The implications of Falstaff's childlike self-love and hedonism from the beginning of *1 Henry IV* compose, in Francis Fergusson's Jamesian analogy, one of a set of "mirrors" reflecting the central action, the search for an effective adjustment between the inner self and the collective social organism. Since the aim of this action is ultimately to "redeem time" (and thus to redeem the times),[5] both in the sense of justifying "history" and in reconciling the audience to its historical role, Falstaff is best seen as a rebel against history, as guilty of *hubris* as he is of Saturnalian misrule.

The Falstaffian mirror, of course, is not entirely separable from the others. In Part One, the opening scenes reflect various inner-outer disturbances for which partial and ineffective cures are proposed. Bolingbroke's opening speech, for example, suggests a relatively easy, pragmatic cure for the illness of the state, which he describes in his own terms, a cure demanding only that the right people get the point quickly enough:

> So shaken as we are, so wan with care,
> Find we a time for frighted Peace to pant
> And breathe short-winded accents of new broils
> To be commenc'd in strands afar remote.

[4] This role has been mentioned occasionally but has not been extensively explored. See D. A. Traversi, *An Approach to Shakespeare* (New York, 1956), p. 32, and *Shakespeare from Richard II to Henry V* (Stanford University Press, 1957), pp. 77 ff.; Stewart, pp. 127 ff.; Auden, p. 25; Williams, p. 363.

[5] Cf. J. A. Bryant, Jr., "Prince Hal and the Ephesians," *Sewanee Review*, LXVII (1959), 204–219; Benjamin T. Spencer, "*2 Henry IV* and the Theme of Time," *University of Toronto Quarterly*, XIII (1944), 394–399; Paul A. Jorgensen, "'Redeeming Time' in Shakespeare's *Henry IV*," *Tennessee Studies in Literature*, V (1960), 101–109.

No more the thirsty entrance of this soil
Shall daub her lips with her own children's blood;
No more shall trenching war channel her fields,
Nor bruise her flowerets with the armed hoofs
Of hostile paces. Those opposed eyes,
Which, like the meteors of a troubled heaven,
All of one nature, of one substance bred,
Did lately meet in the intestine shock
And furious close of civil butchery,
Shall now, in mutual well-beseeming ranks,
March all one way and be no more oppos'd
Against acquaintance, kindred, and allies.
(I, i, 1–16)

Since the sickness lies solely in civil insurrection, the cure is to be a simple restoration of national unity, or rather the appearance of unity. Henry stresses the one nature, one substance of the constituents, the unnaturalness of civil "butchery," and the attractiveness of a united body. His rhetoric attempts to embody and make attractive the rigorous, ceremonial order for which he asks. But the diagnosis is shallow and the appeal, as we eventually learn, partly bogus in that the proposal to engage in a holy war is strategic rather than religious. He hopes simply to call "Fall in!" and see the chaotic crisscrossing of insurrection and "intestine shock" transformed into "well-beseeming ranks," all marching one way.

In thinking about the Prince's "riot and dishonour" and his alliance with Falstaff, Henry reveals almost accidentally that the disturbance runs deeper. He lapses into the kind of wishful dream that characterizes Richard II:

O that it could be prov'd
That some night-tripping fairy had exchang'd
In cradle-clothes our children where they lay,
And call'd mine Percy, his Plantagenet!
(I, i, 86–89)

That he is mistaken about the Prince is perhaps less important than the indication that the rhetoric of politic calculation is not sufficient to draw the community, or even the king, together, as Falstaff easily demonstrates. His wish for a different son appears more and more ironic as we realize that his own "tender conscience" needs a different image to put on display. But he is not simply trying to avert civil chaos through an appearance of public order; he wants also to *be* something different from himself, the follower of "indirect crook'd ways" to an undeserved crown; and he would like his son, who is really very much his, to be his justification. Obviously, if the Prince turns out to be another Richard, the crooked path will only lead back to the same morass; his public ceremonies will turn out to have been private orgies, held in full view of a commonwealth he thinks should not see too much of a king.

The Hotspur mirror reveals an impulsive drive for self-glorification undermining the community without twinges of conscience. Hotspur in a sense bribes the moral sense by making a religion of chivalric virtues; he discovers or manufactures opponents such as the perfumed "popinjay," Henry, and the Prince, against whom he can legally exercise those virtues. He thinks of heroism as a leaping upward to the pale-faced moon and a plunging downward where fathom line could never reach to pluck up maiden-honor, both places suggesting dream fulfillment; but his "vision" is more dynamic than rational. His is an aggressive, individual dream, like those of romance knights, that would make history primarily a chronicle of individual heroic events, incapable of uniting a community except as a collection of followers. (Even so, Hotspur is no further from an adjustment of self and society than John of Lancaster, who has little understanding of personal, subversive tendencies. His strategem at the Forest of Gaultree is justified insofar as Authority needs desperately to keep control, but it cannot, of course, lead to permanent psychic or communal well-being: he submerges the inner self in the machinations of politics, though it reappears now and then, a little strangled, on the surface.)

Falstaff reflects all of these deficiencies, but in a more dangerous form because he has an effective mechanism to handle them. Rather than curing sickness, he explodes tension in laughter, which reconciles us to incongruities without eliminating them. Whereas Hal aims at a comprehensive integration of aggressive and self-transcending tendencies (to borrow Arthur Koestler's terms[6]), Falstaff adjusts to the former—as long as he can—through comic strategies, and grows fat on pretensions to the latter that he sees all around

[6] *Insight and Outlook* (New York, 1949), pp. 57 ff.

him. The "tragedy" he ultimately faces makes such a static adjustment impossible and forces the audience to abandon it, to reach upward toward some sort of extra-personal fulfillment. To prevent our substituting resentment for political insight, Shakespeare makes the "tragedy" implicit throughout in the very nature of the humor. In Falstaff's first appearance in *1 Henry IV*, for example, though the Prince and Falstaff play lightly with the subject of sickness, the disease goes too deep for purely comic adjustment or purgation. If hours were indeed "cups of sack, and minutes capons, and clocks the tongues of bawds, and dials the signs of leaping-houses, and the blessed sun himself a fair hot wench in flame-coloured taffeta" (I, ii, 6–9), time would be unredeemable. (The sun image is soon connected to providential order, an objectively stable and redeemable time, and the "epiphany" of the new king.) To "go by the moon" as Falstaff proposes, is to lose one's will and become as changeable as the sea; it leads to an ebb as low as the foot of the ladder and a flow as high "as the ridge of the gallows" (I,ii,34), not so high as Hotspur plans to leap, but high enough.

The mock interview is perhaps a clearer example in that the tragic undertones that prepare the audience to transcend the sea-moon sickness and accept the duties of *Respublica* are more central to the dramatic *agon*. The scene demonstrates the insufficiency of the comic mode in handling the disturbances of the "times." Whereas comic rebels are ordinarily animated mannerisms of some kind, or collections of them, which the dramatist can set in place without destroying, when Falstaff's "meanings collapse" in absurdity, something besides mannerism and "make-believe" is lost.[7] The make-believe and the mannerisms are part of a Falstaffian ceremony of self-creation that Hal is invited to join at the end of the scene (he has only to concede that his corporeal friend is more or less permanent). In his failure "to make his body and furnishings mean sovereignty" and thus finally to mean "all the world," as Mr. Barber aptly puts it, and in his inability to redeem time through a private ritual divorced from political and religious duties, Falstaff himself is destroyed, first symbolically in mock rejection and finally, of course, in actual "history." The Prince's answer cuts through the comic façade like a precise surgical instrument. If "each repetition of 'sweet Jack Falstaff, kind Jack Falstaff' aggrandizes an identity which the serial clauses caress and cherish" (Barber, p. 182), even though

[7] Barber, p. 189.

caressing with some irony, the entire structure comes down at the Prince's sharp pronouncement, "I do, I will." As a kind of official proclamation, his answer expresses not a timeless dream but a present impulse to reject comic ritual and to seek some other adjustment. Though brief, it has its own rhythm and force; neither self-aggrandizement nor its protective irony can stand against it.

The sacrificial theme is already explicit at this point and already rhetorically effective in that we must begin to choose one commitment in preference to the other, or at least to find some other way to accommodate both. The Prince plans to confront history—which overwhelms a tragic hero and scarcely involves a comic hero at all—by transcending the self. And insofar as he takes the audience with him, he makes it share his distrust of the ironic ritual of self, as through Hotspur it learns to distrust the dream of personal heroism and through John of Lancaster the suffocation of individual honor in the common will.

The Prince's control over impulses of the minute comes primarily through his capacity to see history as a continuous succession of events linking present to past and future. As he learns to control "time," Falstaff more and more loses himself in the present. Living in a timeless, fleeting moment precludes fulfilling future promise, profanes "the precious time," and cuts off the past as a useful, educative force. For to Falstaff, youth is not a time of growth leading continuously to fulfillment; it is adventure, a slim waist, and bells at midnight, seen through a haze of nostalgia (even though that nostalgia can be realistically exploited in others). The present is a rush of officers at the door, interrupting the private life and dragging one off to Shrewsbury. Or it is an attempt to conceal past actions like the performance at Gadshill by re-creating them, with changes, in the present—in a sense "mythologizing" them to accommodate self-respect. And the future will be uncertain because if time is essentially a flow of sack, "minutes capons, and clocks the tongues of bawds," absence will be oblivion: "It grows late," Falstaff laments to Doll; "we'll to bed. Thou't forget me when I am gone" (II, iv, 299, Part Two). The Prince, on the other hand, in the process of validating the future king's future community, expiates a past curse in the processes of time, experience, and growth. When he gets the best of Falstaff, it is only by connecting past and future as one continuum. Ironically, to do so in the rejection scene, he must make himself appear discontinuous:

> Presume not that I *am* the thing I *was*;
> For God doth know, so shall the world perceive,
> That I have turn'd away my former self;
> So will I those that kept me company.
> When thou dost hear I *am* as I *have been*,
> Approach me, and thou *shalt be* as thou *wast* . . .
> (V, v, 60, Part Two)

Falstaff must be made to think he has changed whether he has or not. But Falstaff's blessings would be lost anyway in the essential discontinuity of his own life, in time's always increasing curse: "Thou whoreson little tidy Bartholemew boar-pig," Doll says affectionately, "when wilt thou leave fighting o' days and foining o' nights, and begin to patch up thine old body for heaven?" Falstaff will never be ready for the Totentanz: "Peace, good Doll! do not speak like a death's-head. Do not bid me remember mine end." Which is to say that he attempts to separate present existence from historical continuity, while the Prince submits existence to the controls of honor, duty, public ceremony—in short, social and political tradition.

It is necessity for controls of this kind that makes the sacrifice of Falstaff inevitable. With this in mind, we might think of the history play as a dramatic demonstration of how to counter the disintegrative and antisocial impulses of self through a sense of continuous historical "transcendence." Such transcendence does not necessarily involve freedom from time and the demands of ego—Hal accepts past guilt and future duties, and is personally ambitious—but with some qualifications, as we shall see later, it puts such demands in a meaningful historical framework that liberates hero and audience from any particular demand: a moment in history is less overpowering when connected in sequence with what has passed and what is to come.

Some of the limitations of the function of Falstaff's "tragedy" in the series are implicit in this stress on continuity and tradition. The province of the history play is not the inner world or the world of fable but a historical world like the one outside the theater, engrossed in politics and asking that taxes be paid. Its hero never quite escapes into legend or touches the deepest layers of our sympathy. It is concerned with the redemptive virtues, or lack of them, and leaves unexplored the more absorbing depths of individual motivation that ordinarily occupy tragedy. For this reason, Falstaff's "tragic" slavery to time, like his comic absurdity, is perhaps best interpreted as simply a failure in historical vision, a failure in adjustment to "history." The history play, through its hero or exposure of nonheroes, shows the audience how to make that adjustment.

<2>

Not until his public denunciation of Falstaff does the Prince become the manifest center of community tradition. Before the redemptive process reaches that completion, he must undergo several trials—against Hotspur and the sick king as well as against Falstaff—all of which force him to rise above himself as an apparent rioter-in-time and become someone the world can "perceive," who is without discrepancy between inner self and outer act. As he helps defeat the rebels, he takes over their powers in the manner of a morality-play hero and consigns to the grave their unredeemable qualities—the hidden conspiracies, inner guilt, and aggressive egoism—which cause discontinuity in both personal life and public tradition. At each step he becomes more clearly the purified and evident "continuator" who will assume the inherited crown and weld, after his epiphany, an unbroken chain of order from God to man, past to future. (Quelling political rebellion, of course, is but one of the purgative acts.[8]) In the deaths of both Hotspur and the king, the transfer and purgation which make that chain possible are explicit:

Prince. . . . And all the budding honours on thy crest
I'll crop, to make a garland for my head. (V, iv, 71–72)

King. . . . God knows, my son
By what by-paths and indirect crook'd ways
I met this crown; . . .
To thee it shall descend with better quiet,
Better opinion, better confirmation;
For all the soil of the achievement goes
With me into the earth. (IV, v, 184 ff., Part Two)

[8] Hugh Dickinson oversimplifies the redemptive process, I think, in pinning it entirely on the defeat of Percy. See "The Reformation of Prince Hal," *Shakespeare Quarterly*, XII (1961), 33–46.

King [*Henry* V]. My father is gone wild into his grave
For in his tomb lie my affections;
And with his spirit sadly I survive,
To mock the expectation of the world,
To frustrate prophecies, and to raze out
Rotten opinion, who hath writ me down
After my seeming. (V, ii, 123, Part Two)

The discontinuity between son and father can be resolved completely only when the son becomes father and casts off his childhood, or sublimates its Oedipal impulses, or whatever, on behalf of the "fatherland." Feelings toward the state as a kind of superparent—the "womb of kings" and the fatherland all in one—are much less ambivalent than those toward the king-father. Hence, as the "soil" of the king's achievement is buried, the Prince's own "offending" qualities are purged. As Canterbury recalls in *Henry* V,

Consideration like an angel came
And whipp'd th' offending Adam out of him,
Leaving his body as a paradise
T' envelop and contain celestial spirits.
(I, i, 28)

Canterbury is less than critical of the Prince's strategy, but "consideration's" final banishment of prodigality is clearly to be taken as a purification, the full effects of which are revealed only in *Henry* V. Time and death, which defeat Falstaff, sanctify the lineal descent, wash the blood from the inherited crown, and establish the Prince as vicegerent of cosmic stability.

The rebellious spirit dies differently in each case, but the same general process holds true: in each *agon* the Prince gains tighter control of the "intestine shocks" that disturb both the individual and the nation. In the psychomachian battle of Shrewsbury, Shakespeare brings together the main rebels of Part One and has the Prince collect his honors. The insurrectionists appear misled and willfully blind. Douglas, for example, attacks various false images of the king and supposes Falstaff to be dead. (The Prince is misled in a different way: his address to the "dead" friend is a stylized and symbolic rejection rather than a comic mistake that discredits him.) From these acts, we surmise that Douglas does not have his finger on either the national or the individual pulse. Though in both cases he admittedly has reason for confusion, he cannot tell a true king or a live man. The persistent reappearance of the "kings" suggests that the rightful government is omnipresent and a bit mystifying to the outsider. Despite his huffing and puffing, the House of Lancaster refuses to come down and Falstaff, thinking reluctantly of reforming, springs back up again. Rebellion can do nothing but fly headlong "upon the foot of fear." As the entire fabric of self-seeking masquerading as public interest and moral indignation collapses, history appears to have justified the "crook'd ways" and reformed the rioters.

Once we grant the peculiar way the folk hero has of expelling antitypes and absorbing their strength, we are less likely to dispute the Prince's capacity at Shrewsbury to assume Hotspur's chivalric prowess or, in Part Two, his right to acquire his father's political acuteness. That Henry V likewise absorbs something of Falstaff is more difficult to demonstrate; I think, however, that in a sense the new king has learned from Falstaff. To be sure, the Prince's avowed pretexts for plucking the "base strings" would not indicate a profound educational process; and when he thinks Falstaff dead, his grief is significantly qualified by the disenchanting remark, "O, I should have a heavy miss of thee/If I were much in love with vanity!" which substitutes a contrary-to-fact conditional for regret. (If the lines are spoken as a kind of ritual disclaimer, some of the personal quality disappears; and since Falstaff is not dead, an encomium would be out of place and perhaps suggest that Hal's "I do, I will" was not seriously intended after all.) As a final, apparently gratuitous, insult he threatens to have Falstaff "embowell'd" to suit him for lying beside "noble Percy," which may seem to de-Falstaff what is left (though Falstaff is listening, of course, which makes that threat, too, a mixture of comic and tragic foreboding).

But if the strategy of the history play is to convince the audience that nothing is lost in the state's relentless pursuit of its Manifest Destiny, even sacrifices must pay dividends. Falstaff's vitality must not be entirely lost. It is less easily transferred than Percy's chivalry and the sick king's power, but like these it must be made continuous if it is to survive; its "body" must be made less, its "grace" more. In a sense, then, it is left for *Henry V* to demonstrate the validity of the sacrifices required during the course of the Henry IV plays and *Richard II*, which first began shattering dream worlds in the interest of efficient government: the slaying of individual impulses and anarchist dreams is justified only if public action makes self-fulfillment possible in some other way. Henry V as a public figure thus becomes very central to the series of plays. The audience must have a protagonist of some dimensions, both human and "public," to make the center of its circle. The shell of tradition without inner life is no more binding than the verbal observance of love that Lear forces upon his daughters.

Shakespeare has no trouble making Henry V transcend Hotspur, Henry IV, and himself as truant Prince. Though he has been a comparatively passive and shifting figure at Gadshill and Eastcheap, merely the chief knight at Shrewsbury, and an outsider at the Forest of Gaultree, in *Henry V* he becomes the center and wholesale manipulator of the action. Beyond that, on a few occasions his coolness of judgment and his hot quest for honor are animated by a comparatively high degree of vitality and humanity. I suspect that Shakespeare meant to suggest *vestigia Falstaffi* in places other than the dialogue of Pistol and the Hostess, which is designed to lay to rest whatever miscellaneous emotions might still be getting in the way. The shrewdness, expediency, and courage which Henry has taken from his father and Hotspur are significantly altered in the composite character of the new king, not by what Falstaff has taught him directly, but by what Falstaff represents. Irony and humor, of course, have been suppressed because, as we have seen, these lead to a static adjustment of aggressive tendencies rather than to reform and heroic action. The jest of the tennis balls Henry turns into a provocation for war, or pretends to; the practical joke he sets in motion on the eve of battle he drains of humor the next day, when the king must appear king. But some of the vitality of Eastcheap and Gadshill remains. Henry unites realistic pragmatism, ability to accommodate personal impulses quickly to difficult situations, and the bearing of a man-among-men. In doing so he rises above the average patrician and the inflexible professional hero.

Whatever he might have learned from Eastcheap, Henry seems clearly meant to illustrate the highest potentials of the active life. Even his coldbloodedness can work two ways: it may be an operation of pure, disinterested intelligence taking calculated risks, or it may embrace alternatives and choose the right one out of a comprehensive moral perspective, impossible without some degree of humanity. Spiritual energy is clearly part of his impelling force—though this does not mean that he cannot be shrewd at the same time. In handling the treachery of Cambridge, Grey, and Scroop, to choose a representative example, he is compassionate as well as crafty. Meeting calculation with calculation, he brings the three conspirators to an unavoidable moral recognition and finally to contrition. Though the transformation may seem unbelievable in psychological terms, the idea of shifting the burden of execution to the conspirators themselves is scarcely reprehensible in itself. In the context of the play, they are responsible for their inner values in the same way that soldiers are for their souls upon entering battle: Henry insists that maintaining fine distinctions between what belongs to the community and what is one's own is necessary to the health of both individual and state. Considering the "kingdom's safety" he believes to be the king's first duty; to act more mercifully, as again in the execution of Bardolph, would be soft-hearted cruelty (III, vi, 115). *Given the conspiracy to begin with*, repentance is the highest good salvageable.

Henry thus finds personal fulfillment in the "office" rather than in self-definition. The "affection" which Bradley finds in short supply in him, he reserves for this "happy few, [this] band of brothers"—with himself at the head, of course. But Shakespeare, in the Henry plays at least, does not imply that being public in this way requires sacrificing the "citadel of absolute truth, the inner self."[9] Although it is not difficult to diminish the king by measuring him against later tragic protagonists, he is not without virtues. Seen strictly from the standpoint of adjustment to policy, he compares favorably with other Shakespearian heroes: beside him, Coriolanus is an ego-maniac, Caesar an impostor, Antony unscrupulous (in one play) and weak (in the other), and Brutus confused; even Hamlet, as a Prince, appears unbalanced, deprived by the sickness of his world of shaping the state to his inherent magnanimity. After the tragic hero has departed with the sickness and strength of his egoism upon him, Shakespeare ordinarily has a public figure such as Malcolm or Fortinbras reassemble the scattered energies of the

[9] Ellis-Fermor, p. 54.

community and give it coherence and historical duration. Personal isolation and the shattering of communal bonds he shows to be consequences of seeking too intently the "citadel of absolute truth." Henry is not so destructive or so interesting as that, but his limitations do not necessarily indicate that "Falstaff wins after all."

What they do indicate is not easy to determine, but if we were to ignore them we would tend to make an historic epic of some sort out of an historic drama. It may be that Shakespeare is realistic about the king simply to show the irrelevance of personal flaws in the fully absorbing center of community emotion. The intensity of the myth can be measured by the amount of reality it supports without collapsing, which in Shakespeare can be a good deal. In Henry's case, the myth is reinforced by the authorial chorus and by imagistic patterns and echoes from scripture suggesting an analogy between divine and temporal order. The mirror of Christian kings *in his way* is the mirror of the Christian King: the action of redeeming time imitates the Redemption; the epiphany of the new king imitates the Epiphany; the hierarchal structure of the kingdom imitates cosmic structure. Henry's imitation remains imperfect because the history play, unlike mystery or morality plays, remains essentially indeterminate. But despite these limitations, Henry as folk hero fuses a diversity of individual impulses into a unified, social organism that is more than the sum of uses one segment makes of another.

The prebattle speech (IV, iii, 18) reveals something of how the fusion is accomplished. (Since it is long and familiar, I shall not quote it.) We know from the nighttime dialogues that the king does not ignore the dangers he has put his subjects in, but neither does he allow responsibility to paralyze him. The hard-headed plainness, the blunt wit, and the colloquial idiom of the wooing scene are evident before he reaches the drawing room. We know, too, how far democratic instincts have penetrated, without destroying, distinctions of rank and social level. The main point here is that his rhetoric, despite its hortative battlefield simplicity, catches all of this is in its net. It uses but goes beyond the Hotspurian logic of chivalry and the policy involved in rousing the troops at a crucial moment. The repetition is less mechanical, less calculated than Bolingbroke's, which plays upon the emotions without emotion through an intellectual balance of clauses and a manufactured pattern of images and figures. Henry, like Falstaff in the mock-rejection scene, obviously enjoys words which name and glorify tangible objects close to the center of his self-interest; he savors the names which when sounded in the future will continue to weld into a brotherhood those who were initiated at Agincourt. The difference between his rhetoric of names and Falstaff's ritual is that the former creates a group myth, the latter sanctifies the person and personality of the speaker; one looks forward and the other magnifies the present. But both are adept at word-magic. They add communion to communication, in Allen Tate's phrase, and thus avoid a dehumanized rhetoric that reveals nothing of the inner self and leaves even vital community interests untouched.

Henry's speech is partly a wishful dream of heroism but is unquestionably alive and realistic. It is well suited to the form and purpose of the history play. Like the total action, it argues for the sacrifice of personal life in a communal act which will repay the men "with advantages"—provided, of course, that they believe in the king. It is a national version of finding selfhood by losing it, to be sealed by the ritual of bloodshed which makes all men equal, "gentling" those to whom the king has talked in the darkness and who in no tangible political or economic sense will ever be raised.

In the history play, the function of an "epic" speech such as this is to redeem those times that can imaginatively share in the myth: to shape the present so that men "in their flowing cups," "yearly on the vigil feast," will remember the myth. For such history, Shakespeare implies, is never remote to an audience held by the "muse of fire"; relived in the theater, it will make a nationalistic group once again a "band of brothers."[10] Henry is probably meant

[10] The levels of awareness in an audience thus told that it would reenact what it was in fact re-enacting must have been complex. One of the functions of the Chorus, which provides an unusually elaborate mediation between playwright, audience, and play, is to sharpen awareness of the play as play. The Olivier film version carries the point even further. At the conclusion, "Henry" is suddenly revealed as the actor-who-has-been-king: the "performance" is over and the myth shrinks back into present reality. And since the film begins from a perspective outside the Globe and circles in upon the action, there is a further movement from the Shakespearian to the modern theater. The Elizabethan golden age has been part of the myth; and so the modern audience, finding itself outside both the community of the old king and the world of 1599, must make a double "adjustment." The film becomes not so much an apology for *Respublica* as distant history in two layers.

to be justified both in envying the peasant's "best advantages" and in doing everything in his power to secure his grasp on the crown, even though preventing civil turmoil entails a foreign war. To withdraw from responsibility is impossible, or at least risky, as Lear discovers; to assume it without reservation will violate some things, strengthen others. Pursuing a course inherently contaminating, Henry never quite loses equilibrium or allows public obligations to reduce inner life to mechanism.

<3>

The process of purified absorption undoubtedly has less tangible aspects also. Folk heroes acquire powers, as they mount horses, differently from public school boys:

> I saw young Harry with his beaver on,
> His cuisses on his thighs, gallantly arm'd,
> Rise from the ground like feathered Mercury,
> And vaulted with such ease into his seat
> As if an angel dropp'd down from the clouds
> To turn and wind a fiery Pegasus
> And witch the world with noble horsemanship.
> (IV, i, 104ff., Part One)

(That a rider's control of his mount was a common figure for the soul's control of its body explains away some but not all of the witching skill.) Despite the suggestions of superhuman power in the king, however, Shakespeare's dramatic method in presenting him is at least as close to realism as to the technique of the morality and miracle plays. "Participation" in the communal emotion centered in the king results not only from the king's mythological stature and incantational rhetoric but also from a realistic examination of alternatives in various counteractions or dialectical "plots" that close off other channels.

The attempt to turn "disease" to commodity is one of these counteractions. Nearly everyone in the series from *Richard II* to *Henry V* at one time or another thinks of exploiting the weaknesses of the realm or of other parties in it, partly by conjuring the right spirits and partly by simple political trickery. In *2 Henry IV*, the rebels, having been "o'erset," venture again; the Archbishop of York "turns insurrection to religion" and attempts to capitalize upon "a bleeding land,/ Gasping for life" (I, ii, 207); Northumberland lies, as Rumour says, "crafty sick" and awaiting a time to emerge and redeem his honor when the state seems weak enough to allow it. Falstaff is again the key figure, of course. If he comes on stage asking about time in Part One, in Part Two he appears inquiring about his ailing health and advanced age, both equally beyond fixing but not beyond "use." "A man can no more separate age and covetousness than 'a can part young limbs and lechery," he rationalizes; "the gout galls the one, and the pox pinches the other"; but a "good wit will make use of anything. I will turn diseases to commodity" (I, ii, 256, 277). His inability to do so is the source of both comedy and tragedy, as we have seen. Desire, outliving performance, becomes grotesque, like the clawing of poll by parrot, in the Prince's figure. The pressure of time is unbalancing, as a note of desperation comes into the Eastcheap follies. Hostess Quickly chants imperatively to Doll (who also turns disease to commodity): "O, run, Doll, run; run, good Doll. Come. (*She comes blubbered.*) Yea, will you come, Doll?" (II, iv, 420, Part Two).

The emphasis upon commodity is one side of Falstaff's partly real and partly mock gentleman-capitalist role, which complements his Puritanism. He is a "robber" both of "pilgrims going to Canterbury with rich offerings" and of "traders riding to London with fat purses" (I, ii, 109–110). As Gadshill observes, he goes with "burgomasters" who "pray continually to their saint, the commonwealth; or rather, not pray to her, but prey on her" (II, i, 70–72). His expenses, though hardly frugal, are itemized. Shakespeare apparently attaches this cluster of middle-class values to the aristocrat in order to purge them along with other things that "offend." After Falstaff's death, an increased acquisitiveness characterizes his old group, as it slips further and further toward the periphery of the legitimate community. Pistol *owns* Quickly and advises Nym to get papers on Doll as fast as possible (II, i, 77): "My Love," he commands the Hostess, "give me thy lips./ Look to my chattels and my movables" (II, iii, 50). He plans to sell provisions to the army and thus acquire whatever profits war will afford (II, i, 116). Falstaff had at least held upper and lower levels together; now that he is dead, Pistol says, "we must earn" (II, iii, 5), that is, both "grieve" and make a living.[11] And "earning" as they do leads to petty thievery, even

[11] The economic aspect of Pistol's "earning" are reinforced by his speech a few lines later:

to the gallows.

Shakespeare thus minimizes the kind of bourgeois communal power that economic bonds have in Heywood, Dekker, and other middle-class dramatists. But the spiritual bonds of the medieval community have also weakened, and any dramatist interested in more than individual profit motives must do something with the Goddess Utility on a social scale. Hence Henry, like the Bastard, is made aware of lost spiritual bonds and the power of commodity—a money-minded church plays easily into his hands—but he substitutes for them chivalric and heroic virtues, by and large, rather than middle-class virtues. Because the motives behind Falstaff's desire to turn disease to commodity are primarily egoistic and unheroic, he rejects them and turns to the old framework of higher virtues. (After the Histories, Shakespeare will place "chivalry" in a tragic environment and show it to be disintegrating. Someone like Edmund who has violated the old hierarchies and grown possessive will usually give the death blow. Its potential weakness is already clear in *1 Henry IV* when Hotspur momentarily becomes acquisitive and makes the rebellion—supposedly on behalf of honor—look dangerously like a land grab.) The Henry plays explore the profit motive thoroughly, however, in return subjecting the heroic virtues to Falstaff's utilitarian wit. That honor and criticism of his "betters" should be Falstaff's steady diet is an indication that rank and the chivalric distinctions it is based on can now be threatened from below, as Richard II discovers, without flights of angels coming to

> Look to my chattels and my movables.
> Let senses rule; the word is "Pitch and Pay."
> Trust none;
> For oaths are straws, men's faiths are wafercakes,
> And hold-fast is the only dog, my duck. . . .
> Let us for France; like horse-leeches, my boys,
> To suck, to suck, the very blood to suck!
> (II, iii, 50 ff.)

Rather than ritualizing theft as Falstaff had in his role as Saturnalian king, Pistol turns from ritual—the elegy for Falstaff—to economic "bloodsucking." (The pun on "earn" is the pivot.) And whereas Falstaff's game had attracted and educated the young Prince, the serious business of Pistol and his group cannot hold the "boy," who finally seeks out "some better service" (III, ii, 54). The counteraction has lost its dialectical, Saturnalian function.

their defense. A king who has taken the crown expediently must be especially aware of "what the people are saying": the new freedom to climb entails an increasing danger of falling. Public life on all levels, from Iago-like disputes over status and promotion to the politics of a Coriolanus, is a different and more complicated concern.

With his easy movement among levels—from Eastcheap taverns to prebattle councils—and his threat to make the Prince a career robber of the king's treasury, Falstaff, is a champion of antichivalric flexibility. If it takes a war to "gentle" the lowly, wit levels kings without stirring from the chair. In turning disease to commodity, he attacks more than the economic order, however; he also translates moral distinctions downward to purely physical phenomena, and in doing so indirectly affirms the relentless natural law to which he eventually falls. Commodity and naturalism are closely linked in him, as in Edmund. Though the links are made with more wit than cunning, beneath the humor the way is continually being prepared for the king's comment, "know the grave doth gape/ For thee thrice wider than for other men," a caustic remark that only recapitulates what Falstaff himself has implied:

> *Ch. Just.* Well, the truth is, Sir John, you live in great infamy.
> *Fal.* He that buckles himself in my belt cannot live in less.
> *Ch. Just.* Your means are very slender, and your waste is great.
> *Fal.* I would it were otherwise; I would my means were greater, and my waist slenderer. (I, ii, 156, Part Two)

Through the puns Falstaff tries to convert moral disease to mere physical disproportion, which seems the lesser sin—until the Prince suggests that the wider the "grave" for those "surfeit-swell'd," the less the "grace." His last attempt to convert disease to commodity in working Justice Shallow for a thousand pounds carries him rushing into disaster; ironically, he goes to "cure" the young king, "sick" for him, by taking him for what he can.

In "observingly" distilling his experience, the Prince, too, turns disease to commodity, but differently. What he takes from the public till he repays, and what he takes from his antitypes would have been lost or misused anyway. Theoretically, there is nothing at fault with the strategy provided it is made subject to moral controls. Warwick describes it quite accurately when he remarks that

The Prince but studies his companions
Like a strange tongue, wherein, to gain the language,
'Tis needful that the most immodest word
Be look'd upon and learn'd; . . .
So, like gross terms,
The Prince will in the perfectness of time
Cast off his followers; and their memory
Shall as a pattern or a measure live,
By which his Grace must mete the lives of others,
Turning past evils to advantages. (IV, iv, 67ff., Part Two)

Even Falstaff serves the kingdom "in the perfectness of time"—that is, in the perfection of time redeemed by the new king—because past evils, or evil of any kind, can be turned to advantage by the scrupulously unscrupulous. Henry V can play upon the acquisitive instinct without being corrupted by it. His kind of expediency rejects, but with open eyes, the ways which many realists in the audience knew of "getting ahead."

We can now return to the rejection scene, which brings together many of the aspects of the history play we have observed, and see it from what I think is a slightly different perspective from either "character" or "ritualistic" criticism. If equilibrium between self and society is indeed achieved in it, we should expect to find Falstaff's "death" appearing inevitable; it should serve to unite the community in the theater, as in the play, by ridding it of the egocentrism that has crystallized around Falstaff and his ways of confronting time, seeking commodity, curing disease, and so forth. The rejection scene is the first time, of course, that Falstaff is aware that a tutor and feeder of riots is unwelcome in court. His recognition is thus nicely timed to coincide with and contribute to the final manifestation of the king and the *anagnorisis* of the audience. His defensive masks are stripped off and he is suddenly faced with the blatant fact of public life. His heart, Pistol says, is "fracted and corroborate," which is partly humorous and partly pathetic; it is "killed by the King."

The slayer-king speaks not only as an ex-truant but also as the exemplar of psychological order. Falstaff's appeal, "My king! my Jove! I speak to thee, my heart!" recognizes that the "head" of the temporal order functions on at least three levels simultaneously, as king, Jove, and heart of his subjects; he speaks with the rhetoric of elevated majesty, personal teacher, and last judge.[12] It is significant that the first time we are fully convinced of the unity of Hal's impulses and the wholeness of his character, he is playing his most complex role: he cannot *be* himself until he is king. The disjunction in his former life as a rioter under bond to promise is healed by making the promise reality and by consigning the rest to unreal dream. The discrepancy between present and past appearance has never "really" existed, however, for he *is* the thing he *was*, even if not the thing Falstaff and the kingdom took him to be. His educational process has added to his essential character but not disturbed its underlying continuity.

But the chief dramatic point would seem to be that Shakespeare refuses to negotiate the loss of Falstaff, as Bradley wishes he had (p. 253). The language is harsh because *under the circumstances* it could not have been dramatically effective otherwise: the realities of time and disease which the play has made important must be confronted without evasion, conservatism being more deeply ingrained in the play than Falstaff. Thus, though comedy could not expel "such a kind of man" with a clear conscience, history must contrive to get along without him. If we expect a purely tragic "resolution," however, we shall not be quite prepared for what we receive. Falstaff is too human to be dealt with like Malvolio but not of high enough stature for pure tragedy. The rejection scene lacks the kind of language that could transform the unpleasant "fact" to cathartic poetry, nor does it attempt to do so entirely. The community must be made a charmed circle through another kind of rhetoric, part public speech and part confession, flexible, direct, and capable of embracing reality freed from the "long dream."

Difficulties besides that of the language are involved also. The history play must be plotted so as to satisfy our sense of form as though it had beginning, middle, and end, and yet must somehow be left open. Its subject matter leads to plays in a series rather than to single, self-contained works, and even the series cannot be decisively ended. In the tragical histories, Shakespeare emphasizes the new reign, or England's possibilities if it "to itself do rest but true," or the new unity between "the white rose and the red." In

[12] See Harold Jenkins, *The Structural Problem in Shakespeare's Henry the Fourth* (London, 1956), p. 14.

the rejection scene, he divides attention about equally between the promising community surrounding the new king and the "catastrophe" of personal life.[13] The result is a kind of *concordia discors*; to borrow Canterbury's words, heaven divides

> The state of man in divers functions,
> Setting endeavour in continual motion;
> To which is fixed, as an aim or butt,
> Obedience. (*Henry* V, I, ii, 185 ff.)

But even such formulas as this are not completely "fixed"; they must be tested continually against the circumstances of history. (For this reason I have used the word "adjustment" rather than "reconcilement" or "resolution.") Rather than concluding things once and for all, the history play ends at a plateau or brief breathing space from which the state looks backward with relief but forward with apprehension. Even the glories of Henry V, as the audience knew, were to wither in the continued curse of Henry VI and Richard III. (Despite the apparently romantic-comedy ending of *Henry* V, Shakespeare goes out of the way to recall the future.) And it is doubtful that Elizabethans felt collectively and spontaneously that somehow Elizabeth had fixed mutability once and for all.

The best that *2 Henry IV* can do is make its auditors participants in a historical ceremony which frees them from the gormandizing dream without robbing them of their individual wills. It demands "obedience" but not an absolute regimentation of "diverse functions" and endeavors set "in continual motion." Shakespeare will have his squire of the night's body—and thus the dark, protected center of self-interest—and not have him either, if he can transubstantiate part of him; and failing that, he would not likely suffer

[13] Public duty and private impulse are not "represented" in Hal and Falstaff as in an allegory, of course. If the Prince absorbs some of Falstaff, Falstaff in turn picks up a Lancastrian political device or two. He is well aware of the figure he and his companions will cut when arraigned before the emerging king, for example. Even their tattered clothes he will turn to advantage, appearing "to seem stained with travel and sweating with desire to see him; thinking of nothing else, putting all affairs else in oblivion, as if there were nothing else to be done but to see him" (V, v, 24). We know that the "as if" is justified and that even with Falstaff friendship and patronage go hand in hand: "woe to my Lord Chief Justice" and "Blessed are they that have been my friends."

so much from the incongruity of loving and hating the same man as modern readers might, who are that much farther from gothic ambivalences: who have never experienced the weird illogic of the moralities, which award the official palm to Order and make us remember Riot. He would probably not hesitate, in other words, to choose Order, with whatever ritual can be put in it, over an instinctive anarchy insufficiently protected from the world by comic strategies. And when we consider that such "magic" as Henry performs in redeeming time—and thus as Shakespeare performs in redeeming history—is effective without demanding that we accept simply on faith the night-tripping "elfin guardians,"[14] we can perhaps avoid adding new levels to the schizophrenic feeling for Falstaff. It is not a question of either swallowing duty, sweetly covered with ritual, or rebelling on behalf of all that Falstaff stands for—and feeling dissatisfied in either case: the community which the history play imitates has its own legitimate life.

As to the form of that imitation, we can perhaps let Morgann have the last word after all; for in his role as preromantic critic, he leaves room both for the categories into which we put dramatic types and for the unique, organic form by which a given play "takes in" its audience, sometimes in defiance of normal expectations and tendencies to favor certain elements. He has Aristotle (surprisingly) rebuke such critics-by-generic-rule as Thomas Rhymer who expect the old categories to hold true for all times: "True poesy is *magic*," Aristotle admonishes, "not *nature;* an effect from causes hidden or unknown. To the magician I prescribed no laws; his law and his power are one; his power is his law." Shakespeare, seeing something even in a king who remains alive at the end of the play, made new laws of genre to accommodate him.

[14] Cf. A. P. Rossiter's statement in *Woodstock: A Moral History* (London, 1946), "magic is part of the Tudor world, not least where Monarchy is touched" (p. 12).

GARETH LLOYD EVANS

The Comical-Tragical-Historical Method—Henry IV

IN 2 *Henry IV*, Prince Henry stealthily takes the crown of England from his dying father's bedside and addresses it

The care on thee depending
Hath fed upon the body of my father;
Therefore, thou best of gold art worst of gold:
Other, less fine in carat, is more precious,
Preserving life in medicine potable;
But thou, most fine, most honour'd, most renown'd,
Hast eat thy bearer up. (IV, v, 159)

His words convey a vision of the nature of kingship, and, by implication of the State itself, which is far removed from any other conception of the royal condition in Shakespeare's previous history plays. For Prince Hal the crown does not have the awesome status of a multiple symbol of power, majesty, grief and death. It is for him nearer to being a dangerous bauble, notwithstanding its tacit symbolism. When he discovers that he has too quickly taken it up, he returns it with words which suggest that the greatest offence he has committed is against his father, rather than against the appointed King of England. The simplicity of the gentle "There is your crown" followed by his anguished

God witness with me, when I here came in,
And found no course of breath within your majesty,
How cold it struck my heart!

From *Early Shakespeare,* Stratford-Upon-Avon Studies 3, ed. John Russell Brown and Bernard Harris (London 1961), 145–163. Reprinted by permission of the author and Edward Arnold (Publishers) Ltd.

with its hint of ceremony, leads to the angry irony of his address to the crown, with its bitter counterpointing of "my father" and "Thee." The crown indeed holds awe, majesty, pain and terror, but Hal's expression of these turns abstraction into personalized grief:

> I put it on my head,
> To try with it, as with an enemy
> That had before my face murder'd my father.

The king's reply also significantly suggests a personal reaction to Hal's grief and regret:

> O my son,
> God put it in thy mind to take it hence,
> That thou mightest win the more thy father's love.

Throughout the scene the father-son relationship swells out, giving an additional dimension to the imperial theme. But, and this is important, we have been conditioned from the beginning of *1 Henry IV* to see this dimension. We have been familiar with a royal prince, who himself has been a familiar with a world elsewhere, where he has been "educated" to make trial by experience of the abstractions which must later enclose his life.

The two parts of *Henry IV* encompass two worlds—the world of kingship and ceremony, and the natural world. The connecting link is Prince Hal; he has commerce with both, and it is what the one world teaches him that enables him finally to take up his habitation in the other. In each world he is confronted with living example of kingship—his own father, and his "adopted" father, Falstaff, emperor of the natural. Both "kings" have a kingdom to bequeath—the one the realm of England, the other, a realm of knowledge and experience. Both kings perish so that Hal may come into his kingdoms—the one by the natural order of death, the other by rejection.

In *1 Henry IV* Hal begins his "education." No other prince of England in Shakespeare's histories is shown making himself deliberately a semifugitive from the world of royalty so that he may more certainly and dramatically enter into his heritage with the aura of man and royalty reborn. The process is self-imposed, and in some measure, self-denying, and one ironic result of it is to set up a poignant personal tension between himself and his father. The conscious purpose of Hal is emphasized time and again. For the present his creed reads "wisdom cries out in the streets, and no man regards it," but there is more than a touch of conceit, a sort of satisfied self-seeing in his private ruminations through the stews of London. There is much in Hal that loves flourish and drama. He looks forward to the great rebirth with youthful relish.

> If all the year were playing holidays,
> To sport would be as tedious as to work;
> But when they seldom come, they wish'd for come,
> And nothing pleaseth but rare accidents.
> So, when this loose behaviour I throw off,
> And pay the debt I never promised,
> By how much better than my word I am,
> By so much shall I falsify men's hopes;
> And like bright metal on a sullen ground,
> My reformation, glittering o'er my fault,
> Shall show more goodly and attract more eyes,
> Than that which hath no foil to set it off.
>
> (I, ii, 177–188)

Boyish conceit perhaps, but there is a calculated reasoning about it and a sense of high purpose. Here is a man assuming a false face, putting on a madcap disposition to ensure a desired result. The "reformation" is a calculated effect—its inevitability is a species of faith for Hal—and this self-conscious responsibility is the keynote of his relationship with Falstaff. Hal has never actually sinned—the early remarks about wenching have the flavour of verbal artifice and nothing else.

When the Gadshill plans are made, the whole tone is that of persuasion. There is a strong impression that this is the first time that Hal has ever considered the possibility of an actual indulgence in the nefarious escapades of Falstaff.

> HAL: Well then, once in my days I'll be a madcap.
> FALSTAFF: Why, that's well said.
> HAL: Well, come what will, I'll tarry at home.
> FALSTAFF: By the Lord, I'll be a traitor then, when thou art king.
> HAL: I care not.

POINS: Sir John, I prithee, leave the prince and me alone: I will lay him down such reasons for this adventure that he shall go.

FALSTAFF: Well, God give thee the spirit of persuasion and him the ears of profiting, that what thou speakest may move and what he hears may be believed, that the true prince may, for recreation's sake, prove a false thief. (I, ii, 124–134)

The emphasis here is plain. It is not merely that the prince is having to be persuaded to join in the affair; more pertinently it is the sense that his participation is a kind of formality "for recreation's sake." There was never a less villainous planning than this for Gadshill. It is no more nor less than tomfoolery. Its "chief virtue" is the unmasking of Falstaff's braggadocio cowardice. The action and the results of Gadshill remain carefully within the atmosphere with which the robbery is planned. In no sense is the prince involved in the actual robbery; in every sense he has a care to be disguised—his first words to Poins before the travellers arrive, are "Ned, where are our disguises?" This prince remains unstained—his committal to the world of Falstaff is academic; he observes and learns. Any doors that might lead us to question the actual propriety of Hal are carefully closed by Shakespeare. Hal lays no hands upon the travellers. Their money is returned, the "jest" is all.

Even so Hal's preoccupation with this world, academic though it may be, when contrasted with the idealized Hotspur, and in the light of the anguish of the King who sees nothing but "riot and dishonour" stain the brow of his son, is sufficient not only to sketch the outlines of the personal tensions which are to well up later between father and son, but also to give an ironic depth to the widening theme of rebellion and the need for strong succession.

Yet, because of his self-conscious responsibility Hal has about him something too good to be true. He dips only his fingertips in mud, and Shakespeare is careful to wipe them clean. He has about him the self-conscious pride of the man whose indulgence is very circumspect.

The first appearance of Hal after Gadshill has, however, a different complexion. He and Poins meet together at the Boar's Head to await Falstaff, and there occurs the puzzling action with Francis the drawer. As Dover Wilson says, in *The Fortunes of Falstaff,* "Critics have solemnly entered it up in their black book of Hal's iniquities and accused him on the strength of it of 'heartlessly endangering the poor drawer's means of subsistence.' " Yet it is difficult to find Dover Wilson's cheery explanation that "the main purpose of this trifling episode, apart from giving Falstaff's voice a rest after the roaring and in preparation for the strain of the scene ahead, is to keep the audience waiting agog for him," any more convincing. The actor playing Falstaff has already had a scene—that between Hotspur and Kate—in which to rest his voice. As to keeping the audience "agog" for the fat wonder, surely the Hotspur scene fulfils that purpose, especially since in location and tone it takes our minds sufficiently far away from the fooleries of Gadshill to make a return to that atmosphere seem overdue. And if it were necessary for us to be introduced to the Boar's Head and the Prince in order to set the atmosphere for the arrival of Falstaff, why continue the scene-setting so long with this "trifling episode"? Perhaps the explanation of the scene may lie within the boundaries of the knowledge of the Prince which has so far been vouchsafed to us. He is the pure Prince, the conscious wearer of a mask of very harmless anarchy. Indeed all he has done is to wear a mask—he has not indulged in a dance of anarchy. In this scene, however, it may be suggested that Shakespeare, in order to give some depth of credibility to Hal's sojourn in the kingdom of Falstaff, and to the tension between Henry IV's conception of his wild son and the reality, here shows something more than the academic observer of Falstaff's dominion. Here for a short time the Prince is committed to that dominion in a positive, though still relatively harmless, way. For a short time he relaxes his hold on the conscious curriculum of his "education," and engages with that he had decided to observe. In short, he is drunk.

When Poins asks him where he has been, Hal replies

> With three or four loggerheads amongst three or four score hogsheads. I have sounded the very base-string of humility. Sirrah, I am sworn brother to a leash of drawers . . . (II, iv, 4–6)

In the interim, since Gadshill, Hal has been pursuing his "education" and, like a naughty boy who steals the dregs at a wedding feast, is as much intoxicated by his sense of sin as by what he has drunk. Hal relishes the "dyeing scarlet" of drinking, and that he can "drink with any tinker in his own language." His language has the flush of drinking on its face, and the repetitive sibilants of alcohol, and he has entered into the lovely world of hail-fellow-well-met:

> I am no proud Jack, like Falstaff, but a Corinthian, a lad of mettle, a good boy, by the Lord, so they call me, and when I am king of England, I shall command all the good lads in Eastcheap.

He has the tipsy man's giggly desire for a game, and Francis is the victim. When he asks Poins to call Francis, and Poins does so, Hal, with that pointless verbal backslapping which is the temporary gift of alcohol, murmurs—"Thou art perfect." And the jest with Francis is pointless, it *is* a "trifling episode" in the manner in which much pub gaming is pointless and trifling, and by its pointlessness mitigates the discomfiture of the victim. Even Poins, who has not been with Hal amongst "three or four score hogsheads" cannot fathom the game. "Come, what's the issue?" The truth is that there is no "issue" that Hal could possibly explain to Poins. But Hal is not so tipsy that he does not dimly remember the issue himself. His answer is:

> I am now of all humours that have showed themselves humours since the old days of goodman Adam to the pupil age of this present twelve o'clock at midnight.

Now, in his own mind, he can confirm what he had earlier promised.

> I know you all, and will awhile uphold
> The unyok'd humour of your idleness.
> (I, ii, 168–169)

Drink has taken Hal deeper into the world of Falstaff than he has ever been or ever will be again. In his fuddled state he thinks of Hotspur, but he talks of Hotspur in the language of Falstaff.

> I am not yet of Percy's mind, the Hotspur of the north; he that kills me some six or seven dozen of Scots at a breakfast, washes his hands, and says to his wife "Fie upon this quiet life! I want work." "O my sweet Harry," says she, "how many hast thou killed today?" "Give my roan horse a drench," says he; and answers "Some fourteen," an hour after; "a trifle, a trifle." I prithee, call in Falstaff: I'll play Percy, and that damned brawn shall play Dame Mortimer his wife. (II, iv, 92–100)

This is the same comic-cynical vision that sees honour in terms of "he that died a Wednesday"; in a few moments when Falstaff arrives we are to hear just such another "parcel of reckoning" in Falstaff's monstrous fantasies of the men he fought at Gadshill. The possibilities of Hall disengaging himself from this definite descent into the world of Falstaff are, to say the least, tenuous. Falstaff at bay is Falstaff at his most dangerous. Hal, in the flush of wanting to rub home the discomfiture of Falstaff, faces an adversary adept, not only in the art of verbal escapology, but one, when cornered, capable of taunting, corrupting, verbal sword-play. The great scene in which Falstaff relates his version of Gadshill moves impeccably on two lines which intertwine and separate and intertwine, enfolding in their pattern a rich and total image of the education of Hal, his relationship with Falstaff, and through both a vision of kingship which, when it is seen in relation to the royal world Hal returns to, creates the most moving and mature comment in the history plays. The developments of I, iv, after the entry of Falstaff, are firstly the comic surface where Falstaff and Hal, indeed the rest of the crew of the Boar's Head, exist, as it were, man to man—it is the comedy which unites them; secondly the relationship between Hal and Falstaff which exists below the surface of their comic union and is constantly tending to disunite Hal from the kingdom of Falstaff. Ironically, it is the very advantage which Falstaff attempts to seize through his comic largesse of wit that gradually pushes Hal further away from his world, and actually helps to redeem Hal from slipping further into a state he had vowed merely to observe. Falstaff's great comic flaw is his inability to know when to stop—or rather it is both his strength and his weakness. It gives him his monumental self-glowing status and takes away from him his ability to "hold" his most illustrious subject, Prince Henry.

When he enters, Falstaff is hot, dishevelled and angry. He rouses Hal to a pitch of anger by equating "coward" with "Prince." Hal is caught on the raw, confronted with a direct image of himself coined in the realm of Falstaff. But the heat of anger passes, and Falstaff's imagination gathers strength. Out of his dangerous rage, the monstrous comedy of his account of Gadshill grows. Under the Prince's swift questioning and frustration Falstaff ascends to the highest peak of his comic dominion. The corner into which he has been pushed cannot hold him, and there comes what Dover Wilson calls his "consummate retort,"

By the Lord, I knew ye as well as he that made ye.

There is no doubt that the brilliance of Falstaff's verbal gymnastics during this scene endears him to that part of us which revels in the bright machinations of roguery. Never again was Shakespeare to create such a sustained example of the magnificence of the solitary comic spirit. It rests at the opposite pole of the tragic hero's awareness of self. Where his is self-immolating, self-examining, inward turning, Falstaff's is self-expanding, outward turning, feeding on its own audacity, and gloriously aware of the incredible but magnetic effect it creates. But what is equally plain throughout this scene is that Falstaff is meticulously and unconsciously digging his own grave: his future grows less as he builds himself great. Falstaff's account of Gadshill is a superb essay in the art of cowardice. By the very deviousness of his description he proves the falsity and enormity of his naming Hal a coward. The coward is anatomized here—first his rage at apparent exposure, then his outrageous exaggeration, as if cloud-capped towers of falsehood will hide the earthy truth, and finally the hollow, audacious, magnificent trump-card—the attempt to put himself on the side of the angels.

Hal does not let the meaning of the essay go unmarked, "the argument shall be thy running away."

The relish with which Hal accepts Falstaff's invitation to "stand for" his father the King, and to examine the particulars of his life, is an appetite based less on love of the "game" than on the assurance of his own inviolable, secret purposes.

The mock trial scene is of very great significance since it is the last time that Falstaff is seen "in state" with his chief subject, Hal. His reign over Hal is much shorter than is often admitted, and this scene represents a final audience before a long-drawn-out abdication. Shakespeare allows Falstaff to retain the high comic status he has achieved in his description of Gadshill. Falstaff sits on the throne first. But this overindulgence of his comic craft once again causes a gap to widen between himself and Hal. He takes up his symbols and effects of office: "this chair shall be my state, this dagger my sceptre, and this cushion my crown" (II, iv, 336–337). And the Prince's repetition. 'Thy state is taken for a joined stool, thy golden sceptre for a leaden dagger, and thy precious rich crown for a pitiful bald crown," with its emphasis on "thy," sharply distinguishes comic licence and hard reality. Falstaff plays the game of

King-father to Hal, but turns the occasion once more to his favourite theme, himself. The previous swelling fantasies of Gadshill are forgotten, and the new theme is a mocking catalogue of virtues. Yet there creeps into this feast of fooling a shadow of uncertainty, "If then the tree may be known by the fruit, as the fruit by the tree, then peremptorily I speak it, there is virtue in that Falstaff; him keep with, the rest banish" (380–382).

There is a cold silence implied between this and the Prince's next words. Hal does not reply to the challenge—his mind has leapt to another world of consideration; "Dost thou speak like a king? Do thou stand for me, and I'll play my father."

Hal forces him on to the defensive—once more the shadow falls, and banishment is uttered. It is as if Falstaff is fatally fascinated by the need for an answer. He dare not question, but uses an appealing imperative:

> No, my good lord; banish Peto, banish Bardolph, banish Poins: but for sweet Jack Falstaff, kind Jack Falstaff, true Jack Falstaff, valiant Jack Falstaff, and therefore more valiant, being as he is, old Jack Falstaff, banish not him thy Harry's company, banish not him thy Harry's company; banish plump Jack, and banish all the world.

But he gets an unequivocal answer: "I do, I will."

There are no more dramatic interruptions than that which suddenly cuts across the stage at this point. Bardolph runs in shouting that the sheriff is at the door. Falstaff has been left in an agony of apprehension by Hal's words—he hardly takes in the fact that the law stands outside his door. He says to Bardolph, "Out, ye rogue! Play out the play; I have much to say in the behalf of that Falstaff."

Indeed he has much to say, but nothing ever again that can gainsay what Hal has said. Dover Wilson, observing that following Hal's words the Cambridge and other modern editions supply a stage direction, "*A knocking heard, exeunt Hostess, Francis and Bardolph,*" notes that neither quartos nor Folio supply previous exits for these three, and complains that firstly, this would leave the stage silent for several moments ("which is absurd"), and secondly the direction is unnecessary since Bardolph and the Hostess could exit at any time during the scene unnoticed by the audience. But it may be said that the instinct of the editors is correct. Nothing could be less absurd than a silence at this point, with Falstaff and Hal left alone momentarily until Bardolph runs back with his dread news. Falstaff hardly hears Bardolph, nor the Hostess when she repeats that the sheriff is at the door. He is still alone with Hal. His tone is still pleadingly imperative: "Dost thou hear, Hal? never call a true piece of gold a counterfeit; thou art essentially made without seeming so." Falstaff asks Hal not to mistake his (Falstaff's) counterfeiting (i.e., cowardice) for his real character (a true piece of gold). Hal is one thing while seeming to be another—so, the inference is, why should not he, Falstaff, counterfeit too? This is an interpretation of Falstaff's activities which Hal in the next line completely rejects: "And thou a natural coward, without instinct."

With the intervention of the sheriff, Falstaff leaves and Hal does an office of friendship. He puts the sheriff off the scent. There is, however, an attitude of strong decision about him now. He seems to be slipping away from this world of riot. It is as if he is putting his effects in order before setting out on a journey from which he will not return the same person. He engages his word to the sheriff that Falstaff will answer to the charges; he promises that Falstaff will be answerable if found guilty; he says that all must go to the wars; that the money will be paid back with advantage. As for himself: "I'll go to the court in the morning."

The themes and issues of this great scene irradiate both parts of the play. The magnificence of its comedy, and the meanings which emerge from Hal's verbal encounters with Falstaff make it a scene central to both parts of the play. On the battlefield of Shrewsbury its memory strikes home with a sharp nostalgia, "I fear the shot here; here's no scoring but upon the pate" (V, iii, 30–31). And when Hal meets Falstaff:

FALSTAFF: Nay, before God, Hal, if Percy be alive, thou get'st not my sword; but take my pistol, if thou wilt.

HAL: Give it me: what, is it in the case?

FALSTAFF: Ay, Hal; 'tis hot, 'tis hot; there's that will sack a city.

And Hal finds it to be a bottle of sack. Again in Falstaff's scenes with Shallow and Silence, there is constant backward looking at haunts now deserted. And even in *Henry V* the long aroma of the Boar's Head stretches into the field of Agincourt: "Would I were in an alehouse in London! I would give all my fame for a pot of ale and safety" (III, ii, 12).

But the suffusion of the atmosphere of the tavern throughout the plays is secondary to the depth of effect the action between Hal and Falstaff, within its walls, imposes upon the flow of the historical action. The comic anatomization of kingship and cowardice in their interplay—the interplay between a world of royalty feigning and a counterfeit world which has the greatness of influence thrust upon it by the shrewd audacity of comic genius, the knowledge we receive of Hal and his purposes—all this colours our acceptance of the historical narrative.

The two scenes following, for example, take on a deep irony. The rebellious leaders Hotspur and Glendower, whom we meet immediately afterwards, have no glow of greatness about them. Shakespeare does not make the mistake of creating too great a contrast with the Hotspur whom Hal has pictured in the exaggerated comedy of his intoxication. This Hotspur is a long way in stature from the man we met in the early scenes arguing with the king about prisoners. There he was coldly determined, arrogant, a champion of rights, now he is petulantly mulish, irritating. Hal has seen below the chivalric generalizations of his own father's picture of Hotspur as:

> A son who is the theme of honour's tongue;
> Amongst a grove, the very straightest plant;
> Who is sweet Fortune's minion and her pride
> (I, i, 81–83)

And the proof of Hotspur's other self is revealed in this cavilling taunting youth who rows with Glendower about magic and pieces of land. But, to the king, Hotspur remains the perfect son some "night-tripping fairy" exchanged for his own. When Hal goes to him from the tavern, he is treated to a long regretful diatribe on his own iniquities—his "low desires," "mean attempts," "barren pleasures," words which curiously fit the Hotspur we have just seen. Hal, who keeps his intentions always to himself, does not break his silence. Henry ruminates bitterly on the similarity of Hal's and Richard II's behaviour, and draws a picture of himself in isolated regal splendour—a kind of altar at which all genuflect in awe:

> Thus did I keep my person fresh and new;
> My presence, like a robe pontifical,
> Ne'er seen but wondered at; and so my state,

Seldom but sumptuous, showed like a feast
And won by rareness such solemnity.
(III, ii, 55–59)

Hal's reply is tight-lipped:

I shall hereafter, my thrice gracious lord,
Be more myself.

It is only when the king brings up the name of Hotspur that Hal speaks at length. He does not explain away his "iniquity," but formally avows his determination to startle the king and the world, and Hotspur:

for the time will come,
That I shall make this northern youth exchange
His glorious deeds for my indignities.

The tensions which inhabit this interview arise directly out of the commenting, revealing power of the Boar's Head scene. The King remains within the dim shadows of formal royalty. His picture of himself as Prince and King seems utterly and pathetically remote from the sharp realities of the kind of Prince that Hal is showing himself to be, and the kind of king he may become. Henry cannot see beyond the abstractions that surround royalty, and his stricken gaze falls upon the possibility that his usurping reign can only be succeeded by his stained son. Stuck as he is within ideas of kingship, he could never understand the practicalities of Hal's reasons for temporarily forsaking his world, in order to gouge out of experience a wisdom about men and about himself. Henry's tragedy, unlike that of his predecessor Richard, is seen to be less the result of an insufficiency to fit the royal condition, than complete isolation from the new world which is being born in the person of his son. To a king who can only see himself in terms of a cypher, a symbol, fixed and ceremonial, and all this ironically meaningless in the echo-chamber of usurpation, no other world can offer any meaning. And so Hal relieves the King of some of his grief in the only way in which Henry can understand—in a formal promise to change, and to wreak vengeance on Hotspur.

Hal has already set his face clearly in the direction of a return to a royal world—but on his own terms and of his own building.

Throughout the rest of the history of the reign of Henry IV, the character of Hal constantly gains in integration, while the world of Henry and Hotspur—the political world of usurpation and rebellion—and the world of Falstaff, the anarchic comic, constantly gain a momentum towards disintegration. As the history advances towards the Kingship of Hal, he is seen more and more as a rock of unity, a Prince of total experience, around which the rest distintegrates.

The decay of Falstaff begins most cogently in *1 Henry IV*, III, iii: "Bardolph, am I not fallen away vilely since this last action? do I not bate? do I not dwindle?"

The comic self-sufficiency which made him, in his description of Gadshill, seem inviolable and untouchable for a time, has suffered the calamity of losing its sense of infinity. Falstaff's comic genius needs something equal in magnificence to itself to feed upon. It must have Hal to gorge its pride and joy and exultation. The fact of Hal brings out the greatest in Falstaff. But from now on it has to dive into the deeps of a series of affairs and incidents which are unworthy of his comic wealth. There is in *2 Henry IV* nothing around Falstaff which by its challenging presence can bring a flight of glory into his monstrous words of misrule. After the first Boar's Head scene he meets Hal on several occasions before his public banishment, but he is never allowed to swell as he did once when the young Prince first entered his kingdom. On Hal's second visit to the haunts of Falstaff, the fat man is defeated again by the Prince, and this time on his own grounds—money grabbing. Almost viciously he tries to cast Hal in the image he so desperately wants to see—the image of a Prince of his own misruling realm: "Rob me the exchequer the first thing thou doest, and do it with unwashed hands too." But he gets a dusty answer: "I have procured thee, Jack, a charge of foot" (III, iii, 165). Again on the way to Coventry he meets Hal and is treated to a sharp comment on the shoddiness of his troop. He meets Hal before Shrewsbury, and is reminded that he owes God a death. When Hal visits the tavern in disguise he treats Falstaff to further words about Gadshill and cowardice. The next time he sees Hal he is publicly banished. All that Hal learns from Falstaff about the way of the world is returned to Falstaff, but weighed by a different scale of values and meanings. The comic success of Falstaff as he swells into the fullness of his illusory rule of Hal is one of diminishing returns. We see him more often in *2 Henry IV* but he is not the same man, or rather he is a shadow of the same man—his wit and comedy and triumphs are all at ground level. His largeness now is only comparative, and no longer an absolute, for it cannot but appear large faced with such puny adversaries as Shallow, Silence, Pistol and Doll Tearsheet. He is more given to soliloquy, and his conceit now has something of the bitterness of self-knowledge about it:

> Men of all sorts take a pride to gird at me: the brain of this foolish-compounded clay, man, is not able to invent any thing that tends to laughter, more than I invent or is invented on me. (I, ii, 6)

His tavern world is rich in action, in bawdry, in the machinations of commodity, but it is as far from the tavern world of the first part of the play as Falstaff is from Hal. Like Falstaff this world now seems merely sharp, shrewd, calculating. Its comedy no longer glows, largely because Falstaff, bereft of the Prince, can no longer be content with, perhaps is no longer capable of, superb comic improvisations whose source lay in a feeling of complete satisfaction. By blow after blow Falstaff has been separated from the Prince, and has no place in the new order to come. He is put in direct antagonism to the law, and less obviously as a counterpointing agent to deepen the comic irony between rule and misrule. His "kingship" is as empty as that of Henry's, partly because it knows that the succession is in doubt. The comi-tragedy of Falstaff is that of complete isolation from the new order, but in his isolation he has little of the inertia of Henry. He remains a true if pathetic king, he has usurped nothing though he has tried, and therefore retains energy and a sense of the validity of his own reign: "I shall be sent for soon at night" (V, i, 96).

As the world of Falstaff disintegrates about him, the rebellious world which surrounds the dying king itself disintegrates. There are occasions when it splutters into life, when it seems on the point of taking fire and engulfing all before it, but it exists largely in an atmosphere of endless bickering, questioning and false hopes. As the usurping King, Henry IV, whose sin has bred rebellion, fades away, so rebellion peters out. In *2 Henry IV*, the King speculates on the chaos of the political world; the tone is weary and valedictory:

> O God! that one might read the book of fate,
> And see the revolution of the times
> Make mountains level, and the continent,
> Weary of solid firmness, melt itself
> Into the sea; and, other times, to see
> The beachy girdle of the ocean
> Too wide for Neptune's hips; how chances mock
> And changes fill the cup of alteration
> With divers liquors! O, if this were seen,
> The happiest youth, viewing his progress through
> What perils past, what crosses to ensue,
> Would shut the book, and sit him down and die.
> (III, i, 45)

The King's counterpart is the "crafty sick" Northumberland. His part in the rebellious camp is just as wearied and unconvinced; constantly through the course of the rebellion, his "sickness doth infect the very lifeblood of our enterprise." The inertia of this rebel and his king stem from the same source—conscience. Worcester voices the suspicion:

> it will be thought
> By some, that know not why he is away,
> That wisdom, loyalty and mere dislike
> Of our proceedings kept the earl from hence.
> (*1 Henry IV*, IV, i, 62–65)

But the death-blow is delivered at the battle of Shrewsbury, when the triumphant Prince of Wales stands over the dead Hotspur:

> fare thee well, great heart!
> Ill-weaved ambition, how much art thou shrunk!
> When that this body did contain a spirit,
> A kingdom for it was too small a bound;
> But now two paces of the vilest earth
> Is room enough. (V, iv, 86–91)

He has, too, another office to perform,

> What, old acquaintance! could not all this flesh
> Keep in a little life? Poor Jack, farewell!
> I could have better spared a better man:

O, I should have a heavy miss of thee,
If I were much in love with vanity!
Death hath not struck so fat a deer to-day,
Though many dearer, in this bloody fray.
Embowell'd will I see thee by and by;
Till then in blood by noble Percy lie.
(101–109)

The tone of this is regretful, but curiously as in hindsight. It is as if the apparently actual death of Falstaff is merely the palpable sign for Hal of a departing that occurred some time before:

O I should have a heavy miss of thee
If I were much in love with vanity.

Yet it is Falstaff who does the final symbolic office. He carries Hotspur out of history—the world of comic anarchy, counterfeit to the end, trudges out with the world of misguided chivalry on its back.

At the battle of Shrewsbury Hal emerges as the dominant, dynamic Prince. He has redeemed his promise to his father. He has no rival in courage, his state is established. But there lurks on the edge of his status, his brother John of Lancaster. This cold, professional soldier and prince has no blot or stain on him—he has no wild past to raise a voice of doubt. He is less a threat, than a symbol of solid orthodox political royalty. But even in this sense he is an implied opposite to the free-ranging princeliness of Hal; he must be expunged. Shakespeare waits before wiping out this remnant of an orthodox world, but he prepares the stroke at Shrewsbury. Hal's magnanimity to Douglas is direct and simple—it has about it much of the sense of justice which is seen in Hal's judgment of the traitors before he, as Henry V, embarks for France. In the second climax of rebellion in *2 Henry IV*, John of Lancaster has the initiative to deal with the rebels. He meets them, talks with them, drinks with them, and embraces them in counterfeit amity:

If this may please you,
Discharge your powers unto their several counties,
As we will ours; and here between the armies
Let's drink together friendly and embrace,
That all their eyes may bear those tokens home
Of our restored love and amity. (IV, ii, 61)

He is at his highest peak, but a meanness of spirit, a politic trick, makes him break faith. He has nothing of Hal's correct compassion. He crashes into the wreckage of the world of Henry IV and his rebellious subjects, with his inadequate honour unmasked.

The movement of the two parts of *Henry IV* is implacably towards the raising of the figure of Hal as representative of a different kind of order than either of those which are laid bare and rejected. The dynamic natural, amoral world of Falstaff, and the tired outworn formalistic world of the King and rebels are, both, in a certain sense, chaotic. Neither world knows the other—only we see how the values of both are counterfeit, and how they shed a light one on the other. And only Hal learns the lesson, that the world of the natural, the temporary, and the world of the political and traditional, must both be experienced.

But merely to regard the plays as communicating a vision of life in which the personal natural order and the political order are cynically opposed, with Hal as the emerging champion of the new order, is to ignore the human dramatic warmth which constantly vitalizes them.

Hal has to reject much, and overcome much, to achieve the fullness of kingship. In so far as he does this, he is inevitably a calculating self-conscious "political" manipulator of his own destiny. It has been cogently argued by D. A. Traversi that the kind of success in politics which Hal achieves "implies moral loss, the sacrifice of more attractive qualities in the distinctively personal order." It is certainly arguable that in the rejection of Falstaff there is an acute example of this. But the rejection is clearly laid down from the beginning, and its inevitability must loom larger as Hal grows to the crown. But to sentimentalize the rejection is to falsify the relationship of Hal and Falstaff. On the political level, it is a clear necessity, though on the personal level it seems cold-blooded.

Yet it does less than justice to Hal and it "softens" the presence of Falstaff, to make this distinction too sharp. In the welter of Falstaff's comedy, which endears in its audaciousness, in the working out of the large plan of the prince, it is easy to miss the nature of the essentially personal relationship between the two. The clearly personal ties are not developed—they could not possibly be—and they lie in small corners of the play, but when they are shown, it is almost always through the medium of Hal, and with affection. He covers Falstaff's retreat from the sheriff, he closes the Gadshill affair by seeing that the money is returned: "O my sweet beef, I must still be good angel to thee." His only reaction to Falstaff's claim to have killed Hotspur is the amiable

> For my part, if a lie may do thee grace
> I'll gild it with the happiest terms I have.

His speech to the "dead" Falstaff, for all its punning and implied hindsight, is close and familiar. There is indeed more direct and implied affection in Hal than in Falstaff. In *1 Henry IV*, he bathes in the glow of Hal's presence, but the fire is used to heat not friendship, but the furnace of Falstaff's own wit. When he hears of the death of Henry IV, his reaction is characteristic:

> Away, Bardolph! Come, Pistol, utter more to me; and withal devise something to do thyself good. Boot, boot, Master Shallow: I know the young king is sick for me. Let us take any man's horses; the laws of England are at my commandment. Blessed are they that have been my friends; and woe to my lord chief-justice! (*2 Henry IV*, V, iii, 138)

This is indeed, as D. A. Traversi says, "the voice of appetite." If Hal's appetite is implacably that of a man desiring and shaping a personal destiny and status, it is not unmitigated by an affection for that which supplies its nourishment. Falstaff's appetite consumes without taking a breath of affection. Hal's rejection of Falstaff may seem severe, but it is the end-product of the logic of his advance out of Falstaff's kingdom and out of the empty chaos of the kingdom of Henry IV. The other and final product is the essentially new kingdom of Henry V. This, too, is a formal world, with a ceremonial pattern, but the vital difference is that the pattern now is balanced, rich and all-inclusive. The "education" of Prince Henry has ensured that the new world is one in which the political and the natural are blended, and in which the king actually as well as symbolically is the "father" of all his people, and not a solitary repository of abstractions surrounded by a tight circle of political expediency:

> A largess universal like the sun
> His liberal eye doth give to everyone.

To regard *Henry V* as a disappointing sequel, devoid of the rich variety of characterization, tragic and comic, of *Henry IV* is to ignore the inevitable consequence of that play. Henry V is as aware of the responsibility of the king, as of his subjects; in him justice is implacable but truly just in that it is dispensed without favour; in him honour and chivalry are richer ores, taking their colour and content not from outworn and malleable forms, but from the actualities of the king's faith in his meanest and highest subjects, and his subjects' sense of being involved in the majesty of a kingdom. All this exists because, as Prince Hal, the king breathed the air of the commonalty, and purged royalty of its rootless fever.

In *Henry* V comedy and history dance to the same tune, and there can be little of tragedy in so triumphant a dance. The pattern of movement is all designed to celebrate a "model" kingdom of "inward greatness." Here comic anarchy and political rebellion are mere remnant shreds—Falstaff, Bardolph, Pistol, Cambridge, Scroop and Grey are replaced by a new and joyous orthodoxy—the affirming comedy of Fluellen, and the selfless chivalry of Erpingham, Bedford and Salisbury. The dissenting voices in the new world—Pistol, Bates and the rebellious trio executed at Southampton—are mere irritants which subtly prevent the body of Henry's new kingdom from seeming, dramatically, too hygienically healthy, and thus possessed of the boredom of unremitting perfection. When the king speculates on ceremony on "the sword, the mace, the crown imperial" he utters two words which make his ruminations, otherwise apparently cast in the solitary rhetoric of Henry VI and Richard II, imply a different order of kingship. They are "I know":

I know
'Tis not the balm, the sceptre and the ball,
The sword, the mace, the crown imperial,
The intertissued robe of gold and pearl,
The farced title running 'fore the king,
The throne he sits on, nor the tide of pomp
That beats upon the high shore of this world,
No, not all these, thrice-gorgeous ceremony,
Not all these, laid in bed majestical,
Can sleep so soundly, as the wretched slave,
Who with a body fill'd and vacant mind
Gets him to rest, cramm'd with distressful bread
(IV, i)

The "I know" is the proof of Henry's awareness of the "wisdom that cries out in the streets," it is the legacy of observing the "unyok'd humour" of his kingdom. It gives all his words and his deeds in *Henry V* the justification of a personal involvement and fills his majesty with meaning.

The political "message" of *1* and *2 Henry IV* is the responsibility of rulers and subjects. There is no unique concept of political thought; the play rests like all the histories on certain basic assumptions—the paradox of the fact of kingship and the sin of usurpation, the evil of rebellion, the validity of law and strong government. These were some of the assumptions of Shakespeare's time and in his history plays he dispenses them freely. But these assumptions, which stand in the foreground of his early histories, forming and constricting to their own fixed patterns the dramatic and human fluidity of the plays, are in *Henry IV* in the background—against which a much more fluent and varied drama of human relationships is played out. The history and orthodox political conceptions are modulated and deepened by a vision which adds dimensions to the flat panorama of action and idea.

Certain forces are manipulated by Shakespeare in *Henry IV* which are later to be developed with increasing assurance and subtlety. The most important of these is the use of comedy to deepen and underline the "serious" actions of the play. It is not merely that the "serious" action has a comic parallel—that Falstaff is, as it were, the reverse side of the political coin—but that the comic and the "serious" are mixed so that there is a simultaneous communication of two sides of a character, an idea, an action. Falstaff, both in what he is and in what he speaks, exists on two levels, one which is naturalistically involved in the action, the other which is a comment upon the action. It is through Falstaff that we, as much as Hal, are "educated" to take a closer look at the play's issues. He is too involved and too forceful in his individuality to be a true Fool, but he has in him much which Shakespeare later used in the making of his Fools: the sense of comic isolation, the twin functions of his presence in the play. Like the Fool he is a repository of a species of truth, with the vital difference that whereas the true Fool is not called upon to "prove" his truth, Falstaff cannot help doing so—he has not got the isolated neutrality of Touchstone, Feste and Lear's Fool. They can, by their isolation, which is complete, "cleanse the foul body of th' infected world" without being questioned, for they are not involved deeply with the world they cleanse. Falstaff, through his unconscious "education" of Hal, helps to cleanse the foul body of Henry IV's infected world only at the expense of his own destruction.

In the creation of Hal may be seen the seeds of a conception of character whose first obvious flowering is in Hamlet—the secretive inward-looking temperament in opposition to an external world, the clash between a notion of private purpose and that of public destiny. In Hal the conception is in its infancy, the opposition is not so violent because both private and public destinies are consanguineous; it is not, as in Hamlet, a matter of two utterly different orders of belief and reality in violent opposition. Yet the clash is here, and the nature of its communication has similarities. Like Hal, Hamlet puts on a disposition, like Hal his motive is to disguise his purposes, like Hal he tries to learn by observation, like Hal there is a histrionic flavour in the assumption of his chosen role.

In *Henry IV* the interplay of natural and political, of comic and serious, of private and public, not only suggests the emergence of new dimensions in Shakespeare's plays, but makes of history much more than a chronicle tapestry. It implies an attitude towards the dramatic presentation of life that sees things not in terms of one-dimensional historical narrative, varied by dissociated areas of comic and tragic action and character, but strictly as a unity of comical-tragical-historical.

CLEANTH BROOKS and ROBERT B. HEILMAN

Dramatic Balance in Henry IV, Part I

1. THE PROBLEM OF UNITY

The salient problem in this play must be the problem of unity. To most readers at least, the most important general question which presents itself is this: does the play achieve a real dramatic unity, or is it, after all, merely a not-too-interesting "history" play to which Shakespeare has added, in the interest of amusement, the Falstaff tavern scenes? To state the problem with special reference to Act V, does this last act really succeed in uniting the various threads of interest that run through the play?

The "history" plot is, of course, brought to a conclusion in this act with the decision gained in the Battle of Shrewsbury.[1] But what of the comic underplot? Does it come here into any organic relation with the other elements of the play, or does it remain isolated? What happens to Hotspur when he comes within the orbit of Falstaff? Or what, for that matter, happens to Falstaff when he comes between the "fell incensed points/ Of mighty opposites"? If he affords no more than comic relief, then we are perhaps justified in holding that as a character he is a lucky accident, a character who was, in Shakespeare's original plans, to have

[1] To a temporary conclusion at least, for Shakespeare continued the story in *Henry IV, Part 2,* which the student should read. The two-part arrangement in itself raises the problem of unity in a special form. Suffice it to say here that, whatever the total unity which the two parts taken together may have, this first part has its own special unity which it is our immediate problem here to attempt to define.

Falstaff's death is mentioned in *Henry V*, and he is the central figure in *The Merry Wives of Windsor;* but in this latter play, most critics and scholars agree that he comes closer to the mere buffoon—that he lacks the special quality of character shown in the *Henry* plays.

figured as a sort of jester, but who became something richer and more imaginative than intended. As a matter of fact, one might, pushing this line of argument a step further, contend that Falstaff has actually so far outgrown the needs of the play, strictly considered, that he comes close to destroying it.

It is possible, however, to see Falstaff's role as a more positive one than that of merely diverting us *from* the more serious concerns of the play. It is possible that his function is to define—as well as enrich—the theme of the play. But to explore this possibility will involve a rather careful consideration of his relation to the other characters in the play and a further inquiry into the theme—the total "meaning" of the play.

2. THE SYSTEM OF CONTRASTS IN THE PLAY

If *Henry IV, Part I* does have a principle of unity, it is obviously one which allows for, and makes positive use of, an amazing amount of contrast. There is the contrast between the king's hopes for his son and the life which Prince Hal has actually been leading; the contrast between the pomp and state of the councils at court which are called to debate the state of the realm and those other councils at the Boar's Head which take measures for the better lifting of travelers' purses. Moreover, as we have remarked earlier, Prince Hal and Percy Hotspur are obvious foils for each other; they are specifically contrasted again and again throughout the play. But one of the most important contrasts developed in the play is that between Falstaff and Percy Hotspur.

On one level, it ought to be pretty obvious, the play involves a study in the nature of kingship—not an unduly solemn study, to be sure, but a study, nevertheless, of what makes a good king. In this study, of course, Prince Hal is the central figure, and the play becomes, then, the study of his development.

On this level of consideration, Percy Hotspur not only is Hal's rival but also furnishes an ideal of conduct toward which Hal might aspire (and toward which his father, the king, actually wishes him to aspire). Falstaff represents another ideal of conduct—and here, consequently, finds his foil in Hotspur. (If the pairing of Falstaff and Hotspur seems, at first glance, forced, nevertheless we shall presently see that there is abundant evidence that Shakespeare thought the contrast important and relevant to his purpose.)

Indeed, as Mr. R. P. Warren has pointed out, it is almost as if Shakespeare were following, consciously or unconsciously, the theme of Aristotle's Nichomachaean ethics: virtue as the mean between two extremes of conduct. This suggestion can be used to throw a good deal of light on the relationship of the characters of Falstaff, Prince Hal, and Hotspur to each other.

Consider the matter of honor. Hotspur represents one extreme, Falstaff, the other. Hotspur declares characteristically

> By heaven, methinks it were an easy leap,
> To pluck bright honour from the pale-faced moon, . . .
> (I, iii, 201–202)

Falstaff speaks just as characteristically when he argues in his famous speech on honor: "Well, 'tis no matter; honour pricks me on. Yea, but how if honour prick me off when I come on? how then? Can honour set to a leg? no: or an arm? no: or take away the grief of a wound? no . . . (V. i)

Falstaff's common sense is devastating; but it is also crippling—or would be to a prince or ruler. If it does not cripple Falstaff, it is because Falstaff frankly refuses to accept the responsibilities of leadership. Perhaps he chooses wisely in so refusing. By refusing he achieves a vantage point from which he can perceive the folly and pretentiousness which, to a degree, always tend to associate themselves with authority of any kind.

But Hotspur's chivalry is crippling too. He wants to fight for honor's sake: he will not wait for reinforcements because it will beget more honor to fight without waiting for them; but, on the other hand, he will not fight at all (Worcester fears) if he hears of the king's mollifying offer, for then his pride will be saved, his honor preserved, and the political aspects of the rebellion can go hang; for Hotspur has little or no interest in them. Indeed, Hotspur can rely on the obvious fact that he is fighting merely for honor to gain the forgiveness of the king, though Worcester fears that the forgiveness extended to himself will be only a nominal forgiveness and that the king will be on the lookout for later excuses to injure him.

If one assumes the necessity for leadership (and there is little doubt that the Elizabethan audience and Shakespeare did), then Hotspur points to an extreme which the truly courageous leader must avoid quite as clearly as he must avoid the other extreme represented by Falstaff. True courage, we may say, has as one frontier an unthinking impetuousness like that of Hotspur: it has as its other frontier a kind of calculation, which, if not cowardice, at least results in actions which look very much like cowardice. Falstaff is too "practical"; Hotspur, not "practical" enough.

3. THE "IMMATURITY" OF FALSTAFF AND HOTSPUR

Yet Shakespeare does not give us an oversimplified picture of either extreme. Falstaff redeems himself for most of us by his humor, by his good nature, by his love of life, and perhaps, most of all, by a thoroughgoing intellectual honesty. Hotspur also has his attractive side. There is a kind of abandon, a kind of light-hearted gaiety—in his whole-souled commitment to the pursuit of honor, in his teasing of his wife, and in his laughing at the pompous mystery-mongering of Glendower—which puts him, like Falstaff, *above* the plots and counter-plots that fill up the play.

Yet—if we assume the necessity for leadership and authority—both Falstaff and Hotspur are *below* the serious concerns that fill the play. About both of them there is a childlike quality which relieves them of the responsibility of mature life, a frankness which is the opposite of the pretense and hypocrisy so apparent in the adult world.[2]

This suggestion that there is something childlike and immature about Falstaff and Hotspur must, of course, be heavily qualified. There is a sense in which Hotspur is the epitome of manliness and aggressive masculinity, and certainly he thinks of himself as anything but childish. Moreover, Falstaff, in spite of the war cry with which he sets upon the travelers, "They hate us youth: down with them; fleece them," is old in the ways of vice, and indeed possesses a kind of wisdom which makes the solemn concerns of Henry IV's court appear callow and naïve beside it.

And yet, even so, the pair do not stand quite on the level of the adult world where there are jobs to be done and duties to be performed. They are either below it or else they transcend it; and

[2] If the student, remembering, for example, how "damnably" Falstaff has "misused the king's press," feels disposed to challenge this observation, he should be reminded that the matter in question is not Falstaff's goodness but his frankness and irresponsibility. He has the child's honest selfishness and the child's lack of conscience as he frankly goes after his own ends.

Shakespeare is wise enough to let them—particularly Falstaff—do both. That is, they appear sometimes *childish* in their attitudes and sometimes *childlike*, for Shakespeare exploits both aspects of their characters in the play.

The childlike qualities, of course, are found predominantly in Falstaff—in his vitality and in his preservation of a kind of innocence. But Hotspur, too, has a kind of innocence which sets him apart from the more calculating of his fellow-conspirators. He is impulsive where they are Machiavellian; boyish, in his love of adventure, where they are playing coldly for high stakes. But the childlike innocence (or, if one prefers, the boyish impulsiveness) merges into childish foolhardiness when he insists on fighting the king at Shrewsbury before reinforcements can be brought up.

4. FALSTAFF AT THE BATTLE OF SHREWSBURY

Falstaff is, of course, a far more complex character than Hotspur, or, for that matter, than any other character in the play. But an examination of the childish-childlike aspects of his nature may, even if it will not wholly account for the richness of his personality, lead the student into a further knowledge of that richness. Certainly, it may give us one of the most important clues as to how his character is related to the central problems of the play.

Falstaff as Philosopher. Falstaff, we may say, is like the child in the story who alone was able to detect the fact that the emperor's new clothes were entirely imaginary. With a clarity of vision that is unclouded by reverence towards authority of any kind, the child sees that the emperor is naked, and says so. (Falstaff strips Henry IV quite naked in his famous parody of the king's speech in Act II, iv. King Henry's concern for his son's wicked ways, as we see in Act III, is more than half an extension of his own self-conceit. His son's reputation disturbs him because he regards it as a reflection upon himself.)

Falstaff's clarity of vision, however, is not an effect of cynicism. The spectacle of the world in its nakedness, stripped of its pretensions, does not move Falstaff to bitterness. He can laugh in thorough good humor. And Falstaff does laugh continually through the play as he sees through what is glibly called "honor," through self-righteousness, through the pretensions of royalty. In this sense, like the child, he is fundamentally a moral anarchist. But

Falstaff is—again like the child—not a missionary anarchist. He does not for a moment intend to convert others to his views; he is not the moralist, certainly, nor the inverted moralist, the cynic.

In short, in spite of the fact that he speaks merely to amuse himself and others, Falstaff supplies a brilliant and what is—up to a point—a perfectly true commentary upon the world about him. Falstaff is doubtless the last man in the world to set up for a philosopher; yet his humor, because it does have point and does make a rich commentary upon the world about him, does have a philosophical quality.

Falstaff as Man of Action. But in Act V we see Falstaff as man of action, and this action tests him even as the world of action is tested by Falstaff's commentary. On a battlefield the committed man of action must be prepared to die, but Falstaff does not feel the need to die for any man. He frankly sees no point in dying by Douglas's sword for King Henry. King Henry himself, as Falstaff well knows, is scarcely likely to appreciate such a devotion on Falstaff's part. Hal himself will not lose or retain his chances for the crown by Falstaff's death alone; and the issue, when Douglas challenges him, is certainly death; for Falstaff, in spite of his playful boasting, has absolutely no illusions about his own prowess as a warrior.

Falstaff loses no time in resolving his problem: he contents himself with playing 'possum. From one point of view, this is simply cowardice; from another, Falstaff is being perfectly consistent, and, to be so, risking the imputation of cowardice. In the same situation Blunt declares heroically, "I was not born a yielder, thou proud Scot"; he believes in honor, and so he has his reward, even in death. Falstaff is equally consistent because he does not believe in honor; for him, heroics would be a pretense—phony honor.

The Parallelism of Falstaff and Hotspur. If the student has had any difficulty in seeing and accepting the parallelism between Falstaff and Hotspur, he might reflect that in this last act of the play the author himself has taken some pains to point it up, and may be said to have allowed at least Prince Hal, among the characters, to see it. In this connection Hal's speech over the dead body of Hotspur and his remarks over Falstaff's "dead" body, which he discovers a moment later, are worth careful consideration.

William Empson has pointed out (in his *English Pastoral Po-*

etry) that Hal's remarks here involve a series of puns applying both to largeness of body and to greatness of spirit. Of Hotspur the prince says:

> When that this body did contain a spirit,
> A kingdom for it was too small a bound. . . .
> . . . . this earth that bears thee dead
> Bears not alive so stout a gentleman.

A few lines later, he is saying of Falstaff:

> What, old acquaintance! could not all this flesh
> Keep in a little life? Poor Jack, farewell!
> I could have better spared a better man:
> O, I should have a heavy miss of thee,
> If I were much in love with vanity!
> Death hath not struck so fat a deer to-day, . . .

Hotspur has had too much spirit for the flesh; Falstaff has had so much flesh that it is ironical that the spirit has escaped at all. (The irony is increased, of course, by our knowing that Prince Hal little realizes how truly he speaks: the flesh that Falstaff so comfortably hugs about himself has *not*, as a matter of fact, allowed the spirit to escape.)

Moreover, it is significant that the prince, although he thinks that Falstaff has died in battle, refers to him as a "deer," a hunted animal, who would not fight back but would try to escape from the pursuit of death. From the standpoint of the huntsman (death) he is a fine animal ("so fat a deer"), and to the prince a "heavy loss" (another pun) though "better men" have died for his cause that day.

Is the prince mocking and cold-hearted? Hardly; the jesting farewell is the sort which accords with the jesting and affectionate companionship of the two in the past. It conveys a depth of feeling that perhaps would not be conveyed by a more solemn tribute.

At least Falstaff, who of course hears the prince's tribute, suffers no hurt feelings from the nature of the tribute. He has no shame and no qualms. In fact, only the word "Embowelled" runs the shivers up and down his back. The idea of being embalmed and given a fine burial by the prince stirs no regrets in him that he did not stand his ground and die honorably. Falstaff values his bowels. He is far from done with his gorbelly. Hotspur may have the prince's compliment and the noble burial which, doubtless, the prince intends for him. Falstaff is perfectly satisfied to abide by the choice which he has made.

Falstaff's Failure. Still, from the point of view of the need for responsibility and authority, Falstaff's conduct is childishly frivolous, if not much worse—as is his conduct throughout the battle. On one level, it is very funny when Prince Hal reaches into Falstaff's holster and pulls out a bottle of sack; and the prince himself doubtless smiles as he delivers his reprimand. But the reprimand is deserved: Falstaff won't realize that the battlefield is no place for joking. Indeed, though Shakespeare allows Falstaff his due even here, he has made the case against Falstaff very plain.

Consider the incident in Act V, iv. An Elizabethan audience would not have missed the point when, just after Falstaff has stabbed the dead Hotspur, Prince Hal came on the scene with his younger brother, Prince John, and says to him

> Come, brother John; full bravely hast thou flesh'd
> Thy maiden sword.

The commendation of Prince John applies ironically to "Brother" John Falstaff—here in full view of the audience—whose sword is a "maiden" sword too, which he has just "flesh'd" safely in the dead Percy. The boy prince John has shown himself a man: Sir John Falstaff has shown himself a child.

5. FALSTAFF AND THE WORLD OF HISTORY

The student may possibly object to so heavy an emphasis upon the battlefield scenes: yet our search for the unity of the play demands that we consider carefully this one group of scenes in which all the characters come together. Besides bringing all the characters together, too, the battle scenes subordinate Falstaff, for all his delightfulness, to something larger (somewhat to the resentment of readers to whom Falstaff is a kind of demigod); and this subordination itself is a unifying process.

But the battle scenes do not cancel out the more widely discussed tavern scenes; they qualify the tavern scenes. We may now return to reconsider the tavern scenes in the light of these qualifications.

It is perhaps significant that Falstaff is introduced to us with the line: "Now, Hal, what time of day is it, lad?"—a question which the prince answers with a jest: ". . . What a devil hast thou to do with the time of the day? Unless hours were cups of sack and minutes capons and clocks the tongues of bawds and dials the signs of leaping-houses and the blessed sun himself a fair hot wench in flame-coloured taffeta, I see no reason why thou shouldst be so superfluous to demand the time of the day." The jesting in the prince's speech may not come quite up to the better efforts of Falstaff himself; but the speech, quite apart from the jesting, is perfectly true. It is true in a deeper sense than even the prince realizes.

It is indeed an absurdity for Falstaff to ask the time of day, for Falstaff has properly nothing to do with the world of time. He transcends the time-ridden world of important affairs—the world of appointments to be kept, of tasks to be performed, of responsibilities to be undertaken. Time does not exist in his world. This is not to say, of course, that Falstaff's world is one in which nothing ever happens. For Falstaff, that world is interesting and even exciting. But in it, one is not dogged by time just as the child is not dogged by time in his world.

Falstaff and the King. For Falstaff, each day is a new day, lived for itself. The future does not cast a cloud over the present. This characteristic Shakespeare has emphasized by pointing up a sharp contrast between Falstaff and the king. The king is bedeviled with insomnia; Falstaff is not. Even with the bailiff at the door looking for a "gross fat man" suspected of robbery, Falstaff behind the arras drops off to sleep as naturally as would an exhausted child. Falstaff has nothing to do with time; but Henry, the king, is obsessed with time. The king not only makes history—his life *is* history. In the great tavern scene (II, iv) in which Falstaff plays the part of the king, Falstaff . . . parodies the sententious Euphuistic style which was popular in the period. But the parody involves more than a mere topical allusion: Falstaff is using the parody of style as an instrument for a deeper parody. He is mocking at the kind of seriousness with which authority has to express—and *take*—itself: the carefully balanced antitheses, the allusions to natural history, the appeal to learned authorities, the labored truisms—

e.g., "There is a thing, Harry, which thou hast often heard of, and it is known to many in our land by the name of pitch: this pitch, as ancient writers do report, doth defile; . . ." The fun is good-humored; but the criticism which it turns upon the institutions of authority is penetrating, and, as far as it goes, perfectly fair. Falstaff as "king" in the tavern is a delightful comedian *because* he is a recognizable monarch; that is, he does not use the pose of royalty merely for slap-stick effects.

But Shakespeare, whom we see constantly balancing scene against scene, has the king "counterfeited" once more in the play —on the battlefield, where knights and nobles wear the king's armor. Sir Walter Blunt, so dressed, is accosted by Douglas with "some tell me that thou art a king," and replies with the noble lie, "They tell thee true." He fights with Douglas and dies for the king—doubly. Falstaff appears on the scene immediately and, noticing Blunt's dead body, remarks "there's honour for you!" No aping of the king for him! The king's robes in the tavern play are one thing; the king's coat of arms on the battlefield, quite another.[3]

6. SHAKESPEARE'S ATTITUDE TOWARD FALSTAFF AND THE PRINCE

Here we come to the crucial problem of unity: what attitude, finally, are we to adopt toward Falstaff and the prince? Which is right? With which of the two are our sympathies finally to rest? Those readers who have felt the charm of Falstaff and who have sensed the fact that Shakespeare is not disposed to defend the duplicities of the king are surely right in refusing to dismiss Fal-

[3] There has been of late a tendency to defend Falstaff even here: to say that Falstaff in his debunking of honor is right after all; that Falstaff sees truly through the empty conventions of "honor"; that he refuses to be taken in by the vainglorious pretensions of the usurper, Henry Bolingbroke, to "honor" and to a legitimacy which he does not deserve. Such critics go on to point out that the device of clothing a number of knights so as to counterfeit the king makes rather hollow all the talk about chivalry and honor that goes on with regard to the battle.

But to take this position is to read into the play far more than the play warrants. If the dynastic pretensions of various people in fifteenth-century England seem trivial enough to us, they did not seem so to Shakespeare's audience or to Shakespeare himself. There is nothing in the play to warrant the belief that Shakespeare is bitterly denying the reality of honor and chivalry. Falstaff never rises to a philosophic indictment which will issue in his calling down a "plague on both your houses."

staff as a coward or buffoon. Furthermore, they may be right in feeling that Shakespeare has even revealed in Prince Hal himself a certain cold-blooded calculation.

The probability is that we shall miss the play if we assume that Shakespeare is forcing upon us a choice of the *either-or* variety. Is it not possible that Shakespeare is not asking us to choose at all, but rather to contemplate, with understanding and some irony, a world very much like the world that we know, a world in which compromises have to be made, a world in which the virtues of Falstaff become, under changed conditions, vices, and the vices of the Prince Hal become, under certain conditions, necessary, and thus, in a sense, accommodated to virtue? (One might well reverse the form of this statement. From the point of view of an Elizabethan audience, one would almost certainly have to reverse it thus: Falstaff's vices partake of virtue and the virtues of the prince—an easy camaraderie, a genial understanding, an unwillingness to stand on a haughty dignity—are revealed to him ultimately as vices which must be put away.)

The Two Worlds of the Play. Human beings live in a world of time, and a world in which—except at rare heroic moments—compromises have to be made. Falstaff lives, as we have already suggested, in a world of the eternal present, a timeless world which stands apart from the time-harried world of adult concerns. Yet Shakespeare keeps the balance with complete fairness. Each world has its claims. For the prince to be able to retire for awhile into Falstaff's world is worth something to him. It testifies to his humanity, since Falstaff's world is a part of the human world. It probably makes him a better king than he would be if he followed his more calculating and limited father's wishes. Bathed in the light of Falstaff's world, the coldness, the pomposity, the pretentiousness of the world of high concerns is properly exposed. Yet, after all, men must act; responsibilities must be assumed. To remain in Falstaff's world is to deny the reality of the whole world of adult concerns.

It is ironic, of course, that the human being is thus divided between the claims of two aspects of life. It is ironic, from one point of view, that men must grow up at all—must grow away from the innocence of the timeless and amoral world of childhood into the adult world, where except when crises evoke extraordinary devotion and resolution, compromises and scheming are a regular, and perhaps inevitable, part of human experience. Prince Hal, for example, in entering into the world of affairs, loses something as well as gains something—a matter which the play (particularly in its second part) rather clearly indicates. Falstaff may belong to a world unshadowed by time, but it is not for nothing that Prince Hal appears in a "history" play. He belongs to history—to the world of time—and in the Battle of Shrewsbury he enters into history.

7. HENRY IV AS MATURE COMEDY

The problem of Shakespeare's attitude toward Hal and Falstaff has been argued for a long time, and doubtless will continue to be argued. At the end of *Henry IV, Part Two* the prince, on being crowned, publicly rejects Falstaff, and thus makes formal and explicit what is hinted at at the end of *Part One*. Having arrived at kingship with its serious duties, he can have no more time for such play as the Boar's-Head Tavern afforded. Delightful as Falstaff is, he must now be put by.

The Two Interpretations of Shakespeare's Attitude. With regard to Shakespeare's attitude toward this relationship there have been, in general, two courses taken. The first considers the two plays as constituting a study in the discipline of a young king, a king who was to be celebrated as the ideal king in Shakespeare's *Henry V*. According to this interpretation, the two plays present Falstaff as undergoing a gradual degeneration of character. Thus, it is argued, we lose some of our sympathy for him and are reconciled to the young king's rejection of him.

The second interpretation reverses the first. Here it is argued that Falstaff retains our sympathies to the end. Hal's conduct, on the other hand, is regarded as having, from the beginning, something of Machiavellian policy in it. Hal delights in Falstaff's company during his carefree youth but dashes the old man's hopes rather brutally at the end by publicly disowning him and reading him a rather smug sermon on the subject of good conduct.

Few critics have, of course, accepted either view without some reservations and qualifications, but it may make the issues clearer to state the views in extreme form as is here done. That the matter of our attitude toward the Falstaff-Hal relationship is important comes out clearly if we consult the most recent book on the subject, Dover Wilson's *Falstaff*. Wilson sees the plays as involving basically a study in kingship. Falstaff has to be rejected.

Though, for Wilson, he remains brilliantly witty, even through the whole of *Henry IV, Part Two,* he becomes more boastful, with a correspondent weakening of our sympathy for him. And Wilson defends the terms of the rejection: Hal is not a "cad or a prig." Falstaff, after all, is not visited with a heavy punishment. The king sees to it that he, along with his other "wonted followers," is "very well provided for."

Shakespeare's Balance. To repeat, the present analysis agrees on the need of having the matter both ways. Surely, Wilson is at his soundest when he argues that Shakespeare keeps the balance most impartially between Hal and Falstaff; but perhaps he might, on the whole, have made out a more convincing case had he pressed this argument further still instead of trying to mitigate the terms of Falstaff's rejection or to argue that the later Falstaff becomes less attractive than the earlier Falstaff. Is not the real point this: that in Hal's rejection of Falstaff something is lost as well as gained—that a good king, one grants, must reject Falstaff, but that in the process by which a man becomes a good king, something else—something spontaneous, something in itself good and attractive—must be sacrificed; that growing up is something which man must do and yet that even in growing up he loses, necessarily, something that is valuable?

Shakespeare does not sentimentalize the situation. The rejection is necessary if Hal is to become the king that he ought to be and that England doubtless needs; and yet Falstaff's dashed hopes are presented with due pathos. The sentimentalist will doubtless need to blacken Falstaff's character a little—suppress his sympathy for him—in order to be able to accept his being turned off; or, if he is unable to do this, he will, in order to justify Falstaff's rejection, doubtless have to blacken the prince's character, reading into it more of the "vile politician Bolingbroke" than Shakespeare ever intended. The stern moralist (and he is nearer allied to the sentimentalist than is usually suspected) will do much the same: he will probably applaud the rejection of Falstaff whole-heartedly, or, just possibly and perversely, he will condemn the prince for his acceptance of pomp and power and for his cold heart.

Neither the sentimentalist nor the moralist, then, will be able to accept the play in its fullness. It is possible, of course, that even for the mature reader, the play finally lacks unity—that the balancing of attitudes which has been argued for in this analysis is something which perhaps Shakespeare should have attempted to accomplish but did not, for one reason or another, actually succeed in accomplishing. This, of course, each reader must decide for himself. For the reader who remains unconvinced of any totality of effect, the play will probably remain a collection of brilliant but ill-assorted fragments—the wonderful tavern scenes juxtaposed oddly with passages of dull and pawky history.

For the reader, however, for whom the play does achieve a significant unity it may well seem that here Shakespeare has given us one of the wisest and fullest commentaries on human action possible to the comic mode—a view which scants nothing, which covers up nothing, and which takes into account in making its affirmations the most searching criticism of that which is affirmed. For such a reader, Shakespeare has no easy moral to draw, no simple generalization to make.

Shakespeare's Irony. Moreover, it will be evident that Shakespeare's final attitude toward his characters (and toward the human predicament, generally) is one of a very complex irony, though it is an irony which will be either missed altogether, or easily misinterpreted as an indifferent relativism—that is, a mere balancing of two realms of conduct and a refusal to make any judgment between them. The world which Shakespeare portrays here is a world of contradictions and of mixtures of good and evil. His vision of that world is ultimately a comic vision—if not gaily comic, and surely not bitterly comic, yet informed with the insights of mature comedy, nonetheless. For the comic writer does not attempt to transcend the world of compromises, even though the more thoughtful writer of comedy, as here, may be fully aware of the seriousness of the issues. Comedy, after all, does not treat the lives of saints or heroes: it does not attempt to portray the absolute commitment to ultimate issues—the total commitment which transcends, tragically and heroically, the everyday world that we know. Shakespeare does not present Prince Hal (as he might conceivably do in a tragic treatment) as a callous man, the scion of the "vile politician Bolingbroke." Hal will make a good ruler, and Falstaff would undoubtedly make a very bad ruler. Nor, on the other hand, is Falstaff portrayed as a villain: Falstaff, too, has his case. Falstaff's wit—most of it at least—is not merely amusing, trifling. It constitutes a criticism of the world of serious affairs, a criticism which, on certain levels, is thoroughly valid. The rulers of the world had better not leave it totally out of account.

If the prince must choose between two courses of action—and, of course, he must choose—we as readers are not forced to choose: indeed, perhaps the core of Shakespeare's ironic insight comes to this: that man must choose and yet that the choice can never be a wholly satisfactory one. If the play is a comedy in this sense, then the "comic" scenes of the play turn out to be only an aspect of, though an important aspect of, the larger comedy. To repeat, the reader must decide for himself whether he can accept the play as a fully unified organism. But the reader who can so accept it may well feel that it represents Shakespeare's most sophisticated level of comedy, a comedy, indeed, more fine-grained and "serious" than the romantic comedies such as *As You Like It* and written with a surer touch than the "bitter" comedies such as *All's Well That Ends Well.*

M. M. REESE

Father and Son

Of Hal's three tempters (Falstaff, Hotspur, and Hal's father), Henry IV perhaps comes nearest to success. Despite the family reconciliation at the end of the play, Henry equally with Falstaff and Hotspur offers an idea of political behavior that is at odds with Shakespeare's conception of majesty. We already know something of his hopeless situation. As the author of a violent present he was condemned to be the victim of a violent present, bound with the rebels in an endless chain of circumstance. He could not rule as the strong, pacific king that he had hoped to be, and his plan for a crusade, through which he might expiate his sin, would never be more than an ironically distant mirage. His daily problem was simply to find a means of keeping by force what force had won him.

Long before the end the proud and confident Bolingbroke has shrunk into a sleepless neurotic helplessly revolving the theme of "if only we had known." But this was a weakness that he revealed only to his family and the few counselors he could trust. The public Henry is never unimpressive, and Shakespeare lets us feel that here

Reprinted from *The Cease of Majesty* (1961), pp. 312–317, by permission of St. Martin's Press, Inc., and Edward Arnold Ltd.

is a shrewd, courageous man doing his best in conditions in which, through his own original fault, success was impossible. Unlike King John, he does not require the presence of foreigners to rouse him to kingly gestures. In business he is swift and efficient, and he addresses all rebels in terms that would be impeccable if only he and they could forget that he was once a rebel himself. But they never could forget, and in consequence Henry never possesses the authority for the proper exercise of royal power. He is reduced to shifts. His is a threadbare, makeshift majesty, and his idea of statesmanship aims no higher than the devious manipulation of opposing forces. He is a sort of poor man's Machiavelli, using the gifts and dedicated purpose of political man simply to keep himself in power.

Nothing is more typical of his limited understanding than his failure to perceive his son's true nature. He does not understand Falstaff or Hotspur either, for he is a man who judges by appearances. This, as he now realizes, had been his mistake before he took the throne, when he misjudged the Percies and perhaps misjudged Richard too. But he has not learned wisdom from his failure, and at their first meeting in the play he treats Hal to an extended lecture on the importance of wearing the right sort of public face.

> Had I so lavish of my presence been,
> So common-hackney'd in the eyes of men,
> So stale and cheap to vulgar company,
> Opinion, that did help me to the crown,
> Had still kept loyal to possession
> And left me in reputeless banishment,
> A fellow of no mark nor likelihood.
>
> (III, ii, 39–45)

This is from the man who sufficiently understood the vulgar arts to woo poor craftsmen with the craft of smiles,[1] but his point is clear. The statesman's public behavior should always be suited to the occasion and should avoid familiarity unless the circumstances particularly require it. He goes on to tell the Prince how he won the throne, by an affectation of courtesy and humility that kept his person ever "fresh and new." This he contrasts with the alleged behaviour of Richard, who

[1] *Richard II,* I, iv, 24–36.

Mingled his royalty with capering fools . . .
Grew a companion to the common streets,
Enfeoff'd himself to popularity . . .
So, when he had occasion to be seen,
He was but as the cuckoo is in June,
Heard, not regarded; seen, but with such eyes
As, sick and blunted with community,
Afford no extraordinary gaze
Such as is bent on sun-like majesty
When it shines seldom in admiring eyes.
(III, ii, 63–80)

This, it will be noticed, is purely technical advice, without roots in character or feeling. Henry is admitting his son into the tricky secret of how he formerly drew attention to himself by a policy of deliberate effacement. It has nothing to do with royalty as Hal is coming to understand it, and he makes no comment whatever upon these seamy disclosures. In fact his reply is a definite rebuke:

I shall hereafter, my thrice gracious lord,
Be more myself. (III, ii, 92–93)

Shortly before he dies Henry begs Clarence to use his personal influence with Hal and to encourage those good qualities in him that may restrain his passions. But Henry is by this time too defenseless and disillusioned to have any sanguine hopes about the future, and he continues to torment himself by imagining "the unguided days and rotten times" that will come after him. These anxieties seem to be confirmed when he finds the Prince prematurely wearing the crown, and he falls again into the prolonged and nagging self-pity that would have justified any of his sons in keeping out of his way.

Pluck down my officers, break my decrees;
For now a time is come to mock at form.
Harry the Fifth is crown'd! Up, vanity!
Down, royal state! all you sage counsellors, hence!
And to the English court assemble now,
From every region, apes of idleness!
(Part II, IV, v, 116–121)

He forgets, apparently, the continuous disorder that his own reign has been, and on and on he goes, declaring that Harry will pluck from "curb'd licence" the "muzzle of restraint" until, with appetite roaming unrebuked, the country will again be peopled by its old inhabitants, the wolves.

This is Henry in his accustomed vein, and the significant passage in the scene occurs when he has swiftly and without question accepted the Prince's explanation of his putting on the crown. Persuaded at last that Hal does not intend to waste the crown in dissipation, he gathers his strength to utter "the very latest counsel that ever I shall breathe": the final witness of a king. It turns out to be typical Lancastrian stuff, confounding statesmanship with trickery and proposing to the heir the trumpery devices of a street-corner Machiavelli.

> God knows, my son,
> By what by-paths and indirect crook'd ways
> I met this crown. (IV, v, 182–184)

This is oddly at variance with what Henry has just been saying to Warwick, to the effect that necessity so bowed the state that he and greatness were compelled to kiss (III, i, 73–74), and there is no reason why he should have lied to Warwick, who was the most loyal of his servants. It could be that in the final grip of sickness he had come to accept the least creditable interpretation of his own actions; a diseased mind does make that sort of submission. On the other hand, this is just the kind of inconsistency that Shakespeare often commits for the sake of the immediate effect. He is concerned at the moment with Henry the Machiavellian, who goes on to tell his son by what ambiguous ways he sought to keep the crown thus indirectly got. Hal's throne will be a little more secure, since he comes in the line of inheritance, but recent memories are still fresh and he will not be able to count on anyone. Henry explains how he had tried to divert the enmity of the intriguers who helped him to the throne.

> All my friends, which thou must make thy friends,
> Have but their stings and teeth newly ta'en out;
> By whose fell working I was first advanc'd,
> And by whose power I might well lodge a fear

To be again displac'd: which to avoid,
I cut them off; and had a purpose now
To lead out many to the Holy Land,
Lest rest and lying still might make them look
Too near unto my state. (IV, v, 203–208)

So much for the pretended crusade: it was just a trick to turn the more dangerous of his former friends from inquiring too closely into his own title. Since these men are only tamed and not subdued, he recommends the same technique to Hal:

Therefore, my Harry,
Be it thy course to busy giddy minds
With foreign quarrels; that action, hence borne out,
May waste the memory of the former days.
(IV, v, 208–211)

The Prince is thus advised to seek an excuse for campaigns overseas as a means of preventing civil war at home, but once again he avoids direct comment on these proposals. To Henry's final prayer that he may be permitted to keep this dubious crown in peace, he simply answers,

My gracious liege,
You won it, wore it, kept it, gave it me;
Then plain and right must my possession be:
Which I with more than with a common pain
'Gainst all the world will rightfully maintain.
(IV, v, 219–223)

These pantomime couplets announce the indefeasible right of possession, a commonplace upon which even King John was able to insist. It is in the circumstances the only conceivable answer, a public and formal acceptance of responsibility. What is significant is that Hal refuses complicity in his father's idea of statecraft.

Hal is moving in the youthful gravity with which he lays the heavy burden on his head (IV, v, 20–46); and even if his previous uncertain relationship with his father makes him protest too much when he explains his action (141–75), he leaves no doubt of the spirit of dedication in which he admits the due of "tears and heavy sorrows of the blood." Joy and vainglorious pride are altogether absent as he receives the crown as an enemy whose cares have killed his father. He takes it as a trust too sacred to be soiled by the politic advice to which he has just been compelled to listen, and his submission to the Lord Chief Justice, in which he formally recants the wildness of his youth, has deeper significance as a repudiation of his father's devious ways:[2]

> There is my hand:
> You shall be as a father to my youth;
> My voice shall sound as you do prompt mine ear,
> And I will stoop and humble mine intents
> To your well-practis'd wise directions.
> And, princes all, believe me, I beseech you;
> My father is gone wild into his grave,
> For in his tomb lie my affections;
> And with his spirit sadly I survive,
> To mock the expectation of the world,
> To frustrate prophecies, and to raze out
> Rotten opinion, who hath writ me down
> After my seeming. The tide of blood in me
> Hath proudly flow'd in vanity till now:
> Now doth it turn and ebb back to the sea,
> Where it shall mingle with the state of floods
> And flows henceforth in formal majesty.
>
> (V, ii, 117–133)

Hal has accepted the principles of justice and the rule of law, and as the bearer of a title in which there was no personal dishonour he would be able to rise above the shifts of "policy." It is his final test and his greatest victory. Neither Falstaff's fleshly seductions nor Hotspur's envious emulation have attached him in quite the same way as the claims of kinship and office exerted by his father, and it would have been easy for an inexperienced youth to confuse craftiness with statesmanship and accept Henry's separation between the private and public faces of a ruler. Hal recognizes this attitude to be false, but without absolutely denying Commodity's place in the conduct of society: there are times when the

[2] It is significant that Hal is not implicated in the treachery committed in Gaultree Forest (IV, ii). It is evidently Prince John who inherits the parental notions of statecraft.

most honest of rulers has to dissemble and times when he must be more ruthless than a private citizen need ever be.

Hal will be a good king because events have schooled him in knowledge and responsibility. He realizes what the "polish'd perturbation, golden care" will mean in the denial of human instinct and the acceptance of loneliness and impersonality. Youth's warm impulses must be steeled into disciplined courage and dedicated to honourable ends. He will have to judge all causes with a "bold, just, and impartial spirit" that despises the short cuts which authority always knows how to find. It is required of him also that he shall know his people in all their strength and weakness, so that he and they may live together in the harmonious relationship that is the supreme condition of majesty. Hal understands all this; and with understanding he has the drive to success—there is no harm in calling it ambition—without which all these other qualities are only ornaments.

RAYMOND H. RENO

Hotspur: The Integration of Character and Theme

In reaction to the "psychologizing" of Shakespeare's characters in the nineteenth century, a number of contemporary critics tend to see the problem of character in Shakespeare largely in terms of the relation of character to theme. L. C. Knights, for example, indicates that the most profitable way to examine a Shakespeare character is to see him as embodying certain attitudes or values which the play as a whole explores.[1] While there is much to recommend an approach which insists on the role of character within the total design of the work, the method Knights urges has one notable drawback: it has much to say about theme but little about charac-

From *Renaissance Papers, 1962,* pp. 17–25. Reprinted by permission of the author and the editor of *Renaissance Papers.*

[1] "The Question of Character in Shakespeare," in *More Talking of Shakespeare,* ed, John Garrett (London, 1959), pp. 55–69.

ter. It works best where character is relatively simple, as in the comedies, but it is quite inadequate for the examination of complex figures like Angelo, Hamlet, or Othello, figures which clearly require some sort of psychological analysis. At the same time, psychological analysis is inadequate to the consideration of general design, that "organization of parts with relation to an idea"[2] which seems accessible only to thematic criticism. The problem, therefore, is to relate Shakespeare's complex characters to the total design of the works in which they figure without pursuing irrelevancies of the kind Knights parodies in the title of his famous essay, "How Many Children Had Lady Macbeth?" and yet without reducing the characters to merely allegorical representations of theme. Here it seems to me we might profitably employ the principle inherent in Coleridge's dictum that in a work of art "the many, *still seen as many,* become one"—the principle that form ("the total structural integration of the work itself"[3]) does not violate the individual integrity of the parts that are made to coalesce under the pressure of a dominant idea. Adapted to the problem of the complex character, this principle suggests that such a character relates to theme not by representing it, as in allegory, but by embodying it so as to articulate it through the unique psychological pattern of the character himself. The complex character, in other words, is an imitation of theme on the level of psychology.

To take Hotspur as an illustration of this kind of imitation of theme in *1 Henry IV*, we may observe that he reflects the play's major theme of disorder in that he is himself a figure of disorder whose every word and action proclaim what Worcester charges him with following his quarrel with Glendower: "want of government" (III, i, 182). "Mad" and "drunk with choler" (I, iii, 138, 129), he is a "harebrained Hotspur, governed by a spleen" (V, ii, 19) and ruled by "humors" (III, i, 232). Two scenes in particular define the nature of this disorder. In the first of these (I, iii), his pride injured by the King's peremptory command that he deliver up his prisoners, he loses self-control to the extent of having to be restrained from bolting after Henry to roar defiance in the royal ears, and throughout the rest of the scene displays himself as a "wasp-

[2] Hereward T. Price, *Construction in Shakespeare,* University of Michigan Contributions in Modern Philology, No. 17 (May 1951), p. 16.

[3] Karl Beckson and Arthur Ganz, *A Reader's Guide to Literary Terms* (New York, 1960), p. 64.

stung and impatient fool," breaking into a "woman's mood," and tying his ear to no tongue but his own. Indeed, his language itself reflects his disorders as it churns into the mere chaos of

> In Richard's time—what do you call the place—?
> A plague upon it, it is in Gloucestershire,
> 'Twas where the madcap Duke his uncle kept,
> His uncle York, where I first bowed my knee,
> Unto this king of smiles, this Bolingbroke—
> When you and he came back from Ravensburgh.
> (241–246)

The passage that most clearly defines the nature of his disorder, however, is the cry he utters in plunging after the King: "I will ease my heart,/Albeit I make a hazard of my head" (127–128). Quite clearly, within Hotspur rages a psychomachia, a rebellion of the heart against the head which threatens to bring the whole of his single state of man to ruin.

The second scene I wish to examine is that moment before Shrewsbury (IV, i) when the rebels receive the news that because of illness, Northumberland, Hotspur's father, will not be able to join them. The thematic movement here involves the association of a personal disorder with a general condition and the extension of that disorder into an organism larger than the merely human. Northumberland's illness is related to the state of the times, which are not "whole" or in health, and seen as spreading throughout the entire rebel army. An "inward sickness," as Hotspur calls it, it attacks "the very lifeblood of [the] enterprise" and thus courses throughout the rebel body until it infects even the extremities, those allies whom Northumberland cannot now draw by "deputation." His loss is, then, a "perilous gash, a very limb lopped off."

In this context occurs a discussion which again introduces the theme of disorder in terms of an inversion of the faculties. Worcester sees Northumberland's withdrawal as likely to cast a doubt on the rebel cause in that people may think that Northumberland was motivated by "wisdom, loyalty, and mere dislike" of the rebels' proceedings. This will, he argues, "breed a kind of question in our cause" and allow "the eye of reason" to pry in upon them. But their cause, he reminds the others, cannot abide "strict arbitrament." Reason, in other words, threatens to ruin them.

Nothing could make it more clear how little their cause can abide the eye of reason than Hotspur's counter-argument that Northumberland's absence, far from being a loss, is an enormous gain. It will "lend a luster and more great opinion" to the enterprise, for men will think that if the rebels, without Northumberland, dare stand against the King, then with him they "shall o'erturn" the state "topsy-turvy down." Therefore, Hotspur concludes, "all our joints are whole." To which Douglas, mirroring Hotspur's very mode of thought, responds enthusiastically: "As *heart* can *think*." The source of Hotspur's logic, in other words, is not the head but the heart; and the psychomachia noted earlier has progressed to the point where the lower faculty, no longer merely a threat to the higher faculty, has usurped the higher faculty's office and function. When we note that Hotspur is attempting to usurp the sphere occupied by the Prince of Wales, we observe once more the extension of a personal disorder into a body politic.

Yet, the engagement of Hotspur's character with the play's major theme is more intricate and meaningful than my comments so far have indicated. To approach this more complex relationship, I would like to draw into a pattern a number of aspects of his character suggested at various points in the play.

Following his outbreak against the King in I, iii, Hotspur learns, apparently for the first time, that Richard II had proclaimed Edmund Mortimer, Hotspur's brother-in-law, heir to the throne. This information prompts Hotspur to show his uncle and father "the line and the predicament" wherein they "range under this subtle King" and to urge them to "redeem" their "banished honors." Worcester interrupts to speak of the plot he and Northumberland have already conceived, but his reference to it as a "secret book" containing "matter deep and dangerous" evokes from Hotspur an outbreak proclaiming his eagerness to let honor "grapple" with danger. On this, Northumberland comments acutely: "Imagination of some great exploit/Drives him beyond the bounds of patience." Ignoring his father, Hotspur pursues the theme of honor:

> By Heaven, methinks it were an easy leap,
> To pluck bright honor from the pale-faced moon,
> Or dive into the bottom of the deep,
> Where fathom line could never touch the ground,
> And pluck up drowned honor by the locks,

> So he that doth redeem her thence might wear
> Without corrival all her dignities. (201–207)

The passage confirms Northumberland's diagnosis as it reveals a Hotspur carried by fancy beyond the spheres proper to human life and into areas symbolic of disorder. But the passage also suggests imagination in a sense other than fancy, a sense Worcester indicates in a comment as perceptive as Northumberland's: Hotspur, he wryly observes, "apprehends a world of figures here,/But not the form of what he should attend." Thus Worcester defines Northumberland's term "imagination" with respect to "figures" or "images."

At this point the pattern I referred to earlier begins to emerge. To see Hotspur as driven beyond the bounds by his apprehension of a world of images is to understand, I believe, precisely what "honor" means for him. It means image—nothing more nor less than what Falstaff calls it in his famous catechism on honor at Shrewsbury (V, i, 129–139): a "scutcheon," an image painted for men to see. In a word, reputation. And so Hotspur himself, albeit unknowingly, defines it as he calls on his father and uncle to revenge themselves on the King:

> Shall it for shame be spoken in these days
> Or fill up chronicles in time to come,
> That men of your nobility and power
> Did gage them both in an unjust behalf . . . ?
> (I, iii, 170–173)

"Redeem/Your banished honors," he urges them, "and restore yourselves into the good thoughts of the world again" (180–182). Practical men, raising a "head" to save their heads (281), Northumberland and Worcester have little interest in reputation. But for Hotspur it is an obsession, and he sees it in terms of something he would *wear*, as though it were a badge or "scrutcheon" to set him off in the eyes of others. Thus before his encounter with Hal at Shrewsbury, he regrets that Hal's "name in arms" (which is, of course, the technical meaning of scutcheon) is slight as it is, so trivial a prize for him to gain.

Hotspur's passion for honor amounting, then, to the apprehension of a world of knightly images, his obsession finds its major concretion in the image he would project of himself as the very embodiment of chivalry: the knight on horseback. "Come, wilt thou see me ride?" he asks his wife (II, iii, 94), a question which in a sense he puts to all the world. "That roan," he tells her in the same scene, "shall be my throne"; and when she asks, "What is it carries you away?"—beyond, that is, the bounds—his answer is "Why, my horse, my love, my horse" (70–71).

As honor, therefore, dissolves into reputation and then into image and the figure of the horseman, the shape of Hotspur's character gradually emerges from the splendid rhetoric that hides it. It stands quite nakedly revealed when he suddenly discovers a threat to his image of himself as the icon of chivalry. On the eve of Shrewsbury, after learning that the King's armies are on the march, he scornfully asks of Hal: And what of Bolingbroke's son,

> The nimble-footed madcap Prince of Wales,
> And his comrades, that daffed the world aside
> And bid it pass? (IV, i, 95–97)

What he hears in reply is incredible, a shock to that world of figures he has constructed and in which he wears, without corrival, all the dignities of honor. "I saw young Harry," Vernon answers,

> with his beaver on,
> His cuisses on his thighs, gallantly armed,
> Rise from the ground like feathered Mercury,
> And vaulted with such ease into his seat
> As if an angel dropped down from the clouds
> To turn and wind a fiery Pegasus,
> And witch the world with noble horsemanship.
> (104–110)

"No more, no more," Hotspur protests, "Worse than the sun in March/This praise doth nourish agues" (111–112).

If Hotspur were not a figure of disorder ruled by spleen and passion, he could never allow himself to reveal what this cry of anguish makes clear: the essential emptiness within him. For what this protest makes evident is his recognition of Hal's claim to the throne he has always regarded as rightfully his, the throne Douglas had in mind a few moments earlier when he called Hotspur the "king of honor." The throne at stake is, of course, the horse, with all its associations with knighthood and Hotspur's image of himself as the embodiment of chivalry. In this context we recall his earlier declaration that "that roan shall be my throne" (II, iii, 65).

Thus the most profound wrench to Hotspur's self-esteem derives from the fact that in his eyes Hal has already usurped that throne. Hotspur's conception of honor, we have observed, is based on his image in the eyes of other men. Now Hal has become, at least in the eyes of Vernon, the observed of all observers, and in effect, then, has already fulfilled the promise he made to his father "to make this Northern youth exchange/His glorious deeds for my indignities" and "render every glory up—/Yea, even the slightest worship of his time" (III, ii, 145–146, 150–151). Worship, honor, reputation, his image in the eyes of other men—these Hotspur in his own mind has already lost to Hal. From this point forward, Hotspur sees the battle of Shrewsbury as a personal conflict between himself and Hal, for now he must redeem his lost honor.

The pain evident in Hotspur's response to Vernon's glowing description of Hal springs, then, from a sense of outraged justice. This man who has usurped his image is the man Hotspur formerly contemned as a "sword-and-buckler Prince of Wales" deserving only to be "poisoned with a pot of ale." What cries out in Hotspur is, I suggest, the sense of violent outrage a man experiences who has paid the price of winning but who has not won, who sees the prize go to another who has not paid the price. It is the outcry of the athlete who has put himself through a spartan discipline only to see the race won by a playboy who has trained in bars and taverns and nightclubs. It is, finally, the agony of the man who has come to learn that he who labors is not always rewarded and that often the rewards go to the merely lucky, the man who has been given the natural talent and the grace without having to earn them. Hotspur has sold himself to his world of values, the world of chivalry. That world Hal, the truant to chivalry, has daffed aside and bid pass; but now it turns to him anyway, prostituting itself and offering those riches Hotspur has so desperately coveted.

But Hotspur's cry suggests more than outrage; it suggests envy, which in turn suggests a powerful, although suppressed, conviction of his own inadequacy. If so—and the pattern is once again that of a man obsessed with his own image—then what we observe at the very center of Hotspur is merely a terrible emptiness. Honor, therefore, becomes finally a mask; behind it, nothing.

In Hotspur as a man without a center informed by a mere negativity, we have his final integration with the major theme of the play. The state in *1 Henry IV* is likewise without a center. Bolingbroke is a man without substance, a chameleon politician. Like Hotspur, he too is obsessed with reputation and lectures Hal at length on that theme. He is further like Hotspur in that he too affects image: he is one who stole courtesy from heaven, dressed himself in humility, and won the crown by keeping his person fresh and new, his presence like a robe pontifical and his state seldom but sumptuous. While Richard lost his power by projecting his image as a "skipping King," Bolingbroke plucked allegiance from men's hearts by affecting an image or mask of "solemnity" (III, ii, 39–60). The political world of *1 Henry IV* is altogether a world of appearance and image and mask, where the garment of the rebellion is faced with some fine color that may please the eye (V, iv, 74–75), where the poor abuses of the time seek "countenance" (I, ii, 134–135) but where the King hath many marching in his coats (V, iii, 25), and where, as Falstaff says, to counterfeit is to be "the true and perfect image of life indeed" (V, iv, 114–117)—of life, that is, in this latter age, these "days of villainy" (III, iii, 148).

Without a center, this world is subject to mere anarchy in the shape of appetite. To extend Gadshill's words in the innyard scene, men "Pray continually to their saint, the commonwealth; or rather, not pray to her, but prey on her, for they ride up and down on her, and make her their boots" (II, i, 70–73). You may buy land now as cheap as stinking mackerel, and indeed you may also buy a commodity of good names. The whole household of the kingdom, to draw from the innyard scene once more, "is turned upside down since Robin Ostler died" (II, i, 9–10), since, that is, the deposition and assassination of Richard II. Degree has been broken and now everything includes itself in power,

> Power into will, will into appetite,
> And appetite, a universal wolf,
> So doubly seconded with will and power,
> Must make perforce a universal prey.
> (*Troilus and Cressida*, I, iii, 119–123)

Without substance and center, degree broken within him, Hosspur, like the state, is also ravaged by appetite. In this respect he stands in an analogical relationship to Falstaff; both are instances of that appetite which the breaking of degree has unleashed. In terms of appetite the play brings the two men together by the lines which conclude Hal's interview with his father (III, ii) and which open the immediately following scene. Encouraged by Hal's promise to reform (to don, we might note, "a garment of blood" and to cover his face with a "bloody mask"), the King closes the interview by urging haste, for "Advantage feeds him fat while men delay." The reference here is to the rebels, and, of course, to Hotspur. As though on cue, Falstaff, the incarnation of appetite, enters in the following scene and alludes to himself in words which amount to an echo of the King's: "Bardolph, am I not fallen away vilely since this last action? Do I not bate? Do I not dwindle?" That he hasn't bated is perfectly clear, but Bardolph's remark a moment or so later establishes the connection: "Why, you are so fat, Sir John, that you must needs be out of all order, out of all reasonable compass." On the Elizabethan stage, the negligible interval between the scenes would have effected a montage of Falstaff upon the not yet faded image of the rebels in the King's closing line and thus have brought Falstaff and the rebels together as creatures of appetite and disorder.

The analogy continues most meaningfully when we note that both Falstaff and Hotspur see the war as an opportunity for satisfying their appetites. Falstaff pursues profit, of course, fattening himself by abusing the King's press damnably. "Tut, never fear me," he tells Hal on the road to Shrewsbury. "I am as vigilant as a cat to steal cream" (IV, ii, 51–52). Hal agrees: "I think to steal cream indeed, for thy theft hath already made thee butter" (53–54). For Sir John, the war is not a "fray" but a "feast," and he sees his soldiers, therefore, as food—sacrifices to his appetite (as well, of course, as to the appetites of hungry politicians): "Tut, tut, good enough to toss; food for powder, food for powder" (58–59).

Hotspur likewise sees the King's soldiers as sacrifices, but to his appetite for glory, and to his rage to redeem his honor and image. "Let them come," he exclaims following his protest against Vernon's description of Hal:

> They come like sacrifices in their trim,
> And to the fire-eyed maid of smoky war
> All hot and bleeding shall we offer them.
> The mailed Mars shall on his altar sit
> Up to the ears in blood. (IV, i, 112–117)

They are to be sacrificed to an idol, mailed Mars on his altar: in other words, to Hotspur's image of himself as the embodiment of chivalry, the armed knight on horseback. That it is his obsession with his image which prompts this outbreak is clear from the fact that it follows Vernon's description of Hal and his comrades as "glittering in golden coats, like *images*" (IV, i, 100) and particularly, of course, the image Vernon has drawn of young Harry, gallantly armed, witching the world with noble horsemanship. It is, then, to his appetite for reputation and his desperate hunger to redeem his honor and his image that Hotspur would sacrifice "all hot and bleeding" the entire kingdom: "And appetite, a universal wolf . . . Must make perforce a universal prey."

In the final analysis, the integration of Hotspur with the theme of disorder in *1 Henry IV* derives from the fact that without a substantial center, informed by the merely negative—his empty envy and suppressed conviction of inadequacy—and with the hierarchy of his faculties deranged, he, like the kingdom, is ravaged by appetite and driven headlong to ruin. But we must also observe that as a leader, and indeed as the chief fomenter of the rebellion, he is a major source of the disorder bringing "pell-mell havoc and confusion" (V, i, 82) to the kingdom. Thus the disorder in the little world of man reaches out to rend and deracinate the larger world of the state. In this way, character and theme engage in a relationship of the greatest complexity and power; for theme becomes, then, not simply an analogy of character, but its projection into the entire structure of the play.

JOHN MASEFIELD

Hal—the Unheroic Hero

Prince Henry, afterwards Henry V, has been famous for many years as "Shakespeare's only hero." Shakespeare was too wise to count any man a hero. The ways of fate moved him to vision, not heroism. If we can be sure of anything in that great, simple, gentle, elusive brain, we can be sure that it was quickened by the thought of the sun shining on the just and on the unjust, and shining none the less golden though the soul like clay triumph over the soul like flame. Prince Henry is not a hero, he is not a thinker, he is not even a friend; he is a common man whose incapacity for feeling enables him to change his habits whenever interest bids him. Throughout the first acts he is careless and callous though he is breaking his father's heart and endangering his father's throne. He chooses to live in society as common as himself. He talks continually of guts as though a belly were a kind of wit. Even in the society of his choice his attitude is remote and cold-blooded. There is no good-fellowship in him, no sincerity, no whole-heartedness. He makes a mock of the drawer who gives him his whole little pennyworth of sugar. His jokes upon Falstaff are so little good-natured that he stands upon his princehood whenever the old man would retort upon him. He impresses one as quite common, quite selfish, quite without feeling. When he learns that his behaviour may have lost him his prospective crown he passes a sponge over his past, and fights like a wild cat for the right of not having to work for a living.

Reprinted from *William Shakespeare* (New York, 1911), pp. 111–113. Title supplied by Ed.

WILLIAM B. HUNTER, JR.

Prince Hal, His Struggle Toward Moral Perfection

Aside from Hamlet, I doubt whether another character in English literature has been the object of greater discussion than the fat knight, that reverend vice Sir John Falstaff. Somewhat like the melancholy Dane, he has been all things to all men. Sentimentalists see him as basically a good fellow, rejected at the end of the

From *South Atlantic Quarterly,* L (January 1951), 86–95. Reprinted by permission of the author and Duke University Press. Originally entitled "Falstaff," the essay has been retitled by the author for its appearance here.

Henry IV plays by the prudish new King Henry V and finally killed by this blow. Perhaps they are led astray by admiration for the tremendous humor of the man, a quality which by and large they do not possess. One must remember that the frequently repeated testimony as to the cause of his death—"The King has killed his heart"—is spoken by Mistress Quickly, a most inaccurate reporter, as witness her lines in the same scene on Sir John's "burning quotidian tertian"—a fever never experienced in this world even in the fanciful catalogues of diseases which the Renaissance has bequeathed us. A broken heart is doubtful in that old ruffian's case; the final results of overindulgence are more plausible.

Recent critics are, by and large, more sensible in their discussions of this "tun of man." They have been at pains to point out that he derives from a whole family tree of rascals: the court jester, the braggart soldier, the character of Vice in the earlier morality plays. John Dover Wilson, one of the most stimulating and daring of modern judges, has put forward this view, which seems eminently sensible. But the estimate of Falstaff is not one which can be reckoned apart from those of the other characters. If he is really an old scalawag with a heart of gold beating some feet beneath his rough hide, the Prince becomes, in Professor Bradley's words, a man ready "to use other people as a means to his own ends"—a heartless prig. His transformation to Shakespeare's picture of him later as the ideal king, Henry V, is as great as that visited upon St. Paul and an improbable transformation upon the stage even between plays. On the other hand, if Falstaff is really evil, there is the opportunity for the moral rehabilitation of Prince Hal which Shakespeare seems to have intended; a truly good man would have, perforce, to shun Sir John. Shakespeare himself has clearly defamed the fat rascal in Part II. To take but one instance: the impressment scene, only briefly described in Part I, is given in realistic detail in the sequel. The groundlings, subject themselves at times to just such a recruiting sergeant, would not have looked upon Falstaff thereafter with any real affection.

Professor Wilson has given an able exposition of such points as these. But he has mostly left out of account the fact that in the first play there is a third participant in this mighty drama: Henry Percy, the Hotspur of the North. Many people have contrasted Hotspur with Prince Hal to the latter's detriment; as many have compared the Prince with Falstaff; but only a few critics have considered all three together and hence have tried to present the whole of their drama instead of only part of it. A complete theory must account for all three in the First Part; for Falstaff, Hal, and the Chief Justice in the Second Part; and for a consistent development of Hal's character into that of Henry V in the final play of the group.

A clue in Part I lies in certain clear contrasts between Hotspur and Falstaff which must have been deliberate. Both speak of honor, though they have, of course, two very different ideas on the subject. The speeches are about equally well known. First, Hotspur asserts in almost extravagant terms the nobility of personal honor —a subject which links him with medieval chivalry:

> By heaven, methinks it were an easy leap
> To pluck bright honour from the pale-fac'd moon,
> Or dive into the bottom of the deep,
> Where fadom line could never touch the ground,
> And pluck up drowned honour by the locks.

Falstaff takes the exactly opposite position. Before he enters the Battle of Shrewsbury he rejects honor as a personal ideal. Why should he seek death, he asks:

> Well, 'tis no matter; honour pricks me on. Yea, but how if honour prick me off when I come on? How then? Can honour set to a leg? No. Or an arm? No. Or take away the grief of a wound? No. Honour hath no skill in surgery then? No. What is honour? A word. What is that word honour? Air. A trim reckoning! Who hath it? He that died a Wednesday. Doth he feel it? No. Doth he hear it? No. 'Tis insensible then? Yea, to the dead. But will it not live with the living? No. Why? Detraction will not suffer it. Therefore I'll none of it. Honour is a mere scutcheon.

Later, standing over the body of Sir Walter Blunt, he reiterates the same point of view.

Now surely, since Falstaff's speeches are soliloquies, we may look upon them as genuine utterances from character, as are all of Shakespeare's mature soliloquies. These who sympathize with Honest Jack either fail to note the real meaning of the lines or interpret them as mere clever exhibitionism. But why should they not be taken at face value? If so taken, we must condemn their speaker unless we disagree with the Elizabethans upon the value of a personal code of honor. Falstaff is clearly deficient in this prime attribute.

More difficult to see is that Hotspur's honor is not the ideal goal either. Hotspur, like Mercutio, is one of Shakespeare's most attractive creations. Everyone regrets his early passing. In this admiration we tend to forget that his honor in the long run destroys him; more important, that it leads him into situations where he shows up badly. At his very first appearance he insists because of his honor on keeping prisoners whom, the play implies, the King can rightly demand. Later in the same scene he even angers his father and uncle by a similar hotheaded insistence. As Worcester says of him:

> He apprehends a world of figures here,
> But not the form of what he should attend.

In Act III he very nearly breaks up the conspiracy by insulting Glendower and demanding his rights to the last tithe. His father, Northumberland, calls him "a wasp-stung and impatient fool" to "break into this woman's mood," and Worcester again corrects him to his face:

> In faith, my lord, you are too wilful-blame,
> And since your coming hither have done enough
> To put him [Glendower] quite besides his patience.
> You must needs learn, lord, to amend this fault.
> Though sometimes it show greatness, courage, blood—
> And that's the dearest grace it renders you—
> Yet oftentimes it doth present harsh rage,
> Defect of manners, want of government,
> Pride, haughtiness, opinion, and disdain;
> The least of which haunting a nobleman
> Loseth men's hearts, and leaves behind a stain.

The noble Hotspur has an excess, which occasionally leads him astray and which does not serve him in the long run. Falstaff possesses a deficiency in the same virtue.

The presence of both the excess and the deficiency of a virtue naturally suggests Aristotle's comprehensive theory of ethics. In this book, which he addressed according to tradition to his son Nicomachus, Aristotle presents his famous theory that virtuous action or good action exists as a mean between two extremes both of which are vicious. Virtue, he says, to quote from the translation of W.D. Ross, "must have the quality of aiming at the intermediate." More particularly, "it is a mean between two vices, that which depends on excess and that which depends on defect; and again it is a mean because the vices respectively fall short of or exceed what is right in both passions and actions." For one example, he holds that "it is possible to desire honour as one ought, and more than one ought, and less." As to the mean of honor, he writes in a later chapter that it must be recognized, though unnamed; "now men desire honour both more than they should and less; therefore it is possible also to do so as one should; at all events this is the state of character that is praised, being an unnamed mean in respect of honour. Relatively to ambition it seems to be unambitiousness, and relatively to unambitiousness it seems to be ambition." These words seem to fit admirably with the words and actions of Hotspur and Falstaff.

If this be true, the golden mean, the ideal pattern of action in the play, must be Prince Hal, who is later to become the ideal king of England and in doing so must reject both extremes. The evidence is not far to seek. His enemy, Vernon, testifies to his excellence just before the battle. Throughout the play the young Prince does not falter, nor does he brag of his exploits. He "conquers" Falstaff at Gadshill against odds, just as he does Hotspur when he kills him in the last act. Never does the audience question his personal integrity. The clincher is his criticism of the honor of both Falstaff and Hotspur in Mistress Quickly's tavern. There he and Poins reveal to the world Falstaff's "cowardice" in running away at Gadshill. Most critics agree that Falstaff is not a coward: "he will not fight longer than he sees reason," as Poins says. On the other hand, in comparison with the Prince in the scene at the Boar's Head, he is surely panicky at the thought of fighting the rebels: "Tell me, Hal, art not thou horrible afeard? Thou being heir apparent, could the world pick thee out three such enemies . . . ? Art thou not horribly afraid? Doth not thy blood thrill?" If not the critics, at least the Prince thinks him serious and returns him a scornful answer.

Earlier in the same scene Hal laughs at Hotspur's excessive concern for honor. To Poins he confesses ironically, "I am not yet of Percy's mind, the Hotspur of the North; he that kills me some six or seven dozen of Scots at a breakfast, washes his hands, and says to his wife, 'Fie upon this quiet life! I want work.' " Even more telling is his comparison of his deeds with those of Hotspur when he is vowing to his father that he will reform: "I will redeem all this on Percy's head," he avers, and goes on:

And that shall be the day, whene'er it lights,
That this same child of honour and renown,
This gallant Hotspur, this all-praised knight,
And your unthought-of Harry chance to meet.
For every honour sitting on his helm,
Would they were multitudes!

The Prince, as mean, is fundamentally opposed to both extremes, which, in turn, are most contrary to each other. As Aristotle says, "the greatest contrariety is that of the extremes to each other, rather than to the intermediate." It is thus not surprising that when they meet at last on the field of battle, Falstaff should commit the indefensible act of stabbing the dead Hotspur. Even in death he seems to fear him. We see the Prince's rejection of both extremes in the course of the two parts of *Henry IV:* of Hotspur when Hal kills him at the end of the First Part; or Falstaff when he disowns him at the same moment of the Second Part. Together, then, the two plays show the Prince choosing and practicing the ideal mean and preparing for his emergence as ideal king.

If this analogy with Aristotle's ethics is justified, it may be helpful to look further into his series of moral virtues. Honor is by no means the only one. In each case we should expect the Prince to approach the golden mean of proper action and either Hotspur or Falstaff or both to represent the vicious extremes. Consider for example the mean of liberality as opposed to prodigality and meanness. It can hardly be denied that the Prince is liberal, Falstaff prodigal, and Hotspur mean at least once in the aforesaid argument over the division of spoils with Glendower and the other conspirators. A similar comparison might be made of the moderation of Hal's good temper with Hotspur's irascibility and Falstaff's utter lack of the quality. Indeed, Hal loses his temper only at the illegal destruction of his baggage train by the French in *Henry V;*

there, since he "is angry at the right things and with the right people," he is still virtuous in Aristotle's eyes. Another of the virtues is temperance. It is doubtful whether any other character in English literature is as intemperate as is Falstaff; on the other hand, the Prince is moderate. Even a sense of humor appears as a mean in the *Ethics;* the contrast with the buffoon and the boor, marked between Falstaff and Prince John in the Second Part, is emphasized where the former says of the younger claimant to the throne just after an exit, "I would you had but the wit. 'Twere better than your dukedom. Good faith, this same young sober-blooded boy doth not love me; nor a man cannot make him laugh. But that's no marvel; he drinks no wine."

According to Aristotle the magnanimous or proud man represents the sum of all the virtues. Ross translates *megalopsychia* as *pride,* but *magnanimity* avoids the unpleasant connotations of this word. The magnanimous man, says Aristotle, "must be good in the highest degree"; his characteristic is "greatness in every virtue." Here appears the real key to Prince Hal, since magnanimity "seems to be a sort of crown of the virtues; for it makes them greater, and it is not found without them." Hence it is quite difficult to be truly magnanimous. Besides the need for perfection in all the virtues, Aristotle adds that this type of man is not disdainful or insolent—nor is he fond of just any danger. He will, however, "face great dangers, and when he is in danger he is unsparing of his life, knowing that there are conditions on which life is not worth having. And he is the sort of man to confer benefits, but he is ashamed of receiving them." Just so does Hal conduct himself during and after the Battle of Shrewsbury; he does not falter from danger even when his father warns him away. And he is willing to free the noble Douglas and give Falstaff the credit for killing Hotspur.

The magnanimous man, furthermore, will readily give help to anyone, gets along with all classes of people, and is "unassuming towards those of the middle class." He does not try for ordinary rewards but is "sluggish" and "holds back" unless great issues are at stake. Such a paragon is not overwhelmed by admiration, nor mindful of wrongs, nor a gossip, nor one who asks favors. All in all, one need not ask a better description of Henry as Prince and King. True, his father thought that he was a wastrel. True, Hotspur scorned him—to his sorrow—but then the extreme is opposed to the mean. True, Falstaff thinks that he will control the kingdom when the Prince comes to power. Even Poins, who is actually closer to Hal's real thoughts than Falstaff, cannot fathom his true character. Yet these are partial or biased witnesses. From the much-debated soliloquy which ends his first appearance the audience itself is never in any doubt that the Prince is in fact good, whatever others may think of him. If we accept this interpretation, he presents such a moral character as can properly develop into an ideal king. Nor must we at the same time denigrate the more popular and human—because sinning—Hotspur and Falstaff.

If the First Part of the play represents the final rejection by death of Hotspur, the Second Part witnesses the rejection of the other extreme in Falstaff—a neatly symmetrical arrangement. But if this is true, we have a long five acts without a worthy opponent for Sir John to replace the dead Hotspur. Instead the one vicious extreme in the play is now opposed to the Lord Chief Justice, representative of law and order. He is clearly not the opposite vicious extreme, for the new King Henry V sides with him and carries out such policies as the Justice would sponsor, e.g., the execution of Nym and Bardolph for robbing a church during the French campaign. The theory of the moral unity of the plays would thus break down, since there is no opportunity for the development of anything more than justice versus injustice. Apparently Falstaff will have to carry on alone.

It must be admitted that the sequel is not as dramatically powerful as the First Part. Under the impact of success, Shakespeare probably gave Falstaff a proportionately much greater part. But there are two significant differences btween the two plays. First, the Prince, who had been Falstaff's close companion in the earlier play, appears with him in the later for but part of a single scene besides the renunciation. Shakespeare seems to have made a deliberate effort to keep them apart, probably to avoid smirching the character of the man about to be crowned. The result accounts for the falling off in Falstaff's wit in the Second Part. In the previous play that "bolting hutch of beastliness" had an equal for cleverness in the Prince, who called on Sir John's best for wit combats; in the Second Part he has only the immensely inferior Bardolf or Shallow or the ladies. As a result, he is reduced to soliloquy—a more contrived and hence less successful form of amusement.

Even so, the "swollen parcel of dropsies" retains a moral function in this play. If we turn over a few chapters in the *Nicomachean Ethics,* we come to the last of the moral virtues, justice, represented in the play by the Lord Chief Justice, whom the Prince meets on stage only in the final act. Now justice, Aristotle says, is different from the other virtues. In the first place, it divides into the lawful, or universal justice, and the fair and equal, or particular justice. As to the lawful, it is "complete virtue" in relation to our neighbor; it is "complete virtue in its fullest sense, because it is the actual exercise of complete virtue." So conceived, justice becomes "not a part of virtue, but virtue entire; nor is contrary injustice a part of vice but vice entire." Like Falstaff, "the worst man is he who exercises his wickedness both towards himself and towards his friends."

This, then, is the legal aspect of justice. In the particular sphere Aristotle devotes a good deal of space to determining just how each man should conduct himself with respect to other men. His argument is a little long for summary, but the conclusion is that "Justice is a kind of mean, but not in the same way as the other virtues, but because it relates to an intermediate amount, while injustice relates to the extremes." The just man acts by choice to give "what is equal in accordance with proportion"; injustice, on the contrary, is "related to the unjust, which is excess and defect, contrary to proportion, of the useful or hurtful. For which reason injustice is excess and defect, viz. because it is productive of excess and defect," quite an exact description of Sir John's failings. Indeed, the "just is the proportional; the unjust is what violates the proportion"; Falstaff qualifies in both plays as an example of the latter failure. As Bardolph says of his size, "You must needs be out of all compass—out of all reasonable compass, Sir John." One may even, Aristotle adds, "voluntarily, owing to incontinence, be harmed by another who acts voluntarily, so that it would be possible to be voluntarily treated unjustly." The scenes with the Hostess in Part II seem an explicit recognition of this characteristic of injustice. Actually, it is important to observe that Falstaff's relations with her are not primarily self-indulgent but a means of escaping arrest and—so to speak—protecting his financial interests. As Aristotle adds, "if one man commits adultery for the sake of gain and makes money by it," he is unjust in comparison with the man who does it merely for pleasure. So it is that Falstaff fears the law—it is an important source too of his wit—and has no better conception of it than "old father antic."

Clearly the Lord Chief Justice represents just action in both Aristotelian senses. His early warnings to Falstaff stress his excesses, but they go unheeded. Unlike the audience, the Justice believes with Falstaff that the new King Henry is on the side of the unjust; Falstaff says on learning of the coronation, "the laws of England are at my commandment. Blessed are they that have been my friends, and woe to my Lord Chief Justice." So when Henry meets the symbol of law and order, the Justice pleads his case: he represents the person and authority of the crown:

> The image of his power lay then in me;
> And in th' administration of his law,
> While I was busy for the commonwealth,
> Your Highness pleased to forget my place,
> The majesty and power of law and justice,
> The image of the King whom I presented.

These lines almost exactly represent Aristotle's reason why law is above the sway of any individual: "we do not allow a *man* to rule, but *rational principle,* because a man behaves thus in his own interests and becomes a tyrant." So would Falstaff have done. The true magistrate is the "guardian of justice" and as such will have no exceptional material reward; instead, he is due "honour and privilege; but those for whom such things are not enough become tyrants." As the new king says:

> You are right, Justice, and you weigh this well.
> Therefore still bear the balance and the sword;
> And I do wish your honours may increase.

So it is that the moral struggle develops in Aristotelian terms through the two *Henry IV* plays to eventuate in the actuality of an ideal king whose perfections had been foreshadowed through these first two plays. Henry V is not essentially different from Prince Hal, though he has matured and seems less human, perhaps because of the absence of close human associates; as king it is noteworthy that he is not represented as being intimate with any other characters. He has succeeded in avoiding the vicious extremes and practices the golden mean of virtue.

This is not, of course, to say that these plays are to be interpreted as a moral allegory, though some elements of the morality plays survive in them. Anyone who tries to limit Falstaff by a label and to say that he can be mounted like a dead elephant is doomed to falsify the evidence. He is far too real to be circumscribed by any pat formula. The suggestion that he fits into the moral pattern of the plays should not be interpreted as meaning that we can exhaust his significance by tacking the name of extreme to him. A girth like his can contain a multitude of considerations. Rather, the ethical mean here advanced should indicate the belt which set a limit to proportion and gave direction to the moral element of all these plays. At the same time, Hal's importance, so often overlooked, comes to the fore. He is the key character, though this position has not been often accorded him; we must agree with Dr. Johnson, that the Prince is the real hero of both the comic and tragic parts. Neither as Prince nor King does he catch the imagination and sympathy as do Hotspur and Falstaff. But real virtue is not spectacular, and we children of Adam do not find it particularly enticing. "Men," as Aristotle noted, "think that acting unjustly is in their power, and therefore that being just is easy. But it is not."

J. DOVER WILSON

Falstaff and the Plan of Henry IV, Part I

Henry IV, a play much neglected by both actors and critics, offers to our view the broadest, the most varied, and in some ways the richest champaign in Shakespeare's extensive empire. Much of this, and not the least alluring stretches, must be ignored in what follows, or barely glanced at; Glendower's do-

From *The Fortunes of Falstaff* (New York, 1944), pp. 15–35. Reprinted by permission of Cambridge University Press. Title added by Ed.

main [1] in Part I, for example. Many characters can hardly be touched; I shall have little to say about Ancient Pistol or Mistress Quickly, Hotspur or Prince John. The more subtle aspects of the play, its poetry, its dramatic light and shade, what may be called its atmospheric effects; all matters of first importance to anyone concerned in tracing the development of Shakespeare's art in the crucial and largely unexplored period that divides *Richard II* from *Hamlet:* these also lie beyond my present scope. The task I have set before me is at once narrow and simple. I am attempting to discover what Professor Charlton has called "the deliberate plan of Shakespeare's play" and, if such a plan existed, how far he succeeded in carrying it into execution.

My title, *The Fortunes of Falstaff*, will suggest the method to be followed. I propose to look for the outlines of Shakespeare's scheme by tracing the career of the knight of Eastcheap. This does not mean that I think him of greater structural consequence than Prince Hal. On the contrary, Falstaff's career is dependent upon Hal's favour, and Hal's favour is determined by that young man's attitude towards his responsibilities as heir to the throne of England. Yet if the Prince's choice spans the play like a great arch, it is Falstaff and his affairs that cover most of the ground.

The title I have selected has, moreover, the convenience of comprising the fortunes, or misfortunes, of the fat rogue outside the pages of Shakespeare. There are, for instance, his pre-natal adventures. He tells us that he "was born about three of the clock in the afternoon, with a white head and something of a round belly"; but all the world now knows that he was walking the boards in an earlier, pre-Shakespearian, incarnation, as a comic travesty of Sir John Oldcastle, the famous Lollard leader, who was historically a friend and fellow-soldier of Prince Hal in the reign of Henry IV, but was burnt as a heretic by the same prince when he became King Henry V. He still retained the name Oldcastle, as is also well known, in the original version of Shakespeare's play; until the company discovered, or were forcibly reminded, that the wife of the

[1] I refer to III, i of Pt. I, which was headed "The Archbishop of Bangor's House in Wales" by Theobald and later editors, though without any warrant in Shakespeare. Glendower behaves like a host throughout the scene, which is clearly a family party.

proto-protestant martyr they were guying on the public stage was the revered ancestress of the Cobhams, powerful lords at Elizabeth's court. Worse still, one of these lords was not only of strongly protestant bent, but also, as Lord Chamberlain, actually Shakespeare's official controller. Hasty changes in the prompt-book became necessary. How far they extended beyond a mere alteration of names can never be determined, though it seems possible that references to some of Oldcastle's historical or legendary characteristics would require modification. It is even more likely (as Alfred Ainger was, I believe, the first to point out) [2] that traces of Lollardry may still be detected in Falstaff's frequent resort to scriptural phraseology and in his affectation of an uneasy conscience. Of this I shall have something to say later.

First of all, however, I wish to deal with Falstaff's ancestral fortunes of a different kind. As he shares these to a large extent with Prince Hal, a consideration of them should prove helpful in bringing out the main lines of the plot which it is our object to discover.

RIOT AND THE PRODIGAL PRINCE

Falstaff may be the most conspicuous, he is certainly the most fascinating, character in *Henry IV*, but all critics are agreed, I believe, that the technical centre of the play is not the fat knight but the lean prince. Hal links the low life with the high life, the scenes at Eastcheap with those at Westminster, the tavern with the battlefield; his doings provide most of the material for both Parts, and with him too lies the future, since he is to become Henry V, the ideal king, in the play that bears his name; finally, the mainspring of the dramatic action is the choice I have already spoken of, the choice he is called upon to make between Vanity and Government, taking the latter in its accepted Tudor meaning, which includes Chivalry or prowess in the field, the theme of Part I, and Justice, which is the theme of Part II. Shakespeare, moreover, breathes life into these abstractions by embodying them, or aspects of them, in prominent characters, who stand, as it were, about the Prince, like attendant spirits: Falstaff typifying Vanity in every sense of the word, Hotspur Chivalry, of the old anarchic kind, and the Lord Chief Justice the Rule of Law or the new ideal of service

[2] V. Alfred Ainger, *Lectures and Essays*, 1905, i, pp. 140–55.

to the state.[3]

Thus considered, Shakespeare's *Henry IV* is a Tudor version of a time-honoured theme, already familiar for decades, if not centuries, upon the English stage. Before its final secularization in the first half of the sixteenth century, our drama was concerned with one topic, and one only: human salvation. It was a topic that could be represented in either of two ways: (i) historically, by means of miracle plays, which in the Corpus Christi cycles unrolled before spectators' eyes the whole scheme of salvation from the Creation to the Last Judgement; or (ii) allegorically, by means of morality plays, which exhibited the process of salvation in the individual soul on its road between birth and death, beset with the snares of the World or the wiles of the Evil One. In both kinds the forces of iniquity were allowed full play upon the stage, including a good deal of horse-play, provided they were brought to nought, or safely locked up in Hell, at the end. Salvation remains the supreme interest, however many capers the Devil and his Vice may cut on Everyman's way thither, and always the powers of darkness are withstood, and finally overcome, by the agents of light. But as time went on the religious drama tended to grow longer and more elaborate, after the encyclopaedic fashion of the middle ages, and such development invited its inevitable reaction. With the advent of humanism and the early Tudor court, morality plays became tedious and gave place to lighter and much shorter moral interludes dealing, not with human life as a whole, but with youth and its besetting sins.

An early specimen, entitled *Youth*[4] and composed about 1520, may be taken as typical of the rest. The plot, if plot it can be called, is simplicity itself. The little play opens with a dialogue between Youth and Charity. The young man, heir to his father's land, gives insolent expression to his self-confidence, lustihood,

[3] In what follows I develop a hint in Sir Arthur Quiller-Couch's *Shakespeare's Workmanship*, 1918, p. 148: "The whole of the business [in *Henry IV*] is built on the old Morality structure, imported through the Interlude. Why, it might almost be labelled, after the style of a Morality title, *Contentio inter Virtutem et Vitium de anima Principis.*"

[4] *The enterlude of youth,* ed. by W. Bang and R. B. McKerrow, Louvain, 1905.

and contempt for spiritual things. Whereupon Charity leaves him, and he is joined by Riot,[5] that is to say wantonness, who presently introduces him to Pride and Lechery. The dialogue then becomes boisterous, and continues in that vein for some time, much no doubt to the enjoyment of the audience. Yet, in the end, Charity reappears with Humility; Youth repents; and the interlude terminates in the most seemly fashion imaginable.

No one, I think, reading this lively playlet, no one certainly who has seen it performed, as I have seen it at the Malvern Festival, can have missed the resemblance between Riot and Falstaff. The words he utters, as he bounces on to the stage at his first entry, give us the very note of Falstaff's gaiety:

> Huffa! huffa! who calleth after me?
> I am Riot full of jollity.
> My heart is as light as the wind,
> And all on riot is my mind,
> Wheresoever I go.

And the parallel is even more striking in other respects. Riot, like Falstaff, escapes from tight corners with a quick dexterity; like Falstaff, commits robbery on the highway; like Falstaff, jests immediately afterwards with his young friend on the subject of hanging; and like Falstaff, invites him to spend the stolen money at a tavern, where, he promises, "We will drink diuers wine" and "Thou shalt haue a wench to kysse Whansoeuer thou wilte"; allurements which prefigure the Boar's Head and Mistress Doll Tearsheet.

But Youth at the door of opportunity, with Age or Experience, Charity or Good Counsel, offering him the yoke of responsibility, while the World, the Flesh, and the Devil beckon him to follow them on the primrose way to the everlasting bonfire, is older than even the medieval religious play. It is a theme to which every generation gives fresh form, while retaining its eternal substance. Young men are the heroes of the Plautine and Terentian comedy which delighted the Roman world; and these young men, generally under the direction of a clever slave or parasite, disport themselves, and

[5] riot= "wanton, loose, or wasteful living; debauchery, dissipation, extravagance" (*O.E.D.*). Cf. the Prodigal Son, who "wasted his substance with riotous living" (Luke xv. 13).

often hoodwink their old fathers, for most of the play, until they too settle down in the end. The same theme appears in a very different story, the parable of the Prodigal Son. And the similarity of the two struck humanist teachers of the early sixteenth century with such force that, finding Terence insufficiently edifying for their pupils to act, they developed a "Christian Terence" by turning the parable into Latin plays, of which many examples by different authors have come down to us.[6] In these plot and structure are much the same. The opening scene shows us Acolastus, the prodigal demanding his portion, receiving good counsel from his father, and going off into a far country. Then follow three or four acts of entertainment almost purely Terentian in atmosphere, in which he wastes his substance in riotous living and falls at length to feeding with the pigs. Finally, in the last act he returns home, penniless and repentant, to receive his pardon. This ingenious blend of classical comedy and humanistic morality preserves, it will be noted, the traditional ratio between edification and amusement, and distributes them in the traditional manner. So long as the serious note is duly emphasized at the beginning and end of the play, almost any quantity of fun, often of the most unseemly nature, was allowed and expected during the intervening scenes.

All this, and much more of a like character, gave the pattern for Shakespeare's *Henry IV*. Hal associates Falstaff in turn with the Devil of the miracle play, the Vice of the morality, and the Riot of the interlude, when he calls him "that villainous abominable misleader of Youth, that old white-bearded Satan," [7] "that reverend Vice, that grey Iniquity, that father Ruffian, that Vanity in years," [8] and "the tutor and the feeder of my riots." [9] "Riot," again, is the word that comes most readily to King Henry's lips when speaking of his prodigal son's misconduct.[10] And, as heir to

6 V. C. H. Herford, *The Literary Relations between England and Germany in the Sixteenth Century*, 1886, ch. III, pp. 84–95.

7 Pt. I, II, iv, 412; cf. l. 398: "Thou art violently carried away from grace, there is a devil haunts thee in the likeness of an old fat man."

8 *Ibid.* II, iv, 404.

9 Pt. II, V, v, 63.

10 Cf. Pt. I, I, i, 85: "Riot and dishonour stain the brow / Of my young Harry"; Pt. II, IV, iv, 62: "His headstrong riot hath no curb," IV, v, 135: "When that my care could not withhold thy riots, / What wilt thou do when riot is thy care?"

the Vice, Falstaff inherits by reversion the functions and attributes of the Lord of Misrule, the Fool, the Buffoon, and the Jester, antic figures the origins of which are lost in the dark backward and abysm of folk-custom.[11] We shall find that Falstaff possesses a strain, and more than a strain, of the classical *miles gloriosus* as well. In short, the Falstaff-Hal plot embodies a composite myth which had been centuries amaking, and was for the Elizabethans full of meaning that has largely disappeared since then: which is one reason why we have come so seriously to misunderstand the play.

Nor was Shakespeare the first to see Hal as the prodigal. The legend of Harry of Monmouth began to grow soon after his death in 1422; and practically all the chroniclers, even those writing in the fifteenth century, agree on his wildness in youth and on the sudden change that came upon him at his accession to the throne. The essence of Shakespeare's plot is, indeed, already to be found in the following passage about King Henry V taken from Fabyan's *Chronicle* of 1516:

> This man, before the death of his fader, applyed him unto all vyce and insolency, and drewe unto hym all ryottours and wylde disposed persones; but after he was admytted to the rule of the lande, anone and suddenly he became a newe man, and tourned al that rage into sobernesse and wyse sadnesse, and the vyce into constant vertue. And for he wolde contynewe the vertue, and not to be reduced thereunto by the familiarytie of his olde nyse company, he therefore, after rewards to them gyuen, charged theym upon payne of theyr lyues, that none of theym were so hardy to come within x. myle of such place as he were lodgyd, after a day by him assigned.[12]

There appears to be no historical basis for any of this, and Kingsford has plausibly suggested that its origin may be "contemporary

[11] In particular, the exact significance of the Vice is exasperatingly obscure. Cf. the discussion by Sir E. K. Chambers (*Medieval Stage*, ii, pp. 203–5), who concludes "that whatever the name may mean . . . the character of the vice is derived from that of the domestic fool or jester." I hazard the suggestion that it was originally the title or name of the Fool who attended upon the Lord of Misrule; *v.* Feuillerat, *Revels of the time of Edward VI*, p. 73: "One vyces dagger & a ladle with a bable pendante . . . deliuerid to the Lorde of Mysrules foole."

[12] Fabyan's *Chronicle*, 1516, p. 577.

scandal which attached to Henry through his youthful association with the unpopular Lollard leader" Sir John Oldcastle. "It is noteworthy," he points out, "that Henry's political opponents were Oldcastle's religious persecutors; and also that those writers who charge Henry with wildness as Prince find his peculiar merit as King in the maintaining of Holy Church and destroying of heretics. A supposed change in his attitude on questions of religion may possibly furnish a partial solution for his alleged 'change suddenly into a new man.'" [13] The theory is the more attractive that it would account not only for Hal's conversion but also for Oldcastle's degradation from a protestant martyr and distinguished soldier to what Ainger calls "a broken-down Lollard, a fat old sensualist, retaining just sufficient recollection of the studies of his more serious days to be able to point his jokes with them."

Yet when all is said, the main truth seems to be that the fifteenth and early sixteenth centuries, the age of allegory in poetry and morality in drama, needed a Prodigal Prince, whose miraculous conversion might be held up as an example by those concerned (as what contemporary political writer was not?) with the education of young noblemen and princes. And could any more alluring fruits of repentance be offered such pupils than the prowess and statesmanship of Henry V, the hero of Agincourt, the mirror of English kingship for a hundred years? In his miracle play, *Richard II*, Shakespeare had celebrated the traditional royal martyr; [14] in his morality play, *Henry IV*, he does the like with the traditional royal prodigal.

He made the myth his own, much as musicians adopt and absorb a folk-tune as the theme for a symphony. He glorified it, elaborated it, translated it into what were for the Elizabethans modern terms, and exalted it into a heaven of delirious fun and frolic; yet never, for a moment, did he twist it from its original purpose, which was serious, moral, didactic. Shakespeare plays no tricks with his public. He did not, like Euripides, dramatize the stories of his race and religion in order to subvert the traditional ideals those stories were first framed to set forth. Prince Hal is the prodigal,

[13] C. L. Kingsford, *The First English Life of King Henry the Fifth*, 1911, pp. xlii, xliii.

[14] V. pp. xvi–xix, lviii–lix of my Introd. to *Richard II*, 1939 ("The New Shakespeare").

and his repentance is not only to be taken seriously, it is to be admired and commended. Moreover, the story of the prodigal, secularized and modernized as it might be, ran the same course as ever and contained the same three principal characters: the tempter, the younker, and the father with property to bequeath and counsel to give. It followed also the fashion set by miracle, morality and the Christian Terence by devoting much attention to the doings of the first-named. Shakespeare's audience enjoyed the fascination of Prince Hal's "white-bearded Satan" for two whole plays, as perhaps no character on the world's stage had ever been enjoyed before. But they knew, from the beginning, that the reign of this marvellous Lord of Misrule must have an end, that Falstaff must be rejected by the Prodigal Prince, when the time for reformation came. And they no more thought of questioning or disapproving of that finale, than their ancestors would have thought of protesting against the Vice being carried off to Hell at the end of the interlude.

The main theme, therefore, of Shakespeare's morality play is the growing-up of a madcap prince into the ideal king, who was Henry V; and the play was made primarily—already made by some dramatist before Shakespeare took it over—in order to exhibit his conversion and to reveal his character unfolding towards that end, as he finds himself faced more and more directly by his responsibilities. It is that which determines its very shape. Even the "fearful symmetry" of Falstaff's own person was welded upon the anvil of that purpose. It is probably because the historical Harry of Monmouth "exceeded the meane stature of men," as his earliest chronicler tells us; "his necke . . . longe, his body slender and leane, his boanes smale," [15]—because in Falstaff's words he actually was a starveling, an eel-skin, a tailor's yard, and all the rest of it—that the idea of Falstaff himself as "a huge hill of flesh" first came to Shakespeare.[16] It was certainly, at any rate in part, in order to explain and palliate the Prince's love of rioting and wantonness

[15] Kingsford, *op. cit.* p. 16.

[16] Ainger tries to persuade himself that there was a tradition associating the Lollard, Oldcastle, with extreme fatness; but his editor, Beeching, is obliged to admit in a footnote that he is not aware of any references to this fatness before Shakespeare; *v.* Ainger, *op. cit.* pp. 126–30.

that he set out to make Falstaff as enchanting as he could.[17] And he succeeded so well that the young man now lies under the stigma, not of having yielded to the tempter, but of disentangling himself, in the end, from his toils. After all, Falstaff *is* "a devil . . . in the likeness of an old fat man," and the Devil has generally been supposed to exercise limitless attraction in his dealings with the sons of men. A very different kind of poet, who imagined a very different kind of Satan, has been equally and similarly misunderstood by modern critics, who no longer believing in the Prince of Darkness have ceased to understand him. For, as Professor R. W. Chambers reminded us in his last public utterance,[18] when Blake declared that Milton was "of the Devil's party without knowing it," he overlooked the fact, and his many successors have likewise overlooked the fact, that, if the fight in Heaven, the struggle in Eden, the defeat of Adam and Eve, and the victory of the Second Adam in *Paradise Regained*, are to appear in their true proportions, we must be made to realize how immeasurable, how indomitable, is the spirit of the Great Enemy. It may also be noted that Milton's Son of God has in modern times been charged with priggishness no less freely than Shakespeare's son of Bolingbroke.

Shakespeare, I say, translated his myth into a language and endued it with an atmosphere that his contemporaries would best appreciate. First, Hal is not only youth or the prodigal, he is the young prodigal *prince*, the youthful heir to the throne. The translation, then, already made by the chroniclers, if Kingsford be right,

[17] Cf. H. N. Hudson, *Shakespeare: his Life, Art and Characters* (ed. 1888), ii, p. 83: "It must be no ordinary companionship that yields entertainment to such a spirit [as Prince Hal's] even in his loosest moments. Whatever bad or questionable elements may mingle with his mirth, it must have some fresh and rich ingredients, some sparkling and generous flavour, to make him relish it. Anything like vulgar rowdyism cannot fail of disgusting him. His ears were never organised to that sort of music. Here then we have a sort of dramatic necessity for the character of Falstaff. To answer the purpose it was imperative that he should be just such a marvellous congregation of charms and vices as he is." See also A. H. Tolman, *Falstaff and other Shakespearian Topics*, 1925, and W. W. Lawrence, *Shakespeare's Problem Comedies*, 1931, p. 64 (an interesting contrast between Hal and Falstaff, Bertram and Parolles).

[18] *Poets and their Critics: Langland and Milton* (British Academy Warton Lecture), 1941, pp. 29–30.

from sectarian terms into those more broadly religious or moral, now takes us out of the theological into the political sphere. This is seen most clearly in the discussion of the young king's remarkable conversion by the two bishops at the beginning of *Henry* V. King Henry, as Bradley notes, "is much more obviously religious than most of Shakespeare's heroes," [19] so that one would expect the bishops to interpret his change of life as a religious conversion. Yet they say nothing about religion except that he is "a true lover of the holy church" and can "reason in divinity"; the rest of their talk, some seventy lines, is concerned with learning and statecraft. In fact, the conversation of these worldly prelates demonstrates that the conversion is not the old repentance for sin and amendment of life, which is the burden, as we have seen, of Fabyan and other chroniclers, but a repentance of the renaissance type, which transforms an idle and wayward prince into an excellent soldier and governor. Even King Henry IV, at the bitterest moments of the scenes with his son, never taxes him with sin, and his only use of the word refers to sins that would multiply in the country, when

> the fifth Harry from curbed licence plucks
> The muzzle of restraint.[20]

If Hal had sinned, it was not against God, but against Chivalry, against Justice, against his father, against the interests of the crown, which was the keystone of England's political and social stability. Instead of educating himself for the burden of kingship, he had been frittering away his time, and making himself cheap, with low companions

> that daff the world aside
> And bid it pass.

In a word, a word that Shakespeare applies no less than six times to his conduct, he is guilty of Vanity. And Vanity, though not in the theological category of the Seven Deadly Sins, was a cardinal iniquity in a young prince or nobleman of the sixteenth and seventeenth centuries; almost as heinous, in fact, as Idleness in an apprentice.

[19] *Oxford Lectures*, p. 256.

[20] Pt. II, IV, v, 131.

I am not suggesting that this represents Shakespeare's own view. Of Shakespeare's views upon the problems of conduct, whether in prince or commoner, we are in general ignorant, though he seems to hint in both *Henry IV* and *Henry V* that the Prince of Wales learnt some lessons at least from Falstaff and his crew, Francis and his fellow-drawers, which stood him in good stead when he came to rule the country and command troops in the field. But it is the view that his father and his own conscience take of his mistreadings; and, as the spectators would take it as well, we must regard it as the thesis to which Shakespeare addressed himself.

When, however, he took audiences by storm in 1597 and 1598 with his double *Henry IV* he gave them something much more than a couple of semi-mythical figures from the early fifteenth century, brought up to date politically. He presented persons and situations at once fresh and actual. Both Hal and Falstaff are denizens of Elizabethan London. Hal thinks, acts, comports himself as an heir to the Queen might have done, had she delighted her people by taking a consort and giving them a Prince of Wales; while Falstaff symbolizes, on the one hand, all the feasting and good cheer for which Eastcheap stood, and reflects, on the other, the shifts, subterfuges, and shady tricks that decayed gentlemen and soldiers were put to if they wished to keep afloat and gratify their appetites in the London underworld of the late sixteenth century. It is the former aspects of the old scoundrel that probably gave most pleasure to those who first saw him on the stage; and, as they are also those that we moderns are most likely to miss, I make no apology for devoting most of the rest of this chapter to an exposition of them.

SWEET BEEF

Riot invites Youth, it will be remembered, to drink wine at a tavern, and tavern scenes are common in other interludes, especially those of the Prodigal Son variety. But Shakespeare's tavern is more than a drink-shop, while his Riot is not only a "huge bombard of sack" but also a "roasted Manningtree ox with the pudding in his belly."

The site of the Boar's Head tavern in Eastcheap is now as deep-sunk in the ooze of human forgetfulness as that of the palace of Haroun. But it was once a real hostelry, and must have meant much to Londoners of the reigns of Elizabeth and James. Records are scanty, but the very fact that Shakespeare makes it Falstaff's headquarters suggests that it was the best tavern in the city. And the further fact that he avoids mentioning it directly, though quibbling upon the name more than once,[21] suggests, on the one hand, that he kept the name off the stage in order to escape complications with the proprietors of the day, and on the other that he could trust his audience to jump to so obvious an identification without prompting. In any event, no other tavern in Eastcheap is at all likely to have been intended, and as Eastcheap is referred to six times in various scenes, there can be little real doubt that what Falstaff once calls "the king's tavern" [22] is the famous Boar's Head, the earliest known reference to which occurs in a will dating from the reign of Richard II.[23] Whether there is anything or not in Skeat's conjecture that the Glutton in *Piers Plowman* made it the scene of his exploits like Falstaff,[24] it was a well-known house of entertainment more than two hundred years before Shakespeare introduced it into his play, and had come therefore by his day to be regarded as a historic hostelry, for which reason it was probably already associated in popular imagination with the floating legends of the wild young prince. What, however, seems to have escaped the attention of modern writers is that the house, with a name that symbolized good living and good fellowship above that of any other London tavern, was almost certainly even better known for good food than for good drink.

Eastcheap, there is plenty of evidence to show, was then, and had long been, the London centre at once of butchers and cookshops. Lydgate, writing in the reign of Henry V, puts the following words in the mouth of his *London Lyckpenny:*

[21] V. Pt. I, II, iv, 100: "That damned brawn"; Pt. II, I, i, 19: "Harry Monmouth's brawn"; II, ii, 143 : "Doth the old boar feed in the old frank? / At the old place, my lord, in Eastcheap"; and II, iv, 224 "Thou whoreson little tidy Bartholomew boar-pig."

[22] Pt. I, II, ii, 49. This designation perhaps implies a claim to royal patronage on the proprietor's part, possibly connected with the quasi-historical incident known as the Hurling in Eastcheap, an affray which arose among their retinue while Hal's brothers, the princes John and Thomas, were taking supper at a tavern (unnamed) in Eastcheap, on St John's Eve, 1410, as is related by Stow (*v.* Kingsford, *op. cit.* p. xxxix).

[23] V. "East Cheap" in Sugden's *Topographical Dictionary to the Works of Shakespeare.*

[24] V. note on *Piers Plowman,* Passus v, l. 313, ed. Skeat (Clarendon Press).

Then I hyed me into Estchepe;
One cryes 'rybbes of befe and many a pye';
Pewter pots they clattered on a heap;
There was a harp, pype, and minstrelsy.

The street was famed, in short, not only for meat and drink, but also for the "noise" of musicians, which belonged to "the old Tauerne in Eastcheap" in *The Famous Victories*, and which "Mistress Tearsheet would fain hear" in Part II of *Henry IV*.[25] As for "rybbes of befe," though we never see or hear of Falstaff eating, or desiring to eat, anything except Goodwife Keech's dish of prawns[26] and the capon, anchovies and halfpenny worth of bread recorded with "an intolerable deal of sack" in the bill found upon him while asleep,[27] Shakespeare none the less contrives to associate him perpetually with appetizing food by means of the imagery that plays about his person. For the epithets and comparisons which Hal and Poins apply to him, or he himself makes use of, though at times connected with his consumption of sack, are far more often intended to recall the chief stock-in-trade of the victuallers and butchers of Eastcheap, namely meat of all kinds, and meat both raw and roast.

Falstaff is once likened to a "huge bombard,"[28] once to a "hogshead,"[29] once to a "tun,"[30] and twice to a "hulk," that is, to a cargo-boat; the nature of the cargo being specified by Doll, who protests to Mistress Quickly, "There's a whole merchant's venture of Bourdeaux stuff in him, you have not seen a hulk better stuffed in the hold."[31] But beyond these there is little or nothing about him in the vintner's line. When, on the other hand, Shakespeare promises the audience, through the mouth of his Epilogue in Part II, to continue the story, with Sir John in it, "if you be not too much cloyed with fat meat," the phrase sums up the prevailing image, constant in reference though ever-varying in form, which the physical characteristics of Falstaff presented to his mind's eye,

[25] Pt. II, II, iv.
[26] *Ibid.* II, i, 94
[27] Pt. I, II, iv, 479–485.
[28] *Ibid.* II, iv, 402.
[29] Pt. II, II, iv, 59
[30] Pt. I, II, iv, 399.
[31] Pt. II, II, iv, 59–61

and which he in turn was at pains to keep before the mind's eye of his public. Changes in London, and even more, changes in the language, have obliterated all this for the modern reader, so that what was intended, from the first, as little more than a kind of shimmering half-apprehended jest playing upon the surface of the dialogue, must now be recovered as a piece of archaeology, that is, as something long dead. The laughter has gone out of it; yet I shall be disappointed if the reader does not catch himself smiling now and again at what follows.

"Call in Ribs, call in Tallow" is Hal's cue for Falstaff's entry in the first great Boar's Head scene; and what summons to the choicest feast in comedy could be more apt? For there is the noblest of English dishes straightaway: Sir John as roast Sir Loin-of-Beef, gravy and all. "Tallow," a word often applied to him, generally in opprobrium, is not rightly understood, unless two facts be recalled: first, that it meant to the Elizabethans liquid fat, as well as dripping or suet or animal fat rendered down; second, that human sweat, partly owing perhaps to the similarity of the word to "suet," was likewise thought of as fat, melted by the heat of the body. The most vivid presentation of Falstaff served up hot, so to say, is the picture we get of him sweating with fright in Mistress Page's dirty linen basket, as it was emptied by her servants into the Thames; and though *The Merry Wives* does not strictly belong to the Falstaff canon, the passage may be quoted here, as giving the clue to passages in *Henry IV* itself. For however different in character the Windsor Falstaff may be from his namesake of Eastcheap, he possesses the same body, the body that on Gad's Hill "sweats to death, and *lards* the lean earth, as he walks along." [32]

"And then," he relates to the disguised Ford,

> to be stopped in, like a strong distillation, with stinking clothes that fretted in their own grease! Think of that, a man of my kidney! think of that—that am as subject to heat, as butter; a man of continual dissolution and thaw; it was a miracle to 'scape suffocation. And in the height of this bath, when I was more than half stewed in grease, like a Dutch dish, to be thrown into the Thames, and cooled, glowing-hot, in that surge, like a horse-shoe. Think of that—hissing hot: think of that, Master Brook! [33]

[32] Pt. I, II, ii, 95–96.
[33] *Merry Wives of Windsor*, III, v, 103–12.

The "greasy tallow-catch," [34] again, to which the Prince compares him, much to the bewilderment of commentators, betokens, I believe, nothing more mysterious than a dripping-pan to catch the fat as the roasting joint turned upon the spit before the fire. Or take the following scrap of dialogue:

> L. CHIEF JUSTICE. What, you are as a candle, the better part burnt out.
> FALSTAFF. A wassail candle, my lord, all tallow—if I did say of wax, my growth would approve the truth.
> L. CHIEF JUSTICE. There is not a white hair on your face, but should have his effect of gravity.
> FALSTAFF. His effect of gravy, gravy, gravy.[35]

Falstaff's repeated "gravy" is a quibble, of course. But it is not just a feeble jest upon his table manners, as seems to be usually assumed: it follows upon the mention of "tallow" and refers to the drops of sweat that never cease to stand upon his face. In fact, to use a seventeenth-century expression, applicable to one bathed in perspiration, he may be said perpetually to "stew in his own gravy." [36]

Indeed, he glories in the fact. Was it not, according to the physiological notions of the time, the very warrant of his enormous vitality? Never is he more angered to the heart than when the Prince likens him one day to a dry withered old apple-john. His complexion is merely sanguine; heat and moisture mingle to form the element he moves in; except in moods of mock-repentance he leaves to baser earth the cold and dry of melancholy.[37]

Once we have the trick of it, all sorts of other allusions and playful terms of abuse are seen to belong to the same category, while the analogy between that vast carcase, as a whole or in its parts, and roasts of various kinds is capable of almost infinite elaboration. "Chops," for instance, as he is twice called,[38] carries

[34] Pt. I, II, iv, 206.
[35] Pt. II, I, ii, 155–61.
[36] *V. O.E.D.* "gravy."
[37] *V.* p. 224, *Edinburgh University Journal,* Summer 1942 (art. on "Shakespeare's Universe").
[38] Pt. I, I, ii, 118; Pt. II, II, iv, 211.

the double significance of "fat cheeks" and "cutlets"; "guts," the Elizabethan word for "tripe," is an epithet that occurs no less than five times; [39] and "sweet beef" as a term of endearment [40] requires no explaining. Nor is he only served up as beef; pork, still more appropriate to the Boar's Head, though brought in less often, provides some magnificent examples. The term "brawn," which means a large pig fattened for the slaughter, is applied to him on two occasions; [41] on his return from Wales the Prince, enquiring of Bardolph, "Is your master here in London? . . . Where sups he? doth the old boar feed in the old frank?" [42] refers to the familiar inn-sign; Falstaff himself declares that he walks the streets followed by the diminutive page "like a sow that hath overwhelmed all her litter but one"; [43] last, and best of all, when Doll salutes him between her "flattering busses" as her "whoreson little tidy Bartholomew boar-pig," [44] she is alluding to the tender sweet-fleshed little sucking-pigs which formed the chief delicacy at Bartholomew Fair.

The mention of Bartholomew Fair, the most popular annual festivity of Elizabethan and Jacobean London, may be linked with two other comparisons, which take us beyond the confines of Eastcheap and help to bestow on Falstaff that "touch of infinity" which Bradley discovers in him, associating him, as they do, with feasting on a vast and communal scale. The first, already quoted above, is the Prince's description of him as a "Manningtree ox with the pudding in his belly," [45] in other words, as an ox roasted whole and stuffed with sausages, after the fashion of the annual fairs at Manningtree, an Essex town famed for the exceeding fatness of its beasts. But the extremest inch of possibility is reached by Poins when he asks Bardolph "How doth the Martlemas, your master?" [46] Martlemas, or the feast of St Martin, on 11 November, was in those days of scarce fodder the season at which most of

[39] Pt. I, II, iv, 205, 235, 403; *ibid.* III, iii, 136, 138.
[40] Pt. I, III, iii, 158.
[41] Pt. I, II, iv, 100; Pt. II, I, i, 19.
[42] Pt. II, II, ii, 143.
[43] *Ibid.* I, i, 11–12.
[44] *Ibid.* II, iv, 224–5.
[45] Pt. I, II, iv, 403.
[46] Pt. II, II, ii, 100.

the beasts had to be killed off and salted for the winter, and therefore the season for great banquets of fresh meat. Thus it had been for centuries, long before the coming of Christianity,[47] and thus it remained down to the introduction of the cropping of turnips in the eighteenth century. In calling him a "Martlemas" Poins is at once likening Falstaff's enormous proportions to the prodigality of fresh-killed meat which the feast brought, and acclaiming his identity with Riot and Festivity in general.[48] But perhaps the best comment upon Falstaff as Martlemas comes from Spenser's procession of the seasons in the Book of Mutabilitie. His November might almost be Falstaff himself, though the dates prove that the two figures must be independent:

> Next was Nouember, he full grosse and fat,
> As fed with lard, and that right well might seeme;
> For, he had been a fatting hogs of late,
> That yet his browes with sweat did reek and steem,
> And yet the season was full sharp and breem.[49]

One might go to the other end of the scale and point out that the objects Falstaff chooses as a contrast to his person, objects excessively thin, wizened or meagre, are likewise often taken from the food-shops. There is, for instance, the shotten herring, the soused gurnet, the bunch of radish, the rabbit-sucker or poulter's hare, and wittiest of all perhaps, the carbonado—the rasher of bacon, we should say—which he will only allow Hotspur to make of him, if he is foolish enough to come in his way.[50] But enough to have shown that by plying his audience with suggestions of the choicest food that London and Eastcheap had to offer, whenever the person of Falstaff is mentioned, Shakespeare lays as it were the physical foundations of his Falstaff myth.

The prodigiously incarnate Riot, who fills the Boar's Head with his jollity, typifies much more, of course, than the pleasures of the table. He stands for a whole globe of happy continents, and his laughter is "broad as ten thousand beeves at pasture." [51] But

[47] V. Sir E. K. Chambers, *Medieval Stage,* ch. XI, "The Beginning of Winter."

[48] I owe this point to the late Lord Ernle: writing in *Shakespeare's England* (i, p. 356), he notes: "To Shakespeare's mind the prodigious plenty of Martlemas suggested Falstaff in its proportions."

[49] *The Faerie Queene,* Bk. VII, canto vii, st. 40.

[50] Pt. I, V, iii, 56.

[51] George Meredith, *The Spirit of Shakespeare.*

he is Feasting first, and his creator never allows us to forget it. For in this way he not only perpetually associates him in our minds with appetizing images, but contrives that as we laugh at his wit our souls shall be satisfied as with marrow and fatness. No one has given finer expression to this satisfaction than Hazlitt, and I may fitly round off the topic with words of his:

> Falstaff's wit is an emanation of a fine constitution; an exuberance of good-humour and good-nature; an overflowing of his love of laughter and good-fellowship; a giving vent to his heart's ease, and over-contentment with himself and others. He would not be in character, if he were not so fat as he is; for there is the greatest keeping in the boundless luxury of his imagination and the pampered self-indulgence of his physical appetites. He manures and nourishes his mind with jests, as he does his body with sack and sugar. He carves out his jokes, as he would a capon or a haunch of venison, where there is *cut and come again;* and pours out upon them the oil of gladness. His tongue drops fatness, and in the chambers of his brain "it snows of meat and drink." He keeps perpetually holiday and open house, and we live with him in a round of invitations to a rump and dozen. . . . He never fails to enrich his discourse with allusions to eating and drinking, but we never see him at table. He carries his own larder about with him, and is himself "a tun of man." [52]

MONSIEUR REMORSE

Like all great Shakespearian characters Falstaff is a bundle of contradictions. He is not only Riot but also Repentance. He can turn an eye of melancholy upon us, assume the role of puritan sanctimony, and when it pleases him, even threaten amendment of life. It is, of course, *mock*-repentance, carried through as part of the untiring "play extempore" with which he keeps the Prince, and us, and himself, entertained from beginning to end of the drama. And yet it is not mere game; Shakespeare makes it more interesting by persuading us that there is a strain of sincerity in it; and it almost completely disappears in Part II, when the rogue finds himself swimming on the tide of success. There is a good deal of it in Part I, especially in the earliest Falstaff scenes.

> But, Hal, I prithee, trouble me no more with vanity. I would

[52] *Characters of Shakespeare's Plays* (Hazlitt's *Works,* ed. A. R. Waller and A. Glover, 1902, i. 278).

to God thou and I knew where a commodity of good names were to be bought.

Thou hast done much harm upon me, Hal—God forgive thee for it: before I knew thee, Hal, I knew nothing, and now am I, if a man should speak truly, little better than one of the wicked: I must give over this life, and I will give it over: by the Lord, an I do not, I am a villain. I'll be damned for never a king's son in Christendom.[53]

One of his favourite poses is that of the innocent, beguiled by a wicked young heir apparent; he even makes it the burden of his apologia to the Lord Chief Justice at their first encounter. It serves too when things go wrong, when resolute men who have taken £1000 on Gad's Hill are left in the lurch by cowardly friends, or when there's lime in a cup of sack:

There is nothing but roguery to be found in villainous man, yet a coward is worse than a cup of sack with lime in it. A villainous coward! Go thy ways, old Jack, die when thou wilt, if manhood, good manhood, be not forgot upon the face of the earth, then am I a shotten herring. . . . There lives not three good men unhanged in England, and one of them is fat, and grows old. God help the while! a bad world, I say. I would I were a weaver—I could sing psalms or anything.[54]

But beside this talk of escaping from a wicked world and the toils of a naughty young prince, there is also the pose of personal repentance. At his first entry Poins hails him as Monsieur Remorse, an indication that this is one of his recognized roles among Corinthians and lads of mettle. And we may see him playing it at the opening of Act 3, Scene 3, when there is no Hal present to require entertaining.

Well, I'll repent, and that suddenly, while I am in some liking. I shall be out of heart shortly, and then I shall have no strength to repent. An I have not forgotten what the inside of a church is made of, I am a peppercorn, a brewer's horse. The inside of a church! Company, villainous company, hath been the spoil of me.

Such passages, together with the habit of citing Scripture, may

[53] Pt. I, I, ii, 70–73, 80–85.
[54] *Ibid.* II, iv, 111–119.

have their origin, I have said, in the puritan, psalm-singing, temper of Falstaff's prototype—that comic Lollard, Sir John Oldcastle in the old *Henry IV*. But, if so, the motif, adapted and developed in Shakespeare's hands, has come to serve a different end. In this play of the Prodigal Prince it is Hal who should rightly exhibit moods of repentance; and on the face of it, it seems quite illogical to transfer them to Falstaff, the tempter. Yet there are reasons why Hal could not be thus represented. In the first place, as already noted, repentance in the theological sense, repentance for sin, is not relevant to his case at all, which is rather one of a falling away from political virtues, from the duties laid upon him by his royal vocation. And in the second place, since Henry V is the ideal king of English history, Shakespeare must take great care, even in the days of his "wildness," to guard him from the breath of scandal. As has been well observed by a recent editor: "His riots are mere frolics. He does not get drunk and is never involved in any scandal with a woman."[55] And there is a third reason, this time one of dramatic technique not of morals, why the repentance of the Prince must be kept in the background as much as possible, viz. that as the only satisfactory means of rounding off the two parts, it belongs especially to the last act of the play.

Yet Monsieur Remorse is a good puppet in the property-box of the old morality, and may be given excellent motions in the fingers of a skilful showman, who is laying himself out, in this play especially, to make fun of the old types. Why not shape a comic part out of it, and hand it over to Falstaff, who as the heir of traditional medieval "antics" like the Devil, the Vice, the Fool, Riot and Lord of Misrule, may very well manage one more? Whether or not Shakespeare argued it out thus, he certainly added the ingredient of melancholy, and by so doing gave a piquancy to the sauce which immensely enhances the relish of the whole dish. If only modern actors who attempt to impersonate Falstaff would realize it!

[55] V. p. xi of *1 Henry IV*, ed. by G. L. Kittredge (Ginn & Co). I fancy Hal is just a little tipsy at the beginning of Pt. I, II, iv, but the point is, in general, sound enough, and the more striking that the chroniclers do not hide the fact that Prince Henry was given to sexual intemperance; *v.* Kingsford, *op. cit.* p. 17: "he exercised meanelie the feates of Venus and of Mars, and other pastimes of youth, for so longe as the Kinge his father liued."

Falstaff, then, came to stand for the repentance, as well as the riotous living, of the Prodigal Son. And striking references to the parable, four of them, seem to show that his creator was fully aware of what he was doing. "What, will you make a younker of me? shall I not take mine ease in mine inn but I shall have my pocket picked?"[56] Sir John indignantly demands of Mistress Quickly, on discovering, or pretending to discover, the loss of his grandfather's seal-ring. The word "younker" calls up a scene from some well-known representation of the parable, in picture or on the stage, a scene to which Shakespeare had already alluded in the following lines from *The Merchant of Venice:*

> How like a younker or a prodigal
> The scarféd bark puts from her native bay,
> Hugged and embracéd by the strumpet wind!
> How like a prodigal doth she return,
> With over-weathered ribs and ragged sails,
> Lean, rent, and beggared by the strumpet wind![57]

Equally vivid is Falstaff's description of the charge of foot he led into battle at Shrewsbury as so "dishonourable ragged" that "you would think that I had a hundred and fifty tattered prodigals, lately come from swine-keeping, from eating draff and husks."[58] And seeing that he calls them in the same speech "slaves as ragged as Lazarus in the painted cloth, where the Glutton's dogs licked his sores," we may suppose that, here too, he is speaking right painted cloth, from whence he had studied his Bible;[59] an inference which seems borne out by his third reference, this time from Part II. Having, you will remember, already honoured Mistress Quickly by becoming indebted to her for a hundred marks, that is for over £65, he graciously condescends to borrow £10 more from her. And when she protests that to raise the sum she must be fain to pawn both her plate and the tapestry of her dining-chambers, he replies: "Glasses, glasses, is the only drinking—

[56] Pt. I, III, iii, 69–70. "The alternative title for the Prodigal Son was the 'younger,' as the alternative for the good brother was the 'elder' " (Richmond Noble, *Shakespeare's Biblical Knowledge,* p. 277).

[57] *The Merchant of Venice,* II, vi, 14–19; cf. 3 *Henry VI,* II, i, 24: "Trimmed like a younker, prancing to his love."

[58] Pt. I, IV, ii, 27–31.

[59] Cf. *As You Like It,* III, ii, 271: "I answer you right painted cloth, from whence you have studied your questions."

and for thy walls, a pretty drollery or the story of the Prodigal or the German hunting in waterwork is worth a thousand of these bed-hangers and these fly-bitten tapestries."[60] This is not just the patter of the confidence-trickster; Falstaff, we must believe, had a real liking for the Prodigal Son story, or why should that tactful person, mine Host of the Garter Inn, have gone to the trouble of having it painted, "fresh and new," about the walls of the chamber that he let to the greasy philanderer who assumed the part of Sir John, in Windsor.[61] Not being a modern critic, the good man could not know that his guest was an impostor.

But jollification and mock-repentance do not exhaust Falstaff's roles. For most of *Henry IV* he plays the soldier, taking a hand in a couple of campaigns, the first culminating in the death of Hotspur at Shrewsbury, and the other in the encounter between Prince John and the Archbishop of York at Gaultree Forest, where the rebels are finally overthrown. In both of these he performs the useful dramatic function of supplying the light relief, and in so doing he exhibits himself as at once the supreme comic soldier of English literature and a variation of a time-worn theme, the *miles gloriosus* of Plautus. . . .

[60] Pt. II, II, i, 143–7.

[61] *The Merry Wives,* IV, v, 7.

ARTHUR C. SPRAGUE

Gadshill Revisited[1]

For about a hundred and eighty years after Sir John Falstaff for the first time ran roaring from Gadshill, the fact of his cowardice was taken for granted. Falstaff was immensely popular with readers and playgoers alike. In the seventeenth century, allusions to him are far more numerous, by actual count, than those to any other Shakespearian character,[2] and the terms in which he is referred to are quite unambiguous. "A thrasonical puff, and emblem of mock valour," Tom Fuller calls him;[3] and Dryden, not, I think, inaccurately, describes him as "old, fat, merry, cowardly, drunken, amorous, vain, and lying." Yet Falstaff's individuality, as Dryden perceived, lay elsewhere:

> That wherein he is singular is his wit, or those things he says . . . unexpected by the audience; his quick evasions, when you expect him surprised, which, as they are extremely diverting of themselves, so receive a great addition from his person.[4]

And Dr. Samuel Johnson, agreeing with Dryden, pronounces Falstaff a coward and defines his wit as consisting "in easy escapes and sallies of levity."[5]

It was not until 1777 that heresy began. In that year appeared a long essay of a good deal of subtlety, and even charm, *On the Dramatic Character of Sir John Falstaff*, by Maurice Morgann.

From *Shakespeare Quarterly*, IV (April 1953), 125–137. Reprinted by permission of the author and the Shakespeare Association of America.

[1] A paper read at the Shakespeare Conference at Stratford-on-Avon in August 1951.

[2] G. E. Bentley, *Shakespeare and Jonson* (Chicago [1945]), chap. vii.

[3] *The History of the Worthies of England*, ed. P. Austin Nuttall (London, 1840), II, 455.

[4] "An Essay of Dramatic Poesy," in *Dramatic Essays*, "Everyman's Library," p. 43.

[5] *The Plays of William Shakespeare*, ed. Johnson (London, 1765), IV, 356.

Morgann, a middle-aged civil servant of "uncommon powers," acknowledges that his book was written on a dare, and he dreads that it might be taken, as, indeed, it was by many, as a mere exercise in paradox. He recognizes "how universally the contrary opinion prevails"; and that "the appearances" in this case are all against him. Falstaff is involved, almost immediately, "in circumstances of apparent dishonour"; he is called a coward; is seen "in the very act of running away," and "betrayed into those *lies* and *braggadocioes,* which are the usual concomitants of cowardice in military men, and pretenders to valour." What was more, these things are "thrust forward, pressed upon our notice as the subject of our mirth." [6] The grounds for his own belief that Sir John was no coward were of quite another sort, and he asks patience of the reader while he sets forth what "lies so dispersed, is so latent, and so purposely obscured" [7]—the "secret impressions upon us of courage." [8]

Though Morgann's ideas were to prevail, they were not unopposed in his own day. A carefully reasoned reply by Richard Stack appeared in *The Transactions of the Royal Irish Academy.* Dr. Johnson's opinion was twice asked and given. "Why, Sir," Boswell quotes him as saying, "we shall have the man come forth again; and as he has proved Falstaff to be no coward, he may prove Iago to be a very good character." [9] Thomas Davies, too, the actor and bookseller, spoke out, and the point he made was, I think, a telling one: "If the knight is proved to be a man of courage, half the mirth he raises is quite lost and misplaced." [10] What is more curious, Falstaff on the stage remained unregenerate. As he had once been, in this matter of cowardice, so he has remained right down to the present—though such fine actors as Sir Ralph Richardson and (at Stratford) Mr. Anthony Quayle and the late Roy Byford, have dispensed with most of the traditional buffoonery which once disfigured the role.

We have come, indeed, to a parting of ways, the actors keeping straight on as they had been going, the critics, with few excep-

[6] *An Essay on the Dramatic Character of Sir John Falstaff* (London, 1820), pp. 2, 3.

[7] *Ibid.*, p. 4.

[8] *Ibid.*, p. 13.

[9] James Boswell, *Life of Samuel Johnson,* ed. G. B. Hill and L. F. Powell (Oxford, 1934), IV, 192 note.

[10] *Dramatic Miscellanies* (London, 1784), I, 272.

tions, straying obscurely to the left. Nor was Morgann, with his notion of appearance and reality, his "secret impressions" of courage, a safe guide. Thus, William Lloyd would have Falstaff's delightfully spontaneous rejoinder to the Prince's "Where shall we take a purse tomorrow, Jack?" "Zounds, where thou wilt, lad! I'll make one," a bit of crafty duplicity, with the speaker fully conscious of the incongruity of what he says.[11] And Hazlitt fancies that Falstaff's bill, with its "out-of-the-way charge for capons and sack with only one half-penny-worth of bread," may have been planted for the Prince to find.[12] (One might question, with equal propriety, whether at the moment of the reading of the bill Sir John, for all his snoring, was really asleep!)

The starting point for such divagations remains the denial of what in the theater seems obvious, the fact of cowardice. Yet Bradley and even Kittredge are among those who have denied it. Bradley, indeed, is not without misgivings. The manner of Falstaff's flight at Gadshill troubles him, if only in a footnote: "It is to be regretted . . . that in carrying his guts away so nimbly he 'roared for mercy'; for I fear we have no ground for rejecting Henry's statement to that effect." [13] He grants, too, that "Falstaff sometimes behaves in what we should generally call a cowardly way." But conduct is not a certain indication of character. "If the word [coward] means a person who feels painful fear in the presence of danger, and yields to that fear in spite of his better feelings and convictions, then assuredly Falstaff was no coward." [14] As for Kittredge, strangely, as it always seemed to me, he had no doubts whatsoever. Even the roaring at Gadshill he denied, or explained away. For once, dramatic evidence went by the board with him, and his Falstaff was *sans peur*, if not quite *sans reproche*.

Among the minority-critics who have held out for cowardice (and John Bailey was one), the foremost is, of course, Professor Stoll. Time after time he has returned to the question, bringing to it his broad knowledge of popular drama and its enduring conventions.[15] Thus, he shows that Falstaff's behavior on the battle-

[11] *Essays on Shakespeare* (1858), in *1 Henry IV*, Furness Variorum Edition, p. 135.

[12] *Characters of Shakespeare's Plays*, Bohn ed. (1892), p. 135.

[13] *Oxford Lectures on Poetry* (London, 1909), p. 268 note.

[14] *Ibid.*, p. 266.

[15] *Shakespeare Studies* (New York, 1927); "Recent Shakespeare Criticism," *Shakespeare Jahrbuch*, LXXIV (1938); *Shakespeare and Other*

field—his cracking jokes, for instance, or capturing a prisoner of his own, the redoubtable Colevile of the Dale—cannot be taken as evidence of courage, since the mere type-cowards and comic butts of earlier and cruder plays do the like. Sir John's ancestors are a shabby lot, but their existence may as well be acknowledged. In fact, a late-comer to this controversy, who has convinced himself that Falstaff was no braver than he should be, is likely to discover that many of his best arguments have already been used, somewhere, by Mr. Stoll. That they have been so largely disregarded is a little puzzling.

Finally, Professor J. Dover Wilson, though he repeatedly invokes the authority of Johnson in combatting the Romantic critics, is ambiguous on this matter of timidity; or, rather, as it seems to me, he would have it both ways. Falstaff, during the overpowering of the travelers at Gadshill, is described as "dancing with rage, on the fringe of the scuffle," and his subsequent flight becomes as ignominious as the older actors were accustomed to make it. Indeed, if the Gadshill Scene stood alone, Mr. Wilson is satisfied that the audience would accept Sir John as "an absolute coward"—which he will not admit.[16] The representation of cowardice by the right sort of comedian will (he thinks) have produced an effect upon us very different from what might be expected—affection, even, rather than a "jeering contempt." [17] The impression of cowardice is dissolved in the mirth of the Tavern Scene. Falstaff, sensing the plot against him, deliberately exaggerates, winking to the audience at the moment he begins to do so. The groundlings might miss the point; there would be others to whom the question of cowardice was left open to debate. And Falstaff's "magnificent display of stoutness of heart" when the Sheriff comes to arrest him, is "the final answer to the Prince's slanderous story of the events on Gad's Hill, and to our own receding impressions." [18]

Yet as we pass to still later episodes, it is curious to find Mr. Wilson taking issue repeatedly with the contentions of the Mor-

Masters (Cambridge [Massachusetts], 1940); *From Shakespeare to Joyce* (New York, 1944); "Symbolism in Shakespeare," *Modern Language Review*, XLII (1947).

[16] *The Fortunes of Falstaff* (Cambridge and New York, 1944), pp. 44, 45.

[17] *Ibid.*, p. 47.

[18] *Ibid.*, p. 58.

gann school. Falstaff's presence in the thick of battle is no longer accepted as evidence of valor. His "military reputation is not only complete bogus, but one of the best jokes in the whole drama." [19] Had Colevile of the Dale resisted, "we may surmise that another sham death would have followed the exchange of a few blows." [20] Even the turning out of poor swaggering Pistol is left to Bardolph, "while Falstaff, sword in hand, follows up at a discreet distance behind." [21]

On this whole question of cowardice, then, the earlier critics, and the actors, are on one side; the later critics, with few exceptions, on the other. Either, that is to say, Falstaff is an egregious coward; or he is—here there is some want of agreement—a veteran soldier, usually, and a realist in war; trusted, and not wholly undeserving of trust; wily, and of great presence of mind; no Hotspur, of course but just as certainly, not a coward. The chief arguments of Morgann and his followers, the arguments against cowardice, are familiar—Morgann, himself, thought up most of them—and I shall present them only summarily, though I hope with fairness.

There is, first of all, Morgann's bold challenge to the impartial reader: "We all like *Old Jack*" though we so constantly abuse him! But could we like him, vicious as he is, were he actually a coward? Cowardice seems incompatible with our impression of the character as a whole. Our feeling toward Falstaff is altogether different from our feeling toward, say, the cowardly Parolles in *All's Well that Ends Well.*

From impressions and their analysis we pass to inference. Falstaff's military reputation is pointed to with confidence as evidence of desert. Thus, in the dark days before Shrewsbury, the Prince himself entrusts him with the command of a company of foot. Falstaff is present at the King's Council of War; and in the premature account of the outcome of the battle is prominently mentioned among the casualties—"And Harry Monmouth's brawn, the hulk Sir John, Is prisoner." Later we hear of "a dozen Captains" searching anxiously for him while he sups with Mistress Tearsheet. Then, too, a rebel of some note, a knight, Colevile of the Dale, surrenders at once upon hearing who his antagonist is: "I think you are Sir John Falstaff, and in that thought yield me."

[19] *Ibid.*, p. 89.
[20] *Ibid.*, p. 87.
[21] *Ibid.*, p. 107.

Much is made, also, of a relatively inconspicuous episode at the close of the great Tavern Scene in *1 Henry IV*. Bardolph rushes in, with a good deal of nasal clamor, to interrupt the play which Falstaff and Prince Hal are acting: "O, my lord, my lord! the sheriff with a most monstrous watch is at the door"—looking of course, for certain thieves. Falstaff, it is urged, might well be expected to show alarm at this, or even terror. On the contrary, he merely takes hiding behind the arras, where he is presently discovered, not quaking with fear but asleep, and "snorting like a horse."

Later in the same play we have Sir John on the field of battle—and in time, too! He tells us in soliloquy that he has led his poor soldiers where they were slaughtered. He finds himself in the very thick of the fight. Hotspur contends with Prince Hal in single combat. The terrible Douglas suddenly attacks Falstaff. Whereupon Falstaff, no match of course for such an adversary, but never losing his coolness and presence of mind, has recourse to a brilliant stratagem by which he escapes: lives, as is hopefully said of him, to fight another day. As no coward could have slept, earlier, so no coward could now have outwitted death by seeming to die!

The complicated happenings at Gadshill, Morgann takes up last of all, and he admits the possibility that Falstaff in this single instance yielded to a momentary and quite understandable terror (even Bradley, as we saw, was troubled by Sir John's *roaring* as he ran). For an uncompromising defense of the fat hero at this point, one goes to Kittredge. Falstaff, he urges, is under no sort of obligation to fight it out. On the contrary, as a thief caught in the act, it behooves him to take to his heels. "How the fat rogue roar'd!" says Poins, at the end of the Gadshill Scene. But this refers to Falstaff's "vociferous swaggering"—his "Down with them . . . whoreson caterpillars" and so on—as he set upon the travellers—or encouraged poor Bardolph and the others to set upon them! And when the roaring is again mentioned and its precise character specified ("and, Falstaff, you carried your guts away as nimbly . . . and roar'd for mercy, and still run and roar'd, as ever I heard bullcalf"), it is the "only departure from accuracy in Prince Hal's story."

These, then, are the principal arguments which have been used by those who deny that Falstaff was a coward, despite those circumstances of "apparent dishonour" and appearances "singularly strong and striking" which Morgann recognized as likely to sway the judgment of a simple reader. They are arguments which vary a good deal in force; but each of them can, I think, be fairly met.

There is Morgann's argument, first of all, that we could not like "plump Jack" as we do if to his other failings, and quite tipping the balance, were added cowardice. But this is to leave out of account Sir John's years, and it might be added his corpulence. He is obviously disqualified as a combatant—"blasted with antiquity." [22] To expect valor of him is, indeed, to expect too much! And in the Play Scene when, speaking in the person of Prince Hal, he has occasion to praise himself, he makes a point of this: "But for sweet Jack Falstaff, kind Jack Falstaff, true Jack Falstaff, valiant Jack Falstaff, and therefore more valiant being, as he is, old Jack Falstaff. . . ." Nor need the argument remain hypothetical. For it is quite obvious that Dr. Johnson liked Falstaff, though recognizing the rogue's numerous vices and insisting upon his cowardice.

As for his military reputation, I am tempted merely to repeat Professor Dover Wilson's comprehensive description of it as "complete bogus" and "one of the best jokes in the whole drama." Colevile of the Dale has only to learn who his antagonist is, and yields without striking a blow. (His alacrity in yielding does not, indeed, escape comment: "It was more, his courtesy than your deserving," says Prince John to Falstaff, unpleasantly enough.) But if Pistol, the complete coward, is able to take a prisoner on the field of battle, why not his old master, the better man of the two? And Colevile, though his words are not abject like those of Pistol's Frenchman, seems scarcely formidable. Falstaff speaks of him with suspicious emphasis as "a most furious knight and valorous enemy" and of his own "pure and immaculate valour" in taking such a prisoner. Perhaps, the first tribute is as unsubstantial as the second?

But the Prince entrusted Falstaff with the command of a company shortly before Shrewsbury? And this same company, it might be answered, will afford occasion for one of Sir John's happiest monologues; is fully justified, in terms of dramatic economy, by the use made of it! The Prince, too, seems to take the matter lightly. "I'll procure this fat rogue a charge of foot," he says, adding, not I think without relish, "and I know his death will be a march of twelve score." He wants to see Falstaff larding the lean earth

[22] 2 *Henry IV*, I, ii, 207.

once more! Meanwhile, there will be the pleasure of telling him the news:

> I have procured thee, Jack, a charge of foot.
> *Falstaff*. I would it had been of horse.

Later, by the way, Hal entrusts dispatches of obvious importance to—of all messengers—Bardolph!

He slept behind the arras—slept soundly and snored. Now this fact has been taken as incontestable proof of high fortitude on the snorer's part. But is it? I would not so far belittle Sir John's sagacity as to believe that what even a minor member of the gang (Gadshill) recognized would not have been perceived by Falstaff—that on this particular expedition they stole "as in a castle, cocksure." [23] The Prince of Wales, deeply involved as he is, himself, must needs "(if matters should be look'd into) for [his] own credit sake make all whole." Falstaff might well sleep soundly, and, sleeping, contribute to the forwarding of the plot by allowing his pockets to be picked. What is natural in itself has reason as well in the economy of the play as a whole; most of dramatic technique (as I have come to believe) consisting in a playwright's ability to kill more than one bird with a single stone.

Falstaff's behavior at Shrewsbury and Gadshill remains to be considered. At Shrewsbury, then, he led his ragamuffins where they were peppered; is found, himself, where the fighting is fiercest, and escapes death by means of a quite legitimate stratagem. The passing allusion to the destruction of the ragamuffins is impressive when taken out of context. Nor would I impute a sinister motive to old Jack and believe that the securing of their death pay was his object here.[24] Were this so, one would expect some intimation of it in the text. They fell, in any case, almost to a man—and it is convenient for the playwright certainly, and perhaps for Sir John, to have them out of the way. Meanwhile, the soliloquy in which we hear of their fate is worth examining. "Though I could scape shot-free at London," Falstaff begins, "I fear the shot here." Then, starting at the sight of one who has paid his score—"There's honour for you!" "I am as hot as molten lead," he mutters, "and as heavy too. God keep lead out of me! I need no more weight than mine

[23] *1 Henry IV*, II, i, 77.
[24] Cf. J. W. Fortescue, in *Shakespeare's England*, I, 123.

own bowels." For an Elizabethan audience—for, I think, any popular audience—the character of the speech will already have been determined. It is addressed to them, designed for their amusement—a comic monologue spoken by one who does, indeed, "fear the shot" and who will have recourse to whatever shifts he can devise to save that precious carcass of his.

Such shifts and stratagems, far from being incompatible with cowardice on the stage, were its familiar concomitants. Not to go further for an illustration, one turns to *The Famous Victories of Henry the Fifth.* In the old play of that name, well known, it would seem, to Shakespeare, the "Clown" Dericke is an egregious coward; yet he has his wits about him, and most of all when his need is greatest. He boasts of having tickled his nose with a straw, gained in this way the title of "the bloodie souldier," and so escaped combat duty.[25] Taken prisoner, ignominiously enough, during the raid upon the English camp at Agincourt, he manages by an elaborate and very implausible trick to secure his captor's sword, "*hurles him downe*" and is about to kill him when the Frenchman escapes in turn. "What, is he gone?" says Dericke, "Masse, I am glad of it. For, if he had staid, I was afraid he wold have sturd again, and then I should have beene spilt." [26]

"Enter *Douglas.* He fighteth with *Falstaff,* who falls down as if he were dead." I recall a very good performance of *1 Henry IV* at an American repertory theater before a small audience. In the row behind me were two very young girls who clearly had not read the play but, as clearly, were greatly enjoying it. And the happy comment of one of them, wholly spontaneous as it was, delighted me: "He's playing possum!" It came, as I noted, a moment or two after Sir John's descent. To her, as to a good many in that first audience of long ago, he must have seemed to have died indeed. And when, upon the talk of embowelling, Falstaff rose, there came amusement and relief. Though the expedient he practiced was, as an eighteenth-century critic stated, "very natural to a coward," [27] and one which an unfortunate fat man of the same name repeats in *The Merry Wives of Windsor,* it is not, I should say, conclusive evidence of cowardice any more than it is of valor. Relief and

[25] *Chief Pre-Shakespearean Dramas,* ed. J. Q. Adams (Boston, etc. [1924]), p. 688.

[26] *Ibid.,* pp. 686, 687.

[27] Richard Stack, in *1 Henry IV,* Furness Variorum Edition, p. 417.

amusement come first, and beyond such feelings I doubt if the ordinary spectator goes. Long ere this, he will have made up his mind on the matter of cowardice and will interpret this episode accordingly. And if we, away from the theater, disputing as we do over niceties, are in need of further enlightenment, it comes in the speech immediately following. "The better part of valour is discretion," Falstaff rationalizes. Then, as he looks about him, come thoughts of another sort. "Zounds, I am afraid of this gunpowder Percy, though he be dead. How if he should counterfeit too, and rise?" And, accordingly, to "make him sure," he will thrust his sword into the dead body. If, he adds as an afterthought, he takes upon himself the glory of having slain Hotspur, he may succeed in brazening it out. "Why may not he rise as well as I?" he repeats. There is a double incentive for what he does—fame, yes, but caution as well. Tom Davies who, knowing as he did a great deal about the practical theater, remained undazzled by the brilliance of Maurice Morgann, gave this passage the emphasis it deserves: "If any proof of [Falstaff's] timidity be yet wanting, we have, in this scene, such as bids defiance to all question; for Falstaff, not satisfied with seeing the dead body of Percy before him, to make all sure, wounds the corpse in the thigh." [28]

The circumstances of the Gadshill robbery Morgann, for obvious reasons, examined last of all. In the play, it is of some consequence, however, that the episode comes very early. Shakespeare's practice in matters of exposition is remarkably consistent. Facts and impressions, once imparted, are rarely contradicted, and then in quite unmistakable terms. Even Iago, who for a few moments may appear to have something of a case against his master, a still unknown Moor, is soon shown in his true colors as a designing villain. What is more, the cowardice of Falstaff is not lightly referred to, or joked about; it receives in the Gadshill episode what amounts, in dramatic terms, to demonstration.

As Poins outlines the plan, he and the Prince are to set upon Falstaff, Bardolph, Peto, and Gadshill, and rob them of their newly acquired booty. The Prince, not unnaturally, wonders whether "they will be too hard for us"—four men against two. But Poins reassures him:

> Well, for two of them, I know them to be as true-bred cowards as ever turn'd back; and for the third, if he fight longer than he

[28] *Dramatic Miscellanies, I,* 273.

> sees reason, I'll forswear arms. The virtue of this jest will be the incomprehensible lies that this same fat rogue will tell us when we meet at supper: how thirty, at least, he fought with; what wards, what blows, what extremities he endured; and in the reproof of this lies the jest.

Thus, two things are promised: that Falstaff, to translate understatement by understatement, is not likely to do much fighting; and that, in keeping with his timidity and making it truly diverting, his tales of prowess afterwards will be infinite ("incomprehensible"). Hal is satisfied—and, indeed, Poins knows his man!

At Gadshill, Falstaff has first to endure the distress of being deprived of his horse—that unfortunate animal!—but being Falstaff is soon able to play upon the familiar theme of his own bulk quite as happily as his tormenters. He hears that the travelers are numerous. "Zounds," he cries, "will they not rob us?" And the Prince: "What, a coward, Sir John Paunch?" "Indeed," he answers, "I am not John of Gaunt, your grandfather; but yet no coward, Hal." "Well, we leave that to the proof." And the proof is soon forthcoming. The travelers, easing their legs by walking down the hill, are pounced upon and relieved of their money, Falstaff setting up a prodigious clamor while this is going on. Once more, to keep these complicated happenings clear, the prince comments:

> The thieves have bound the true men. Now could thou and I rob the thieves and go merrily to London, it would be argument for a week, laughter for a month, and a good jest for ever.

But Falstaff, returning with the booty, is full of satisfaction:

> Come, my masters, let us share, and then to horse before day. An the Prince and Poins be not two arrant cowards, there's no equity stirring. There's no more valour in that Poins than in a wild duck.

It is the note he will sound insistently at the beginning of the Tavern Scene. They are the cowards, not he! He may even believe it, himself. Then,

> *as they are sharing, the Prince and Poins set upon them. They all run away, and Falstaff, after a blow or two* [he is, of course, less nimble than the rest], *runs away too, leaving the booty behind them.*

> PRINCE. Got with much ease. Now merrily to horse.
> The thieves are scattered, and possess'd with fear

So strongly that they dare not meet each other.
Each takes his fellow for an officer.
Away, good Ned. Falstaff sweats to death
And lards the lean earth as he walks along.
Were't not for laughing, I should pity him.

POINS. How the fat rogue roar'd!

So in *A Midsummer Night's Dream*, Bully Bottom's companions had fled in panic at sight of the ass's head.

George Bartley, a distinguished Falstaff of the early years of the last century and for a long time stage-manager at Covent Garden Theatre, is described as "a courteous, discreet gentleman." He had, nevertheless, a very low opinion of the intelligence of audiences.

> "Sir," he would say . . . , "you must first tell them you are going to do so and so; you must then tell them you are doing it, and then that you have done it; and then, by G-d" (with a slap on his thigh), "*perhaps* they will understand you!" [29]

Shakespeare in the present instance might almost be anticipating the precautions recommended. We are told what will happen; told, as well, what has happened. And if the actual encounter can scarcely be interpreted while it is taking place, it is, in Shakespeare's theater, no encounter of phantom-shapes, of dimly outlined silhouettes, but one clearly visible by honest daylight. Misunderstanding could not well have existed. "But yet no coward, Hal. . . . Well, we leave that to the proof."

More still was promised: "the virtue of this jest . . . the incomprehensible lies." And Falstaff fairly outdoes expectation. In the study, one may forget or overlook, the visual impressiveness of his entrance. He and his followers carry battered weapons, their clothes are stained with blood ("Tell me now in earnest," the Prince asks later, "how came Falstaff's sword so hack'd?" and Peto explains, "Why, he hack'd it with his dagger, and said he would swear truth out of England but he would make you believe it was done in fight, and persuaded us to do the like"). It is he, Sir John, who makes complaint, "A plague of all cowards, I say." Deserted, as he found himself, by those who should have fought beside him, he had yet borne himself magnificently and escaped only "by miracle." Poins had prophesied he would claim to have fought with "thirty, at least," and he reaches fifty—"two or three

[29] J. R. Planché, *Recollections and Reflections* (London, 1872), II, 208.

and fifty upon poor old Jack." Then, before the fun of the mounting figures is yet exhausted, he is led to mention casualties: "two rogues in buckram . . . pepper'd." The same two, as we recognize, who are so eagerly listening to him now, who can wait, nonetheless, and give their great fish more line, for he is surely caught!

For the actor to wink at his audience, somewhere here, as Mr. Dover Wilson would have him do, seems to me purely arbitrary. (The meaning of innumerable passages in Shakespeare could be perverted by means of extra-textual winkings, and it is to be hoped that the present vogue for imagining them does not spread to tragedy!) Arbitrary, and also confusing, dividing the audience at a moment when they should be at one and sharing their pleasure as good audiences ever do. Above all, for Sir John to appear conscious of his danger thus, is to anticipate our pleasure in his escape. Whereas, if we are to judge from the text alone, this comes as a magnificent surprise. He seems doomed.

> PRINCE. Mark now how a plain tale shall put you down. Then did we two set on you four and, with a word, outfac'd you from your prize, and have it; yea, and can show it you here in the house. And, Falstaff, you carried your guts away as nimbly, with as quick dexterity, and roar'd for mercy, and still run and roar'd, as ever I heard bullcalf. . . . What trick, what device, what starting hole canst thou now find out to hide thee from this open and apparent shame?
>
> POINS. Come, let's hear, Jack. What trick has thou now?

And then, and only then (and the actor will not fail to bring out the sudden and dramatic change of speed which marks the moment), Falstaff replies:

> By the Lord, I knew ye as well as he that made ye. Why, hear you, my masters. Was it for me to kill the heir apparent? Should I turn upon the true prince? Why, thou knowest I am as valiant as Hercules; but beware instinct. The lion will not touch the true prince.

Falstaff, as Davies recognized, "is never in a state of humiliation; he generally rises superior to attack, and gets the laugh on his side in spite of truth and conviction." [30] Nevertheless, it is the Prince who recurs to this episode with enjoyment, still gloating over it in *The Second Part of Henry the Fourth*. And Falstaff, having out-

[30] *Dramatic Miscellanies,* I, 237, 238.

done himself with his glorious lion and a prince whose legitimacy is *now,* he says, established (as if there might have been some slight reason to doubt it before!) significantly changes the subject:

> Gallants, lads, boys, hearts of gold, all the titles of good fellowship come to you! What, shall we be merry? Shall we have a play extempore?
>
> PRINCE. Content—and the argument shall be thy running away.
>
> FALSTAFF. Ah, no more of that, Hal, an thou lovest me!

As Professor Waldock asked in *The Review of English Studies* some years ago, "What point would there be in such a reply . . . if Falstaff had had the laugh on them all along?" [31] He has extricated himself—"in spite of truth and conviction"—and we in the audience are glad of it. Yet Poins and Prince Hal were right; and for them Gadshill will be, as prophesied, "argument for a week, laughter for a month, and a good jest for ever."

It will be seen, if we look back, that the arguments of those who have denied that Falstaff was a coward are of many different sorts. For the most part, they are suggestive of the study rather than the playhouse. Some, indeed, are abstract, or even syllogistic, like Morgann's *We do not like cowards; we like Falstaff; therefore, Falstaff is not a coward.* Some, again, are based on inferences, sound enough, perhaps, in real life, but untrustworthy in the case of popular drama, as that a coward is unlikely to be found in the thick of the fighting. Often, it is as if the critics were determined to impose their own sense of naturalness on what, in the theater, is the more effective for being extreme—Falstaff's "incomprehensible" lying, for example. Yet Bradley himself perceived that "Shakespeare's comic world" was one of make-believe, "not merely as his tragic world is, but in a further sense—a world in which gross improbabilities are accepted with a smile. . . ." [32]

It remains possible, of course, that with this great character Shakespeare was not contented to work on a single level; so that at one instant we may be back with the Clowns of primitive drama (with Dericke, say, in *The Famous Victories*) and at another are not far from the amiable philosopher of the romantic critics. Thus, the soliloquy on honor seems to me something more than a very

[31] A. J. A. Waldock, "The Men in Buckram," *Review of English Studies,* XXIII (1947), 19.

[32] *Oxford Lectures on Poetry,* p. 270.

witty apology for the speaker's cowardice—though is it not that, as well? We read of an American actor whose fame is associated with this role:

> the shudder with which Hackett spoke the words about Honor, "Who hath it? he that-*died*-o'Wednesday," with its obvious revulsion from even the thought of death, was wonderfully expressive of *Falstaff's* animal relish of life, and also it was supremely comic.[33]

For the cowardice of Falstaff as a comic assumption gives added point to speech after speech, and to deprive the actors of it is to deprive them of a constant source of merriment. "Where," as John Bailey asked, "would be the humour of 'a plague of all cowards' if the speaker were a brave man? Where would be the fun of the 'plain tale' that put his preposterous boastings down if, as we are told, he never meant to be believed?"[34] I would not defend the farcical enormities which have been committed in Falstaff's name by unworthy comedians. Descriptions of the older stage business, whether at Gadshill or Shrewsbury, are sometimes far from edifying. But suppose, merely for the sake of argument, that Sir John *was* a coward—a fat, old, witty, boastful coward.

Early in the *Second Part of King Henry the Fourth*, he seeks to avoid a meeting with the Lord Chief Justice, attempts to hide, then feigns deafness. "Go pluck him by the elbow," the Justice tells his Servant, who does so. (Kittredge, I remember, used to describe this Servant as the Justice's "personal attendant," a "young lawyer," who "thought a lot of himself.") "Sir John!" And Falstaff, as if shocked: "What? A young knave, and begging? Is there not wars? . . . Doth not the King lack subjects?" and so on, all very humiliating to the young man. "You mistake me, sir," he says, but Falstaff continues—and goes too far.

> Why, sir, did I say you were an honest man? Setting my knighthood and my soldiership aside, I had lied in my throat if I had said so.
>
> SERVANT. I pray you, sir, then set your knighthood and your soldiership aside, and give me leave to tell you you lie in your throat if you say I am any other than an honest man.

[33] William Winter, *Shakespeare on the Stage: Third Series* (New York, 1916), p. 359.

[34] *Shakespeare* (London, New York, and Toronto, 1929), p. 128.

FALSTAFF. I give thee leave to tell me so? I lay aside that which grows to me? If thou get'st any leave of me, hang me; if thou tak'st leave, thou wert better be hang'd. You hunt counter. Hence! avaunt!

Is it not the fact of timidity, here thinly disguised in bluster, which makes the episode diverting? [35]

When the attempt to arrest Falstaff is resisted, a little later, his own part in the ensuing scuffle is not easy to determine. As Professor Shaaber, the Variorum editor, notes, much is left to the actors here; yet he adds, wisely, I think, "There is perhaps a hint in the fact that almost every word Falstaff says is by way of putting Bardolph up to active measures of defense." On the other hand, I should allow Sir John a major share in the routing of Ancient Pistol, in the Tavern Scene. Though Bardolph is at hand, once more, to give assistance, his master seems to have put on a magnificent show of belligerency, at the least; is reported to have hurt Pistol in the shoulder and has to be quieted at last by Doll, who points out that "the rascal's gone." Afterwards, we have speeches of purring self-gratulation ("A rascal bragging slave! The rogue fled from me like quicksilver"), as, to use Mr. Stoll's words, he "prolongs the precious moment, unique and unparalleled in his experience, by continually recurring to it." [36] And perhaps we remember (as we should) Sir John's own description of his opponent earlier in the scene as "a tame cheater. . . . You may stroke him as gently as a puppy greyhound. He'll not swagger with a Barbary hen if her feathers turn back in any show of resistance."

Finally, I would suggest that even single lines and phrases may take on an unexpected impressiveness for us if we return to the earlier conception of the character: to a Falstaff of dexterous evasions and miraculous escapes, lawless in his exaggerations, redoubtable only in repute, and the funnier for being fat and old and a coward. So, in the theater, I have heard Ned Poins lay a sudden emphasis upon two words, just before the Gadshill robbery: "Sirrah Jack, thy horse stands behind the hedge. When thou need'st him, there thou shalt find him. Farewell and *stand fast*"; and their portentousness was of exactly the sort that Sir Toby

[35] Stoll brackets Falstaff's sidling off at this moment with his behavior towards Poins in *1 Henry IV*, II. iv, 131, an episode which seems to me less clear in its implications (*Shakespeare Studies*, p. 421).

[36] *Ibid.*, p. 425.

Belch, sometimes, imparts to a phrase in Sir Andrew's letter: "Fare thee well, and *God have mercy upon one of our souls!*" I conceive, too, of a glint in Falstaff's eye, a certain morbid insistence in his voice, as, at another time, he dwells on the strength of the rebels.

> But tell me, Hal, art not thou horrible afeard? Thou being heir apparent, could the world pick thee out three such enemies again as that fiend Douglas, that spirit Percy, and that devil Glendower? Art thou not horribly afraid? Doth not thy blood thrill at it?

A veteran talking to a young soldier, you may say of the passage—and perhaps it is merely that. Just before Shrewsbury they are talking in a somewhat similar vein.

> FALSTAFF. Hal, if thou see me down in the battle and bestride me, so! 'Tis a point of friendship.

It is delivered with a flourish—almost as if in imagination he saw the Prince of Wales standing over and defending a gallant old soldier wounded (at any rate, *fallen*) in battle. Hal's quibbling reply gives him cold comfort: "Nothing but a Colossus can do thee that friendship. Say thy prayers, and farewell." And Falstaff: "I would 'twere bedtime, Hal, and all well."

The last instance I shall give is from a soliloquy, in which the Elizabethan actor, standing in the midst of his hearers, would have directly and familiarly addressed them. Falstaff speaks of Prince John, who does not appreciate him and cannot be made to laugh. No wonder, he says, for "this same young sober-blooded boy" does not drink as he should:

> There's never none of these demure boys come to any proof; for thin drink doth so over-cool their blood, and making many fish-meals, that they fall into a kind of male greensickness; and then, when they marry, they get wenches. They are generally fools and cowards—which some of us should be too, but for inflammation.

For an instant, the joke has become one between Falstaff and ourselves. He pauses after "cowards"; then, "which some of us" (Sir John himself, no less!) would certainly be too, except (triumphantly) for the effects of drinking sack! And who could accuse him of negligence in that regard? *You thought I was confessing, did you?*

I would not seem to attach an undue importance to these passages. They can be reconciled, each of them, with the Morgann Falstaff. "Would 'twere bedtime, Hal, and all well" is a sentiment which can be responded to by plenty of soldiers on a level quite different from that of comic cowardice. And the loss to the actor—though there is loss—will not be irreparable. On the other hand, it may be that the consensus among early readers and critics deserves more emphasis than I have given it. The burden of proof, as even Morgann recognized, rests upon those who deny cowardice. Samuel Johnson, as I said earlier, referred twice to Morgann's *Essay*. On the second occasion, when it is Malone who records the Doctor's words, they are splendidly comprehensive: "all he shd. say, was, that if Falstaff was not a coward, Shakespeare knew nothing of his art." [37]

[37] Boswell, *Life of Johnson*, iv, 515.

E. M. W. TILLYARD

On the Structure of Henry IV

In an article on *Structural Unity in the two Parts of "Henry IV"* R. A. Law maintains that Part Two is a new structure, an unpremeditated addition. I think so decidedly the other way that I shall treat the two parts as a single play (as Dover Wilson does in the *Fortunes of Falstaff*). Indeed Shakespeare almost goes out of his way to advertise the continuity by keeping the action patently incomplete at the end of the first part. In IV, iv the Archbishop of York is shown preparing for the rebellious action which is the main political theme of Part Two but which is almost irrelevant to Part One. In V, ii there is a probable reference forward to the second part. Here Worcester refuses to inform Hotspur of the king's generous consent to confine the battle to a duel between Hotspur and the Prince and of his generous offer of a

From *Shakespeare's History Plays*, by E. M. W. Tillyard, pp. 264–266. Title added by the Ed.

pardon to all the rebels. Worcester distrusts Henry and probably without reason. Shakespeare was thinking ironically of John of Lancaster's offer of pardon made to the other rebels in the second part, which, though insincere, was trusted. And the first part ends with Henry's sending Prince John and Westmoreland to deal with Northumberland and the Archbishop; an action which is taken up immediately in the second part. Finally, one of the most striking anticipations, pointing to Shakespeare's having planned ahead with much thought, is the talk between Falstaff and the Prince on justice in the scene that first brings them in. The Prince has slipped into the talk of robberies by moonlight an unpleasant reference to the gallows. Falstaff, not relishing it, seeks to turn the conversation with

> And is not my hostess of the tavern a most sweet wench?

But the Prince turns the conversation back to the unpleasant theme. Falstaff again turns the conversation; but the thought of the gallows is too strong for him and he can't help asking,

> Shall there be gallows standing when thou art king? and resolution thus fobbed as it is with the rusty curb of old father antic the law?

The Prince does not say no to this. But the questions are not answered till the end of the second part—indeed they cannot arise again in the first part because the Prince is not yet king—but there Resolution, or Falstaff and his gang, are indeed fobbed with the rusty curb of the Lord Chief Justice or old father antic the law.

The reason why Law wishes to separate the two parts is that he thinks their motives are different. According to him Part One shows the struggle of the Prince and Hotspur culminating in the Battle of Shrewsbury, while Part Two, in strong contrast, shows the Prince in the background not fighting but fought over, as in the Moralities, by the royal household and the Lord Chief Justice on the one hand and by Falstaff, the epitome of the Seven Deadly Sins, on the other. Law was right in seeing the Morality pattern in Part Two, but wrong in not seeing it in Part One likewise. The struggle between the Prince and Hotspur is subordinate to a larger plan.

The structure of the two parts is indeed very similar. In the first part the Prince (who, one knows, will soon be king) is tested in the military or chivalric virtues. He has to choose, Morality-fashion, between Sloth or Vanity, to which he is drawn by his bad companions, and Chivalry, to which he is drawn by his father and his brothers. And he chooses Chivalry. The action is complicated by Hotspur and Falstaff, who stand for the excess and the defect of the military spirit, for honour exaggerated and dishonour. Thus the Prince, as well as being Magnificence in a Morality Play, is Aristotle's middle quality between two extremes. Such a combination would have been entirely natural to the Elizabethans, especially since it occurred in the second book of the *Fairy Queen*. Guyon is at once the Morality figure fought over by the Palmer and Mammon and the man who is shown the Aristotelian allegory of Excess Balance and Defect in Perissa Medina and Elissa. Near the end of the play the Prince ironically surrenders to Falstaff the credit of having killed Hotspur, thus leaving the world of arms and preparing for the motive of the second part. Here again he is tested, but in the civil virtues. He has to choose, Morality-fashion, between disorder or misrule, to which he is drawn by his bad companions, and Order or Justice (the supreme kingly virtue) to which he is drawn by his father and by his father's deputy the Lord Chief Justice. And he chooses Justice. As in the first part the Aristotelian motive occurs, but it is only touched on. After Falstaff has exchanged words with John of Lancaster about his captive Sir John Colevile, he remains on the stage to soliloquise. He calls John a "sober-blooded boy" and blames him for not drinking sack. John is thus cold-blooded and addicted to thin potations, Falstaff himself is warm-blooded and addicted to strong drink. The Prince is the mean, cold-blooded by inheritance but warmed "with excellent endeavour of drinking good and good store of fertile sherris." Temperamentally he strikes the balance between the parsimony of John and the extravagance of Falstaff. He does the same too in his practice of justice. The justice of John of Lancaster in his cold-blooded treatment of the rebels verges on rigour; Falstaff has no general standard of justice at all, Henry V uses his justice moderately in the way he treats his old companions—at least by Elizabethan standards.

M. A. SHAABER

The Unity of Henry IV

The fact that, in the last three or four years, two persuasive and influential critics have offered us interpretations of Shakespeare's *Henry IV* plays which assume that these plays form a unified whole invites us once more to consider this assumption. There is nothing new about it (it is at least as old as Dr. Johnson), but it has rarely been assumed so confidently or worked into so elaborate an interpretation. Since, however, as often as it has been made it has been questioned—among others, by Dr. J. Q. Adams, whose scholarly distinction and rare friendliness we commemorate—it seems desirable to ascertain whether or not Professor Wilson and Dr. Tillyard have been able to put it on a new or a firmer footing.

Professor Dover Wilson proclaimed the unity of the two plays in *The Fortunes of Falstaff* (1943), but without making much attempt to prove it. He says:

> (1) . . . Shakespeare must have kept his intentions for Part II steadily in mind all the time he was writing Part I, and (2) . . . Part II . . . is a continuation of the same play, which is no less incomplete without it than Part II is itself unintelligible without Part I. In any case, the unity and continuity of the two parts is a cardinal assumption of the following study. As we shall find, it is impossible otherwise to make sense of Falstaff's character, to say nothing of Prince Hal's [p. 4].

But in his edition of *1 Henry IV* (1946) he offers some justification of his opinion:

> *1 Henry IV* . . . is . . . patently only part of a whole, inasmuch as at its close all the strands of the plot are left with loose ends. [1] The rebels, Northumberland and Archbishop Scroop,

From *Joseph Quincy Adams Memorial Studies* (Washington, D.C., 1948), pp. 217–227. Reprinted by permission of the Folger Shakespeare Library and the author.

are still at large after the battle of Shrewsbury; and [2] the Archbishop is introduced and given a scene to himself in 4. 4 in order to prepare the audience for the expedition of Prince John in Part 2. [3] The relations of the Prince with his father, eased by the interview in 3. 2 and his brilliant conduct in battle, still await that final clarification which, as Elizabethan auditors acquainted with the merest outline of the life of Henry of Monmouth would know, belonged to the death-bed scene in the Jerusalem chamber. [4] Most striking of all perhaps is that stone of stumbling to modern interpreters, the soliloquy at the end of the second scene of Part 1, which looks forward not only to the coronation of Henry V but also to the rejection of Falstaff, neither of which occurs until the very end of Part 2. If Part 1 be an integral drama, and Part 2 a mere afterthought, the soliloquy is inexplicable . . . In short, the political and dynastic business of this history play, which is twofold, the defeat of the rebels and the repentance of the Prince including his reconciliation with his father, is only half through at the end of Part 1. . . . [5] Yet another indication of planning is the symbolic arrangement, which excludes the Lord Chief Justice from Part 1, though there are indications that he appeared early in the pre-Shakespearian version, restricts that part to the theme of the truant prince's return to Chivalry, and leaves the atonement with Justice, or the Rule of Law, as a leading motive for its sequel [p. x ff.].

Dr. E. M. W. Tillyard, in *Shakespeare's History Plays* (1944), argues for the unity of the two plays as follows:

[6] [Shakespeare keeps] the action patently incomplete at the end of the first part. [7] In IV, iv the Archbishop of York is shown preparing for the rebellious action which is the main political theme of Part Two but which is almost irrelevant to Part One. [8] In V, ii there is a probable reference forward to the second part. Here Worcester refuses to inform Hotspur of the king's generous consent to confine the battle to a duel between Hotspur and the Prince and of his generous offer of a pardon to all the rebels. Worcester distrusts Henry and probably without reason. Shakespeare was thinking ironically of John of Lancaster's offer of pardon made to the other rebels in the second part, which, though insincere, was trusted. . . . [9] Finally, one of the most striking anticipations, pointing to Shakespeare's having planned ahead with much thought, is the talk between Falstaff and the Prince on justice in the scene that first brings them in. . . .

"Shall there be gallows standing when thou art king? and resolution thus fobbed as it is with the rusty curb of old father antic the law?"

The Prince does not say no to this. But the questions are not answered till the end of the second part . . . there Resolution, or Falstaff and his gang, are indeed fobbed with the rusty curb of the Lord Chief Justice or old father antic the law [p. 264 ff.].

It is apparent that 1 and 6, 2 and 7 are the same arguments and that 4 and 9 come to almost the same thing. Except for 8, which I think need not be taken seriously, I shall discuss them seriatim.

[1, 6] The incompleteness assumed by both interpreters is not apparent to me. Of course, the reign of Henry IV is incomplete; as long as Shakespeare chose to make the Battle of Shrewsbury the climax of his play it could not be otherwise. The rebels, to be sure, are not completely quelled, but then they never are. The announcement that they have been thoroughly scotched a moment before Henry IV dies is an invention of Shakespeare's intended, I think, to add a poignant irony to the king's death. But the inheritors of their quarrel rise up against Henry V at the beginning of his reign, and indeed it is the argument of Dr. Tillyard's book that the rebel cause draws its motive from the wrong done Richard II, a wrong which plagues Henry IV and his successors all their lives and is not expiated till the end of the Wars of the Roses. So far as the play is incomplete, it is incomplete because history is an endless chain, and Shakespeare is dramatizing history. And if the theme of *1 Henry IV* is what Dr. Tillyard says it is, I do not understand how the play can be called incomplete.

In the first part [he says] the Prince . . . is tested in the military or chivalric virtues. He has to choose, Morality-fashion, between Sloth or Vanity, to which he is drawn by his bad companions, and Chivalry, to which he is drawn by his father and his brothers. And he chooses Chivalry.[1]

[1] *Op. cit.*, p. 265. I accept this statement of Dr. Tillyard's so as to keep the discussion on the unity of the two plays, but I have uncomfortable misgivings about it. It could equally well be argued that the prince is never really tempted by Sloth and Vanity. He tolerates them; he plays the madcap in their company; but he is never deceived by them. "I know you all," he says, and why may we not take him at his word? Hal does not *choose* Chivalry; he *is* Chivalry from the beginning to the end of the play. There is no visible struggle. The conflict is not between his better and his worser nature, but between his real nature and the common opinion of him. These are not precisely the terms I would choose to

Indeed he does, unequivocally and completely. Fully reconciled with his father, he seems to have set the issue between them completely at rest. I cannot think what need have or could have been added to show that Hal was indeed the true prince.

[2, 7] *1 Henry IV*, IV, iv is very commonly pointed out as a reason for taking the two plays as a unit. It has even been said that this appearance of the archbishop "has no meaning unless his conspiracy was to follow." [2] On the contrary, the scene has an obvious meaning in the dramatic scheme of *1 Henry IV* and is not "almost irrelevant" to it. Its business is to foreshadow the outcome of the Battle of Shrewsbury. There the rebels are to meet with a decisive check, and Shakespeare, after his usual fashion, anticipates what is to come. This scene signifies that the rebel cause is in a bad way indeed if one of its ringleaders has grave misgivings about it. The same thing might have been, and is, signified otherwise, but this is by no means the only place where Shakespeare, even near the end of a play, has brought forward a new character to serve some purpose of the moment and dismissed him as soon as his work was done. If *1 Henry IV* had never had a sequel, Shakespeare, judged by his practice elsewhere, might well have put this scene into his play.

[3, 4, 9] The idea that the relations of the prince and the king, "eased by the interview in 3. 2 and his brilliant conduct in battle," still await "final clarification" is adroitly stated. Much virtue in *eased*. Is there really the slightest hint in *1 Henry IV* that the king and the prince are not completely and triumphantly reconciled? Does "Thou hast redeem'd thy lost opinion" (V, iv, 47) really mean "I feel a bit easier about you than I did before, but the final showdown is still to come"? I cannot think that the impression left by *1 Henry IV* is anything but that of a complete vindication of the prince in his father's eyes. To be sure, in *2 Henry IV* we find him as much misunderstood as ever, but to interpret the first part by the second is what Professor Wilson himself objects to as "the fallacy of omniscience, that is, of treating a play like a historical

---

describe the play, but they seem to me to correspond with Shakespeare's text at least as well as Dr. Tillyard's interpretation. It is amazing how small a place is allowed Hotspur in this interpretation. Dr. Tillyard is right in saying that Hotspur is not the hero of the play, but how can one ignore the fact that his combat with the prince is the climax?

[2] *Shakespeare, Works* (Eversley ed., 1899), vi, 253 ff.

document and collecting evidence in support of a particular reading of character or situation from any point of the text without regard to its relation to the rest."[3] If one does not fall into this fallacy, there is no reason whatever for supposing that the end of *1 Henry IV* is anything but an end. The prince has broken through the clouds "that did seem to strangle him," has falsified men's hopes; the premises from which the play took its start have been carried to a conclusion.

In another sense, however, Professor Wilson and Dr. Tillyard have a point here. There is no doubt that, from the first, Shakespeare knew that the scene at the death-bed of Henry IV and the rejection of Falstaff were parts of the legend of Prince Hal with high dramatic possibilities. But this is really no argument that *2 Henry IV* was conceived and planned with its predecessor. No one thinks that, as he wrote *1 Henry IV*, Shakespeare did not have a sequel in mind—a sequel approximately like the play we know as *Henry V*. I have no notion how clearly Shakespeare had devised a scheme for this sequel while at work on *1 Henry IV*, but, whether clear or highly nebulous, his plan could easily have included the idea of beginning with the rejection of Falstaff or even with the death of Henry IV. The coronation would be a natural starting-place for a history of the reign of Henry V, especially when it is immediately preceded by one highly dramatic episode and followed by another. Therefore, since Shakespeare certainly had a play on Henry V in mind when he wrote *1 Henry IV*, the anticipations in the latter of the death of Henry IV and the rejection of Falstaff cannot be used to prove that he also had *2 Henry IV* in mind, for these episodes might appropriately have begun the projected *Henry V*. If *2 Henry IV* is an unpremeditated sequel, Shakespeare of course transferred them to the new play he was constrained to fabricate.

[5] I cannot say much against Professor Wilson's idea that the appearance of the Chief Justice in *2 Henry IV* is a proof of a unified plan for both plays, for I do not know how an idea of this kind can be proved or disproved. Professor Wilson thinks that the late appearance of the Chief Justice must be the result of planning; I think it could equally well be the result of a search for new material to make a play not contemplated until Falstaff became a tremendous hit. Thought is free, and neither of us can adduce real

[3] *The Fortunes of Falstaff*, p. 3 ff.

evidence to support his point of view. I doubt that Professor Wilson would rest his case on this argument alone and I would not think that I had disposed of his case if I could squelch it utterly.

Besides imputing weakness to the arguments in favor of a unified plan, I submit that there are other reasons for viewing the idea skeptically. The first is the similarity of the structure of the two plays. Structurally *2 Henry IV* is almost a carbon copy of the first play. According to the scene-division of modern editions, there is exactly the same number of scenes in both plays; according to that of the folio, there are three more in the first part. By either count the number of scenes is exactly the same in the first, second, and last acts. What is more impressive, the sequence of scenes developing the historical plot and that of the comic scenes is almost exactly the same. The following table shows the order of the historical and the comic scenes in both plays.

	Part 1	*Part 2*		*Part 1*	*Part 2*
I, i	H	H	IV, i	H	H
I, ii	C	C	IV, ii	C	H
I, iii	H	H	IV, iii	H	C
II, i	C	C	IV, iv	H	H
II, ii	C	(H), C	IV, v		H
II, iii	H	H	V, i	H, C	C
II, iv	C	C	V, ii	H	H
III, i	H	H	V, iii	H, C	C
III, ii	H	C	V, iv	H, C	C
III, iii	C		V, v	H	H, C

In the first two acts the correspondences are remarkably close. I, iii represents a conference of the rebels in both plays; II, iii is a domestic scene among the Percies; II, iv is a tavern scene. The last is, I think, especially significant. In the third act the plan is, in a very general way, the same (historical matter followed by a Falstaff scene), but in *2 Henry IV* the comic material outweighs the historical. In the fourth act the correspondence is perhaps closer than the table shows, for in *2 Henry IV* there are really only two scenes (corresponding to i–iii and iv–v). In both plays the act is devoted to the historical plot except for one irruption on the part of Falstaff. There are real divergences in the fifth act. In *1 Henry IV* the historical and the comic material are interwoven; in *2 Henry IV* they are separated until the last scene. The question is, then, would Shakespeare be more likely to plan the plays in this fashion if he were working out, in a single fit of creation, a play of ten acts or if, after *1 Henry IV* proved a resounding success, he aimed at repeating it? To me the latter view is the more probable.

Another reason for hesitating to see the two plays as one is, I think, the fact that in the second the clock is turned back most flagrantly. At the end of *1 Henry IV* the king and the prince are *en rapport* and united against the Welsh; in *2 Henry IV* we find them estranged all over again so that they must be reconciled a second time. No new cause of misunderstanding is shown; the situation simply reverts to what it was in the beginning. Shakespeare sets the clock back adroitly, but set it back he does. I know that Professor Wilson will have it otherwise: the king and the prince are only tentatively reconciled at the end of *1 Henry IV*; their relations are only "eased." I can only repeat what I have said above, that I defy a candid reader to detect any flaws in the understanding between them as it is presented at the end of *1 Henry IV*. What becomes of the triumphant close of the play if the king and the prince are still somewhat at odds? How could this imperfect sympathy possibly be acted? Thus the question arises, if Shakespeare planned both plays as a whole, would he have planned to bring the king and the prince together, separate them covertly, and then bring them together once more? Would he have invented the reconciliation at the Battle of Shrewsbury, about which *The Famous Victories* and Holinshed are silent, knowing that there was a second reconciliation to come later? Or is it more likely that he would have done what he did because the immoderate popularity of *1 Henry IV* forced him to write an unpremeditated sequel for which he needed the death-bed scene as climax? It is hard for me to believe that an experienced playwright who from the first contemplated making the death-bed scene the climax of his picture of the relations of father and son would have anticipated their reconciliation in his version of the Battle of Shrewsbury and the events leading up to it.

Finally, the question of the unity of *Henry IV* raises larger questions about cyclical plays. Professor Wilson sees the implications of his argument clearly and faces them boldly. "Part II," he says, "was written to be played immediately, or at not more than twenty-four hours' interval, after Part I." [4] And indeed his interpretation is highly esoteric unless the plays were so performed. What is the likelihood that they were?

So far as I know, there are no recorded performances of the two plays on the same day or on successive days before the twentieth century.[5] In the absence of contemporary records of performances of Shakespeare, we have nothing to judge by but Henslowe's * records. They are not decisive. Henslowe records a number of performances of the two parts of *Tamburlaine* on successive days,[6] a few more of a two-part *Hercules* [7] and a two-part *Tamar Cam*,[8] and one of a two-part *Seaser*.[9] But at the same time he also records independent performances of both parts of the same plays. We can infer very little from these facts even if we assume that the Chamberlain's men would always do just what Henslowe's companies did. 1 and 2 *Henry IV* may have been acted both successively and separately in Shakespeare's day.

Perhaps the practice of other playwrights will help us to estimate the likelihood of Shakespeare's having planned *Henry IV* as a unit. In the sixteenth and seventeenth centuries, I cannot find a real example of an integrated cycle of plays, of two or more plays which must be considered as one if their import is to be grasped.[10] I find a number of examples of linked plays and of plays on contiguous subjects, but none of a cycle like Professor Wilson's version of *Henry IV*. The nearest thing would seem to be, strangely enough, Heywood's *Iron Age*, in which the story of the siege of Troy (plus other matter) is divided between the two parts as if the audience were expected to follow it from the beginning, but to speak of the unity of so naïve a cycle is a little absurd. *The Conquest of Granada*

[4] *The Fortunes of Falstaff*, p. 91.

[5] Both parts may have been performed at court during the holiday season of 1612–1613; at least two plays for which the King's men were rewarded—*The Hotspur* and *Sir John Falstaffe*—have been so identified (see Chambers, *The Elizabethan Stage*, iv, 180). But there is nothing to show that they were acted on successive nights.

* Philip Henslowe (d. 1616), a theatrical manager. Ed.

[6] *Henslowe's Diary*, ed. Greg. i, 21–42.

[7] *Ibid.*, i, 24–7.

[8] *Ibid.*, i, 42.

[9] *Ibid.*, i, 24.

[10] I have not considered a few Cavalier two-part plays because I think they must be quite outside any tradition which may throw light on Shakespeare's practice.

almost answers the specifications. The two parts are closely integrated; there is no final resolution of anything at the end of the first and some familiarity with the first is demanded to understand the second. But the fact remains that both parts were often played independently,[11] apparently without baffling audiences or sending them home unsatisfied.*

It would seem then that, if *Henry IV* is a fully integrated unit, it is virtually unique. What Shakespeare did no other playwright of his time attempted. Obviously Shakespeare is by no means debarred from venturing upon untrodden ground and the singularity of such a scheme hardly disproves it. But one may still ask what Shakespeare would have gained by it, what advantage a highly integrated scheme gave him in attracting audiences to the theater. From a purely practical point of view, surely none at all; successive performances, separated by an interval of not more than twenty-four hours, require a degree of cooperation of the audience difficult to obtain. For obviously such a cycle of plays can achieve its full effect only so far as the same audience attends both performances. According to Professor Wilson, any spectator who sees *1 Henry IV* alone goes away unsatisfied and any one who sees *2 Henry IV* alone cannot understand it. Presumably such an outcome must be forestalled. But Professor Wilson cannot suppose that, in the sixteenth century, every member of the audience who saw *1 Henry IV* on Monday was able, even if willing, to come back on Tuesday to see the second part. Or that on Tuesday auditors who could not show that they had seen the first part on Monday were turned away from the door. The practical difficulties of achieving what Professor Wilson requires are very great.

So great, indeed, that I cannot imagine an experienced playwright, in his right wits, doing anything of the kind. I doubt that such a playwright would ever think of writing a play which, by itself, had not sufficient dramatic interest to stand on its own legs, which would be unintelligible without some other play which the audience may not see or have seen, which would not fully reward any audience that happened to gather to see it. This is not to say that there are no links between the two parts of *Henry IV* or that

[11] Dryden, *Works* (Nonesuch ed., 1932), iii, 13.

* Note 12, omitted here, lists a number of two-part plays of the sixteenth and seventeenth centuries each part of which, Professor Shaaber contends, can stand as an adequate dramatic unit. Ed.

the experience of seeing *2 Henry IV* is not the richer for having seen the first part. It is only to say that I cannot square what I think a knowledgeable playwright would do in writing two linked plays with Professor Wilson's description of *Henry IV*, and that therefore I am suspicious of his description. The unity which he attributes to the two plays seems to me to be a theatrical impossibility.[13]

We must conclude, I think, that the unity of the *Henry IV* plays is an assumption which Professor Wilson and Dr. Tillyard have not proved and which implies some things difficult to believe. Accordingly, interpretations of the plays based on their assumptions cannot win a hearty assent.

One word more. I hope I do Professor Wilson and Dr. Tillyard no injustice by inferring that when they defend the unity of *Henry IV* they think they are vindicating Shakespeare's art, they think that a unified *Henry IV* is artistically superior to two plays linked by catch-as-catch-can methods. To that assumption I would demur. The logic of a play is no necessary cause of its greatness and at most but a minor cause. According to Professor Wilson, it is impossible to make sense of Falstaff's character or of the prince's unless we look at the two plays as a unified whole. Let us suppose that he is right. What do we gain? Something which increases or intensifies our enjoyment of Falstaff's antics or the prince's exploits as we watch a performance of the play? I think not. Making sense of the play, rationalizing its diversity is an *ex post facto* operation; it cannot even begin before all the materials which it fits into rational patterns have been unfolded. It seems to me therefore largely a work of supererogation, with some interest of its own but no great importance to the understanding or the enjoyment of drama. Assuming it to be all-important is the capital fallacy of Professor Wilson's and Dr. Tillyard's discussions of the play. What worries

[13] The structure which Professor Wilson attributes to the two plays is, I suspect, equally impossible. According to him (*1 Henry IV*, p. xi ff.), the normal dramatic curve of a five-act Shakespearian play here encompasses ten acts. Now the structure of an effective play presses the spectator forward at an accelerating pace till his interest is carried to the climax and is satisfied by the dénouement. There are minor relaxations of the tension along the way, but there can be no real interruption of this continuous and progressive interest without disastrous results. How is it possible to send him home overnight midway in this continuous and progressive development without seriously impairing its effect? What experienced playwright would ever dream of doing such a thing?

them seems to me largely beside the point. "Part II is itself unintelligible without Part I," says Professor Wilson. Who asks for intelligibility—the kind of intelligibility that Part I can confer on Part II—in a play? "The soliloquy is inexplicable." Who asks to have it explained? "Falstaff's false claim to the *spolia opima* of Harry Hotspur . . . [is] the key to his character in Part 2." [14] Who pays his penny at the door to have keys to character put in his hand? "Once its unity is accepted . . . , it will stand revealed as one of the greatest of dramatic masterpieces." [15] Unity—Professor Wilson's kind of unity—is the test of a masterpiece? It cannot be. For two hundred years captious critics have been trying to make sense of Falstaff's hyperbolical account of the action on Gadshill, trying to make it acceptable to our minds. They have not succeeded. But the scene remains ineffable comedy just the same; in other words, whether the mind can accept it has very little to do with the matter. Sense is only sense; it is not drama. Critics who put so heavy an emphasis on it are barking up the wrong tree. What happens in Shakespeare's plays (like what happens in human life) sometimes defies explanation, especially easy explanation, but if this fact is of any importance to the profound and lasting impressions that the plays make it is because our interest is quickened and our impressions heightened, as in life itself, by what is not transparently clear. Explain away the puzzles, the incongruities, the diversities and you take away some of the amazement, the awe, the sense of the complexity and the inscrutability of life which they excite. We do not need to impose an airtight logical scheme on Shakespeare's plays to justify them artistically; we come much closer to the radiant core of their interest by other avenues of approach.

[14] *1 Henry IV*, p. x f.
[15] *Ibid.*, p. xiii.

FREDSON BOWERS

The Structural Climax in Henry IV, Part I

Shakespeare's plays were plays, first and foremost. Present-day critics, in their search for new areas of exploration, do these plays a disservice by treating them as poems—often as if they were extended lyric poems. Whether a play is in verse or in prose, it is primarily a play and must conform to the laws of the drama, not to criteria that have been set as appropriate for other literary genres. When dramatic structure is neglected for, say, an interest in style, criticism ceases to be dramatic criticism.

Moreover, a concern for dramatic structure acts as a check on another troublesome habit of present-day Shakespearean criticism: the reconstruction of a play—its people and the significance of its action—either in terms of some preconceived aesthetic theory or in terms of the critic's own ingenious sensibility. Both can be peculiarly misleading. The constant awareness that drama imposes certain rules on literature written in its form serves as a check upon mythic theory, or upon quite personal sensibility, forcibly imposed from without on Shakespeare. Any critical method that is external and not inductive runs contrary to the truth that can be sought in Shakespeare from the evidence of his plays as drama. Basically, most laws of drama that are not concerned with simple stagecraft have as their object the manipulation of the audience's point of view. By its nature the drama is perhaps the most highly developed objective literary form in existence, and thus the control of the point of view is a crucial matter. The dramatist must use action as his chief means of working out his story in terms of character. For instance, he can seldom slip into narration, except at the peril of losing the interest of his audience. Even such narrative as may be

From "Shakespeare's Art: The Point of View," in *Literary Views,* ed. Carroll Camden (Chicago, 1964), pp. 45–58. Reprinted by permission of the author and William Marsh Rice University. Title added by Ed.

required to transmit vital facts about the antecedent action—what is technically known as the exposition—cannot be managed in the playwright's own person but must come from the mouth of one or more characters. Yet the audience cannot always be immediately certain that the account these characters give is an accurate one. When dramatic persons are not mere sticks, or automatons, they participate in the nature of all humanity, the chief characteristic of which is to be fallible. Their information may not be wholly accurate; or if it is, their personal reactions may color the interpretation in a manner that should lead an audience to view the account with some caution.

Indeed, when the interpretation of fact is involved, an audience learns to be especially wary of accepting the statement of any dramatic character as infallible truth. When in the opening scene of Shakespeare's *Antony and Cleopatra* Philo and Demetrius discuss Antony's visible subjection to Cleopatra, it is important to recognize that they are Romans. Two Egyptians, like Charmion and Iras, take the opposite position. Which is the audience to believe, or should it believe neither as representing the whole truth?

The peculiar condition of the dramatic form is that the playwright must work exclusively through the words and actions of a series of fallible characters. He can never speak in his own person, else he is breaking the form. Since characters fail if they are simple authorial mouthpieces, and the play is likely to fail with them, the major dramatic problem is to convey to the audience, within the rules of the game, what the dramatist wants it to believe. Moreover, these ideas (in other words, the dramatist's point of view) must be conveyed in such a manner that the audience is unaware that it is being manipulated and directed into certain channels of belief. Today in the experimental theater a dramatist may quite deliberately refuse to impose any point of view upon the play so that the audience is a free agent and can react in whatever unpredictable and various ways it chooses. That indeed may become the very point of the play—the deliberate withdrawal of any attempt at dramatic control over the audience's reactions to, or interpretations of, the events it is watching on the stage.

The Shakespearean drama does not have a twentieth-century soul in this respect. Ordinarily, like every other Elizabethan dramatist, Shakespeare was concerned to control for his own ends the reactions of his audience. He does so, of course, in respect to the audience for which he wrote, and he usually took particular care to control their view of character and of action. Thus if we follow the various ways by which he manipulated his audience in order to maintain his control, we can come upon some useful critical insights, for we shall have clear-cut evidence about Shakespeare's conscious intentions. Surely, before a critic proceeds to unconscious intentions (important as they may be), he had better settle first what the author was consciously trying to impress upon his audience. Such information will offer a factual basis, and for this reason the dramatist's art is singularly important to construe.*

* * * * *

. . . nothing approaches plot as a means of enforcing the dramatist's point of view. The plot of a play is that series of interconnecting incidents, or actions, by means of which the main story is presented. Plot in Aristotle's phrase is "the structure of the incidents" (*Poetics* vi, 9). To Aristotle, "Tragedy is an imitation, not of man, but of an action and of life, and life consists in action, and its end is a mode of action, not a quality. . . . Character determines men's qualities, but it is by their actions that they are happy or the reverse. Dramatic action, therefore, is not with a view to the representation of character: character comes in as subsidiary to the actions. Hence the incidents of the plot are the end of a tragedy; and the end is the chief thing of all" (vi, 9–10).

If plot is indeed the end of a tragedy, then we must look to the dramatist to utilize action in contrived episodes to lead the audience to the correct understanding of his theme, or purpose, in the full plot. The working-out of the plot has various incidents that serve as stations on the way. Of all these, that incident in the plot that one calls the climax, or crisis, is the most significant, for in it will reside the main action or decision that in a comedy will eventually lead the ending to come out well for the chief persons, and in a tragedy to come out ill. Since such a turning point must automatically be a significant action—else the play will be trivial, or quite meaningless—it behooves a critic to isolate this episode from the surrounding incidents of the plot. Once this crisis incident can be identified, the major significance of the plot may be determined

* In the passages omitted here, Professor Bowers discusses the device of a "touchstone character," like Enobarbus, Horatio, or Don Pedro, "whose important function is to act as an intermediary and translator between the audience and the events of the play."

and an important part of the total meaning of the play thereby assessed.

* * * * *

To my mind, the high point of subtlety in Shakespeare's treatment of the climax as the key to point of view appears in *1 Henry IV*. Truly, if critics had observed the implications of this scene, much misapprehension about the play would have been prevented. In terms of the plot the climax can only be Act III, Scene ii, in which, seemingly, King Henry weans Hal from his dissolute life and sets him on the road to Shrewsbury, the conquest of Hotspur, and the acceptance of his duties as Prince of Wales. By himself, it is implied, King Henry cannot subdue the rebels. By himself, Hal can have no national forces to lead. A scene of high drama can be anticipated in which the father pleads with his son to join him against a common danger: and, on the surface, Shakespeare gives us just that. The King reproves his son for his wild courses and refuses to accept Hal's submission, perhaps because he thinks it too coldly offered. Hal's formal request for pardon receives a quick "God pardon thee!" and sixty-odd lines of further reproof mixed with a lesson on kingship. Hal quietly promises to be himself, that is, to reform. But the King pushes on as if the Prince had not spoken, and delivers the ultimate insult that he really expects Hal, through fear, to join Hotspur's party against him. Stung at last, Hal forsakes his formal protestations and in an emotional speech vows to defeat Percy and reconcile himself to his father by his deeds. Immediately Henry clinches his victory with,

> A hundred thousand rebels die in this!
> Thou shalt have charge and sovereign trust herein.

Every indication points to Henry's having prepared this interview with particular care, as was his way, leaving nothing to chance. The rising tide of his emotion, and finally the obviously calculated insult at the right moment, are characteristic of his methods. Are we to believe, then, that the King has truly won over his son by this contrivance, has broken down Hal's indifference, detached him from Falstaff and the idle tavern life that was corrupting him and returned the Prince to the great world of affairs that was to be the training for the hero-king Henry V? If we are to believe so, then we must take it that a real conflict of wills was present and that it was resolved in classic fashion in a turnabout of motive and action, a true peripeteia. The King would have been right, and Hal wrong. Hal would have been convinced of the error of his ways by the force of his father's speech and would have been, in a manner of speaking, converted.

Such a scene might well have been an exciting and significant one; but Shakespeare did not write it so. The true point of this climax is that no peripeteia takes place. Hal makes no decision that he had not previously planned. With or without this scene the play would have had the same ending, for a few hours before, Hal had formally decided to reconcile himself to his father and to join in subduing the rebels.[1] There is no tug of war in which Hal is placed between Falstaff and what he represents, and King Henry and what he represents. The famous "I know you all" soliloquy, at the very beginning of the play, effectively disposes of any dramatic suspense that might have developed from a genuine inability in the Prince to make up his mind about his future. From the start of the play, therefore, Shakespeare has deliberately cast off the legitimate suspense that might have been generated by a lack of Hal's firm commitment. The soliloquy shows Hal to be plain enough. He is amusing himself for the nonce. When an emergency arises he will break through the clouds like the sun and show himself in his true majesty. He is not in the least deceived by Falstaff, nor does he have more than a partial interest in their tavern life.

I pass over the possible moral question that modern sensibility has quite wrongly raised in connection with this soliloquy. Neither Shakespeare nor his audience were egalitarians, nor was it demeaning to accept the fact that kings were not common men fully responsible to the ordinary law. Kings had their own code of conduct, and the responsibility for their actions was primarily to God. We can be confident that Shakespeare would have been surprised to hear the modern denigration of Hal on the basis of this speech. It is not a character speech at all, as Kittredge has observed, but a time-saving plot device, rather on the clumsy side, deliberately to remove from the audience any suspense that Hal was actually committed to his low-life surroundings. A comparison, indeed, may be made with the fifth soliloquy in *Hamlet*,

[1] Hal to Poins at the end of II, iv: "I'll to the court in the morning. We must all to the war. . . . "

'Tis now the very witching time of night,
When churchyards yawn, and hell itself breathes out
Contagion to this world. . . .

This soliloquy has no other purpose than to prevent the audience from feeling an illegitimate suspense in the closet scene that is to follow. When Hamlet promises that the soul of the matricide Nero from feeling an illegitimate suspense in the closet scene that is to Gertrude but use none, he is warning the audience that he plans to take a very high line with his mother and, in effect, to frighten her into repentance—a feat that he actually performs. But the audience must not fear for the Queen's life no matter how violently he behaves.[2]

When a playwright deliberately throws away dramatic suspense, one of his main stocks in trade, it is well to look into his motives. In *Hamlet* it is clear that Shakespeare for very good reasons is determined that the audience should not take the wrong point of view about Hamlet's violent actions in the closet scene. So concerned is he with manipulating the audience to guide the reactions he wants in an episode yet to come that he is willing to sacrifice part of the superficial drama of the scene in order to emphasize to the audience the true nature of the conflict between mother and son.

Similarly, the outright manipulation of the audience was a necessity in *1 Henry IV*. The standard pattern of the plot would have produced a Prince Hal more acted upon than acting himself. Suspense would have developed from his indecision before the three ways of life open to him, each with its separate and conflicting ideals. Then in the climax he would have brought the play to a successful conclusion with his victory at Shrewsbury. This is a possible plot, but it is not Shakespeare's. Recent critics are so occupied with abusing Hal as a cold-blooded prig that they fail to see what Shakespeare was desperately trying to convey in his shaping of the action into a plot. What kind of a play is it in which the Prince from the start reveals to the audience his whole future course of action and therefore destroys the pleasurable uncertainty the audience would feel in the development of the suspense and its resolu-

[2] Bowers, "Hamlet's Fifth Soliloquy, III.ii.406–417," *Essays in Shakespeare and Elizabethan Drama in Honor of Hardin Craig*, ed. R. Hosley (Columbia: University of Missouri Press, 1962), pp. 213–222.

tion? What kind of a play is it in which, faced with three laws of life, Hal chooses all, and none? What kind of a play is it in which the climax goes through all the motions of a decision, but no decision is actually made, for none is needed?

The answer is an obvious one. This is a play about a future hero-king who rose far above ordinary humanity. As in the old fairy tale of the Bear's Son, this future hero had a wild and careless youth, which Shakespeare is concerned to rationalize.[3] We could scarcely expect him to take personally the primitive beef-and-blood picture of Hal in *The Famous Victories*. Hal is to rise superior to the Machiavellian kingship of his father, even though Henry's policy was aimed at a strong central monarchy that any Tudor subject knew was absolutely required for peace and stability. He is to rise superior to Hotspur's narrow chivalric code of honor based on the outmoded feudal ideals that could become a force for evil when used without intelligence. Moreover, the practical value of these ideals was being made obsolete by the nascent central royal authority. He is to rise superior to the chaotic forces of the self-seeking pleasure that denies responsibility in favor of hedonism, as embodied in Falstaff. Three principles of self-seeking are portrayed in this play, each trying to control the future king.[4]

Shakespeare's difficulty in some part resembled that of Milton in *Samson Agonistes* in that his hero can demonstrate superiority for most of the play only by endurance in the rejection of false values offered to tempt him—that is, by a refusal to be acted upon from without—until the time comes for his own positive individual action that cuts the knot and resolves the whole dramatic problem. Once we learn to read the plot, we see what Shakespeare intends to convey to us through the action. Indeed, he was so concerned to insure the audience's point of view that he ventured in the "I know you all" soliloquy to erect the plainest signpost he could contrive. He thereby tried to avoid the confusion that would have lain in any

[3] If anything, Shakespeare shows Hal revolting against the principles of his father and dissociating himself from them by his refusal to join in the court life. This is, in brief, the rationalization of Hal's low-life career.

[4] In this sense Falstaff and his crew represent in concentrated form the commons, which are antigovernment, since their duty is to be governed, generally contrary to their true desires. Thus they avoid responsibility as much as possible and concentrate on their private concerns. Hotspur allows his feudal ideals to overcome his patriotism; the commons are, in their own self-seeking way, equally unpatriotic.

suspense about Hal's future course. In the action he deliberately shows Hal as a committed man biding his time. The time comes, and Hal makes his anticipated move toward the life of superior glory that lay ahead for him. King Henry may think he has converted his erring son, but Shakespeare tells us the contrary in his plot. That the climax is no climax, in respect to any decision not made before, should alert us to Shakespeare's clear intentions. Hal is his own man, and as his own man he chooses his own course of action in his own way. He is not influenced in any manner by the attempts of others to engage him, because from the start he knows the synthesis that lies ahead for him in the ideals of kingship, chivalry, and the proper use of materialism. This is what Shakespeare tells us through the plot, and we should pay attention to its evidence. . . .

D. A. TRAVERSI

Henry IV, Part I: *History and the Artist's Vision*

The increased volume of work which has recently been devoted to Shakespeare's series of English historical plays has not been without its uses. In particular it has served to bring these works decisively out of the sphere of patriotic commonplace to which they had often been consigned by relating them firmly to the political conceptions of the Elizabethan period. The work, however, is not without dangers of its own. There is a very real risk that erudition, in its efforts to relate the plays to their period, may end by obscuring the personal contribution that makes them most valuable as works of art. For these plays—and more especially those dealing with the reign of Henry IV and his son—contain something of far deeper and more permanent significance than the social and political commonplaces of a departed age; they illuminate these com-

Reprinted from "Henry IV—Part I," *Scrutiny*, XV (December 1947), 24–35, by permission of the author. The essay has been revised in minor details by the author for its appearance here. Title added by Ed.

monplaces by the same profoundly personal vision which, at a more mature stage, developed further to produce Shakespeare's greatest plays. The true artist, when circumstances induce him to approach political problems, brings with him a concern for permanent human values which, while never limited to the momentary issue, may be none the less profoundly illuminating to those who can combine a serious interest in contemporary developments with the preservation, often equally necessary, of a proper detachment. To bear this truth in mind and to trace in detail the unfolding of a personal interpretation of his inherited theme is to throw light upon an important stage in the development of Shakespeare's art.

The broad conception of the whole trilogy, initially accepted by Shakespeare as his starting-point, is clear enough. It emerges generally speaking from historical and dramatic works previously in existence and fits in with the current conceptions of the age. The three plays, as well as *Richard II* which preceded them, are evidently conceived as studies in kingship. The royal office is plainly regarded throughout as basing its claims to obedience upon divine ordination. The power of the King, a power conveyed upon him by God, is conferred as a guarantee of social order and of that acceptance of "degree" which cannot be denied without plunging society into anarchy and chaos. This conception is already clearly present in the opening scene of the first part of *Henry IV*. Bolingbroke, newly come to the throne, is weighed down from the first by recent memories of feudal anarchy and internal war. His opening speech has for its background the bitter memory of "civil butchery," of strife between armies "All of one nature, of one substance bred," clashes within the body politic that can only serve to wound and destroy it. Finding his country still "shaken" and made "wan with care" by these civil disasters, it is his desire and duty to propose a higher aim in the following of which the factions so recently at one another's throats may find a common unity. It is for this reason and in this spirit that Henry calls his barons, united under the "blessed Cross," to the liberation of the sepulchre of Christ. The crusade will serve both to calm the political passions which Henry himself exploited to reach the throne and to provide a foundation for the national unity which he now as King sincerely desires.

It is at this point that Shakespeare, though still using traditional conceptions, begins to unfold a personal interpretation of his historical material. In calling for a crusade Henry is moved by motives in which selfish calculation are oddly mixed with a true desire for the general good. As crowned King he genuinely wishes to follow his vocation by uniting his subjects in a worthy and religious enterprise; but as usurper he hopes that his proposal will "busy giddy minds with foreign quarrels" (*Part II*, IV, v) and so distract attention from the way in which he himself came to the throne. In other words—and here Shakespeare's thought is clearly working on traditional lines—Henry's desire to play properly the part of a King is hindered past mending by a flaw in the way in which he came to the throne. His overthrow and murder of Richard II, a crime not only against common humanity but still more against the divine foundation of order centred on the crown, fatally produces the very strife and division which he now aims at ending. No sooner has he stated his purpose than "heavy news" comes "all athwart" from Wales to force for the first time what will turn out to be a life-long postponement of Henry's project. The reign which opens with the call to a crusade ends, after years of weariness and disillusion with death in a room "called Jerusalem" which is fated to be his nearest approach to the Holy Land; and in between it has seen little but rebellion, plot and counterplot, and battles where victory serves only to sow the seed of further domestic strife.

If the whole conception of these plays could be summed up in this way their interest would lie only in the skill with which Shakespeare had unfolded what was, after all, a completely traditional scheme. The fact is, however, that his real conception, far from ending here, has its true beginning at this point. Its true originality begins to appear when the political is over-shadowed by the personal interest. Henry IV is punished for his past sins not only as King in the weariness which increasingly overtakes him and in the growing sense of impotence which sometimes raises him to moments of tragic intensity, but as father in the most intimate concerns of his life. It is here that Shakespeare, still using inherited and familiar material, shows the true originality of his conception. For Prince Hal who is destined to become the incarnation of political competence and to achieve all his father's desires, is at the same time "a scourge" in the hands of God, a continual reminder to Henry of his "displeasing service" in the past. This disappointment, which accompanies the father through his own life and is not wholly dispelled by his apparent transformation at Shrewsbury, is related ultimately to unresolved contradictions in the family character. Henry's first speech to his son (III, ii) is most revealing in its remarkable blend of true personal pathos and political calculation. The former shades indeed almost insensibly into the latter. That the father is genuinely wounded by his son's behaviour, that he is moved with "tenderness," that he "hath desired to see" him more often, is certain; but as we read the long speech we cannot help suspecting that the speaker's only true *moral* criterion is *political* success. To say this is to put one's finger upon the motive that impels the House of Lancaster all through these plays. Henry's criticism of the prodigality of Richard, "the skipping king," is expressed with a linguistic freshness that draws freely upon the vernacular—"*carded* his state," "*capering* wits," "glutted, gorged, and full"—and reflects the keenness of his interest in the intricacies of political behaviour. That interest is a constant feature of the family. Behind it, however, Shakespeare is careful to convey a significant note of falseness and moral deficiency. Bolingbroke, in his own words, "*stole* all courtesy from heaven," "dressed" himself in a humility which is clearly less a moral virtue than the conscious device of policy. For Henry the criterion of morality tends always to be success; and that being so, it is not surprising that his son should have learned from the first to separate the promptings of humanity from the necessities of political behaviour and that filial tenderness in him should exist side by side with a readiness to subject all personal considerations to public achievement. In the realization, born of bitter experience, that the quest for this achievement can be an illusion lies the secret of the tragic note which dominates the father's later years.

These considerations illuminate considerably Shakespeare's conception of Prince Hal and show that the developments later revealed in *Henry V* [1] are already substantially present in his father. It might almost be said, indeed, that the motives which underlie the behaviour of the family throughout the trilogy are revealed in the Prince's opening soliloquy (I, ii). These motives in turn spring at least in part from the nature of the material which the dramatist inherited. In writing his play Shakespeare's freedom of conception was faced by what might have seemed at first sight a grave limitation: the necessity of squaring his account of the Prince's character with a traditional story as naïve in its moral values as it was familiar in all its details. The Prince, as Shakespeare found him in the popular account on which he based his

[1] I have tried to interpret the spirit of this play in a previous article in *Scrutiny*, March 1941.

play, was an outstanding example of the familiar story of the dissolute young man who underwent a kind of moral conversion when faced by grave responsibilities and finally made good in the great sphere of political action to which he was called. The story, conceived in these terms, was too familiar and too popular to be ignored by a practical dramatist; on the other hand its conception of human character and motive was too naïvely optimistic to appeal to a Shakespeare moving at this stage towards the mood that was shortly to produce *Hamlet*. Faced with this dilemma Shakespeare chose to accept the very improbability of the story and to turn it to account. The Prince, from his very first appearance, looks forward to a reformation which, just because it is too good to be true, is seen to be moved by a political calculation which clearly reflects the character of his father. If his character is to change, as he announces in his very first soliloquy, it is because a transformation of this kind will attract popularity: for "nothing pleaseth but rare accidents." The whole process of "reformation," as the Prince himself describes it, has a surface quality which Shakespeare is clearly concerned to emphasize. It is seen "glittering" with metallic speciousness over previous faults, "like bright metal on a sullen ground"; and its purpose, above all, is to "*show* more goodly" and "attract more eyes." The conversion, thus transformed from an edifying example to an instrument of political success, enters fully into the permanent characteristics of the House of Lancaster. The future Henry V, already regarded as an example of the perfect political figure, begins by consciously abstaining from the finer aspects of human nature; for behind Shakespeare's acceptance of a traditional story lies the conviction that success in politics implies a spiritual loss, commonly involves the sacrifice of more attractive qualities which are distinctively personal.

The character of the Prince as it is developed through the play brings home this conception with a variety of detail. It is the character of a man whose keen if limited intelligence is placed consistently at the service of his political interests. If the politician is not so much a man of intellectual subtlety and spiritual discernment as one who can envisage with clarity the practical end of his activities and devote all his faculties without division to its attainment then the Prince is a complete example of the type. His intelligence is of the kind that, operating entirely in the practical order, sees through all pretences and evasions to the concrete issues that underlie them. Hotspur's reputation does not blind him to his failings, and when he now describes him he at once conforms to his own assumption of a cynical tone—appropriate to the "humours" of his tavern associates—and stresses the lack of imagination which we have just witnessed in his rival's attitude to his wife. Hotspur is the man who "kills me six or seven dozens of Scots at a breakfast" and then complains of his quiet life, like Douglas whose prowess in battle is filled out, in the popular imagination, with adornments which strike Hal, in his ironical detachment, as simply absurd:

PRINCE. He that rides at high speed and with his pistol kills a sparrow flying.
FALSTAFF. You have hit it.
PRINCE. So did he never the sparrow. (II, iv).

For the Prince Douglas is an enemy, but his attitude would not have been different had he been an ally. In either case the firm if limited judgment would be based on the same clear narrow principles of expedience. His intelligence is of the kind that judges all men by their value in relation to a coldly conceived political scheme; that is the reason both for his success and his inhumanity.

This detachment in the Prince's attitude towards friend and foe is based in turn upon a series of moral deficiencies which Shakespeare is concerned to stress from the first moment. His relationship to those around him, invalidated by the peculiar mental reservation which invariably accompanies it, is necessarily unsatisfactory. The Prince is to all appearances capable of sinking himself into his surroundings and meeting his "low" associates on their own level; but his attitude to them, when he is alone and expresses his inmost feelings, shows a certain false humility that is most revealing: "I have sounded the very base-string of humility. Sirrah, I am sworn brother to a leash of drawers; and can call them all by their christen names, as Tom, Dick, and Francis" (II, iv). The confidence with which he moves among the "lower orders"—I choose the phrase, with all its implications of set purpose—expresses itself, moreover, in a peculiar and typical tone. The quality of many of his observations upon those whom he encourages to regard themselves as his friends reflects a coarseness which is, in the true sense of the word, vulgar and thoroughly characteristic of his entirely amoral personality. Shakespeare brings this home to us in numerous apparently petty turns of phrase: "If there come a hot June and this civil buffeting hold, we shall buy maidenheads as they buy hob-nails, by the hundreds" (II, iv). Spoken of itself in one of the tavern scenes of this play we might pass over phrasing of this type; but Shakespeare brings us into contact with the kind of feeling that prompted it too often for us to ignore it in the long run. Falstaff, whose relationship to the Prince lies at the heart of the whole play, is the particular butt of a kind of intensity in grossness which is surely revealing. After the trick played on him at Eastcheap, he "*lards* the lean earth as he walks along" (II, ii); and in the great parody of the relationship between the King and his son the Prince heaps upon him such a list of epithets as "bolting-hutch of beastliness," "swollen parcel of dropsies," "huge bombard of sack" and "stuffed cloak-bag of guts" (II, iv). The insistence upon this type of imagery, so lacking in the spontaneous imaginative warmth that characterizes Falstaff's fleshliness, is certainly intentional. It is as though the Prince, whose every action is based on calculation, felt for Falstaff, who represents in himself the vitality and the weakness of human flesh, the semi-conscious repulsion felt by the cold practical intellect for something which it can neither understand, ignore, nor, in the last resort, use. The Prince, echoing Falstaff's idiom, brings to it a cold, efficient intensity that points to an underlying aversion. The flesh, with which the finished politician needs to reckon, is nevertheless an object of repulsion to him. Beneath the burlesque and the rowdiness we may already look forward to the ultimate rejection of Falstaff. That rejection indeed is actually anticipated in the same scene. Falstaff, in a plea that is not less pathetic for being a parody based on monstrous presumption, concludes by begging the Prince not to banish him: "banish plump Jack and banish all the world" (II, iv). Banish Falstaff, in other words, and banish everything that cannot be reduced to an instrument of policy in the quest for empty success. It is true to the Prince's character and to the tragedy of his family that he already replies without hesitation "I do, I will."

The tracing of a common destiny working itself out through character in the actions of the family of Lancaster is, then, an essential part of Shakespeare's conception. It is not, however, the whole. In many of the political plays written by Shakespeare at this period we are aware that the individuals whose actions are represented are in fact bound together in character as different aspects of an embracing whole; their virtues and their faults, their successes and failures are inter-dependent parts of a world whose unity is to be sought in the author's experience projected into the complete conception of the play. In *Troilus and Cressida,* as I have tried to show elsewhere,[2] this unity of characters connected by complementary qualities and related imagery is obviously of fundamental importance; but it exists already in the Second Part of *Henry IV* and is at least foreshadowed in the first. For the rebel leaders in this play, when they attempt to translate their aspirations into action, are affected by a flaw not fundamentally dissimilar from that which dominates the royal camp. If Henry IV's kingship is rendered sterile in its higher aspirations by the fact that his seizure of the crown involved the murder of his predecessor and was prompted by egoism the same is true of those who, having helped to bring him to the throne, now wish to see his power curbed or destroyed. The part played by the rebels in Henry's rise to power is stressed from the very beginning. It is, indeed, a chief point in the presentation of their case. Worcester, whose first appearance involves a clash with the King, refers in his very first speech to:

> that same greatness too which our own hands
> Hath holp to make so portly. (I, iii).

A little later in the same scene Hotspur puts the relationship in less flattering terms. He describes his associates as the "base second means," "the cords, the ladder, or the hangman" involved in Richard's murder and is at pains to emphasize that what they have done is criminal, committed in "an unjust behalf." The fact is that it was desire for power which prompted the rebel leaders to crime, and now it is mutual fear, itself the consequence of crime, that makes their clash inevitable. Henry, conscious that his own power was criminally obtained, cannot help suspecting that those who once followed their own interest in dethroning a king may do so again; and the rebels (or the more reflective of them) understand that the King must think in this way and that they themselves can therefore never be safe. The result is an endless mistrust, the consequences of which continue until they fatally conclude at Shrewsbury. The preliminaries of that battle are in themselves highly significant. Both sides at heart desire peace, the rebels because they know they are not strong enough to win, the King because he realizes in the light of experience that the disunity in his kingdom is

[2] *Scrutiny*, December 1938.

not one which battle, however victorious, can resolve. Reason, indeed, demands peace and unity; but the consequences of the original crime against order and therefore against reason are still there and need to work themselves out in blood. The King makes Worcester and Vernon a generous offer of peace, seeing in peace a restoration of natural order based on the free recognition of just and beneficent authority. His behaviour in doing so is that proper to a King. He uses the familiar image of the planets to drive home his contrast between selfish anarchy and ordered peace:

> will you again unknit
> This churlish knot of all-abhorred war?
> And move in that obedient orb again
> Where you did give a fair and natural light.
> And be no more an exhaled meteor,
> A prodigy of fear, and a portent
> Of broached mischief to the unborn times? (V, i).

Henry speaks here as he had spoken at the opening of the Crusade, as a King fulfilling the terms of his vocation. He calls for unity, using the accepted imagery; but the origins of his power, which he would now wish to forget, make themselves felt in their endless consequences to frustrate the lawfulness of his intentions.

Worcester's reaction to the offer serves to bring out a parallel weakness in the rebel camp. In the figure of Worcester Shakespeare sought to study the type of the political courtier. Persuasiveness and reason, born of cunning and experience, are his gods; in the early scenes we see him restraining the impetuosity of Hotspur basing his argument on the very appeal to expediency that Henry himself uses to his son; for Hotspur's impatience, he tells him, is such that it "loseth men's hearts" (III, i) and compromises their chances of success. Yet Worcester, all reason and moderation as he appears, is a rebel and, being a rebel in the name of interest, he is driven to exclude the operation of reason as the most dangerous enemy of his projects. For reason, according to the original conception, is necessarily on the side of order, of kingship, and rebellion owes its origin to the promptings of selfish passion against rational restraint. Worcester stresses this flaw in their position to his fellow-conspirators:

> For well you know we of the offering side

Must keep aloof from strict arbitrement,
And stop all sight-holes, every loop from whence
The eye of reason may pry in upon us. (IV, i).

Rebellion, according to the convention which Shakespeare accepted as the starting-point of his political plays, is based upon the exclusion of reason, though it takes a rebel as rational as Worcester so to define it. Priding himself on his realistic attitude to political events, he is yet driven first to shut out reason and then to conceal the fact that peace has been offered by the King and that the battle itself has become unnecessary. The reasons he gives to Vernon are highly significant:

It is not possible, it cannot be,
The king should keep his word in loving us;
He will suspect us still, and find a time
To punish this offence in other faults . . . .
. . . treason is but trusted like the fox
Who, ne'er so tame, so cherish'd and lock'd up,
Will have a wild trick of his ancestors. (V, ii).

Worcester's distrust, like Henry's tragedy, has its roots far in the past. It owes its existence to the original crime against Richard by which the bond of freely accepted rule once broken, the seeds of disorder and suspicion are sown to work themselves out on both sides in mutual destruction. The combatants in either camp at Shrewsbury invoke "honour" and other lofty sanctions to justify their cause; but the reality is that crime born of self-interest on either side has born fruit in unnecessary bloodshed.

Shakespeare's treatment of the rebel leaders is designed to drive home these points as they reveal themselves in the details of character expressed in action. If their handling of the campaign is futile and their motives based on an unhappy mixture of fear and self-seeking the divisions that make their common action impossible spring from the dubious foundations of a cause conceived in egoism and executed without conviction. Of their moral and intellectual qualities we are left in no doubt. Glendower is a mixture of superstition, vanity and incompetence whose self-regard prompts him to look everywhere for insults and makes it impossible for him to collaborate honestly with his fellow-conspirators; Douglas is as the

Prince has described him, a brainless butcher as contemptuous of the reasoning of others as he is himself incapable of rational thought. Throughout the rebel camp before the battle there exists the familiar division between the counsels of reason, which cannot see beyond timidity and selfish fear, and those of passion, which drive those possessed by them to actions which cannot be justified upon the slightest reflection. Reason prompts Northumberland and Glendower to withhold their forces in order not to commit themselves to the common cause at the decisive moment, just as it has caused Vernon and Worcester to conceal the King's offer of peace; passion drives Hotspur and Douglas to accept battle against better advice on hopeless terms and to despise the reasonable counsels of strategy as inspired by "fear and cold heart." In this world of political sordidness and folly Hotspur stands out as a figure relatively attractive. That he is not without a critical eye is proved by his understanding of the nature of Glendower (III, i) and by his incisive description of the courtly popinjay who brought him the King's demand for his prisoners after his victory at Holmedon (I, iii). In both cases the justice of his comment is reflected in a vivid vernacular phrasing that guarantees its genuineness. Yet, in spite of these qualities, Hotspur remains a rebel and time shows him to be the instrument of politicians more calculating than himself. A warrior and man of action, the cause for which he fights is one whose moral basis cannot be reasonably sustained; so that his motives, far from being adequate, reduce themselves to an acceptance of the rhetorical idea of honour which prompts him, whenever it is mentioned, to emotional outbursts which contrast completely with Worcester's tight-lipped calls to reason and calculation. We are reminded of the Trojans in *Troilus and Cressida* with their facile surrenders to emotion leading to the acceptance of a cause indefensible in reason. At Shrewsbury Hotspur falls on behalf of policies less creditable than those his own nature should have been capable of accepting. His death leaves us with a sensation somewhere between the tragic and the ironic, adequately summed up in the contrasted attitude contained in his conqueror's brief words—"For *worms, brave* Percy" (V, iv). It is simply one aspect of the futility which is the real meaning of the battle of Shrewsbury, in which the rebels fail to achieve their end and at the same time prevent the King from obtaining the unity for which he is *now*, but too late, genuinely striving.

So far we might call the First Part of *Henry IV* an acute political study based on a personal elaboration of ideas rooted in traditional thought. But Shakespeare's most individual contribution to his material lies in the figure of Falstaff. Falstaff is given in the play a position of peculiar significance which enables him to transcend the political action in which he moves and to provide a sufficient comment on it. He serves, in a sense, as a connecting-link between two worlds, the tavern world of comic incident and broad humanity in which he is at home and the world of court rhetoric and political intrigue to which he also has access. So situated in two worlds and limited by neither, Falstaff is thus used as a commentator who passes judgment on the events represented in the play in the light of his own superabundant comic vitality. Working sometimes through open comment, sometimes even through open parody, his is a voice that lies outside the prevailing political spirit of the play, that draws its cogency from the author's own insight expressing itself in a flow of comic vitality. He represents, we might say, all the humanity which it seems that the politician bent on the attainment of success must necessarily exclude. That humanity, as it manifests itself in the tavern scenes, is full of obvious and gross imperfections; but the Falstaff of the play, whilst he shares these imperfections, is not altogether limited by them. His keen intelligence, his real human understanding, his refusal to be fobbed off by empty or hypocritical phrases—all these are characteristics that enable him to transcend his world and to become the individual expression of the conscience of a great and completely serious artist. In the elaboration of this point we approach the very heart of Shakespeare's conception in this play.

The true nature of Falstaff becomes most apparent when we realize that he comes to be in this series of plays a complete and significant contrast to the figure of the Prince. The full force of this contrast probably only became apparent to Shakespeare as he proceeded with his trilogy; but something of it is present from the first. It becomes fully clear for the first time in the scene of tavern parody when the two men caricature the relationship of Henry IV and his son (II, iv). Falstaff's behaviour after ascending his mock throne at Eastcheap in a scene which parodies by anticipation the real one shortly to take place (III, ii) envelops that relationship at once in the atmosphere of the popular stage, of the "harlotry players," to use the Hostess' own words, and provides us with a new standpoint from which to consider the central political theme. The description he gives of the Prince, using his father's supposed words, is in itself a criticism, realistic and sardonic, of the whole family: "That thou art my son, I have partly thy mother's word, partly my own opinion, but chiefly a villanous trick of thine eye, and a foolish hanging of thy nether lip, that doth warrant me." It is not thus that Henry does actually speak to his son, nor is it true to say that the relationship between them is of this kind. That relationship is on the contrary truly tragic, and becomes more so as the father grows older and more conscious of the weariness that besets him through life; but the disillusioned clarity, even the coarseness, of Falstaff's description corresponds to something really present, that makes itself felt time and again in the Prince's attitude towards his life in the taverns and is a symptom of the detached inhumanity which is one ingredient of his political sense. This is not the Prince as he is, but it is one true aspect of him as seen by an eye clear and unfailing in its realism in the world in which this aspect is most in evidence. To bring out that aspect in those who surround him is the first of Falstaff's functions in the play.

The second is to provide on the basis of this clarity of vision a criticism of the whole political action, both on the loyalist and rebel side, which leads up to the dubious battle in which it concludes. In this action, and especially in its warlike phases, Falstaff is involved without being of it or subdued to the spirit, now cynical, now wordily "honourable," in which it is habitually conceived. His comments on the motives of the rebels are characteristically clearheaded; his reaction to Worcester's disclaimer of responsibility for the rising is summed up in the phrase "Rebellion lay in his way, and he found it" (V, i). More revealing still, because based on sentiments more deeply human beneath the comic vision, is his attitude towards the pressed troops placed under his command to lead into battle. He has, as always, no particular illusion about the nature and the origins of this human material, "the cankers of a calm world and a long peace" (IV, ii); but his very account of them in the same speech as "discarded unjust serving-men, younger sons to younger brothers, revolted tapsters, and ostlers tradefallen," together with many other references, implies an awareness of social issues possessed by no other character in the play. This awareness is based in its turn upon Falstaff's outstanding quality, the capacity for human sympathy which marks him out in a world of calculation and inspires the respect for human life implied in his magnificent ironic reply to the Prince when the latter sums up his contingent as so many "pitiful rascals"—"Tut, tut; good enough to toss; food for powder, food for powder; they'll fill a pit as well as better; tush, man, mortal men, mortal men" (IV, ii). For the Prince as for all his world, soldiers are mere pawns, the wretched instruments of political calculation to be considered from the point of view of their possible efficiency in the tasks imposed upon them by their leaders; for Falstaff alone they are human victims, individuals exposed to the manipulations of discreditable interests, "mortal men" and as such to be respected after detached and unsentimental scrutiny in the very sordidness of their tragedy. It is his sense of humanity in its weakness and its irreducibility that prompts Falstaff's behaviour in the battle. Precisely because he is so human himself in his very irony he has no desire to die, to pay the debt of death "before his day" (V, i); and precisely because he can realize in others the human desire to survive which he feels so strongly in himself he is keenly aware that "honour" in the mouths of politicians who have been brought to battle by a combination of past selfishness and present refusal to face their responsibilities is an empty word and a delusion. "I like not such grinning honour as Sir Walter hath" (V, iii) is his final comment, at once human and dispassionate, on the waste implied in a battle based on causes so suspect; and inspired by its spirit he moves through the conflict without being subdued to its tone, viewing it and himself with characteristic frankness and dominating it, when all is said and done, by the very force of his vitality.

These observations bring us to a third characteristic of Falstaff, the one which is perhaps the ultimate source of his strength and the key to Shakespeare's deepest conception in this play. There is in Falstaff a true and rare combination of the warm, alert humanity we have already noted with a background, sometimes accepted and sometimes rebelled against, but continually present, of inherited Christian tradition. It is reasonable to suppose that the latter element makes itself felt in a spontaneous acceptance of the inheritance, still not so distant from Shakespeare, of the mediaeval religious theatre. We may sense the presence of this inheritance in the readiness with which Falstaff in his phrasing draws upon images and ideas which derive their force from their relation to crucial moments in the familiar Christian drama. When he calls upon his tavern companions to "watch to-night, pray to-morrow" (II, iv) the effect of the phrase depends largely upon its relation to the originally Christian ethic; when in the same scene he greets the news of the arrival of the King's messenger with "What doth gravity out of his bed at midnight?" it is not fanciful to seek in "gravity" a personification of the kind familiar in the bearded, solemn figures of the old morality plays. Falstaff's utterances, indeed, are steeped in tradition, at once religious and theatrical, of this kind. He shares with his audience a whole world of imagery, drawn upon in such phrases as that in which his troops are described as "slaves as ragged as Lazarus in the painted cloth, where the glutton's dogs licked his sores" (IV, ii). This common inheritance itself gives him reality by contrast with the orators and politicians of the verse scenes of this play. The ease with which the theatrical passes into the religious reference is clearly seen in his comment on Bardolph's nose (III, iii), to which he refers as "a Death's head or a *memento mori*"—"I never see thy face but I think upon hell-fire and Dives that lived in purple." In such phrases we feel what the strength of a still living popular tradition could offer to the dramatist. Assimilated into his utterances it enables Falstaff to bring to his criticism of the political action around him a realism that, in its profounder moments, is neither self-regarding nor cynical, but that derives from a balanced view of man's destiny and in particular of the peculiar complexity of spiritual motives. At his best Falstaff, recognizing his own faults, gives them a taste of tragic significance by relating them to the familiar but profound spiritual drama of mankind worked out in the individual between birth and death, in mankind between the Creation and the Last Judgment: "Thou knowest in the state of innocency Adam fell; and what should poor Jack Falstaff do in the days of villainy? Thou seest I have more flesh than another man, and therefore more frailty" (III, iii). To take this too seriously would be as naïve as it would be short-sighted to deny it all seriousness. Falstaff's tone is in part ironical, mocking as usual; but the reference to the physical flesh here is subsidiary to the spiritual meaning of the word sanctioned by Christian theology, and it is in the sense of the relationship between the two, a relationship comprehending dependence and separation in a single unity, that Falstaff acquires his full stature. Such were the advantages for Shakespeare of inheriting—I say inheriting because the question of personal belief need not arise—a set of spiritual conceptions at once simple enough to be popular and sufficiently profound to cover the wealth of human experience. We need not say—should not say—that Falstaff simply accepts the Christian tradition. Part of him, what we may call the flesh, clearly does not; but the tradition is there, alive in his utterances and giving him even in his refusal to conform a vitality that enables him to dominate the play. We shall see this Christian background deepened and developed in the Second Part of the play.

L. C. KNIGHTS

Henry IV *as Satire*

Henry IV does not fit easily into any of the critical schemata,* though "incongruity" has served the critics in good stead. But, at any rate, since the time of Morgann, Falstaff has received a degree of sympathetic attention (how we love the fat rascal!) that distorts Shakespeare's intention in writing the two plays. We regard them as a sandwich—so much dry bread to be bitten through before we come to the meaty Falstaff, although we try to believe that "the heroic and serious part is not inferior to the comic and farcical." Actually each play is a unity, sub-plot and main plot cooperating to express the vision which is projected into the form of the play. And this vision, like that of all the great writers of comedy, is pre-eminently serious. It is symptomatic that Hazlitt, defending Shakespeare's tragedies against the comedies, said, "He was greatest in what was greatest; and his *forte* was not trifling."

The first speech of the King deserves careful attention. The

Pt. II of "Notes on Comedy" from *The Importance of Scrutiny*, ed. Eric Bentley (New York, 1948). Reprinted by permission of the author and the publisher, George W. Stewart, Inc. Title added by Ed. The essay first appeared in *Scrutiny*, I (March 1933), 356–367.

* That is, the various theories about comedy discussed by Professor Knights earlier in his essay. Ed.

brittle verse suggests the precarious poise of the usurper:

So shaken as we are, so wan with care,
Find we a time for frighted peace to pant,
And breathe short-winded accents of new broils
To be commenced in stronds afar remote.

The violence of the negative which follows suggests its opposite:

No more the thirsty entrance of this soil
Shall daub her lips with her own children's blood:
No more shall trenching war channel her fields,
Nor bruise her flowerets with the armed hoofs
Of hostile paces.

"Thirsty" contains the implication that the earth is eager for more blood; and when the prophecy of peace ends with the lisping line, "Shall now, in mutual well-beseeming ranks," we do not need a previous knowledge of the plot or of history to realize that Henry is actually describing what is to come. The account of the proposed crusade is satiric:

But this our purpose is a twelvemonth old, . . .
Therefore we meet not now.

Throughout we are never allowed to forget that Henry is a usurper. We are given four separate accounts of how he gained the throne—by Hotspur (I, iii, 160–186), by Henry himself (III, ii, 39–84), by Hotspur again (IV, iii, 52–92), and by Worcester (V, i, 32–71). He gained it by "murd'rous subornation," by hypocrisy, his "seeming brow of justice," by "violation of all faith and troth." Words expressing underhand dealing occur even in the king's account to his son:

And then I stole all courtesy from Heaven,
And dress'd myself in such humility
That I did pluck allegiance from men's hearts.

There is irony in the couplet that concludes the play:

And since this business *so fair* is done,
Let us not leave till all *our own* be won.

The rebels, of course, are no better. The hilarious scene in which the plot is hatched (I, iii, 187–299) does not engage much sympathy for the plotters, who later squabble over the expected booty like any long-staff sixpenny strikers. Their cause does not bear prying into by "the eye of reason" (IV, i, 69–72), and Worcester, for his own purposes, conceals "the liberal kind offer of the King" (V, ii, 1–25). But this is relatively unimportant; there is no need to take sides and "like Hotspur somewhat better than the Prince because he is unfortunate." The satire is general, directed against statecraft and warfare. Hotspur is the chief representative of chivalry, and we have only to read his speeches to understand Shakespeare's attitude towards "honour"; there is no need to turn to Falstaff's famous soliloquy. The description of the Mortimer-Glendower fight has just that degree of exaggeration which is necessary for not-too-obvious burlesque, though, oddly enough, it has been used to show that Hotspur "has the imagination of a poet." But if the image of the Severn—

> Who then, affrighted with their bloody looks,
> Ran fearfully among the trembling reeds,
> And hid his crisp head in the hollow bank—

is not sufficient indication, the rhyme announces the burlesque intention:

> He did confound the best part of an hour
> In changing hardiment with great Glendower.

There is the same exaggeration in later speeches of Worcester and Hotspur; Hotspur's "huffing part"—"by Heaven methinks it were an easy leap"—did not need Beaumont's satire.* In the battle scene the heroics of "Now, Esperance! Percy! and set on," the chivalric embrace and flourish of trumpets are immediately followed by the exposure of a military dodge for the preservation of the King's life. "The King hath many marching in his coats."—"Another King! They grow like Hydra's heads."

The reverberations of the sub-plot also help to determine our attitude towards the main action. The conspiracy of the Percys is

* See the "Induction" to *The Knight of the Burning Pestle* by Francis Beaumont and John Fletcher. Ed.

sandwiched between the preparation for the Gadshill plot and counterplot and its execution. Poins has "lost much honour" that he did not see the "action" of the Prince with the drawers. When we see the court we remember Falstaff's joint-stool throne and his account of Henry's hanging lip. Hotspur's pride in himself and his associates ("Is there not my father, my uncle and myself?") is parodied by Gadshill: "I am joined with no foot land-rakers, no long-staff sixpenny strikers . . . but with nobility and tranquility, burgomasters and great oneyers." The nobles, like the roarers, prey on the commonwealth, "for they ride up and down on her and make her their boots."

The Falstaff attitude is therefore in solution, as it were, throughout the play, even when he is not on the stage; but it takes explicit form in the person and speeches of Sir John. We see a heroic legend in process of growth in the account of his fight with the men in buckram. The satire in the description of his ragged regiment is pointed by a special emphasis on military terms—"soldiers," "captain," "lieutenant," "ancients, corporals . . . gentlemen of companies." His realism easily reduces honour to "a mere scutcheon." Prince Henry's duel with Hotspur is accompanied by the mockery of the Douglas-Falstaff fight, which ends with the dead and the counterfeit dead lying side by side. If we can rid ourselves of our realistic illusions and their accompanying moral qualms we realize how appropriate it is that Falstaff should rise to stab Hotspur's body and carry him off as his luggage on his back.

The satire on warfare, the Falstaff attitude, implies an axis of reference, which is of course found in the gross and vigorous life of the body. We find throughout the play a peculiar insistence on imagery deriving from the body, on descriptions of death in its more gruesome forms, on stabbing, cutting, bruising, and the like. We expect to find references to blood and death in a play dealing with civil war, but such references in *Henry IV* are far more pervasive than in a war play such as *Henry V*. In the first scene we hear of the earth "daubing her lips with her own children's blood." War is "trenching"; it "channels" the fields and "bruises" the flowers. "The edge of war" is "like an ill-sheathed knife" which "cuts his master." Civil war is an "intestinal shock," and battles are "butchery." We learn that the defeated Scots lay "balk'd in their own blood," and that "beastly shameless transformation" was done by the Welsh upon the corpses of Mortimer's soldiers. Later Hotspur mentions the smell of "a slovenly unhandsome corpse," and we hear of Mortimer's "mouthed wounds." So throughout the play. The dead Blunt lies "grinning," Hotspur's face is "mangled," and Falstaff lies by him "in blood." Falstaff's "honour" soliloquy insists on surgery, on broken legs and arms.

To all this Falstaff, a walking symbol, is of course opposed. "To shed my dear blood drop by drop i' the dust" for the sake of honour appears an imbecile ambition. Falstaff will "fight no longer than he sees reason." His philosophy is summed up when he has escaped Douglas by counterfeiting death: "S'blood! 'twas time to counterfeit, or that hot termagant Scot had paid me scot and lot too. Counterfeit? I lie, I am no counterfeit: to die is to be a counterfeit; for he is but the counterfeit of a man who hath not the life of a man; but to counterfeit dying, when a man thereby liveth, is to be no counterfeit, but the true and perfect image of life indeed." The same thought is implicit in the honour soliloquy.

Once the play is read as a whole, the satire on war and policy is apparent. It is useful to compare the first part of *Henry IV* with *King John* in estimating the development of Shakespeare's dramatic power. *King John* turns on a single pivotal point—the Bastard's speech on commodity; * but the whole of the later play is impregnated with satire which crystallizes in Falstaff. Now, satire implies a standard, and in *Henry IV* the validity of the standard itself is questioned; hence the peculiar coherence and universality of the play. "Honour" and "state-craft" are set in opposition to the natural life of the body, but the chief body of the play is, explicitly, "a bolting-hutch of beastliness."—"A pox on this gout! or a gout on this pox, I should say." Other speeches reinforce the age-and-disease theme which, it has not been observed, is a significant part of the Falstaff theme. Hotspur pictures the earth as an "old beldam"

> pinch'd and vex'd
> By the imprisoning of unruly wind
> Within her womb.

Again, he says:

> The time of life is short;
> To spend that shortness basely were too long,

* II, i, 561–598. Ed.

If life did ride upon a dial's point,
Still ending at the arrival of an hour.

The last two lines imply that no "if" is necessary; life does "ride upon a dial's point," and Hotspur's final speech takes up the theme of transitoriness:

But thought's the slave of life, and life time's fool:
And time, that takes survey of all the world,
Must have a stop.

There is no need to emphasize the disease aspect of Falstaff (Bardolph's bad liver is not merely funny). He "owes God a death." He and his regiment are "mortal men." It is important to realize, however, that when Falstaff feigns death he is meant to appear actually as dead in the eyes of the audience; at least the idea of death is meant to be emphasized in connexion with the Falstaff-idea at this point. No answer is required to the Prince's rhetorical question,

What! old acquaintance! could not all this flesh
Keep in a little life? Poor Jack, farewell!

The stability of our attitude after a successful reading of the first part of *Henry IV* is due to the fact that the breaking-down process referred to above is not simple but complex; one set of impulses is released for the expression of the Falstaff-outlook; but a set of opposite complementary impulses is also brought into play, producing an effect analogous to that caused by the presence of comedy in *King Lear* [1] (compare the use of irony in *Madame Bovary*). *Lear* is secure against ironical assault because of the irony it contains; *Henry IV* will bear the most serious ethical scrutiny because in it the "serious" is a fundamental part of the "comic" effect of the play. (The second part of *Henry IV* is no less interesting. No one has yet pointed out that drunkenness, lechery, and senile depravity (in II, iv, for example) are *not* treated by Shakespeare with "good-natured tolerance." Shakespeare's attitude toward his characters in 2 *Henry IV* at times approaches the attitude of Mr. Eliot towards Doris, Wauchope, etc., in *Sweeney Agonistes.* Northumberland's monody on death (I, i) needs to be studied in order to understand the tone of the play.)

[1] See the admirable essay on "Lear and the Comedy of the Grotesque" in *The Wheel of Fire,* by G. Wilson Knight.

MADELEINE DORAN

Imagery in Richard II *and in* Henry IV †

It is a commonplace that the development of Shakespeare's style is away from verbal ingenuity and exuberance for their own sake and towards concentrated expression under control for dramatic ends. What I shall have to say here is nothing very new in itself, but it may be said in such a way as to give new significance to an old subject. I shall be concerned only with imagery, and with that only in two plays which come at crucial stages in Shakespeare's poetic and dramatic growth: *Richard II* about 1595, at the end of his "experimental" years, and 1 *Henry IV* a year or two later, when he has unmistakably attained his majority. Most of the work on Shakespeare's imagery has had to do with its content and its distribution. But the quality of an image—its fabric and structure and relation to its immediate context—is also interesting and may, as is recognized, be important in revealing something of the poetic process. Much may yet be done in the way of examining Shakespeare's images from this intensive point of view.

On reading the First Part of *Henry IV* immediately after *Richard II* one is struck, along with evidences of greater maturity in other matters, by the difference in the handling of the images. I shall begin with a general statement which will obviously need qualification and if pushed too far will distort the picture, but

From *Modern Language Review*, XXXVII (April 1942), 113–122. Reprinted by permission of the Modern Humanities Research Association and the author. Footnotes have been renumbered.

† It will be evident in this paper how much I owe to the rather pervasive influence in our time of I. A. Richards and William Empson. But I wish to acknowledge a more specific debt to E. M. W. Tillyard's profoundly stimulating book, *Poetry Direct and Oblique*, London, 1934. Some of the terms I use (*directness, statement, obliquity*) will be recognized as coming from him. Since it is the point of view of the book as a whole that has been important to me, I can give references to particular pages only in a few instances.

which, for convenience, has nevertheless to be made at the outset. It may be said that the images in *Richard II* tend to be direct or explicit, complete, correspondent, point by point, to the idea symbolized, and separate one from another; whereas the images in *1 Henry IV* tend to be richer in implicit suggestion and in ambiguity, not fully developed, fluid in outline and fused with one another.

These qualities will be evident in the following illustrations:

RICHARD. I have been studying how I may compare
This prison where I live unto the world:
And for because the world is populous
And here is not a creature but myself,
I cannot do it; yet I'll hammer it out.
My brain I'll prove the female to my soul,
My soul the father; and these two beget
A generation of still-breeding thoughts,
And these same thoughts people this little world,
In humours like the people of this world,
For no thought is contented. The better sort,
As thoughts of things divine, are intermix'd
With scruples and do set the word itself
Against the word:
As thus, 'Come, little ones,' and then again,
'It is as hard to come as for a camel
To thread the postern of a small needle's eye.'
Thoughts tending to ambition, they do plot
Unlikely wonders; how these vain weak nails
May tear a passage through the flinty ribs
Of this hard world, my ragged prison walls,
And, for they cannot, die in their own pride.
Thoughts tending to content flatter themselves
That they are not the first of fortune's slaves,
Nor shall not be the last; like silly beggars
Who sitting in the stocks refuge their shame,
That many have and others must sit there;
And in this thought they find a kind of ease,
Bearing their own misfortunes on the back
Of such as have before endured the like.

Thus play I in one person many people,
And none contented. (*Richard II*, v, v, 1–32)

Except for the compact and allusive "do set the word itself Against the word," etc. (ll. 11–13), which at once strikes one because it is so unlike the style of the rest of the play, the passage is explicit throughout. Notice the completeness of the image on the peopling of the world with thoughts, and with the equation of terms—brain to mother, soul to father, thoughts to children with all varieties of temperament who will in turn grow up to breed more of their kind, equally discontented. And then the discontented thoughts are enumerated one by one, each equated with an image more or less fully worked out. In the remainder of the speech, not quoted, it will be recalled how extensively treated is Richard's conceit of himself as a clock. With such a subject, requiring a listing of ideas, the separation of the images is perhaps not as indicative as in some other places. All of Richard's long speeches tend to show this succession of separate images [1] and it may be objected that from the speeches of a character so specially conceived as is Richard we have no right to draw too general conclusions about Shakespeare's style. To this point I shall return later. But it may be noted here that the qualities I have been remarking on in the passage quoted occur generally in the speeches of other characters throughout the play, though Richard's long speeches afford the best examples to illustrate the presence of all of them in any one place.[2] Now consider this passage from 1 *Henry IV:*

The skipping King, he ambled up and down
With shallow jesters and rash bavin wits,
Soon kindled and soon burnt; carded his state;

[1] See III, ii, 144–56; III, iii, 143–71; the speeches in the deposition scene, IV, 1.

[2] For other noteworthy examples of fully worked out images see the latter half of Bolingbroke's speech in III, iii (ll. 54–67), where he first compares the meeting of himself and Richard to the meeting of fire and water, and then compares Richard's appearance to that of the sun; also the Queen's and Bushy's talk about her premonition of sorrow (II, ii), where Bushy compares her emotionally distorted visions to the view of a "perspective," and where the comparison of her premonitions to a child she is about to be delivered of runs throughout the whole episode.

Mingled his royalty with cap'ring fools;
Had his great name profaned with their scorns
And gave his countenance, against his name,
To laugh at gibing boys and stand the push
Of every beardless vain comparative;
Grew a companion to the common streets,
Enfeoff'd himself to popularity;
That, being daily swallowed by men's eyes,
They surfeited with honey and began
To loathe the taste of sweetness, whereof a little
More than a little is by much too much.
So, when he had occasion to be seen,
He was but as the cuckoo is in June,
Heard, not regarded—seen, but with such eyes
As, sick and blunted with community,
Afford no extraordinary gaze,
Such as is bent on sunlike majesty
When it shines seldom in admiring eyes;
But rather drows'd and hung their eyelids down,
Slept in his face, and rend'red such aspect
As cloudy men use to their adversaries,
Being with his presence glutted, gorg'd, and full.
(III, ii, 60–84)

Notice the rapid succession of images, the quick suggestion rather than elaboration in such compact and elliptical lines as "To laugh at gibing boys . . ." (ll. 66–67) and "Enfeoff'd himself to popularity" (l. 69), the fusion of one image with another: the skipping and capering with the quick burning of faggots ("rash bavin") and with the adulteration suggested by carding; the enfeoffment with the idea of surfeit (itself boldly linked with eyes), it in turn with the common sight of the cuckoo in June and with the drowsiness of men in constant sunshine, and this latter image shifting ground with "cloudy men." In contrast to the way in which the firm outlines of the images in Richard's speech hold the mind within certain limits set by the close equation of idea and image, the rapidity, complexity, and fluidity of the images in Henry's speech help (as well as their substance) to increase their obliquity. Fewer doors are closed.

It is obvious that the interweaving of images such as one finds in the following speech of the Duchess of Gloucester is not the same thing as the fusion in the speech from *Henry IV* just quoted:

> Edward's seven sons, whereof thyself art one,
> Were as seven vials of his sacred blood,
> Or seven fair branches springing from one root:
> Some of those seven are dried by nature's course,
> Some of those branches by the Destinies cut;
> But Thomas, my dear lord, my life, my Gloucester,
> One vial full of Edward's sacred blood,
> One flourishing branch of his most royal root,
> Is crack'd, and all the precious liquor spilt,
> Is hack'd down, and his summer leaves all faded,
> By envy's hand and murder's bloody axe.
>
> (*Richard II*, I, ii, 11–21)

The vials and the branches retain their distinctness, and their relation to the idea is rather tediously explored. Again, take a genuinely complex figure from *Richard II:*

> for within the hollow crown
> That rounds the mortal temples of a king
> Keeps Death his court, and there the antic sits,
> Scoffing his state and grinning at his pomp,
> Allowing him a breath, a little scene,
> To monarchize, be fear'd and kill with looks,
> Infusing him with self and vain conceit,
> As if this flesh which walls about our life
> Were brass impregnable, and humour'd thus
> Comes at last and with a little pin
> Bores through his castle wall, and farewell king!
>
> (III, ii, 160–70)

"Death" hesitates ambiguously in "Keeps Death his court" between Death as a ruler holding court and Death as a jester holding the real power in the king's court, then shifts certainly to "Death the antic" (still *within* the hollow crown), and then shifts again to a borer from without. Set this passage against one from *Henry IV:*

> Those opposed eyes
> Which, like the meteors of a troubled heaven,

All of one nature, of one substance bred,
Did lately meet in the intestine shock
And furious close of civil butchery,
Shall now in mutual well-beseeming ranks
March all one way and be no more oppos'd
Against acquaintance, kindred, and allies. (I, i, 9–16)

Here the fusion of images results in a syntactical boldness seldom found in *Richard II*. Moreover, for all the complexity of structure in the passage on Death, the images are fully explicatory; whereas in the passage from *Henry IV* the meanings of "opposed eyes" and "meteors of a troubled heaven" are almost wholly implicit.

The differences observed in the passages already quoted are exhibited in certain other ways, namely, in respect to similes, allegorically handled metaphor, and words retaining both a literal and a figurative meaning.

My first impression was that similes were more common in *Richard II* than in *Henry IV*. In a simile, stated as an equation, there is, at least formally, no fusion of idea and image. A closer examination of the two plays does not, in point of fact, bear out my first impression of greater frequency of similes in *Richard II*. But numerical difference is not so important as the character of the similes themselves, and it is true that in *Henry IV* there are fewer fully extended similes of the type here illustrated from *Richard II*:

See, see, King Richard doth himself appear,
As doth the blushing discontented sun
From out the fiery portal of the east,
When he perceives the envious clouds are bent
To dim his glory and to stain the track
Of his bright passage to the occident. (III, iii, 62–7) [3]

Two examples of a similar kind in *Henry IV* occur in set speeches, and two occur in a passage where a scene is being vividly described.[4]

[3] Similar extended similes in *Richard II* occur at II, ii, 16–24; III, ii, 6–11; IV, i, 181–89; V, i, 29–34; V, ii, 23–28.

[4] (1) Prince Hal's soliloquy (I, ii) and Glendower's courtly promise to Mortimer of a song from his daughter (III, i, 213–19); (2) Vernon's comparison of Prince Hal mounting his horse to Mercury or an angel mounting Pegasus, and Hotspur's comparison of the coming of the king's forces to sacrifices to the maid of war, etc. (IV, i, 104–10, 113–17).

But most of the similes in *Henry IV* are brief and colloquial: they are the "unsavoury similes" applied by Hal and Falstaff to one another; the homely comparisons in the talk of Falstaff and his companions (skin like an old lady's loose gown, withered like an old apple John, roaring like a bullcalf, ragged as Lazarus, vigilant as a cat to steal cream, dank as a dog, stung like a tench); the quick, vivid figures in Hotspur's overflowing speech (fresh as a bridegroom, perfumed like a milliner, tedious as a tired horse or a railing wife, worse than a smoky house). It is characteristic of the style of the play that Hotspur's objection to Kate's swearing (III, i, 245–253), which begins with a simile, "Heart, you swear like a comfit-maker's wife" (itself by no means a simple statement), leads into an image that embodies a whole nest of subsidiary images, complex and confused:

> And givest such sarcenet surety for thy oaths
> As if thou ne'er walk'st further than Finsbury.
> Swear me, Kate, like a lady as thou art,
> A good mouth-filling oath; and leave 'in sooth'
> And such protest of pepper gingerbread
> To velvet guards and Sunday citizens.

It is surely not insignificant that one finds allegorical use of metaphor only in *Richard II*, not in *Henry IV*. Allegory is sustained metaphor.[5] One expects it to have a definite core of statement, of clear correspondence between figure and idea, with however much peripheral suggestion it may be enriched. The little allegory of the garden scene (III, iv), in its exact correspondence of figure and idea, point by point, is explicit and little else. The only places where it achieves obliquity are in the implicit allusion in "our sea-walled garden" (l. 43) to John of Gaunt's speech, and in the allusion to Eden and the fall of man in the Queen's address to the Gardener as Adam (ll. 72–80). In the latter allusion a profounder meaning is suggested than is stated.

In *Henry IV* there are a number of single words which, together with a figurative meaning, retain their literal meaning and greatly enrich the context by this ambiguity. A good example is ***balk'd*** in Henry's statement that

[5] See Tillyard's Chapter IV, "Some Terms Discussed," especially pp. 57–8, 60–2.

> Ten thousand bold Scots, two-and-twenty knights
> Balk'd in their own blood did Sir Walter see
> On Holmedon's plains. (I, i, 68–70)

Professor Kittredge (in his notes to the play) defines a *balk* as "a ridge between two furrows." Hence, the statement means literally that the bodies are "piled up in ridges and soaked in blood"; but it also means that the Scots have been thwarted and defeated. The more immediately apprehended figurative meaning is deepened and modified by the force of the literal meaning. Other words in the play which get a similar re-enforcement from two layers of meaning are *malevolent* (I, i, 97), *countenance* (I, ii, 25), *baffle* (I, ii, 88), *frontier* (I, iii, 19), *nettled* (I, iii, 239), *bombast* (II, iv, 291), *teeming* (III, i, 28), *bootless* (III, i, 67), *common-hackney'd* (III, ii, 40), '*stain'd* nobility' (V, iv, 12). This use of words is not the same thing as the play on John of Gaunt's name in *Richard II* (II, i, 73–84 and 115), although it springs, of course, from the same alertness to the suggestive power of words. In the passage in *Richard II*, the meanings are all made explicit; in *Henry IV*, they are left implicit, without statement, and often without special emphasis. Moreover, the use in question is not the same thing as an implied pun, for in the former the meanings are overlaid and mutually enriching, in the latter generally disparate and incongruous. In a really good pun, of course, the obvious incongruity may cover a deeper congruity, as in Falstaff's remark to Prince Hal, who finds a bottle of sack in Falstaff's pistol case, "There's that will sack a city." But in the use under discussion in the words from *Henry IV*, there is no incongruity.

Words used with this special re-enforcement of meaning are rarer in *Richard II*. An example is *down* in Richard's great climactic speech when he surrenders to Bolingbroke:

> Down, down I come; like glistering Phaethon,
> Wanting the manage of unruly jades.
> In the base court? Base court, where kings grow base,
> To come at traitors' calls and do them grace.
> In the base court? Come down? Down, court! down, king!
> For night-owls shriek where mounting larks should sing.
> (III, iii, 178–83)

But even here, the secondary meaning of *down* is made explicit, and *base* is played upon as Gaunt's name is played upon.[6]

Bearing in mind Coleridge's distinction between *fancy* as "the aggregative and associative power" and *imagination* as "the shaping and modifying power" or "the fusing power," * one is tempted to call the images from *Richard II* so far given fanciful, and those from *Henry IV* imaginative. One need not commit oneself to Coleridge's theory of faculty psychology to find the terms useful as descriptive of differences of effect, by whatever mental operation produced. But the matter is too complex to allow of such a simple distinction. A speech such as the Queen's at the sight of Richard coming on his way to the Tower (v, i, 7–15) is an aggregate of separate images, yet at least two of them, "My fair rose" and "the model where old Troy did stand" are imaginative in their evocation of meanings not stated. Moreover, Richard *is* the rose; the two terms have coalesced and mutually modify one another, *Richard* contributing all that we have seen throughout the play of his fresh colouring, youth, and charm, the *rose* bringing in a whole aura of associations from experience and literature—colour, freshness, fragrance, beauty, youth, sensuous pleasure, love, evanescence, the *carpe diem* ** theme. A passage of similar structure is Gaunt's speech on England (II, i, especially ll. 40–59), where, though the rapidly succeeding images (throne, scepter'd isle, seat of Mars, Eden, fortress, little world, precious stone, nurse, teeming womb) are not fused, they are individually more or less rich in suggestion and the whole speech is intense with feeling. However, I do not wish to raise an issue over terms or make the discussion as complex as their just application would entail. I have approached the matter from a somewhat different point of view and have found a different set of terms to be helpful: distinct and fused, explicit and implicit, extended and quickly suggested, and so on. Briefly, the differences in the handling of the images so far exhibited are the differences between enunciation and suggestion.[7]

[6] See *verge* and *waste*, examples of effective ambiguity, in II, i, 100–15.

* See Chapters XII–XIII of Coleridge's *Biographia Literaria*. Ed.

** See Horace, *Odes*, I. xi. 8: *"carpe diem, quam minimum credula postero"*: enjoy today, trust little to tomorrow. Ed.

[7] Tillyard (op. cit., p. 124) uses these two terms in discussing Shirley's "The glories of our blood and state."

The examples have been carefully selected, of course, to make the point, and, although they are typical, there are many exceptions. Not all the images in *Richard II* are extended, separate, and enunciatory, and not all in *Henry IV* are brief, fused, and more implicit than explicit. It seems to me significant, however, that there are more exceptions in *Richard II* than in *Henry IV*. This is what one would expect if the difference is a sign, not just of the differences between subject-matter and characters, but of the maturing powers of the writer. The later manner is likely to appear long before it becomes predominant, and *Richard II* is at most only two years earlier than *Henry IV*; but once the later manner has been fully achieved, the earlier manner will almost certainly disappear except when it is consciously adopted for some specific purpose: Gertrude's pretty and formalized description of the death of Ophelia comes to mind. (As a parallel case of stylistic development compare Yeats.) There are, for instance, almost no conceits that can be strictly so called in *Henry IV*; the most striking exception is Hotspur's description of the fight between Mortimer and Glendower on the banks of the frightened Severn (I, iii, 95–107), and the effect of rhetorical exaggeration is intended. The king's response is, "Thou dost belie him, Percy, thou dost belie him!"

It is interesting that the exceptions to the type in *Richard II* occur almost always in passages describing what the effect of war will be on English soil:

> For that our kingdom's earth should not be soil'd
> With that dear blood which it hath fostered;
> And for our eyes do hate the dire aspect
> Of civil wounds plough'd up with neighbours' sword;
> And for we think the eagle-winged pride
> Of sky-aspiring and ambitious thoughts,
> With rival-hating envy, set on you
> To wake our peace, which in our country's cradle
> Draws the sweet infant breath of gentle sleep;
> Which so roused up with boisterous untuned drums,
> With harsh-resounding trumpets' dreadful bray,
> And grating shock of wrathful iron arms,
> Might from our quiet confines fright fair peace
> And make us wade even in our kindred's blood;
> Therefore, we banish you our territories. (I, iii, 125–39)

Here the fusion of images is combined with the same sort of syntactical boldness we have observed in the passage from *Henry IV* on opposed eyes.[8] The oblique allusion contained in the imagery of the opening lines of *Henry IV* to these fine passages in *Richard II* re-enforces with powerful effect the sense of continuity established by the explicit allusion to events in the earlier play:

> No more the thirsty entrance of this soil
> Shall daub her lips with her own children's blood.
> No more shall trenching war channel her fields,
> Nor bruise her flow'rets with the armed hoofs
> Of hostile paces. (I, i, 5–9)

The idea of war on English soil was evidently one which called forth from Shakespeare an intense imaginative response.

I said I should return to the objection that the imagery in *Richard II* is what it is because of the kind of character Richard is and therefore should not be pressed for another significance. It is true enough that its appropriateness is so great that anything better to exhibit his character can hardly be imagined. But I should like to raise the question whether or not Shakespeare would have been tempted by just such a figure at any time very much later in his career. The question is not idle. Although I have not carefully examined the imagery of all the early plays with respect to the qualities here considered, I suspect that it will be found to be generally of the same kind as in *Richard II;* certainly it is in *Romeo and Juliet. King John,* though perhaps exceptional in the abundance of imaginative images, is strongly marked, nevertheless, by the elaborate type so frequent in *Richard II.*[9] But in the case of *Richard II,* these characteristics of the imagery are especially striking because they are so beautifully adapted to exhibit the central character. The perfection of the play, within its limits, is the perfection of union between character and a style that Shakespeare had mastered at that stage of his career. He had it at his fingers' ends and he found a character for whom it was dramatically right.

[8] Other vividly imaginative passages in *Richard II* on this subject (only one, however, with the degree of fusion exhibited in the passage quoted) occur at III, iii, 42–8, 93–100, 161–63; IV, i, 137–44.

[9] See Constance's speeches, especially the one on Death, in III, iv; and Arthur's speech on the irons Hubert is heating, IV, i, 60–70.

But 1 *Henry IV* is a stage beyond *Richard II* in the welding of poetic imagination to dramatic need. This is best illustrated in the case of Hotspur. Dr. Tillyard says that there is no profound obliquity in Richard's character and that a good deal of the play is the poetry of statement.[10] Richard's character is exhibited directly. He is a poet and he speaks poetically. But Hotspur is a hater of poetry who speaks some of the most vivid and the most beautiful poetry in the play. In all of Richard's poetical speeches, he has nothing like Hotspur's speech on honour, so loaded with unexpressed meaning. Yet Hotspur's animadversions on poets and poetry remain convincing. It will not do to say that we do not take him at his word. That is a very superficial view of his character and of Shakespeare's art. We do take him at his word if we pay attention to the play. He is an entire man of action, as he says he is, without artistic habits or interests. He is intensely imaginative, certainly, but imagination is not enough to make a poet. Whereas Richard's speeches are the poems that Shakespeare puts into his mouth as his own compositions, Hotspur's speeches are Shakespeare's poetry to express the mind of a character who could not himself compose a poem at all. This is a very high degree of obliquity in the use of artistic means. It is accomplishment of an altogether different order from the minor perfection of *Richard II*.

It might prove fruitful to examine the imagery of the rest of the plays from the point of view I have suggested in this paper. Miss Spurgeon and Professor G. Wilson Knight have already shown, in different ways, how the "modifying and shaping power" of the imagination has in the great tragedies produced a kind of running imagery contributory to the tone of each play. One would expect this same power to produce, along with greater boldness in syntax and greater condensation in statement, greater concentration, greater fluidity of outline, and greater suggestiveness in the imagery. The highest achievement of the "fusing power" of the imagination one feels to be, however, not complexity, but something beyond—utter simplicity of form to express multiplicity of meaning. One thinks of *Antony and Cleopatra*, part of whose great obliquity surely arises from its imagery. *Rich* is not an adequate word to describe it. At its greatest, it is evocative of things that can have no statement:

[10] Op. cit., p. 244.

there is nothing left remarkable
Beneath the visiting moon.

MILTON CRANE

The Worlds of Prose and Verse in Henry IV, Part I

Nowhere in Shakespeare are the boundaries of two worlds so clearly delimited by the use of prose and verse as in the *Henry IV* plays (1597, 1598). The scenes relating to the historical matter are in verse, the scenes of Falstaff and his followers in prose. There are trifling exceptions: the conventional usages, as in Hotspur's letter (II, iii); Hotspur's short comic dialogue with his lady (III, i), with its startling shifts between prose and verse; and the mock verse of Pistol. One can hardly say of plays which fall so neatly into two actions and two spheres of influence that the form of either action is basic and the form of the other is the exception. Between the two worlds lies a huge and fundamental opposition, but each is autonomous within itself; Pistol's verse in the Boar's Head tavern is burlesque, not a sadly distorted recollection that the "serious business" of the play is going on elsewhere in verse.

Falstaff is Shakespeare's most brilliant speaker of comic prose, as Hamlet is his most gifted speaker of a prose which defies categories. But why does Falstaff speak prose? This may seem an idle question: Falstaff is a clown, although a nobleman, and must therefore speak prose; he must, furthermore, represent "the whole world" that Hal has to banish before he can become England's Harry, and Falstaff must therefore be opposed in every conceivable way to the world of high action and noble verse in which Hal is destined to move. But beyond all this, Falstaff speaks prose because it is inconceivable that he should speak anything else. He is the incarna-

Reprinted from *Shakespeare's Prose* by Milton Crane, pp. 83–89, by permission of The University of Chicago Press. Published 1951. Title added by Ed.

tion of realism, who, in George Orwell's words, "sees very clearly the advantages of staying alive with a whole skin . . . He it is who punctures your fine attitudes and urges you to look after Number One, to be unfaithful to your wife, to bilk your debts, and so on and so forth."[1] He is the soldier who carries, not unlike Bernard Shaw's Bluntschli, a bottle of sack in his holster, and who remains on the battlefield to question the meaning of honor after the rest have gone forth to seek it. Verse in his mouth is but a mockery of verse, and as such he speaks it. Prose in Shakespeare's earlier chronicle-histories has been the rough speech of Jack Cade and his ragamuffins. Falstaff's prose is the very honey of Hybla. The devil may speak through him, but such is his utterance that the angels are easily worsted.

Burlesque lies near the heart of Shakespearean comedy, from *The Comedy of Errors* to *As You Like It*. In the two *Henry IV* plays, the Falstaff-plot offers the broadest conceivable burlesque on the serious action. Falstaff derides the chivalric ideal, the forms of noble behavior, the law itself; he robs the travelers, suffers himself to be robbed in turn without fighting, and at last lies grossly and complacently about the whole affair and is totally unabashed at being found out. He is an unrepentant sinner, and, notwithstanding, is handsomely rewarded for his evil life until the moment of his banishment. He is a particularly noisome stench in the nostrils of the godly. His burlesque of their world is conducted on every plane: he robs them, flouts their ideals, and corrupts their prince. And, because he is in such constant opposition to their world, it is only fitting that he should never really speak its language. The powerful contrast is expressed on the level of speech as on every other, and thus Falstaff speaks prose because of what he represents as well as what he is.

Most of the characters can be assigned easily enough to one group or the other—Hal's position remaining always ambiguous—but Hotspur's case is somewhat odd. He accepts the code completely; he is honor's fool, and is killed for it. But he is a very downright man, whose hard and realistic common sense makes him impatient with both poetry and milk-and-water oaths; language must speak clearly, directly, and forcefully, or he will have none of it. It is therefore inevitable that he should speak the very best of lan-

[1] George Orwell, "The Art of Donald McGill," in *Dickens, Dali and Others* (New York, 1946), p. 136.

guage, and that especially in verse. His verse is so hard, colloquial, and simple that he really has no need for prose. George Rylands says that Hotspur's speech marks an important stage in the development of Shakespeare's verse style, a stage at which Shakespeare incorporated into his verse many of the qualities of his prose.[2] And yet one feels that Shakespeare must have known what he was about when he made Hotspur speak much more verse than prose. Hotspur belongs, after all, to the world of the knights, and he must speak their idiom even if only to mock them in it. Occasionally he uses prose, and very well, as in the prose letter in II, iii—a furious stream of prose: letter, comment, and vituperation, all well jumbled together. But as soon as Lady Percy enters, we have verse dialogue. The prose of this first long monologue should perhaps be put down to a combination of conventional epistolary prose and the dramatic necessity for continuing the letter scene in prose, even after the reading of the letter is finished.

In III, i, where Hotspur taunts and enrages the fiery Glendower, he begins in broken verse:

> Lord Mortimer, and cousin Glendower,
> Will you sit down?
> And uncle Worcester. A plague upon it!
> I have forgot the map. (III, i, 3–6)

Glendower's reply has been rearranged as most irregular verse by Pope from the prose of the Quartos. Hotspur's next speech is in prose, whereas Glendower at once breaks into the pompous, inflated verse so characteristic of him. Hotspur then varies between prose and verse; the length of the individual speech appears to be the only determinant. Thus he says at first:

> Why, so it would have done at the same season, if your mother's cat had but kitten'd, though yourself had never been born. (18–20)

But, a moment later, he goes on:

> And I say the earth was not of my mind,
> If you suppose as fearing you it shook.
> . . . .

[2] H. W. Rylands, *Words and Poetry* (London, 1928), pp. 147, 148.

O, then the earth shook to see the heavens on fire,
And not in fear of your nativity.
Diseased nature oftentimes breaks forth
In strange eruptions; oft the teeming earth
Is with a kind of colic pinch'd and vex'd
By the imprisoning of unruly wind
Within her womb, which, for enlargement striving,
Shakes the old beldame earth and topples down
Steeples and mossgrown towers. At your birth
Our grandam earth, having this distemp'rature,
In passion shook. (22–23, 25–34)

After Glendower's reply, Hotspur returns to prose for a two-line retort, and, a little later, speaks verse again. Hotspur's prose in this scene appears to be restricted to short gibes, whereas he speaks verse when he becomes aroused.

He uses prose again, briefly, toward the end of the scene, when he jokes with his wife and reproaches her for her genteel swearing. It is difficult to assign any specific reason for this prose, largely because of the general uncertainty of media in this passage (225–258). Hotspur speaks prose, then verse, then prose again; after the Welsh lady's song, Hotspur's protest against his lady's "in good sooth" begins in prose and drops suddenly into verse. His last speech is again in prose. The Quartos and Folio disagree on the setting of the mixed speech. The Quartos have

Not yours, in good sooth? Heart! you swear like a comfit-maker's wife. 'Not you, in good sooth!' and 'as true as I live!' and 'as God shall mend me!' and 'as sure as day!'

And givest such sarcenet surety for thy oaths
As if thou ne'er walk'st further than Finsbury,
Swear me, Kate, like a lady as thou art,
A good mouth-filling oath; and leave 'in sooth'
And such protest of pepper gingerbread
To velvet guards and Sunday citizens.
Come, sing. (245–254)

which is the form generally accepted by modern editors. The Folios; however, make verse of lines 245–247, ending the lines at *sooth? wife, live,* and *day*. The Quartos are doubtless correct in their reading; but one's confusion finds honorable precedents.

The Prince, in general, takes his cue from his company, speaking prose in the tavern and verse in the court with equal facility. His one violation of this division is, consequently, all the more striking. He enters in V, iii, to find Falstaff moralizing over the corpse of Sir Walter Blunt. Hal is now no longer the boon companion, but the valiant knight, and reproves Falstaff in straightforward verse. Falstaff replies with a jest in prose, and the rest of the scene—a matter of a half-dozen speeches—is wound up in prose. But Falstaff himself has brought his prose into a verse scene, one of noble words and deeds, and he has used Sir Walter's "grinning honour" as a telling proof of his conclusions in his own catechism of honor. The scene thus contains a double contrast between prose and verse, and the old use of prose and verse characters within a single scene is here given a new and effective turn.

In V, i, Falstaff is for the first time brought into the world of the court, and at once sets about his favorite task of deriding it. Worcester pleads his innocence, and to the King's ironic question about the rebellion, "You have not sought it! How comes it then?" (V, i, 27), Falstaff interjects a reply: "Rebellion lay in his way, and he found it." Only Hal's injunction to remain quiet keeps Falstaff from making further comments on the action of the scene. He must needs hold his peace until the nobles have left, but immediately thereafter rediscovers his vein. Hal is short with him, for he is keenly aware of the seriousness of the situation. And so Falstaff must wait for even Hal to leave before he can make his most devastating comment on the ideals of a world he so ambiguously serves.

Shakespeare was too keen a dramatist not to have understood that the most powerful impression a scene creates in the mind of an audience is the final one. The first scene of Act V begins with King Henry, Worcester and the rest; but it ends with Falstaff. The *dramatic* point of the scene is well made and the main action is appreciably advanced. But at the side, and attempting always to intrude, is Falstaff, and when the rest have left, he has the stage entirely to himself. The net effect is produced not by the heroics of the nobles, but by the cynical realism of Falstaff. This is not to say that Falstaff dominates the play as he dominates this scene; as Professor Van Doren has well expressed it: "History is enlarged here to make room for taverns and trollops and potations of sack, and the heroic drama is modified by gigantic mockery, by the roared voice of truth; but the result is more rather than less reality, just as a cathedral, instead of being demolished by merriment among its aisles, stands more august."[3]

Hal must, as he says, "imitate the sun," and Falstaff's charm must be made so great as to convince the spectator that Hal's enjoyment of low life is not caused by a natural preference for the stew or the alehouse. But so charming (to use the word strictly) is Falstaff that Hal's necessary renunciation of him cannot be anything but priggish. The more obvious viciousness of Falstaff's actions in *2 Henry IV* is an indication that Shakespeare was obliged to degrade deliberately the tempter who had succeeded only too well. The damage, as far as the reader or spectator is concerned, is past repair.

[3] Mark Van Doren, *Shakespeare* (New York, 1939), p. 116.

U. C. KNOEPFLMACHER

The Humors as Symbolic Nucleus in Henry IV, Part I

In her classic study of Shakespeare's imagery, Miss Caroline Spurgeon argued that both parts of *Henry IV* were "curiously free from any continuous imagery."[1] Although Miss Spurgeon and subsequent critics have touched on the sun imagery which portrays Hal's rise from a riotous young man to the future Henry V, and although symbolic elements from older morality plays have been detected in *1 Henry IV*, her assertion that the play carries no "under-

From *College English*, XXIV (April 1963), 497–501. Reprinted with the permission of the National Council of Teachers of English and Ulrich C. Knoepflmacher.

[1] *Shakespeare's Imagery and What It Tells Us* (New York, 1936), p. 215.

tone of running symbolic imagery" has virtually remained unchallenged throughout the years.[2] I should like to suggest that Shakespeare's subtle metaphoric use of the Elizabethan theory of humors provides the basis for a symbolic nucleus which binds the play's abundant references to blood, sickness, and the four elements to those related to heavenly bodies and to time, and stresses the Christian import of Prince Hal's trancendence. These seemingly disjointed images have a common function: they serve to distinguish the identity of the prince from those characters who, like his father, Hotspur, or Falstaff, are hopelessly enmeshed in a protean world of changes and "counterfeit"; they punctuate the conversion of a companion of thieves into an ideal Christian monarch; and they help to resolve the basic paradox posed by Hal's uncertain claim to a usurped throne.

According to the theories fashionable in Shakespeare's time, the distemper of a patient was determined by the preponderance of one or more of the four humors. The melancholic humor, corresponding to the element of "Earth," was cold and dry; the phlegmatic humor, corresponding to "Water," was cold and moist; the choleric humor, "Fire," was hot and dry; and the sanguine humor, "Air," was hot and moist. In *1 Henry IV*, the opposition between a world of mutability and a world of static truths is depicted through the contrast between King Henry, Hotspur, and Falstaff on the one hand, and Prince Hal on the other. The humors of the King, of Hotspur, and of Falstaff are fragmented, causing their identities to merge and overlap. The Prince, on the other hand, is the man whose humors are well commingled. He shakes off his adopted "intemperance" in order to become "of all humors that showed themselves humors since the days of goodman Adam." The nature of the "base contagious clouds" above which he must rise is depicted in the first three scenes of the play through the unbalance of humors which exists in the characters of the King, Hotspur, and Falstaff, the "foils" to his "glitt'ring" reformation.

The opening speech of *1 Henry IV* is that of a melancholic man, a shaken King, "wan with care," who prescribes a crusade to the Holy Land as the sole remedy for "the intestine shock" suffered by

[2] But see Madeleine Doran, "Imagery in *Richard II* and in *Henry IV*," *Modern Language Review*, XXXVII (1942), 113–122, and Wolfgang H. Clemen, *The Development of Shakespeare's Imagery* (London, 1951), pp. 74–86.

his own, disease-ridden country. England, he assures his audience, has now recovered from its fever: "No more the thirsty entrance of this soil/Shall daub her lips with her own children's blood." But Henry knows that infection will not abate as long as he is England's king. More blood-letting is in store. The King's melancholic speech is an imposture, for the grave and sober ruler hides the crime of a young man who was once, like the Hotspur he admires but resents, "drunk with choler." The England described by the King is thirsty, hot, and dry: "the land is burning." His identification with Hotspur and his deprecation of his son are highly ironic, for he praises his future rival as "sweet fortune's minion and her pride," revealing his own ambitious temper beneath the mask of the responsible ruler. By the third scene of Act I, the King has revealed his true humor: his "blood hath been too cold and temperate," and he clashes angrily with the man he would have liked to have had as a son. The fester implanted by this "ingrate and cankered Bolingbroke" promises to spread over his kingdom, mocking the hopes of his son and his own yearning to wash away his stains at the site of Christ's "bitter cross."

If King Henry changes from feigned melancholy to open choler, his rival, young Harry Percy, lapses from a choleric outburst of temper into the most sanguine of hopes. The King's elements are Earth and Fire; Hotspur's are Fire and Air. Eager to dethrone his King, ready to leap through the skies to pluck "bright honor from the pale-faced moon,"[3] willing to fly like a thunderbolt, "hot horse to horse," Hotspur is himself the "unruly wind" with which he taunts Glendower's allusions to heavenly fires. For Hotspur, like the King, is "altogether governed by humors." His unbounded optimism, which later causes him to convert his father's "inward sickness" into the "very bottom and the soul of hope," is called a "spleen" both by his wife and his uncle.[4] It is the young Percy's sickness, and not his father's, which ultimately draws the "very lifeblood" of the rebels' enterprise. The "ague" which Vernon's praise of Hal, that other son of a sick father, nourishes in Hotspur's heart is not cured until he is chilled by the "earthy and cold hand

[3] Cf. Falstaff: "What is that word honor? Air—a trim reckoning!"

[4] Although the word "spleen" is used here in the sense of "capriciousness," its secondary meaning of "melancholy" is also implicit. Lady Percy at first imputes "thick-eyed musing and cursed melancholy" to her lord when he, like the King, bends his eyes "upon the earth." Her diagnosis is disproven as soon as Hotspur vaults on his horse with the battle-cry of "esperance."

of death." After his death, Percy's airy "spirit" leaps upward; his body, however, finds room enough in "two paces of the vilest earth." He has fought for the wrong element.

If the first scene of Act I opens on the humor of Melancholy only to give way to the Choler predominant in scene three, the scene wedged in between introduces the humor of Phlegm. Lethargic, drowsy, and "fat-witted with the drinking of old sack," a yawning Falstaff asks for the time of day. His element is Water, or, more properly wine. He and his band of thieves belong to a world as inconstant as that of the King who deprived Richard of his throne and that of the "noble" rebels led by Hotspur who haggle over their "promises" like the coarse assembly at the Boar's Head Tavern. Falstaff and his men are "governed as the sea is, by our noble and chaste mistress the moon, under whose countenance we steal." As the leader of the "moon's men" who hope to share the King's coins, Falstaff, "that trunk of humors," is the mock-opposite of Hotspur, who meets with his associates under the light of the moon to spoil the King of his realm.[5] Hotspur, always "on fire to go," despises any "frosty-spirited rogue" who is a coward; Falstaff, in turn, shuns the heat of battle as much as the portents of hellfire on Bardolph's burning nose. His "instinctive" coldness, however, prolongs his life on earth. Though sending his "mortal men" amidst the enemy's fire with the abandon of a Hotspur, Falstaff refuses to pay God the death he owes. After Hotspur's body has been drained of its humors, Falstaff stabs the dried-up remains of "this gunpowder Percy" in order to obtain an "honor" from the King.

Falstaff mistakenly assumes that Prince Hal's blood "thrills" at the mere thought of "that spirit Percy" as much as his own. But the Prince's blood is of a different sort. The King's choler provokes "civil butchery" and the death of loyal followers, armed in his "likeness"; Hotspur's sanguine temper leads to his own destruction and to that of Worcester and Vernon; Falstaff's "instinct" prompts him to massacre his band of ragamuffins. This blood-letting cannot cure England. It is only the blood of a man who can adopt and then cast off the "intemperance" implanted on his country by his father that can placate England's "thirsty soil." The disease which wrecks

[5] Glendower, whose "humor" is crossed by Hotspur, augurs success: "The moon shines fair; you may away by night." But Hotspur has already contested with him "a huge half-moon" of the land that they, in the manner of Falstaff's thieves, are sharing in advance.

the parched nation also bars Hal from the throne. By wearing a Christlike "garment all of blood" and by staining his favors in "a bloody mask," Hal must redeem England by redeeming himself. He must recover the "sunlike majesty" lost by his father:

> I know you all, and will awhile uphold
> The unyoked humor of your idleness.
> Yet herein will I imitate the sun,
> Who doth permit the base contagious clouds
> To smother up his beauty from the world,
> That, when he please again to be himself,
> Being wanted, he may be more wond'red at
> By breaking through the foul and ugly mists
> Of vapors that did seem to strangle him.

Hal's speech is ostensibly aimed at Falstaff and his crew. But it marks his dissociation from all the "contagious" vapors that he must leave behind him in his transcendence. Hal's metaphoric metamorphosis into the rising sun is presented through a series of images which are indirectly related to the humors of King Henry, Hotspur, and Falstaff.

The humor of Choler was associated by the Elizabethans with the symbols of the sun and of Mars; the sun itself was regarded as an emblem for earthly and divine kingship. It is significant that neither King Henry nor Hotspur is depicted as being sunlike. The King identifies his country's illness (and thus his own) with "the meteors of a troubled heaven," meteors which, according to Bardolph's ready gloss, portend, "Choler, my lord, if rightly taken." King Henry asks the rebellious Worcester to "move in that obedient orb again" and "be no more an exhaled meteor." And, in a double-edged analogy in which he compares himself "to Percy now" and his son to the deposed Richard II, whose "sunlike majesty" was "soon kindled and soon burned," he proudly likens his youthful self to "a comet" who "was wond'red at" while the rightful king surrounded himself with "cloudy men," who, like the phlegmatic Falstaff, "drowsed and hung their eyelids down." Hotspur, a "Mars in swathling clothes," is also denied sunlike attributes. Associated also with the capricious "moon" which governs Falstaff's nightly exploits, Hotspur is a "star" which cannot keep its "motion in one sphere" with that of the rising Prince of Wales. Of the three Harries in *1 Henry IV*, it is the Prince alone who can truly "imitate the sun." For it is the divinely ordained "majesty" of Richard II, if not his weakness as a ruler, which is to be recovered by the future Henry V.

Hal's sunlike rise and his concomitant detachment from the earthly vanities of all other characters is presented in two separate cycles. The first takes place in scenes one, two and four of Act II, and portrays Hal's gradual ascendancy over the "thieves of day's beauty," Falstaff's "minions of the moon." The second cycle takes place at Shrewsbury where, after Hal's displacement of Hotspur and his assumption of properties absent in his father, it becomes evident that the "true prince" will become a Christian monarch faithful to his promise to "redeem time."[6] The first of these cycles begins at night and ends in the early dawn; the second begins at dawn and ends in "the closing of some glorious day." The sequence in Act II is marked by allusions to time which reveal the confusion of all characters but Hal. A carrier believes it to be "four by the day," but, when questioned by Gadshill, reverses himself ("I think it be two o'clock"). After the robbery and the plunder by the "two rogues in buckram" has taken place, Hal still pretends to "drive away the time till Falstaff come." But he plays a cat-and-mouse game with Francis the drawer of ale, which clearly prefigures his later charade with Falstaff. As he kicks away the hesitant Francis, the Prince concludes that the time has come: "I am now of all humors that have showed themselves humors since the old days of goodman Adam to the pupil age of this present twelve o'clock." From that point on Hal begins his ascent. The "true prince" has taken over, as he mocks Falstaff's "instinct" and obliquely announces his separation from his former companion. When the Sheriff who looks for Falstaff takes his leave with a "good night, my noble lord," the Prince retorts, "I think it is good morrow, is it not?" The officer is puzzled: "Indeed my lord, I think it be two o'clock." The scene ends with the exchange of "good morrow" between Hal and a respectful Peto. Falstaff is sound asleep, but the prince has divested himself of the nightly humor of idleness and is ready to become the rising sun that breaks "through the foul and ugly mists." He will face his father and then meet Hotspur at a fixed "dial's point," at the appointed "hour."

[6] For a discussion of the full Christian implications of Hal's promise, consult Paul A. Jorgensen, "'Redeeming Time' in Shakespeare's *Henry IV*," *Tennessee Studies in Literature*, V (1960), 101–109.

It is at Shrewsbury that Hal's rise is completed. Hotspur, in "the heat of blood," wants to bid battle at night. But it is at dawn, under a sun that begins to peer "bloodily," that Worcester decides to betray his nephew, knowing that he and not Hotspur, "shall pay for all." In the battle that ensues, Hal's rescue of the King and his recovery of his father's "lost opinion" is subordinated to a more significant redemption which is couched in Christian terms. For in imitating the "blessed sun of heaven," the "son of England" also imitates heaven's "Son."[7] Rising "from the ground" on a "fiery Pegasus," the Prince is said to resemble an "angel dropped from the clouds." Hal's sojourn among thieves has been a deliberate one, and his willingness to meet Hotspur in single combat, "to save the blood on either side," is in direct contrast to his father's readiness to sacrifice followers spuriously dressed in the King's "coat" and "title." It is Hal who must regain this title. While the King ostentatiously invokes God to "befriend" his "just cause," Hal pleads his own cause on the battlefield. His combat with Hotspur, like that of Edgar and Edmund in *King Lear*, is not only fought for the "proud titles" that he stands to gain. It is a struggle in which he must test whether providence will restore him to the place in the divine hierarchy from which he has been removed by his father's crime.

Hal's rise, in imitation of the sun and the Son, is parodied by Falstaff's "counterfeit" resurrection. But the Prince is now aloof. Not even Falstaff's false claim for a "reward" for his own "valor" in killing Hotspur can prompt him into anger. The "true prince" has detached himself from the "double man" who asks mockingly whether the truth is not the truth. Hal has become wholly indifferent to the rewards disputed by thieves, noble and ignoble; for he has benefited from his apprenticeship and paid back Falstaff's money "back again with advantage." The play's numerous allusions to rewards, ransoms, reckonings, payments, purses, coins of all denominations, "pennyworths" turning into a "thousand pounds," become meaningful only through Hal's transcendence:

> Lay not up for yourselves treasures upon earth, where moth and rust doth corrupt, and where thieves break through and steal.
> But lay up for yourselves treasures in heaven, where neither

[7] Hal's metamorphosis is his indirect answer to Falstaff's ironic pun: "Shall the blessed sun of heaven prove a micher and eat blackberries? A question not to be asked. Shall the son of England prove a thief and take purses? A question to be asked."

moth nor rust do corrupt, and where thieves do not break or steal. (St. Matthew, VI, 19–20)

1 Henry IV ends with the glimpse of a sunlike Prince who has already broken through "the foul and ugly mists/Of vapors that did seem to strangle him." The "vapors" still remain. The figure of Falstaff, clinging greedily to the mangled corpse of Hotspur, provides a grotesque contrast to the "fair rites of tenderness" uttered by the Prince for his antagonist's spirit. King Henry's vengeful execution of Worcester, whom he accuses of bearing himself unlike a "Christian," is the ugly counterpart of Hal's release of Douglas, "ransomless and free." Falstaff and the King are "still much in love with vanity." The civil butchery is not ended. But a new sun has arisen. It is the spilled blood of a new Hal, armed in the cross of St. George, and not the proposed pilgrimage to the far-away tomb of Christ, which has "salved" the "long-grown wounds" of his "intemperance" and of the England that is to be his own.

ARTHUR C. SPRAGUE

Henry the Fourth, Part I *On-Stage*

On January 9, 1700, "the Wits of all qualities" assembled at the theatre in Lincoln's Inn Fields to see Thomas Betterton as Sir John Falstaff in a revival of *The First Part of King Henry IV*. Members of the Kit Kat Club had taken a side box. The expectations of the audience were high. Nor were they disappointed, for it was generally agreed that this favourite actor, once an esteemed Hotspur, had now "hitt the humour of Falstaff better than any that have aimed at it before."[1]

From *Shakespeare's Histories: Plays for the Stage* (London, 1964), pp. 50–72. Reprinted by permission of the author and The Society for Theatre Research.

[1] Letter of Villiers Bathurst, quoted in G. Thorn-Drury, *More Seventeenth Century Allusions to Shakespeare* (London, 1924), p. 48; E. L. Avery, "*1 Henry IV* and *2 Henry IV* during the First Half of the Eighteenth Century," *Journal of English and Germanic Philology*, XLIV (1945).

Betterton was followed by Quin, and from his time until the passing of John Henderson, a famous *laughing* Falstaff, in 1785, *Henry IV* remained among the most popular of all Shakespeare's plays.[2] At the turn of the century, it was still being shown with some frequency but those who, like the big Stephen Kemble and George Frederick Cooke, now essayed Falstaff were increasingly subjected to criticism. They lacked "unction," it was said, were not like Henderson. Henderson himself, on reconsideration, was found censurable. "This is a play," Elizabeth Inchbald wrote in her introduction to *1 Henry IV* in 1808, "which all men admire, and which most women dislike. Many revolting expressions in the comic parts, much boisterous courage in some of the graver scenes, together with Falstaff's unwieldy person, offend every female auditor." A further difficulty is implicit in what is said about Falstaff in the *Memoirs* of Charles Mathews. It was a hard role in which to gain success, not only because of the physical exhaustion involved in performing it but also because of the high expectations of readers.[3] And many readers by now had fallen under the influence of Maurice Morgann.

Morgann's *Essay on the Dramatic Character of Sir John Falstaff* (1777) deserves to be read for its urbanity and for the zest and skill with which the writer maintains a paradox. Yet it did much harm, looking forward, in its detachment of a character from his place in the play, its frequent confounding of an artistic creation with reality, to such absurdities as *The Girlhood of Shakespeare's Heroines*. This new Falstaff seemed unplayable, too. And though Morgann ridiculed the exaggeration with which the Knight was presented on the stage, the tradition of making the most of Sir John's timidity remained unbroken. No earlier critic had had doubts on the matter. Nor had Dr. Johnson now. "If Falstaff was not a coward," he said after reading Morgann, "Shakespeare knew nothing of his art."[4]

[2] Mr. Hogan's figures for the entire eighteenth century put *1 Henry IV* ahead of even the most popular of Shakespeare's comedies (*Shakespeare in the Theatre 1701–1800,* II, 717).

[3] Mrs. Charles Mathews, *Memoirs of Charles Mathews,* 4 vols. (London, 1839), II, 284. Mathews undertook the part at the Haymarket in 1814. Criticism of the stage Falstaff began within a few months of the publication of Morgann's book. *The London Review* for November 1777 took Henderson to task for showing in his face "symptoms of fear, from the vulgar notion of the knight's cowardice." A review of the *Essay* had appeared in the May issue of the same periodical.

[4] Boswell, *Life of Johnson,* ed. G. B. Hill and L. F. Powell (Oxford, 1934), IV, 515. In a lecture, "Gadshill Revisited," printed in *The*

In the course of the nineteenth century the play greatly declined in popularity, though for a time one could still see such excellent actors as J. P. Kemble and Macready in the character of Hotspur, or Phelps, Barry Sullivan, and, through many years, Hackett in Falstaff. Frank Marshall, writing in 1888, remarked that *1 Henry IV* had for some time been "virtually dead to the stage"; and Archer, in February 1896, called attention to the fact that after "twenty years' sedulous theatre-going" in London he had had to travel to Manchester in order to see it.[5] In April of the same year, when Beerbohm Tree was about to give some matinées of Shakespeare's history, Archer addressed an open letter to him in *The Daily Chronicle* urging that it be produced "in its integrity." With "four entr'actes averaging seven minutes apiece" (what a wearisome business those entr'actes used to be!) there would still be time between half-past two and half-past five for a nearly complete text; one lacking chiefly, as Archer goes on to explain, the episode with Francis, the last third of the scene in which Glendower figures, and Act IV, Scene iv (the Archbishop of York and Sir Michael). In reply Tree accepts the suggestion that IV, iv should be omitted—as should also, he adds, the Carriers Scene at the beginning of the second act. Posing as a conservative, he defends both the episode with Francis and the Welsh scene. Without, however, still heavier cutting, he fears that the performance will last for three hours and a half, rather than three, and speaks of his obligation to "the great public," who must under no circumstances be bored. When the production finally took place, Archer was full of enthusiasm, welcoming even the interpolation of battle tableaux reminiscent of the days of Charles Kean.[6] Shaw, who disliked the acting heartily, and

---

Shakespeare Quarterly, IV (1953), 125–137, I attempt to show how valuable the *datum* of cowardice is to the actor playing Falstaff.

[5] *The Henry Irving Shakespeare*, III, 334; *Theatrical World of 1896*, p. 33. See also *The Athenaeum*, April 5, 1890, for the play's want of appeal (because of its "slight feminine interest" and the fact that we are likely to side with Hotspur and the rebels against "the prince whose associates have been cutpurses and drunkards"). Productions at Oxford in 1885 (the initial venture of the O.U.D.S.) and Cambridge (by the A.D.C.) in 1886 should be mentioned. For these, see Claud Nugent in *Amateur Clubs and Actors*, ed. W. G. Elliot (London, 1898), pp. 183, 184, and *The Cambridge Review*, VIII (1886), 112, 115, 116.

[6] Archer, *op. cit.*, 86–106, 141–150.

said as much, yet granted that the play had been "accepted from Shakespeare mainly as he wrote it."[7]

Today playgoers with memories of a respectable length should have no difficulty in recalling good performances of *1 Henry IV*. Perhaps those given in London and New York by the Old Vic Company in 1945–1946 will come first to mind. The production (by John Burrell) was straightforward and unpretentious. The cast, headed by Richardson as Falstaff and Olivier as Hotspur, was of extraordinary strength, including such accomplished players (some of them at that time relatively unknown) as Margaret Leighton, Nicholas Hannen, Harry Andrews, Miles Malleson, George Rose, and the late George Relph. "There are few traps in this play for producers," Herbert Farjeon once wrote.[8] Certainly there are wonderful chances in it for actors.

It is safe to assume that among those who first saw *Henry IV* some at least knew little or nothing about Richard's time or how Henry Bolingbroke had gained the throne. And on these matters they were kept waiting.[9] There had been civil strife of some sort, they learned—the King refers to this in his opening speech—but it was over now and he hoped soon to set off on a crusade. The heightened yet plastic style which he uses becomes him and he seems a good and able king. Characters who will soon be important are now mentioned for the first time, and the manner in which they are introduced is not without interest. Thus, Glendower is "the irregular and wild Glendower" (later, even more impressively, he will be "that great magician, damn'd Glendower") and Hotspur, so likeable in the theatre, so frequently scolded by scholars, is at first no more than "gallant" and "young"—though, presently, as the King goes on to praise him he becomes everything that the other Harry, the prodigal Prince of Wales, is not. For like many of Shakespeare's opening scenes this one is continually looking towards the future.

The beginning of Scene ii is a little puzzling. Sir John's first words,

[7] *Our Theatres in the Nineties*, II, 132. In 1914, it was noted that after each of the fifteen scenes in which Tree then divided the play, "down came the curtain, up went the lights, and the band played" (*The London Shakespeare League Journal*, January 1915).

[8] *The Shakespearean Scene* (London [1949]), p. 91.

[9] As if to supplement Shakespeare, Michael Langham's production at Stratford, Ontario, in 1958, began with Henry being crowned and presently hearing of the assassination of Richard.

"Now, Hal, what time of day is it, lad?" seem neither like a phrase of greeting nor a fragment of conversation suddenly overheard, as that between Iago and Roderigo at the beginning of *Othello*. Stephen Kemble may have been right, therefore, in having the fat Knight discovered on a couch, "as if awaking."[10] On the stage, the fashion of Falstaff's clothes has changed little with the generations, as a glance at the famous frontispiece to *The Wits* (1662) will show. They seem, however, to have become less pronounced in colour. "It has long been a stage custom," Winter writes, "to attire him chiefly in red color. This is because red is a 'large' color: it fills the eye."[11] An "old English dress" of "scarlet and buff" is prescribed for him in Oxberry's edition (1822), and five years later Prince Pückler-Muskau was impressed by Charles Kemble's "dress of white and red,—very 'recherché,' though a little worn."[12]

Beerbohm Tree's Falstaff was really too fat; Samuel Phelps's not quite fat enough, it might be, though most happily proportioned.[13] Stephen Kemble and Roy Byford, are Falstaffs who have needed no stuffing. On March 23, 1832, the last night of the old Providence Theatre, when Thomas Hilson was to represent the character, he used such a quantity of "packing" that he found it impossible to mount the narrow stairs from his dressing room, below the stage, and had to ascend by means of a trap. Charles Blake, the historian of the Providence stage, observes with some relief that such an accident could no longer happen to an "actor playing *Falstaff*, who has now merely to don an india rubber undersuit, which can be inflated to any required size."[14] The new method was not, however, without its hazards. Hackett, who in his early days had worn "a

[10] *Shakespeare and the Actors*, pp. 83, 84, and cf. Dover Wilson's note in the New Cambridge edition of the play.

[11] *Shakespeare on the Stage, Third Series*, p. 376.

[12] *A Regency Visitor*, ed. E. M. Butler (London, 1957), p. 268. The elaborately described costume for Falstaff in Lacy's edition (*c.* 1864) is of red, white, and blue, with gauntlets, cane, and the inevitable brown boots.

[13] *The Theatrical Journal*, VII, 243 (August 1, 1846), suggests the desirability of "a little more stuffing," though objecting strongly to the "notion that Sir John must be made a prize hippopotamus in size." For the naturalness of his proportions, see Towse, *Sixty Years of the Theater*, p. 49.

[14] H. O. Willard, *History of the Providence Stage 1762–1891* (Providence, 1891), pp. 112, 113 (this incorporates Blake's history, published in 1868).

heavy padding or stuffing of curled hair," and suffered much, in consequence, when the weather was hot, came to Edinburgh as a visiting star equipped for Falstaff with "an immense paunch" which fitted his costume "to perfection, but was filled with air." At Edinburgh (alas!) he had made enemies among the resident company, and one of them "pricked a hole in his false abdomen, not large enough to make it collapse all at once, but by degrees." The plot succeeded all too well. "He continued to decrease in size till at last there came a rush of wind and the stomach disappeared altogether, the actor finishing the scene as best he could and the audience convulsed with laughter."[15]

During the first half of Scene ii, Falstaff and Prince Hal are alone together. To us, who know the future, their talk may possess meanings which a first audience could not have detected. The mere thrust and parry of such nimble wits must once have been delight enough. There is constant shifting of ground. What has Falstaff to do with daytime? What gracious titles under an enlightened monarch will be bestowed on highwaymen? Why are they rightly called the moon's men? To what can Sir John's melancholy be best compared? (The Prince wins this round with Moorditch, which some of the Elizabethan spectators would have passed on their way to the theatre.) It is talk for talk's sake, unaccompanied by action and not (I think) to be punctuated by bursts of laughter.

In his promptbook, Barry Sullivan wrote "Bus Falstaff Ha! Ha! IMMODERATELY," at Prince Hal's allusion to "the ridge of the gallows"; and at Falstaff's own sally about calling the Hostess to a reckoning, the actor again scrawled "oh! oh ha ha Ha Ha &c." Had he been challenged in the matter, he would doubtless have cited tradition—and perhaps named Henderson. Yet Henderson's constant laughter, in this role, did not escape rebuke. Henry Mackenzie took exception to it in *The Lounger*, May 20, 1786:

> A late excellent actor, whose loss the stage will long regret, used to represent the character of Falstaff in a manner different from what had been uniformly adopted from the time of Quin

[15] Lester Wallack, *Memories of Fifty Years* (New York, 1889), pp. 194–196; Hackett, *Notes, Criticisms, and Correspondence upon Shakespeare's Plays and Actors* (New York, 1863), pp. 313, 314; *Lincoln and the Civil War in the Diaries and Letters of John Hay*, ed. Tyler Dennett (New York, 1939), p. 138.

> downwards. He exchanged the comic gravity of the old school, for those bursts of laughter in which sympathetic audiences have so often accompanied him. From accompanying him it was indeed impossible to refrain; yet, though the execution was masterly, I cannot agree in that idea of the character.[16]

William Richardson in his *Essay* on Falstaff was equally convinced that "the guise or raiment" in which the bouncing Knight clothed his wit was "grave and even solemn."[17] The views of these early critics have come to be shared, it would seem, by actors. Certainly the better Falstaffs whom I remember have laughed seldom, and never boisterously.

With the coming of Poins, the spirit of the scene changes to one of animation and expectancy. What will happen at Gadshill is foretold with great particularity. Falstaff's want of courage is to be demonstrated; but to Poins, at any rate, "the virtue of this jest will be the incomprehensible lies that this same fat rogue will tell us when we meet at supper." And these lies, once more, are anticipated: "how thirty, at least, he fought with; what wards, what blows, what extremities he endured; and in the reproof of this lies the jest."[18]

As for the famous soliloquy with which the scene ends—

> I know you all, and will awhile uphold
> The unyok'd humour of your idleness—

it is not, I am convinced, to be translated literally in terms of character. A good deal of the abusive criticism to which Prince Hal was subjected in the eighteen-nineties, and after, may be ascribed to

[16] Chalmers, *British Essayists,* XXXI, 125.

[17] *Essays on Shakespeare's Dramatic Character of Sir John Falstaff* . . . (London, 1789), p. 35. See also William Maginn, *Shakespeare Papers* (London, 1859), pp. 51, 56, 57 (he cites 2 *Henry IV*, V, 1, 91 ff., with good effect).

[18] Technically, nothing could be more straightforward than the preparation here for scenes to come. Yet S. B. Hemingway, in *The Shakespeare Quarterly,* October 1952, would have Falstaff listening, unobserved, to Poins and Hal. "One little stage-direction," he suggests, "*may* have dropped out of our text." See, however, Miss Helen Gardner, "Lawful Espials," *Modern Language Review,* July 1938, on the pains customarily taken by Shakespeare to indicate that what is spoken is being overheard when eavesdroppers are at work.

misunderstandings of this sort.[19] Rather, the dramatist is assuring his English audience that this wayward young Prince will emerge untarnished as the splendid King Harry of fame and at the same time is inviting them to detect certain ironies in later scenes which might otherwise pass unperceived. On the stage, the speaking of the lines has sometimes been accompanied by business—the Prince strumming a lute, for instance, or rolling dice—as if to disguise the fact that it was soliloquy. In Michael Langham's Canadian production, on the contrary, realism was defied and Prince Hal seated himself on his father's throne as he began to speak. So, conceivably, he did when the play was first performed—or, more likely, coming down-stage into the midst of his auditors and addressing them, changed his manner to fit the change from prose to verse. Style, it can never be said too often, is one of the most trustworthy guides we have in the interpretation of Shakespeare's characters.

Hotspur's presence is felt almost at once in the scene which follows. In creating this character Shakespeare owed little to his sources. The name Hotspur, which suits its possessor, is given there; he is a soldier of high courage and (in Daniel's *Civil Wars*) is young. Yet tucked away, where it is unlikely to be noticed, in Holinshed's account of the middle years of the reign of Richard II, is one brief episode in which he is already himself.

> Shortlie after, by the counsell of those lords and knights that remained about the king, the lord Henrie Percie, sonne to the earle of Northumberland, was sent to the seas, to beate backe the attempts of the enimies, but he was slenderlie appointed to atchieue anie great enterprise. This was doone of some enuious purpose, bicause he had got a name amongest the common people, to be a uerie hardie and ualiant gentleman, as well among Englishmen, as Scots. But he either ignorant, or not much waieng of that which they craftilie had imagined against him, boldlie and ualiantlie executed the businesse inioined him. . . .[20]

Shakespeare, one can be all but certain, read the passage, and profited from it.

His Hotspur is very likeable, in this early scene, as we compare

[19] Shaw, e.g., calls the Prince "deliberately treacherous" in his relations with Falstaff, Mrs. Quickly, and Doll (*Our Theatres in the Nineties,* II, 128, 129).

[20] *Chronicles* (1587), III, 455, under the year 1387.

him with those crafty politicians, his father and uncle; with the nerveless fop of his story, or the threatening, apprehensive King. At the end of the history, Shakespeare is kind to him, too, and he dies young. Hotspur successful, would soon become intolerable.[21] As it is, he is a figure of romance, made real for us through his eccentricity; and we listen without grudging to his widow's rapturous eulogy of him in 2 *Henry IV*.

> By his light
> Did all the chivalry of England move
> To do brave acts. He was indeed the glass
> Wherein the noble youth did dress themselves.
> He had no legs that practis'd not his gait;
> And speaking thick (which nature made his blemish)
> Became the accents of the valiant.

Now "thick" here means hurriedly, quickly, as when Imogen bids Pisanio "say, and speak thick,"[22] but by German actors the word came to be understood otherwise—and they *stammered* in the part.[23] At His Majesty's, in November 1914, Matheson Lang was induced by Tree to stammer, and the innovation caught on at once, though Poel in the *London Shakespeare League Journal* (I, 27) protested with reason that there was "no authority for it in the text." Balliol Holloway in 1923 and Giles Isham eight years later were other Hotspurs who stammered.[24] Then, in 1945, Laurence Olivier in a brilliant performance of the part at the Old Vic found an effec-

[21] In the study, as I suggested, Hotspur has sometimes been very shabbily treated, as notably by Charlton, who maintains that his honour, whatever its "moral basis," renders him "a menace to himself, to his friends, and to the world of his time"—*Falstaff* (Manchester, 1935), pp. 39–42.

[22] III, ii, 58 (cf. *All's Well*, II, ii, 47). *The Monthly Mirror* for December 1797 took exception to Kemble's *"pop, pop, pop, pop, popinjay"* as "a refinement too artificial to be characteristic of the natural impetuosity of *Harry Percy*." I once took this to mean that the actor stammered in the part, but had he done so the fact would pretty certainly have been brought out by his numerous critics.

[23] Cf. C. J. Sisson, *New Readings in Shakespeare* (Cambridge, 1956), II, 45, 46. In the Eschenburg translation, the reading is *"das Anstossen mit der Zunge."*

[24] London *Times*, July 23, 1923; M. C. Day and J. C. Trewin, *The Shakespeare Memorial Theatre* (London and Toronto [1932]), p. 217.

tive variation on the practise, a slight hesitation before the letter "w." This became pitiful when Hotspur died.

> O, I could prophesy,
> But that the earthy and cold hand of death
> Lies on my tongue. No, Percy, thou art dust,
> And food for—
> PRINCE. For worms, brave Percy.

Michael Redgrave, on the other hand, when he undertook Richard II and Hotspur at the Royal Shakespeare Theatre in 1951, chose for the latter a north country accent with "thick 'r's." This helped him, he found, to identify himself with the role (it was wholly unlike the manner of Richard) and served also, as was desirable in the interests of Prince Hal, to keep Percy from becoming too completely the play's hero.[25]

Unfortunately, such experiments as these are likely to obscure the real individuality of Hotspur's speech and to dim his poetry.[26]

As for the other characters who appear in this third scene, the actor who plays the King has a mark to shoot at in what Cibber tells us about Edward Kynaston, "that when he whisper'd the following plain Line to *Hotspur*, 'Send us your Prisoners, or you'll hear of it!' he convey'd a more terrible Menace in it than the loudest Intemperance of Voice could swell to."[27] The Kings whom I can recall did little with the line, such menace as they conveyed coming a moment earlier. The scene ends on a high pitch of defiance:

> HOTSPUR. O, let the hours be short
> Till fields and blows and groans applaud our sport!

Then, without pause, I think, we pass to neighbour Mugs's great yawn at the beginning of the first scene in Act II.

Beerbohm Tree's omission of this later scene (in 1896) was deplored by Shaw, who would have had many readers of the play on

[25] Michael Redgrave, *The Actor's Ways and Means* (Melbourne, London, and Toronto, 1953 [1954]), pp. 43, 44. John Neville, in Seale's production at the Old Vic in 1955, stammered once more, this time on the "m" sound (*Illustrated London News*, May 14, 1955).

[26] Davies could praise the Hotspur of Spranger Barry for his "rapid and animated expression" (*Dramatic Miscellanies*, I, 227).

[27] *Apology*, ed. Lowe, I, 125, 126.

his side.[28] For here, time is annihilated and the inn-yard at Rochester present to our senses, with Charles's wain still shining over the new chimney. In most of the acting editions, in Bell, for instance, Kemble, and Oxberry, the first part of the scene, as far, that is, as the Carriers' departing "to call up the gentlemen," is retained, Gadshill's subsequent encounter with the Chamberlain going by the board. The unintelligibility to a modern audience of Gadshill's jargon is partly to blame for this cut. But what fine sounding jargon it is! And, for sense, the significant point is made that on the present expedition, with a Prince as their companion, they "steal as in a castle, cocksure." (Falstaff, not surprisingly, therefore, will remain unperturbed when, later, the Sheriff "with a most monstrous watch" descends upon Eastcheap.)

The scene of the Gadshill robbery is remarkable for the skill with which so much complicated action is brought to the stage and its progress there kept clear. The demonstration of Sir John's cowardice is—in the theatre, at any rate—complete and enduring. And if at times exponents of the part have yielded to temptation and indulged in certain excesses, the usual treatment of the episode in recent years has left little excuse for complaint.[29] It is a joy to recall Roy Byford (in Bridges-Adams's production) as we saw him, in silhouette, rushing about, just out of harm's way, during the robbery. The mysterious whistling early in the scene coming, perhaps, now from one side of the stage, now the other, and Falstaff's abuse of those "fat chuffs" and "whoreson caterpillars," the travellers, should also be memorable. His ready assumption of youth, at this moment, youth underprivileged and angry, is too delightful to be sacrificed, as it usually is, to mere clamour.[30]

"O, let the hours be short" . . . Hotspur had wished when last we saw him. Now as he waits they seem very long indeed. In his impatience, he identifies the letter from which he is reading with its prudent author, and I have seen him fling it down, and then kick it about the stage, as he rails. Yet already the note of warning has been struck, and it will sound often in our ears before the destruction of

[28] *Our Theatres in the Nineties,* II, 132.

[29] For the excesses, see Sprague, *Shakespeare and the Actors,* pp. 84, 85, and *The Stage Business in Shakespeare's Plays: A Postscript* (London [Society for Theatre Research], 1954), pp. 9, 10.

[30] In productions where pictorial illustration is admitted, there is much to be said for showing a distant gallows in this scene, as was done by Margaret Webster (in 1939) and John Burrell (in 1945–1946).

these doomed men at Shrewsbury. As for Lady Percy, she was contrasted much to her disadvantage with Portia by Mrs. Jameson: "Lady Percy," she decided, "is evidently accustomed to win more from her husband by caresses than by reason . . . she has no real influence over him." (Upon which, Kittredge remarked that "Hotspur would have been as little likely to confide in Portia as Brutus to take Lady Percy into his confidence.")[31] On the stage she will be, one hopes, young, attractive, and very much in love with her husband, as in his way he is with her. She should not on any account be burly and shrewish.

The great Tavern Scene has a certain shapeliness in itself, moving as it does through two climaxes from its lively prologue in the confounding of poor Francis to the very quietest of quiet endings. In the theatre, there is little danger of our wasting pity on Francis; the eager stupidity of the drawer seems an appropriate subject for demonstration.[32] Poins remains curious when this has been concluded. What, he asks, was the point of the jest? To which the Prince of Wales replies in effect that it had no point.

> I am now of all humours that have showed themselves humours since the old days of goodman Adam to the pupil age of this present twelve o'clock at midnight.

The words are almost like a stage direction. For Hal, whatever he is to become later, must not be grave now; must make us feel that he is savouring present joys. J Ranken Towse remembered the Hal of Walter Lacy as "the embodiment of reckless, irresponsible gayety, of humorous mischief without a trace of malice in it." But also, "in his most roystering moods he never quite forgot his princely dignity."[33] Of the actors whom I recall in the part, Richard Burton suggested most nearly the future King Henry the Fifth—but he was never merry.

In the study it is possible to forget or overlook the visual impres-

[31] Mrs. Jameson, *Characteristics of Women* (1832), quoted in *Variorum Edition,* p. 475; Kittredge, ed., *Julius Caesar,* in *Sixteen Plays,* p. 823.

[32] Charlton, taking a wholly different view of the episode, accuses Hal of "heartlessly endangering the poor drawer's means of subsistence" (*Falstaff,* p. 11). For a gag of some antiquity, "six and eight pence," pronounced by Francis, at line 109, instead of the expected "Anon, anon, sir," see Sprague, "Falstaff Hackett," *Theatre Notebook,* IX (1955), 62.

[33] *Sixty Years of the Theater,* p. 66.

siveness of Falstaff's entrance in this scene. He and his followers carry battered weapons, their clothes are stained with blood ("Tell me now in earnest," the Prince asks, later, "how came Falstaff's sword so hack'd?" and Peto explains, "Why, he hack'd it with his dagger, and said he would swear truth out of England but he would make you believe it was done in fight, and persuaded us to do the like"). It is he, Sir John, who makes complaint. "A plague of all cowards, I say." Deserted by those who should have fought beside him, he had yet borne himself magnificently and escaped only "by miracle." Poins had prophesied he would claim to have fought with "thirty, at least," and he reaches fifty—"two or three and fifty upon poor old Jack." Then, before the fun of the mounting figures is exhausted, he is led to mention casualties: "two rogues in buckram . . . pepper'd." The same two, as we recognize, who are so eagerly listening to him now, who can wait, nonetheless, and give their great fish more line, since he is surely caught!

For the actor to wink at his audience, somewhere here, as Professor Dover Wilson would have him do, seems to me not only arbitrary (the meaning of innumerable passages in Shakespeare could be perverted by extra-textual winkings) but also confusing.[34] "Nay then, I have an eye of you," says Hamlet, aside, to assure us that he is not being deceived by the blandishments of Rosencrantz and Guildenstern. Surely, were Falstaff suspicious at this moment he would have said as much. Nor must there be any spoiling by anticipation of the glory of his escape, when escape will seem impossible.

The Falstaff of stage tradition, as it existed at the end of the eighteenth century, say, or the beginning of the nineteenth, entered with an air of gravity and "importance." This was succeeded, however, by one of confusion as Henry very simply and destructively told his story.[35] "What trick," he concludes, "what device, what starting hole canst thou now find out to hide thee from this open

[34] A number of sentences in this and the preceding paragraph appeared first in "Gadshill Revisited," *Shakespeare Quarterly*, IV (1953), 133. See also Wilson, *The Fortunes of Falstaff* (Cambridge and New York, 1944), pp. 51 ff.

[35] See Gentleman's notes in Bell's *Shakespeare; European Magazine*, for October 1802 (on Stephen Kemble); Mrs. Mathews, *Memoirs of Charles Mathews*, II, 287; *Edinburgh Dramatic Review*, VIII (1824), 167 (Charles Kemble); George Darley, in Cumberland edition (Elliston).

and apparent shame?" And Poins, as if certain there would be no answer (how, indeed, could there be!) adds cheerfully: "Come, let's hear, Jack. What trick hast thou now?" I like to think that Garrick's lines on James Quin in the Abbey Church in Bath refer to this moment:

Clos'd be those eyes, the harbingers of wit,
Which spake before the tongue what *Shakespear* writ.

For when Quin played Falstaff, not only was his "expressive eye" commended, but in this very passage his "glow of feature and expression."[36] It is remarkable, indeed, how often in descriptions of early performances of this play Sir John's *eyes* are mentioned.[37] The shrewd glances of Anthony Quayle come to mind, and those still more recently of Eric Berry, but modern stage lighting has not always encouraged actors to do much with their eyes.

Before delivering the exultant "By the Lord, I knew ye" . . . Falstaff has often lowered a shield behind which he has been hiding his face, to show it wreathed in smiles; and even more often, from Quin's time, indeed, he has introduced an anticipatory "Ha! ha! ha! d'ye think I did not know ye?" of his own composition. Both the action and the (I suppose) reprehensible gag have persisted into the present century. Mr. Allan Wilkie confessed that he had used the latter in his Australian productions back in the twenties ("it helped the situation greatly and as you say it is dignified by tradition") and in the early fifties Sir Donald Wolfit found the shield business effective. (What was more, it gave him a chance to wipe his face: Falstaff, we sometimes forget, is one of the most exhausting of Shakespearian roles.) Yet the conceiving of this magnificent means of escape need not be withheld from us. I think of the rapturous excitement with which Roy Byford marked the moment; of the succession of emotions which Douglas Campbell's face displayed before at last we saw it illumined. "By the Lord, I knew ye" . . . and then, "The lion will not touch the true prince."

[36] Gentleman, *The Dramatic Censor,* II, 396, 397.

[37] See, e.g., Victor, *History of the Theatres of London and Dublin,* 2 vols. (London, 1761), II, 67, 68 (Quin); Bell's *Shakespeare,* IV, 69 note (Quin); Tate Wilkinson, *Memoirs,* IV, 79 (Quin); Davies, *Dramatic Miscellanies,* I, 250 (Shuter); Boaden, *Kemble,* I, 301 (Henderson); Planché, *Recollections and Reflections,* I, 34 (Dowton;); *Dramatic Tatler,* Edinburgh, 1829, No. X, p. 37 (Charles Kemble); George Darley, in Cumberland edition (Elliston).

Prince Hal's idea of giving a play (earlier it had been with himself as Hotspur and Falstaff as Lady Percy) is now mentioned again, this time by the fat knight:

> What, shall we be merry? Shall we have a play extempore?
> PRINCE. Content—and the argument shall be thy running away.
> FALSTAFF. Ah, no more of that, Hal, an thou lovest me!

Had he really won the contest from the Prince and Poins, as many critics would have us believe, why, one asks, should he now be so reluctant to have the subject mentioned? In the theatre, however, no difficulty exists. Everyone, except Jack himself, enjoys the thought of his having larded the lean earth as he fled. So the critic of *The Edinburgh, Dramatic Review*, April 21, 1824, in giving examples of Charles Kemble's *vis comica* could write: "next to his ridicule of that 'eternal bonfire,' *Bardolph's* nose, we must say, that we were most delighted with his plea *ad misericordiam*, when he deprecates any farther allusions to his exploits upon *Gadshill:* it might have melted the heart of the most 'flinty hearted villain,' who had any conception of the redeeming properties of wit and humour."[38]

The Play Scene was rarely included in performances from the seventeen-hundreds till the late eighteen-hundreds. Now and again, it was restored briefly, as at Covent Garden, February 24, 1802, when *The Theatrical Repertory* decided that it had "a good effect,"[39] but actors had come to think of it as unserviceable. So when Hackett spent the evening of December 13, 1863, with Abraham Lincoln, the President

> was particularly anxious to know why one of the best scenes in the play that where Falstaff & Prince Hal alternately assume the character of the King, is omitted in the representation. Hackett says it is admirable to read but ineffective on stage, that there is generally nothing sufficiently distinctive about the actor who plays Henry to make an imitation striking.[40]

[38] VIII, 179.

[39] Page 378. See also Hogan, *Shakespeare in the Theatre,* I, 177, 178; II, 250, and *The Times,* July 29, 1846, quoted in Pascoe's *Dramatic List,* London, 1879, p. 261.

[40] *Lincoln and the Civil War in the Diaries and Letters of John Hay,* 138 (this passage was used by Berkelman, "Lincoln's Interest in Shakespeare," *Shakespeare Quarterly,* II [1951], 309). "The players are con-

That Sir John and the Prince have an audience for their play should be borne in mind. Francis is certainly there, Peto and Poins, and for a time, we may suppose, Bardolph.[41] Falstaff addresses them as he ascends his throne, "Stand aside, nobility," and again, it may be, when he and Hal exchange roles, "Judge, my masters," though at that moment conceivably he calls upon the larger audience close to the stage. (So, it has been happily suggested, his "hear you, my masters. Was it for me to kill the heir apparent?" was occasioned by the uproar in the theatre, the spontaneous, unquenchable laughter, which one still hears, sometimes, even now, at the Knight's escape from humiliation.)[42] The ready correction of his age—"some fifty, or, by'r Lady, inclining to threescore"—seems likely, also, to have been made out of deference to some expression of incredulity on the part of the onlookers. It would be like Poins to object.

In several recent productions of *Henry IV*, the earliest at the Royal Shakespeare Theatre in 1951, the play within the play has taken on a sudden earnestness after Hal succeeds Falstaff as King. The subject under discussion has shifted. The emotion with which the participants speak is now their own. Even those about them feel the tension, which is broken by knocking and the return of Bardolph. The effectiveness of this interpretation is beyond question. What may be questioned is the moment at which the change takes place. In Douglas Seale's production at the Old Vic in 1955 the climax of the fun was reached in Falstaff's apology for himself. It was only upon his mention of banishment ("Banish plump Jack, and banish all the world") that the Prince spoke quietly but with a weight of meaning, "I do, I *will*."[43] This withholding of the note of seriousness until almost the end of the episode is, I think, preferable to the method followed at Stratford. There Hal began to de-

sistent," Charles Knight observes in recording the cutting of this scene and III, i: "Their intolerance of poetry and of wit are equal"–*Studies of Shakspere* (London, 1849 [1868]), p. 168.

[41] It is questionable how long Bardolph remains (see J. Dover Wilson, ed., *1 Henry IV*, p. 155, and cf. Sisson, *New Readings in Shakespeare*, II, 32, 33).

[42] Cf. Ronald Watkins, *On Producing Shakespeare* (London [1950]), p. 144.

[43] J. C. Trewin, in *The Illustrated London News,* May 14, 1955, Mary Clarke, *Shakespeare at the Old Vic 1954–55*, p. 160, Audrey Williamson, *Contemporary Theatre 1953–1956*, pp. 118, 119.

nounce his companion almost at once with a mounting violence which seemed out of keeping with the neatly patterned arrangement of the words. "Wherein is he good, but to taste sack and drink it? wherein neat and cleanly, but to carve a capon and eat it? wherein cunning, but in craft? wherein crafty, but in villany?"

The close of the Tavern Scene gives us perfectly the feeling of reaction after excitement. It is cheerful still, though the Prince and Poins (it has regularly been Poins, in the theatre, not Peto) are quite conscious of the approaching war. In their possession of the fat Knight's papers a new joke is already hatching. Meanwhile, the most amusing of all the off-stage sounds called for in Shakespeare's plays, at once soothing and tremendous, goes on and on: Falstaff, "fast asleep behind the arras, and snorting like a horse."

In an earlier chapter, I suggested that a producer of *Richard II* might be judged, in the first instance, by what he did with the Gardeners Scene. The Welsh Scene in *1 Henry IV* is, perhaps, even more exacting. This was long neglected. Betterton omitted the later part of it (from the return of Glendower with Lady Percy and Lady Mortimer) and it had wholly disappeared from the stage by the end of the eighteenth century. "A wild scene," Francis Gentleman calls it, "which is properly rejected in representation."[44] Creswick at the Surrey Theatre restored it in September 1855, and Phelps, at Drury Lane in 1864, when Lewis Carroll was entranced by Edith Wynne's singing of the Welsh song.[45] Yet Archer, a full generation later, was quite willing to have a cut made in the text just here. "In Act III., Sc. 1," he wrote, in his open letter to Tree, "from 're-enter Glendower with the ladies' onward, we cannot recapture the Elizabethans' delight in the Welsh gibberish and 'Welsh song sung by Lady Mortimer,' for the sake of which the scene exists. The theatre is not the place for studies in the archaeology of humour." Tree, to his credit, replied that he found the episode "full of charm and beauty" and would not be dissuaded from keeping it.[46]

[44] Note in Bell's edition, p. 103; cf. Davies, *Dramatic Miscellanies,* I, 255, and John Heraud, *Shakspere his Inner Life,* London, 1865, p. 201.

[45] *The Athenaeum,* September 22, 1855; Lewis Carroll, *Diaries,* London, 1953, p. 212 (April 1, 1864).

[46] *Theatrical World of 1896,* pp. 91 ff. In defending this "scene of love and song," Tree admittedly had in mind the particular character of his matinée audiences.

In performance, the clash of temperaments between Hotspur and Glendower is easy to enjoy.

GLENDOWER. I can call spirits from the vasty deep.
HOTSPUR. Why, so can I, or so can any man;
But will they come when you do call for them?

The sole danger is that of exaggeration. For the portentousness of the Welshman's manner need not in itself be ridiculous.[47] The Cibbers, Colley and Theophilus, both of whom played it, are unthinkable in the part. Irony is present, besides humour, in the quarrelling of these rash men over the division of a country not yet theirs. We should be made to feel, indeed, that they are doomed; that this is a final parting they are taking with their wives, its pathos only half concealed beneath the cheerful banter which Hotspur keeps up with Lady Percy. Nor does the variety of the scene end even here. Mortimer, as he speaks of

ditties highly penn'd,
Sung by a fair queen in a summer's bower,
With ravishing division, to her lute,

and Glendower as he translates for his daughter, a moment later, startle us with poetry of a sort unheard elsewhere in the play and strangely moving here.

The awaited interview between the King and Prince Hal might seem, when it comes, to be imperilled by our memories of an earlier passage. But the image of Falstaff in his great chair, the pillow he wears as crown inclined rakishly over one eye, assuring the madcap Prince that he does not now speak to him "in drink, but in tears," need not recur to the imagination as Henry Bolingbroke begins to chide his son. In the theatre we live far more completely in the moment than is generally acknowledged. The reality of the King's emotion is at once apparent, as is the aptness of the parallel he draws from history, from Richard's time. A new theme has crossed and reinforced that of the two Harries, now familiar to us. When at last the Prince begins his answer—"Do not think so. You shall not find it so"—the words must seem wrung from him. One would like

[47] That Hotspur's conduct in this scene deserves condemnation is urged by Gareth Lloyd Evans in *Stratford-Upon-Avon Studies* 3 (1961), p. 154. Few playgoers would agree.

to believe that "Sir" John Hill was accurate in the description he gives of Ryan's delivery of this speech:

> We see nothing of the player in it: 'Tis nature itself. The contrition the resolution, the gallantry, and the solemnity express'd in it, all succeed one another as they wou'd do in real life; and we are ready to believe ourselves carry'd back to old times, and hearing the first sentiments of that noble daring that afterwards carry'd *Harry the Fifth* thro' the conquest of *France*, breathing themselves out of his own full heart.[48]

It is upon notes of haste and urgency that this scene closes. As the King says, "Advantage feeds him fat while men delay," Falstaff enters—or, as I think, is discovered—talking mournfully with Bardolph about reformation, and his loss of weight "since this last action." On the stage, Bardolph is likely to be valetting him, giving particular attention, it may be, to his master's belt, which he is attempting to lengthen. The tone of the scene is relaxed and almost domestic. Soon, however, it changes. The bustling entrance of Mrs. Quickly is followed by an exchange of accusations—charge and counter-charge—between Sir John and her; and the Prince, to whom both appeal, seems master of the situation. As once before, he is confident that Falstaff can be put down by a plain tale—and tells it. Rather than "bonds of forty pound apiece" and an ancestral ring, the Knight's pocket had contained only "tavern reckonings, memorandums of bawdy houses," and a little sugar. "Art thou not ashamed?" he cries. Sir John's reply needs careful attention if it is to keep its point. At the beginning his manner is partly rueful, partly one of gentle remonstrance. On "thou seest I have more flesh than another man, and therefore more frailty," he pauses, only to pounce the next instant with every word telling. "You confess then, you pick'd my pocket?" And for perhaps the only time in the play, Hal is without an answer. "It appears so by the story," he says, lamely enough, for want of one.[49]

Turning now upon the Hostess with an overpowering show of magnanimity and forgiveness, Jack fairly bundles her off the stage. His "Now, Hal, to the news at court" is, perhaps, to be spoken loudly, for her benefit (much as Hamlet after his confidences with

[48] *The Actor,* London, 1750, pp. 217, 218.

[49] Cf. William Richardson, *Essays on Shakespeare's Dramatic Character of Sir John Falstaff . . . ,* p. 47.

the First Player will sometimes raise his voice for the benefit of Rosencrantz and Guildenstern: "Follow that lord—and look you mock him not") then, seeing that poor Damc Partlct has indccd gone, he adds, quickly, "For the robbery, lad—how is that answered?" What he hears is encouarging.

> PRINCE. I am good friends with my father, and may do anything.
>
> FALSTAFF. Rob me the exchequer the first thing thou doest, and do it with unwash'd hands too.

And Bardolph, whose mind is charmingly literal, says "Do, my lord." At Sadler's Wells in 1856 action accompanied the words. Bardolph, according to Samuel Phelps's promptbook, "X's eagerly to Prince who rebukes him—Bardolph retires up." The scene ends with two couplets, the Prince going out on the first—

> The land is burning; Percy stands on high;
> And either they or we must lower lie—

and Falstaff lingering for the second,

> Rare words! brave world! Hostess, my breakfast, come,
> O, I could wish this tavern were my drum!

That we should hear the drum at this moment is natural enough, and the reappearance of the Hostess, all smiles, bringing in Sir John's breakfast will be resented only by purists.[50]

From the beginning of the fourth act, our sense of a destination grows strong and all roads lead to Shrewsbury. New characters appear, in Vernon and the Douglas. Vernon has the shining description, admired by Dr. Johnson, "All furnish'd, all in arms," which for too many scholars exists chiefly as "context" for one of the most famous of Shakespearian cruxes. Douglas, on the other hand, is likely to disappoint an imaginative reader of the play when he comes to see it performed. Merely as a role, it demands a good deal of the actor without promising him much in return. Meanwhile, we have had a glimpse of Falstaff's leisurely progress toward the field of battle. For his entrance, when Hackett performed the part, "Over

[50] The breakfast business was used in Burrell's Old Vic production. A silly variation is one by which Mrs. Quickly uncovers an immense dish containing a single small egg. The drum is called for in Oxberry's edition (*c.* 1822) and Lacy's (1864).

the hills and far away" used to be played, very slowly, by a drum and fife.[51] Presently, Sir John begins to tell us about his activities. Quin distinguished himself in this soliloquy,[52] which suited his sternly unromantic interpretation of the speaker; Quin and also Henderson. Boaden recalls the latter with relish.

> He stands before me with the muster of his recruits legible in his eye, and I hear the fat and chuffy tones by which he added humour to the ludicrous terms of the poet's description. "Such as fear the report of a caliver, worse than a struck fowl, or a *hurt wild duck*." "Such *toasts and butter*." . . . The burst of laughter he excited by this, which he did not hurry, but seemed mentally to enjoy, as the images rose in succession, were beyond measure delightful. He made his audience for the time as intelligent as himself, and a syllable of pleasure was not lost upon them.[53]

We should be conscious of the proximity of the poor rascals as their captain talks of them, and in John Burrell's Old Vic production their dreary marching song was heard, just off-stage. Originally "Greensleeves," the tune had been worn down into a monotonous grumbling. And like themselves, it was more ludicrous than pathetic.[54] Later in the scene Phelps brought out the contrast between Sir John's easy manner toward Prince Hal—his "How now, mad wag," and so on—and his careful "My good Lord of Westmoreland." This was a touch, Morley decided, which stamped the Knight "as a man well born and bred."[55]

As for the brief scene between the Archbishop of York and the mysterious Sir Michael, it becomes defensible at once if we think of its bearing on the play which follows—the *Second Part* rather than the first.[56] The importance of the approaching battle gains em-

[51] "Falstaff Hackett," *Theatre Notebook*, IX (1955), and Lacy's acting edition.

[52] John Hill, *The Actor* (London, 1750), p. 207.

[53] James Boaden, *Memoirs of Mrs. Siddons* (Philadelphia, 1827), p. 62.

[54] More recently still, in at least two productions, some of the recruits have been shown us, but with more loss, I thought, than gain.

[55] Henry Morley, *The Journal of a London Playgoer* (London, 1891), p. 275.

[56] The scene has been defended by R. A. Law, "Structural Unity in the Two Parts of *Henry the Fourth*," *Studies in Philology*, XXIV (1927), 226, and H. Edward Cain, "Further Light on the Relation of *1* and *2 Henry IV*," *Shakespeare Quarterly*, III (1952), 31, 32.

phasis, too, by what we now hear, as its outcome is made even more certain than it seemed before. Robert Hardy was the Archbishop at Stratford in 1951. He cannot have had many predecessors in the part.

The presence of Jack Falstaff at the King's council of war (V, i) has sometimes been found embarrassing. His single line, "Rebellion lay in his way, and he found it," is best spoken aside to Prince Hal, as Pücker-Muskau noticed it was spoken at Covent Garden in 1827. He was impressed, indeed, by the whole treatment of this scene, which had a propriety wanting in German productions.[57] At Hal's words, "I have a truant been to chivalry," Sir John may make expostulating gestures, without offence; but it is very questionable whether at the command, "Hence, therefore, every leader to his charge," his behaviour should be that described in one of the Hackett promptbooks: "Falstaff starts up, looks off . . . and vapours as if motioning his men."[58] As for the Prince's "Peace chewet, peace," it is a rebuke without severity, whether *chewet* means jackdaw or a particular sort of mince pie.[59]

Near the beginning of the present chapter I pointed out that early critics of the histories were in no doubt as to the cowardice of Falstaff and that on the English stage he has regularly been played as amusingly deficient in courage. Thus Elizabeth Montagu in the seventeen-sixties and James H. Hackett, a century later, have much the same point of view towards the Knight's catechism. Mrs. Montagu was a little shocked, indeed:

> Gluttony, corpulency, and cowardice are the peculiarities of Falstaffe's composition. . . . As the contempt attendant on these vices and defects is the best antidote against any infection . . . so it was very skilful to make him as ridiculous as witty, and as contemptible as entertaining. The admirable speech upon

[57] *A Regency Visitor,* pp. 269, 270.

[58] This is from Hackett's 1828 book ("Falstaff Hackett"). For a piece of atrocious business involving the King and a drum, see *Shakespeare and the Actors,* p. 89.

[59] Cf. John Palmer, *Political Characters of Shakespeare* (London, 1952), p. 194; and Harold Jenkins, *The Structural Problem in Shakespeare's Henry the Fourth* (London [1956]), p. 19. I cannot accept the latter's view that this remark, even remotely, foreshadows the rejection of Falstaff.

> honour would have been both indecent and dangerous from any other person.[60]

Hackett shuddered at the words "he that-*died*-o' Wednesday," and although "wonderfully expressive of *Falstaff's* animal relish of life" it was a comic shudder as well.[61]

How much the actor of a minor part can do towards bringing out the meaning of a passage is well illustrated by Vernon's praise of Prince Hal in V, ii. Vernon has gone with Worcester to negotiate with the King, and the terms which the King offers them have been unexpectedly generous. Peace is beginning to seem possible, after all, when Worcester acts to prevent it. Their offence, he explains to Vernon, is not of a sort to be forgiven.

> My nephew's trespass may be well forgot;
> It hath the excuse of youth and heat of blood,
> And an adopted name of privilege—
> A hair-brain'd Hotspur, govern'd by a spleen.
> All his offences live upon my head
> And on his father's.

Vernon does not oppose him when he concludes, realistically, that the King's offer must be suppressed.

> VERNON. Deliver what you will, I'll say 'tis so.

When, however, he must listen to Worcester's careful misrepresentation of what was said at the parley, it will be for the actor to bring out his sense of humiliation and disgust. Then comes the mention of how Harry Monmouth had challenged Hotspur to single combat, and Vernon is happy in the chance to speak out at last.

> HOTSPUR. How show'd his tasking? Seem'd it in contempt?
> VERNON. No, by my soul. I never in my life
> Did hear a challenge urg'd more modestly . . .

and so on, till Hotspur checks him:

[60] *Essay on the Writings and Genius of Shakespear Compared with the Greek and French Dramatic Poets*, second edition (London, 1770), pp. 107, 108.

[61] William Winter, *Shakespeare on the Stage, Third Series* (New York, 1916), p. 359. Bridges-Adams used to introduce (he once wrote me) "a bang of villainous saltpetre off-stage toward the end of Falstaff's Honour speech." That made "the old thing jump out of his skin."

Cousin, I think thou art enamoured
Upon his follies.

In the theatre, all this can become transparently clear. It is not always so, in the study.[62] Kemble, by the way, made a shift at this point, postponing the return of Douglas, with his "Arm, gentlemen! to arms!" so that it now followed the speeches of Vernon and Percy. This improvement on Shakespeare was commended by Archer but seems not to have been appreciated by Beerbohm Tree.[63]

That Hotspur and the rest are being armed throughout the latter part of the same scene and that this action contributes to our sense of the imminence of battle may be overlooked by a mere reader. And on the royalist side, one captain enters the fray almost without armour. *Punch* in an inquiry headed "How Fat Was Falstaff?" took notice of this curious convention, some years ago, describing the Knight unsentimentally as "a corpulent dotard doing battle amongst a covey of tanks."[64] The explanation is obvious. "I need no more weight than my own bowels," Sir John remarks; and the demands upon his strength and nimbleness are, indeed, becoming excessive. Attacked by the Douglas, he must fall down "as if he were dead"—must to the uninitiated seem dead. Then he revives. Perhaps the old actors made rather too much of his trepidation at the moment of doing so. Charles Kemble, as described in the Edinburgh *Dramatic Tatler*, April 9, 1829, merely followed tradition here. When Hal after his eulogy of Percy leaves the stage,

> the Knight, who is lying upon the ground, his shield covering his face, gently moves his sword as a sign of his existence. He then gradually withdraws the shield from before his face—not, however, without several interruptions from the "din of battle," as it sweeps along in the distance. Jack's undoubted

[62] I am remembering, particularly, the fine performance of Vernon by Frank Duncan with the Old Vic Company in 1946; cf. also George Skillan's acting edition, p. 66, and John Bailey, *The Continuity of Letters* (Oxford, 1923), p. 76.

[63] *Theatrical World of 1896*, p. 145. The shifting of "Now, Esperance! Percy! and set on," to the end of the scene (which Archer also commends), goes back to Bell's edition. Both changes are regularly introduced in nineteenth-century acting texts, like Oxberry's and Lacy's.

[64] February 27, 1946. See also Winter, *Shakespeare on the Stage: Third Series*, p. 377.

want of courage—his radical cowardice—is here displayed in the most unequivocal manner. At length he grows a little braver —he touches his heart, and, after much exertion, he manages once more to get upon his legs.

Jack's most exhausting task remains to be performed. For if he is to fulfill the clear demands of the text he must get Percy's body on his back, becoming so involved with it that he can refer to himself, understandably, as "a double man," and at the end of the scene must bear his "luggage" triumphantly from the stage. No wonder if Charles Kemble, like some actors before him and many after, fairly admitted defeat.[65]

The completeness of this history in itself, however much it may gain in meaning when we think of it as part of a larger whole, must not be ignored. Too much importance is sometimes attached, it may be, to Hal's rescue of his father. Certainly this episode, Shakespeare's own invention, should not be omitted in performance, as it has often been, but quite as certainly it receives little emphasis in the play. The King and his son, we remember, were already reconciled well before the battle. The awaited meeting of Hotspur and the Prince of Wales is another matter. In the theatre, this may still retain something of its first excitement even when we have seen *Henry IV* many times over.

HOTSPUR. If I mistake not, thou art Harry Monmouth.
PRINCE. Thou speak'st as if I would deny my name.
HOTSPUR. My name is Harry Percy.
PRINCE. Why, then I see
A very valiant rebel of the name.

Hotspur is most lovable, dying, and Hal's "Fare thee well, great heart!" rings true, for the Prince in victory is both modest and generous. And Falstaff? "If I do grow great," he says, "I'll grow less; for I'll purge, and leave sack, and live cleanly, as a nobleman should do." In the first audience, I make no doubt, many believed him.

[65] *Ibid.* (For the business in this scene, see also *Shakespeare and the Actors*, pp. 90, 91.) George Skillan in a note to his acting edition calls the old stage direction ("*He takes up Hotspur on his back*") impractical, but I have seen it followed to the letter, as by an admirable Falstaff, Harry Sheppard at the Hedgerow Theatre in 1940.

II

SAMUEL JOHNSON

The Unimitable Falstaff

. . . *Falstaff* unimitated, unimitable *Falstaff*, how shall I describe thee? Thou compound of sense and vice; of sense which may be admired but not esteemed, of vice which may be despised, but hardly detested. *Falstaff* is a character loaded with faults, and with those faults which naturally produce contempt. He is a thief, and a glutton, a coward, and a boaster, always ready to cheat the weak, and prey upon the poor; to terrify the timorous and insult the defenceless. At once obsequious and malignant, he satirises in their absence those whom he lives by flattering. He is familiar with the prince only as an agent of vice, but of this familiarity he is so proud as not only to be supercilious and haughty with common men, but to think his interest of importance to the duke of *Lancaster*. Yet the man thus corrupt, thus despicable, makes himself necessary to the prince that despises him, by the most pleasing of all qualities, perpetual gaiety, by an unfailing power of exciting laughter, which is the more freely indulged, as his wit is not of the splendid or ambitious kind, but consists in easy escapes and sallies of levity, which make sport but raise no envy. It must be observed that he is stained with no enormous or sanguinary crimes, so that his licentiousness is not so offensive but that it may be borne for his mirth.

The moral to be drawn from this representation is, that no man is more dangerous than he that with a will to corrupt, hath the power to please; and that neither wit nor honesty ought to think themselves safe with such a companion when they see *Henry* seduced by *Falstaff*.

From *The Plays of William Shakespeare* (London, 1765), IV, 356. Title added by Ed.

MAURICE MORGANN

The Courage of Falstaff

I do not clearly discern that Sir *John Falstaff* deserves to bear the character so generally given him of an absolute Coward; or, in other words, that I do not conceive *Shakespeare* ever meant to make Cowardice an essential part of his constitution. . . . Cowardice *is not* the *Impression* which the *whole* character of *Falstaff* is calculated to make on the minds of an unprejudiced audience; tho' there be, I confess, a great deal of something in the *composition* likely enough to puzzle, and consequently to mislead the Understanding. . . . It is strange . . . that it should now be a question, whether *Falstaff* is or is not a man of Courage; and whether we do in fact contemn him for the want, or respect him for the possession of that quality: And yet I believe the reader will find that he has by no means decided this question, even for himself.—If then it should turn out that this difficulty has arisen out of the Art of *Shakespeare,* who has contrived to make secret Impressions upon us of Courage, and to preserve those Impressions in favour of a character which was to be held up for sport and laughter on account of actions of apparent Cowardice and dishonour, we shall have less occasion to wonder, as *Shakespeare* is a Name which contains All of Dramatic artifice and genius. . . . Perhaps, after all, the *real* character of *Falstaff* may be different from his *apparent* one; and possibly this difference between reality and appearance, whilst it accounts at once for our liking and our censure, may be the true point of humour in the character, and the source of all our laughter and delight. We may chance to find, if we will but examine a little into the nature of those circumstances which have accidentally involved him, that he was intended to be drawn as a character of much Natural courage and

From *An Essay on the Dramatic Character of Sir John Falstaff* (1777) reprinted from *Eighteenth Century Essays on Shakespeare,* ed. D. Nichol Smith (Glasgow, 1903), pp. 218–231. Title added by Ed.

resolution; and be obliged thereupon to repeal those decisions which may have been made upon the credit of some general tho' unapplicable propositions. . . . With respect to every infirmity, except that of Cowardice, we must take him as at the period in which he is represented to us. If we see him dissipated, fat,—it is enough;—we have nothing to do with his youth, when he might perhaps have been modest, chaste, *"and not an Eagle's talon in the waist."* But *Constitutional Courage* extends to a man's whole life, makes a part of his nature, and is not to be taken up or deserted like a mere Moral quality. It is true, there is a Courage founded upon *principle*, or rather a principle independent of Courage, which will sometimes operate in spite of nature; a principle which prefers death to shame, but which always refers itself, in conformity to its own nature, to the prevailing modes of honour, and the fashions of the age.—But Natural courage is another thing: It is independent of opinion; It adapts itself to occasions, preserves itself under every shape, and can avail itself of flight as well as of action. . . . That Courage which is founded in nature and constitution, *Falstaff*, as I presume to say, possessed;—but I am ready to allow that the principle already mentioned, so far as it refers to reputation only, began with every other Moral quality to lose its hold on him in his old age; that is, at the time of life in which he is represented to us; a period, as it should seem, approaching to *seventy*.—The truth is that he had drollery enough to support himself in credit without the point of honour, and had address enough to make even the preservation of his life a point of drollery. The reader knows I allude . . . to his fictitious death in the battle of Shrewsbury. This incident is generally construed to the disadvantage of *Falstaff*: It is a transaction which bears the external marks of Cowardice. . . . Whatever there may be of dishonour in *Falstaff*'s conduct, he neither does or says any thing on this occasion which indicates terror or disorder of mind: On the contrary, this very act is a proof of his having all his wits about him, and is a stratagem, such as it is, not improper for a buffoon, whose fate would be singularly hard, if he should not be allowed to avail himself of his Character when it might serve him in most stead. We must remember, in extenuation, that the executive, the destroying hand of *Douglas* was over him: *"It was time to counterfeit, or that hot termagant Scot had paid him scot and lot too."* He had but one choice; he was obliged to pass thro' the ceremony of dying either in jest or in earnest; and we shall not be surprized at the event, when we remember his propensities to the former.—Life (and especially the life of *Falstaff*) might be a jest; but he could see no joke whatever in dying: To be chopfallen was, with him, to lose both life and character together: He saw the point of honour, as well as every thing else, in ridiculous lights, and began to renounce its tyranny. . . . The Courage of *Falstaff* is my Theme: And no passage will I spare from which any thing can be inferred as relative to this point. . . . And so with that attention to truth and candour which ought to accompany even our lightest amusements I proceed to offer such proof as the case will admit, that *Courage* is a part of *Falstaff's Character*, that it belonged to his constitution, and was manifest in the conduct and practice of his whole life.

A. C. BRADLEY

The Rejection of Falstaff

The bliss of freedom gained in humour is the essence of Falstaff. His humour is not directed only or chiefly against obvious absurdities; he is the enemy of everything that would interfere with his ease, and therefore of anything serious, and especially of everything respectable and moral. For these things impose limits and obligations, and make us the subjects of old father antic the law, and the categorical imperative, and our station and its duties, and conscience, and reputation, and other people's opinion, and all sorts of nuisances. I say he is therefore their enemy; but I do him wrong; to say that he is their enemy implies that he regards them as serious and recognises their power, when in truth he refuses to recognise them at all. They are to him absurd; and to reduce a thing *ad absurdum* is to reduce it to nothing and to walk

From *Oxford Lectures on Poetry* by A. C. Bradley, pp. 262–268.

about free and rejoicing. This is what Falstaff does with all the would-be serious things of life, sometimes only by his words, sometimes by his actions too. He will make truth appear absurd by solemn statements, which he utters with perfect gravity and which he expects nobody to believe; and honour, by demonstrating that it cannot set a leg, and that neither the living nor the dead can possess it; and law, by evading all the attacks of its highest representative and almost forcing him to laugh at his own defeat; and patriotism, by filling his pockets with the bribes offered by competent soldiers who want to escape service, while he takes in their stead the halt and maimed and the gaol-birds; and duty, by showing how he labours in his vocation—of thieving; and courage, alike by mocking at his own capture of Colvile * and gravely claiming to have killed Hotspur; and war, by offering the Prince his bottle of sack when he is asked for a sword; and religion, by amusing himself with remorse at odd times when he has nothing else to do; and the fear of death, by maintaining perfectly untouched, in the face of imminent peril and even while he *feels* the fear of death, the very same power of dissolving it in persiflage that he shows when he sits at ease in his inn. These are the wonderful achievements which he performs, not with the sourness of a cynic, but with the gaiety of a boy. And, therefore, we praise him, we laud him, for he offends none but the virtuous, and denies that life is real or life is earnest, and delivers us from the oppression of such nightmares, and lifts us into the atmosphere of perfect freedom.

. . . Falstaff is neither a liar nor a coward in the usual sense, like the typical cowardly boaster of comedy. He tells his lies either for their own humour, or on purpose to get himself into a difficulty. He rarely expects to be believed, perhaps never. He abandons a statement or contradicts it the moment it is made. There is scarcely more intent in his lying than in the humorous exaggerations which he pours out in soliloquy just as much as when others are by. Poins and the Prince understand this in part. You see them waiting eagerly to convict him, not that they may really put him to shame, but in order to enjoy the greater lie that will swallow up the less. But their sense of humour lags behind his. Even the Prince seems to accept as half-serious that remorse of his which passes so suddenly into glee at the idea of taking a purse, and his request to his friend to bestride him if he should see him down in the battle. . . .

* *2 Henry IV*, IV, iii. Ed.

Again, the attack of the Prince and Poins on Falstaff and the other thieves on Gadshill is contrived, we know, with a view to the incomprehensible lies it will induce him to tell. But when, more than rising to the occasion, he turns two men in buckram into four, and then seven, and then nine, and then eleven, almost in a breath, I believe they partly misunderstand his intention, and too many of his critics misunderstand it altogether. Shakespeare was not writing a mere farce. It is preposterous to suppose that a man of Falstaff's intelligence would utter these gross, palpable, open lies with the serious intention to deceive, or forget that, if it was too dark for him to see his own hand, he could hardly see that the three misbegotten knaves were wearing Kendal green. No doubt, if he *had* been believed, he would have been hugely tickled at it, but he no more expected to be believed than when he claimed to have killed Hotspur. Yet he is supposed to be serious even then. Such interpretations would destroy the poet's whole conception. . . .

That Falstaff sometimes behaves in what we should generally call a cowardly way is certain; but that does not show that he was a coward; and if the word means a person who feels painful fear in the presence of danger, and yields to that fear in spite of his better feelings and convictions, then assuredly Falstaff was no coward. . . .

"Well," it will be answered, "but he ran away on Gadshill; and when Douglas attacked him he fell down and shammed dead." Yes, I am thankful to say, he did. For of course he did not want to be dead. He wanted to live and be merry. And as he had reduced the idea of honour *ad absurdum*, had scarcely any self-respect, and only a respect for reputation as a means of life, naturally he avoided death when he could do so without a ruinous loss of reputation, and (observe) with the satisfaction of playing a colossal practical joke. For *that* after all was his first object. If his one thought had been to avoid death he would not have faced Douglas at all, but would have run away as fast as his legs could carry him; and unless Douglas had been one of those exceptional Scotchmen who have no sense of humour, he would never have thought of pursuing so ridiculous an object as Falstaff running. So that . . . Poins is right when he thus distinguishes Falstaff from his companions in robbery: "For two of them, I know them to be as true-bred cowards as ever turned back; and for the third, if he fight longer than he sees reason, I'll forswear arms." And the event justifies this distinction. For it is exactly thus that, according to the original stage-direction, Falstaff behaves when Henry and Poins attack him and the others. The rest run away at once; Falstaff, here as afterwards with Douglas, fights for a blow or two, but, finding himself deserted and outmatched, runs away also. Of course. He saw no reason to stay. *Any* man who had risen superior to all serious motives would have run away. But it does not follow that he would run from mere fear, or be, in the ordinary sense, a coward.[1]

[1] It is to be regretted, however, that in carrying his guts away so nimbly he "roared for mercy"; for I fear we have no ground for rejecting Henry's statement to that effect, and I do not see my way to adopt the suggestion . . . that Falstaff spoke the truth when he swore that he knew Henry and Poins as well as he that made them.

E. E. STOLL

Falstaff as Coward

Falstaff's cowardice appears still more clearly when the Gadshill incident is viewed in detail. There is the testimony of the Prince, Poins, and Falstaff himself. Four times the Prince flatly calls him coward to his face. The only time he attempts to deny it—on Gadshill—the Prince replies, "Well, we leave that to the proof"; and it comes speedily. Clearer nothing could be: the question is raised, and Falstaff's roaring and running away the next moment are the all-sufficient answer. . . .

Poins's estimate of Falstaff's character just before this has been subjected to the most undramatic and hair-splitting comment imaginable:—"Well, for two of them, I know them to be as truebred cowards as ever turned back; and for the third, if he fight longer than he sees reason, I'll forswear arms" (I, ii, 158). "As

From *Shakespeare Studies: Historical and Comparative in Method* (New York, 1927), pp. 415–424. Some footnotes have been omitted and those included renumbered.

for the third," echoes Morgann, solemnly; "as if the name of this veteran would have excited too strongly the ideas of courage and resistance." "What stronger evidence can we require," he cries, "than that Poins, the ill-disposed . . . than that this very Poins should not venture to put down Falstaff in the list of cowards?" Humour or the understanding of humour, particularly of that ancient Anglo-Saxon heritage the humour of understatement, which is the Englishman's possession to this hour, seems, as from most of us when saddled and ridden by a theory, to have been frequently withheld from this gifted man,—by a strange irony, the accepted chief expositor, now for a hundred and fifty years, of the foremost humorous character in literature.

Certainly the latter half of Poins's sentence contains no praise, however faint—the whole tone and context of the passage shows this; moreover, it is followed by the remark, still more explicit, about "the incomprehensible lies that this same fat rogue will tell us,—how thirty at least he fought with, and what wards, what blows, what extremities he endured," etc.—"a prediction," Morgann, faithfully but mournfully adds "unfortunately fulfilled, even beyond the letter of it,—a completion more incident, perhaps, to the predictions of a malice than of affection." What could Shakespeare have done with an audience of Morganns? Here or anywhere Poins, or Shakespeare himself in a comedy, is not the man to distinguish between conduct and character, principles and constitution, a skulker and a courageously consistent Epicurean; and the speech in question is a simple truth gilded with a pleasantry. Falstaff himself admits that he was "a coward on instinct," not on principle; and at Shrewsbury says to himself, "I fear the shot here,"—"I am afraid of this Percy," and makes his words good by stabbing the corpse. Against such an interpretation Morgann and his followers murmur, bidding us remember his age and his peculiar philosophy, the corrupting example of his associates, the odds against him, and the suddenness of the assault; but on the Elizabethan comic stage, or any popular stage, where of course there are no relentings towards cowardice . . . nobody confesses to fear but a coward, a child, or a woman. All Shakespeare's cowards, like his villains, bear their names written in their foreheads, and his true men . . . neither know nor understand what fear or dismay is. But the main objection to such considerations, as indeed to the general scheme and tenor of the prevailing Shakespeare criticism, is, as Stack * well says, "its excessive refinement." "Dramatic characters [particularly in comedy, I would add] are not drawn for speculative ingenious men in their closets but for mankind at large." Such extenuations, the motives of malice attributed to "that Poins" and Lancaster, and the "secret impressions" of valour,—all are inferences, "fine-spun deductions," to use Stack's phrase; and the like things in comedy do not count because they have not "a strong and immediate influence. . . ."

Nowhere is it more evident how little Morgann regarded dramatic method and stage-craft than at this early moment in the episode:

PETO. How many be there of them?
GADSHILL. Some eight or ten.
FAL. 'Zounds, will they not rob us?
PRINCE. What, a coward, Sir John Paunch?
FAL. Indeed, I am not John of Gaunt, etc.—(II, ii)

This is found to be hardly more of a confession on his part than the Prince's remark to Poins on his own as they plan their trick in the second scene of Act I: "Yea, but I doubt they will be too hard for us." The latter remark is casual or else made in mockery, but in either case it is meant only to call forth Poins's comment (quoted above) on their companions' timorous natures; whereas this speech of Falstaff's is uttered after the limelight has been turned full upon him—the audience has been apprized of his cowardice, the business is afoot, and the booty at hand. Thus everything has been nicely calculated to give his abrupt exclamation full comic value and "bring down the house," as would be seen by anybody who on principle had not already blurred dramatic perspective and jumbled "values." And Falstaff's retort is, as Stack rightly observes, a witty evasion, an effort to turn the laugh called forth by his timorousness;—not, as Morgann would have it, a hint at his discreetly courageous character, thrown out for the behoof of the audience.

That Falstaff is not dissembling is still more evident from the management of the ensuing incident, in the same scene, and of the scene at the tavern. In the brief and fleeting moment of glory immediately after the robbery of the travellers he calls Poins and

* Richard Stack, author of *Examination of Morgann's Essay on the Character of Falstaff* (1788). Ed.

the Prince cowards, and swaggers. Now the coward charging the brave with cowardice, like the coward boasting of his courage, is a perennial situation, on the stage or off it. . . . Even in our time an audience knows as well what it means when such a charge comes from the lips of one already discredited as when a drunken man declares that he is not drunk and that others are. To clinch the business, immediately upon his words follows the ironical dramatic reversal and traditional comic situation of the robbery of the robber . . . and the fat rogue roaring and running off. What dunce in the audience would now fail to follow the drift? Morgann may think it not roaring if he pleases, for particulars in a play cannot be verified as in a history; but it is difficult to conceive how Poins could now say to the Prince on Gadshill, "How the fat rogue roared" unless he had just been doing it; or the Prince afterwards in Eastcheap could cast it up to Falstaff in the presence of all who heard him, without fear of denial—"roar'd for mercy, and still run and roar'd," and not like a lion, either, but "as ever I heard bull-calf." But to Morgann of course the play is not the whole story!

And when Falstaff with his craven crew, first bursts in, sweating to death, upon Prince Hal and Poins at the Boar's Head, he still cries out on cowards, again and again, as he drinks. Then, once he has caught his breath, come the "incomprehensible lies" of the men in buckram and Kendal green, the acting out of the combat—"wards," "blows," and "extremities"—and the swindling exhibition of battered buckler, bloodied garments, and hacked sword. And just like the coward denying his cowardice and the drunken man denying his drunkenness, he now cries, "I tell thee what, Hal, if I tell thee a lie, spit in my face, call me horse!" "Wilt thou believe me, Hal?" he says on a like occasion, again much misdoubting in his bluster; "three or four bonds apiece and a seal ring of my grandfather's." We have seen him fighting, we know his "old ward" and how he "bore his point," and at these we laugh as at the "eight-penny matter" (for so the Prince will have it) of the bonds and ring. Even if we should suspect him of saying it all for fun, on the spur of the moment, we now learn from blushing Bardolph of "his monstrous devices"—that like the cowardly Dericke of the *Famous Victories of Henry V* [1] he had persuaded them all to tickle

[1] 1585–88. As is well known, Shakespeare was acquainted with the play, and drew from it the traits of Falstaff's cowardice, thievishness, and loose living, the touches of repentance and sanctimoniousness, and his friendship with Prince Hal.

their noses with spear-grass, and to hack their swords with their daggers. As the precious coward Parolles, who thinks also of cutting his garments and breaking his Spanish sword, plans to do, he had given himself some hurts, though "slight" ones, and now swears he had "got them in exploit." [2] Here are all the conventional and traditional tricks of cowardice, and on the exposure of cowardice the comic effect of the scene depends as much as on the reproof of the lies. . . . in the cowardice lies the whole point of twitting him with his boasting lies and excuses;—if in fun Falstaff had run away or lied what fun would there be in confuting him?—but twice in the scene the Prince calls him coward into the bargain, and casts it up to him that he had "hacked his sword and then said it was in fight." [3] "What a slave art thou!" Hal says truly.

Nor by his shifts and evasions, "I knew ye" and "on instinct," does he come off safe and sound. Throughout the rest of the scene, and even in Part II, he and his companions in cowardice are twitted with them.[4] It is the Prince that does the twitting, and the Prince should know. "No more of that, Hal," cries the fat knight, "an thou lovest me"; and that is not the tone of triumph. In the midst of this same scene his cowardice breaks out spontaneously anew. "Zounds," snarls Poins, "an ye call me coward, I'll stab thee." And the knight of Eastcheap sidles off, comically enough giving the words just on his lips the lie: "I call thee coward! I'll see thee damned ere I call thee coward; but I would give a thousand pound I could run as fast as thou canst. . . . Call you that backing of your friends? A plague upon such backing! give me them that will face me!" Just so he falters, and his bluster rings loud but hollow, when in Part II the servant of the Chief-Justice begs leave to tell him that he lies in his throat. "*I* give thee leave to tell me so! If thou gettest any leave of me, hang me!" Calls he this the facing of his foes? He shouts as he retreats, he barks as he runs, he jokes and quibbles to cover up his cowardice and confusion.

Through the rest of the play his cowardice is, as Morgann drolly confesses, still "thrust forward and pressed upon our notice." A coward Shakespeare will have him if Morgann won't. Even now,

[2] See *All's Well,* IV, i, for all these details; cf. Pistol, *Henry V,* V, i, 93–94;

And patches will I get unto these cudgell'd scars,
And swear I got them in the Gallia wars.

[3] II, iv, 237, "Coward"; also lines 219, 441.

[4] II, iv, 254–331.

even after Gadshill, the dramatist, if so he had intended to do, might have let Falstaff retrieve himself, by actions at least, and not merely by wit or ingenuity, and induce the world to believe, what without deeds the world to believe would be little inclined —that his retreat was genuinely strategic, that he ran away only to fight another day, that his cowardice had been a pretence or a venial and momentary aberration. Instead, it is what Morgann will not have it be—if not "constitutional," at least habitual. When he hears the news of the uprising, he ingenuously asks the Prince whether he is not horribly afeard, and in reply is told that the Prince lacks some of his instinct. When told by the Prince that he had been procured a charge of foot, he cries, "Well, God be thanked for these rebels, they offend none but the virtuous. I laud them, I praise them." Like a Stoic, in his own character he finds his consolation. And when he is ordered off to the North he wishes this tavern were his drum; and on the eve of the fray whimpers, "I would 'twere bed-time, Hal, and all well," and then says his catechism of dishonour. Standing by as Prince Hal and Hotspur come together, he proves to be as good at encouraging others to fight as the white-livered Moron and Panurge.[5] Then he falls flat and feigns death as clowns and cowards did in the hour of danger, not in England only but in contemporary Germany, Spain, and Italy; and above all sets the seal on his cowardice by the dastardly blow and by hatching the scheme to take the honour of killing Hotspur to himself. "I'll swear I killed him," he says, "nothing confutes me but eyes and nobody sees me"; and could anything more effectually contradict the opinion that he "stood on the ground of natural courage only and common sense, and renounced that grinning idol of military zealots, honour," than his undertaking, like the pitiful poltroons, Pistol, Parolles, and Bessus,* to filch "bright honour," which the man fallen at his feet had boldly plucked? Men of principle, scorning glory, do not snatch at other men's. Such wreaking of one's self on a dead body, moreover, is, like his "playing possum," one of the established *lazzi* ** of the coward on the stage. . . .

[5] *Princesse d'Élide,* I, iii, intermède, where, perched in a tree, Moron urges on the archers to kill the bear; and Rabelais, II, chap. 29, where Panurge cheers on his master.

* Bessus, a cowardly captain in Beaumont and Fletcher's play *A King and No King.* Ed.

** *Lazzi,* the farcical tricks of stage comedians. Ed.

in Shakespeare's time clowns played pranks on corpses both in England and Germany. Here in the battle, then, is a little heap of *lazzi*, or bits of "business," all stamped as those of a coward, not only intrinsically, but by immemorial custom; and it is difficult to see how Shakespeare could have effaced that impression had he tried.

J. W. DRAPER

Falstaff as an Elizabethan Soldier

Since the sources of *Henry IV* give only the slightest suggestion of Falstaff's character, the present writer proposes to seek his prototype in contemporary society; and, to this end, he presents two hypotheses: that actual Elizabethan conditions furnish ample analogies for the actions, and so for the character, of Falstaff; and that the audience, knowing such actions and such types of character in daily life, would see them, not as dramatic conventions, but as a holding of the mirror up to nature, and so judge them, not with nice ethical reasonings, as Bradley supposes, but in a rough-and-ready fashion, very much as they judged such people and such actions in the world around them.

Shakespeare clearly intended Sir John Falstaff to appear as an army officer; he is shown on a peace footing, with his soldier-comrades and his lady-loves, his food and lodging, his brawling and drinking, his chronic insolvency and his means of evading its consequences; he appears likewise at war, in preparation and recruiting, in military peculation, in actual battle, and in the dubious rewards of victory. Practically all the common elements of a soldier's life are involved, and, in a sense, they comprise practically all that Falstaff does in the three plays in which he appears. Logically then, one should study his character as an army officer, rather

From "Sir John Falstaff," *Review of English Studies*, VII (October 1932), 414–424. Reprinted by permission of the author and The Clarendon Press. Footnotes have been omitted. Title added by Ed.

than in any other group of Elizabethan society; and the following paragraphs propose to show how closely his behaviour squares with the actual doings of officers as depicted in the military books and other literature descriptive of the times.

Army life was on a very low plane, partly because the organisation and the method of recruiting were changing from the feudal to the modern professionalised system, and partly because Renaissance society, without the organised capital of modern industrialism, could hardly finance this new system which political necessity imposed. Soldiers, in consequence, were very little and very irregularly paid; and, as no provision was made for them in peace time or in old age, they often had to live by their wits and turn professional bully or downright highwayman; as Harman says ". . . the hardiest soldiers . . . if they escape all hazards, and return home again, if they be without relief of their friends they will surely desperately rob and steal." * This situation created a vicious circle; officers got their positions by favouritism—very much as Hal procured for Falstaff a "charge of foot"—and sometimes even by actual sale, and mis-used their commissions to enrich themselves. Therefore, men of probity avoided military service; and, therefore, the profession, "dispised of every man," sank lower and lower in the general esteem; Doll Tearsheet was voicing a general sentiment when she declared that captains such as Bardolph made "the word captain odious." Under such conditions, the few chivalrous exceptions, such as Sidney, were all the more conspicuous; and this decadence of army life explains why the worldly-wise Bacon advised Essex to seek civil rather than military preferment.

During war-time, the two main types of peculation practised by captains had to do with recruiting and with the padding of muster-rolls; and Falstaff seems to have been guilty of both.

. . . officers stole from their soldiers; and, even at that, their extravagant and disordered lives sometimes obliged them to pawn their own arms and come into battle, as Falstaff did, without full equipment. They stole the soldiers' pay, and even the money for their food; but the most lucrative form of peculation was the padding of muster-rolls, accomplished by enrolling one soldier in two different "bands" so that the Captain might draw pay for two, or by neglecting to report the dead and missing and so pocket-

* Thomas Harman, author of *A Caveat or Warening for Commen Cursetors* (1573). Ed.

ing their wages. This drawing of "dead pay," as it was called, made it profitable for a commander to lose in battle as many of his men as possible; and Digges declares that some would actually lead soldiers into "some desperate unfeasible Service . . . to have their throats cut, and then, having choice horses to save himself by flight, and his confederate Favorites, with the pay of the dead they may banquet and riot their fill." * Thus Falstaff, in spite of his cowardice, led his men to a place of danger so that "not three" of his "hundred and fifty" were left alive; for, indeed, as he says, he feared the "shot" (tavern-reckonings) of London even more than he did the "shot" of battle; and, knowing this abuse, surely an Elizabethan audience would infer that he had led his men to slaughter so that he might steal their "dead pay." Such were the means by which Bradley's "humorist of genius" attained his "godlike freedom."

If the officer on active service had his financial problems and his dubious ways of meeting them, the officer in peace time was no better off. The rigid system of nobility, clergy and guilds grouped the upper classes into sharply defined, closed corporations; and the widespread vagabondage of the day shows how little was the opportunity of the casual intruder. Society was too tightly organised to assimilate the numbers of soldiers or even of officers who returned from the wars; and the government assumed no responsibility. These outcast soldiers repaired to London, and lived a riotous life, very like that of Falstaff and his crew, sometimes begging from their friends, sometimes robbing as petty thieves, like the well-named Nym, or as highwaymen like Falstaff, and sometimes turning a doubtful penny by acting as "companion" to some wild young nobleman or as bully for some harlot such as Doll. . . .

Surely Shakespeare wrote the Falstaff comedies neither to make his hero the expression of some fine philosophy nor to concoct a clever compound of dramatic convention, although some of his characteristics may come from the tradition of the *miles gloriosus*. He seems rather to have aimed at contemporary realism with a lambent play of laughter. Not only Falstaff but his confederates are soldier-types of the period: Nym, whose very name suggests his "taking" ways; Bardolph, who carried his lantern in his nose; and Pistol, whose fantastic elegancies of speech bespoke a bowing acquaintance with the court; and Falstaff himself, who seems to

* Thomas Digges, *Foure Paradoxes, or Politique Discourses* (1604), pp. 19–20, 48. Ed.

represent the old military aristocracy run to seed, the foil of Henry V, in whom the Elizabethan saw epitomised the Golden Age of valour. Perhaps in Falstaff and his crew Shakespeare wished to satirise, by contrast with this Golden Age, the decadence of his own times, much lamented by Riche and other military writers of the day; but his touch is too light for satire, and his attitude too genial; and so the present writer would rather think that he aimed merely to depict men and things as they are, "to show virtue her own feature, scorn her own image, and the very age and body of the time his form and pressure."

FRANZ ALEXANDER

A Note on Falstaff

He [Falstaff] represents the deep infantile layers of the personality, the simple innocent wish to live and enjoy life. He has no taste for abstract values like honor or duty and no ambition. Man is only partially social. One part of his personality remains individualistic and resents the restrictions of social life and just these restrictions, especially if they go further than one can tolerate them, mobilize all the destructive instincts of man's nature such as discontent, ill spirit and a negative attitude toward the environment. This is the explanation of the popular belief that people who like to eat and drink well—that is to say, who treat the animal in themselves with consideration—are more amiable and less malicious. The opposite is true of the ascetic self-restricting characters often found among political fanatics and exponents of social doctrines for which they sacrifice their lives. Like Robespierre, the fanatic schoolmaster, under the guise of fighting for humanitarian ideals they can take revenge for all their self-imposed restrictions in destroying their opponents en masse. It is seldom difficult to recognize under the thin surface of their rationalizations,

From *Psychoanalytic Quarterly,* II (October 1933), 592–606. Reprinted by permission of the author and the publisher.

their real motives: hatred and revenge. Hotspur unquestionably belongs to this category of fanatic haters. The king offers him full consideration of all his complaints but what he seeks essentially is a fight. The conditions which he proposes to the king are unacceptable, and even his friends call him drunk with fury. He scarcely can await the battle: "Let the hours be short 'til fields and blows and groans applaud our sport."

Hotspur is the exponent of destruction, but destruction which serves not entirely selfish but also collective, that is, caste, interests. Falstaff is the personification of the wholly self-centered pleasure-seeking principle. Although he represents the opposite of destruction, the principle of life, libido, it is the most primitive manifestation of libido, the primary self-centered, narcissistic libido of the child which he stands for.

Prince Henry in the process of maturing must overcome both of these principles. When he kills Hotspur on the battlefield, he overcomes symbolically his own destructive tendency. In killing Hotspur, the arch-enemy of his father, he overcomes his own aggressions against his parent. But he must overcome also the Falstaff in himself if he is to become a fully balanced adult. In the history of the metamorphosis of Prince Henry, Shakespeare dramatically describes the characteristic course of the development of the male. There are two difficult emotional problems which must be solved by everyone in the course of his development; the first is the fixation to the early pregenital forms of instinctual life which expresses itself in oral receptiveness and narcissistic self-adoration. This old fellow, Sir John Falstaff, is a masterful dramatization of such an early emotional attitude. The second difficulty to be overcome is the hatred and jealousy directed against the father. Hotspur, the rebel who strives against the life of the king, is the personification of these patricidal tendencies. In the play, these inner processes find an externalized dramatic expression. After Prince Henry has overcome these two inner—in the drama, external—enemies he becomes an ideal king.

J. I. M. STEWART

The Birth and Death of Falstaff

If Shakespeare does indeed succeed in making the rejection [of Falstaff] palatable to persons adequately aware of traditional matters lying behind the play, it is yet in the theatre that he does so, for that the thing continues to *read* uncomfortably after all Dover Wilson has to say I believe there will be few to deny. What does this mean? It means that although Shakespeare doubtless relied on certain contemporary attitudes to Riot and the like, he relied even more on something perennially generated in the consciousness or disposition of an audience in a theatre—whether they belong to Elizabethan times or to our own. And it is here that I would knit the debate on Falstaff to the theme of the present book. For what I have tried to urge is simply this: that in the interpretation of Shakespeare a study of the psychology of poetic drama (which leads us to understand his *medium*) is at least as important as a study of the contemporary climate of opinion (which gives simply *conditions* under which he worked).

The second point concerns the emphatic and wonderful account in *Henry* V of the death of Falstaff. It is all very well for Dover Wilson to point to the promise of more Falstaff made in the Epilogue to *2 Henry IV* and infer that the subsequent death was a matter of mere theatrical convenience. But surely the Epilogue to *Henry IV* is dramatically altogether less authoritative than the account of Falstaff's passing in the later play; and what Shakespeare there wrote appears to me (because it is so wonderful) much less like an expedient dictated by changes in personnel in his company than the issue of his reflections on the inner significance of what had happened at the close of the earlier drama. "The King has kild his heart," says Mistress Quickly as Falstaff lies dying. "The King hath

From *Character and Motive in Shakespeare* (New York, 1947), pp. 135–139, published by Longmans, Green and Company, Inc., and reprinted by their permission. Footnotes have been omitted. Ed.

run bad humors on the Knight," says Nym, and Pistol at once responds: "*Nym*, thou hast spoke the right, his heart is fracted and corroborate." None of these worthies would cut much of a figure in a witness-box; nevertheless there is no mistaking the dramatic function of the three consenting voices. The truth of the matter is summed here; there follows the new king's dexterous, necessary but none too pleasant entrapping of Cambridge, Scroope and Gray; then comes the tremendous account of Falstaff's end—and after that we are set for Agincourt and the regeneration and triumph of England. It is of set purpose, then, that the rejection of Falstaff is so resounding, so like a killing. And the reverberation of that purpose sounds here in *Henry V*. What is it? There is an allegorical purpose, Dover Wilson says, and with this I agree. But I think, too, that among the "notions and associations . . . gone out of mind" embodied in this "composite myth which had been centuries amaking" there conceivably lies something deeper, something which belongs equally with drama and with magic.

When Shakespeare makes Falstaff die "ev'n just betweene Twelve and One, ev'n at the turning o' th' Tyde," he is touching a superstition, immemorial not only along the east coast of England from Northumberland to Kent but in many other parts of the world too—one shared by Dickens's Mr. Peggotty (who speaks of it expressly) and the Haidas on the Pacific coast of North America. But there is more of magic about Falstaff than this; and Dover Wilson, whom the editing of Shakespeare has schooled in a fine awareness of the reverberations of English words, is more than once well on the scent. "How doth the Martlemas, your Master?" Poins asks Bardolph. And Dover Wilson comments:

> Martlemas, or the feast of St. Martin, on 11 November, was in those days of scarce fodder the season at which most of the beasts had to be killed off and salted for the winter, and therefore the season for great banquets of fresh meat. Thus it had been for centuries, long before the coming of Christianity. In calling him a "Martlemas" Poins is at once likening Falstaff's enormous proportions to the prodigality of fresh-killed meat which the feast brought, and acclaiming his identity with Riot and Festivity in general.

Falstaff, in fact, is the "sweet beef," "the roasted Manning-tree ox with the pudding in his belly," who reigns supreme on the board of the Boar's Head in Eastcheap—"a London tavern . . . almost certainly even better known for good food than for good drink." There is thus from the first a symbolical side to his vast and genuine individuality; and again and again the imagery in which he is described likens him to a whole larder of "fat meat."

> "Call in Ribs, call in Tallow" is Hal's cue for Falstaff's entry in the first great Boar's Head scene; and what summons to the choicest feast in comedy could be more apt? For there is the noblest of English dishes straightaway: Sir John as roast Sir Loin-of-Beef, gravy and all.

Is it not—I find myself asking—as if the "brawn," Sir John, "the sow that hath overwhelmed all her litter but one," were some vast creature singled out from the herd and dedicated to a high festival indeed? But such festivals commemorate more than the need to reduce stock against a winter season. They commemorate a whole mythology of the cycle of the year, and of sacrifices offered to secure a new fertility in the earth.

Now, anthropologists are always telling us of countries gone waste and barren under the rule of an old, impotent and guilty king, who must be ritually slain and supplanted by his son or another before the saving rains come bringing purification and regeneration to the land. Is not Henry IV in precisely the situation of this king? Dover Wilson avers that it is so, without any thought of magical implication:

> . . . his reign and all his actions are overhung with the consciousness . . . of personal guilt . . . a fact that Shakespeare never misses an opportunity of underlining. . . . We see him first at the beginning of act 3 crushed beneath the disease that afflicts his body and the no less grievous diseases that make foul the body of his kingdom.

Perhaps, then, we glimpse here a further reason why the rejection of Falstaff is inevitable—not merely traditionally and moralistically inevitable but symbolically inevitable as well. And this may be why, when in the theatre, we do not really rebel against the rejection; why we find a fitness too in its being sudden and catastrophic. As long as we are in the grip of drama it is profoundly fit that Hal, turning king and clergyman at once, should run bad humours on the knight, should kill his heart. For the killing carries something of the ritual suggestion, the obscure *pathos*, of death in tragedy.

I suggest that Hal, by a displacement common enough in the evolution of ritual, kills Falstaff instead of killing the king, his father. In a sense Falstaff *is* his father; certainly is a "father-substitute" in the psychologist's word; and this makes the theory of a vicarious sacrifice the more colourable. All through the play there is a strong implicit parallelism between Henry Bolingbroke and his policies and Falstaff and *his* policies; and at one point in the play the two fathers actually, as it were, fuse (like Leonardo's two mothers in his paintings of the Virgin and St. Anne), and in the Boar's Head tavern King Falstaff sits on his throne while his son Prince Henry kneels before him. And Falstaff, in standing for the old king, symbolises all the accumulated sin of the reign, all the consequent sterility of the land. But the young king draws his knife at the altar—and the heart of that grey iniquity, that father ruffian, is as fracted and corroborate as Pistol avers. Falstaff's rejection and death are very sad, but Sir James Frazer would have classed them with the Periodic Expulsion of Evils in a Material Vehicle, and discerned beneath the skin of Shakespeare's audience true brothers of the people of Leti, Moa and Lakor.

If this addition of another buried significance to the composite myth of Hal and Falstaff should seem extravagant, or an injudicious striving after Morgann's "lightness of air," let it be remembered that drama, like religious ritual, plays upon atavic impulses of the mind. All true drama penetrates through representative fiction to the condition of myth. And Falstaff is in the end the dethroned and sacrificed king, the scapegoat as well as the sweet beef. For Falstaff, so Bacchic, so splendidly with the Maenads Doll and Mistress Quickly a creature of the wine-cart and the cymbal, so fit a sacrifice (as Hal early discerns) to lard the lean, the barren earth, is of that primitive and magical world upon which all art, even if with a profound unconsciousness, draws.

BIBLIOGRAPHY

The body of comment on Shakespeare is enormous—and ever growing. In his recent bibliography, Professor G. R. Smith lists over twenty thousand references which appeared between 1936 and 1958. The Bibliography that follows is highly selective and, it is hoped, functional. The first part directs the student to those aids by which he can compile a bibliography and pursue whatever facets of Shakespeare he wishes; the second part lists works of fairly broad scope but yet with relevance to *Henry the Fourth, Part I;* and the third part lists works primarily concerned with this play.

<1>

BIBLIOGRAPHICAL AIDS

W. Jaggard, *Shakespeare Bibliography* (1911); W. Ebisch and L. Schücking, *A Shakespeare Bibliography* (1931) plus *Supplement* (1937). *The Cambridge Bibliography of English Literature* ed. F. W. Bateson (1941) plus *Supplement* (1957), ed. G. W. Watson. G. R. Smith, *A Classified Shakespeare Bibliography* 1936–1958 (1963).

Annual bibliographies are published in the following scholarly journals: *Annual Bibliography of English Language and Literature, Journal of English and Germanic Philology, PMLA, Shakespeare-Jahrbuch* (two journals with the same name, one published in Weimar, the other in Heidelberg), *Shakespeare Quarterly* (formerly *Shakespeare Association Bulletin*), *Shakespeare Survey, Studies in Philology,* and *The Year's Work in English Studies.*

STUDY AIDS

E. K. Chambers' *The Elizabethan Stage,* 4 vols. (1923), *Shakespeare: A Survey* (1925), and *William Shakespeare: A Study of Facts and Problems,* 2 vols. (1930); T. M. Parrott, *William Shakespeare: A Handbook* (1934); *A Companion to Shakespeare Studies,* ed. Harley Granville-Barker and G. B. Harrison (1934); Gerald Sanders, *A Shakespeare Primer* (1950); Peter Alexander, *Introductions to Shakespeare* (1964); Alfred Harbage, *William Shakespeare: A Reader's Guide* (1963); Davis S. Berkeley, *A Guide to Shakespeare's Comedies and Histories* (1964); Ronald Berman, *A Reader's Guide to Shakespeare's Plays: A Discursive Bibliography* (1965); and Richard J. Beck, *Shakespeare: Henry IV,* Studies in English Literature, No. 24 (1965).

<2>

THE HISTORY PLAY AND SHAKESPEARE'S "HISTORIES"

F. E. Schelling, *The English Chronicle Play* (1902); C. F. Tucker Brooke, *The Tudor Drama* (1911), chap. x; Irving Ribner, *The English History Play in the Age of Shakespeare* (1957; rev. 1965), contains an extensive bibliography.

Harold Jenkins, "Shakespeare's History Plays: 1900–1951," *Shakespeare Survey*, VI (1953), 1–15, a survey of scholarship; Irving Ribner, "The History Plays," *Seventeenth-Century Newsletter*, XIV (1964), 25, brief review of scholarship since 1946.

J. Dover Wilson, *The Fortunes of Falstaff* (1944); E. M. W. Tillyard, *Shakespeare's History Plays* (1946); Lily B. Campbell, *Shakespeare's "Histories," Mirrors of Elizabethan Policy* (1947); Paul Jorgensen, *Shakespeare's Military World* (1956); D. A. Traversi, *Shakespeare from Richard II to Henry V* (1957); Tom F. Driver, *The Sense of History in Greek and Shakespearean Drama* (1960); M. M. Reese, *The Cease of Majesty* (1961); Clifford Leech, *William Shakespeare: The Chronicles* (1962) and L. C. Knights, *William Shakespeare: The Histories* (1962), both reprinted in *Shakespeare: The Writer and His Work*, ed. Bonamy Dobree (1964); S. C. Sen Gupta, *Shakespeare's Historical Plays* (1964); and A. C. Sprague, *Shakespeare's Histories: Plays for the Stage* (1964).

Useful collections of critical essays are: R. J. Dorius, ed., *Discussions of Shakespeare's Histories: Richard II to Henry V* (1964), and Eugene M. Waith, ed., *Shakespeare: The Histories* (1965).

<3>

EDITIONS

Variorum Edition, ed. S. B. Hemingway (1936) and *Supplement*, ed. G. Blakemore Evans (1956); other editions by G. L. Kittredge (1940), J. Dover Wilson (1946), and A. R. Humphreys (1960).

† The following abbreviations have been used in the entries listed hereafter:

College English	*CE*
English Language Notes	*ELN*
Philological Quarterly	*PQ*
Review of English Studies	*RES*
Shakespeare Quarterly	*SQ*
Studies in Philology	*SP*
Texas Studies in Literature and Language	*TSLL*
University of Texas Studies in English	*TSE*

SOURCES, BACKGROUND, COMPOSITION, AND RELATED MATTERS

In addition to the editions noted above, see Geoffrey Bullough, *Narrative and Dramatic Sources of Shakespeare,* Vol. III (1960), for comprehensive coverage. More limited studies are: Alfred Hart, *Shakespeare and the Homilies* (1934); J. Dover Wilson, "The Origins and Development of Shakespeare's *Henry IV,*" *Library,* XXVI (June 1945), 2–16; Robert A. Law, "The Composition of Shakespeare's Lancastrian Trilogy," *TSLL,* III (1961), 321–327; Laurence Michel, "Shakespeare's History Plays and Daniel: An Assessment," *SP,* LII (1953), 563–567; George B. Johnston, "Camden, Shakespeare, and Young Henry Percy," *PMLA,* LXXIV (1961), 298; W. G. Bowling, "The Wild Prince Hal in Legend and Literature," *Washington University Studies,* Humanistic Series, XIII (1926), 305–334; D. T. Starnes, "More About the Prince Hal Legend," *PQ,* XV (1936), 358–366; C. L. Kingsford, *The First English Life of Henry V* (1911); and Charles Fish, "*Henry IV:* Shakespeare and Holinshed," *SP,* LXI (1964), 205–218; James Monaghan, "Falstaff and his Forebears," *SP,* XVIII (1921), 353–361; J. Dawtrey, *The Falstaff Saga* (1927); J. W. Draper, "Falstaff and the Plautine Parasite," *Classical Journal,* XXXIII (1938), 390–401; D. B. Boughner, "Vice, Braggart, and Falstaff," *Anglia,* LXXII (1954), 35–61; Bernard Spivack, "Falstaff and the Psychomachia," *SQ,* VIII (1957), 449–459; and D. B. Landt, "The Ancestry of Sir John Falstaff," *SQ,* XVII (1966), 69–76.

RECENTLY PROPOSED ANNOTATIONS

Bradbrook, M. C. " 'The Old Lad of the Castle,' " *SQ,* XI (1960), 382–385.

Evans, John X. "Shakespeare's 'Villainous Salt-Peter': The Dimensions of an Allusion." *SQ,* XV (1964), 451–454.

Fisher, Sidney T. *Letter to a University Librarian on Sir John Falstaff* (1960).

Gellert, Bridget. "The Melancholy of Moor-Ditch: A Gloss of 1 *Henry IV,* I.ii.[67–68]," *SQ,* XVIII (1967), 70–71.

Halio, Jay L. "Perfection and the Elizabethan Ideas of Conception," *ELN,* I (1964), 179–182.

Jones, William M. "The Turning of Trent in 1 *Henry IV,*" *Renaissance News,* XVII (1964), 304–307.

Perot, Ruth S. "Shakespeare's 1 *Henry IV,* III, iii, 91–97," *Explicator,* XX (December 1961), item 36.

James L. Sanderson, " 'Buff Jerkin': A Note to 1 *Henry IV,*" *ELN,* III (1966), 92–95.

CRITICAL ESSAYS

The bibliographies appended to the *Variorum* and its *Supplement* list the important studies of the play to 1955. The following list contains critical studies that have appeared since that date.

Auden, W. H. "The Fallen City: Some Reflections on Shakespeare's *Henry IV,*" *Encounter,* XIII (November 1959), 22–31 [repr. in Auden's

The Dyer's Hand (1963)]. Falstaff, the comic symbol for the supernatural order of Charity, contrasted with the temporal order of Justice symbolized by Hal.

Bass, Eben. "Falstaff and the Succession," *CE*, XXIV (1963), 502–506. *Richard II* and the *Henry IV* plays develop the theme of deposition: unlike Richard, Hal rejects Vanity symbolized in Falstaff and saves himself from deposition.

Berkeley, David, and Donald Eidson. "The Theme of *Henry IV, Part I*," *SQ*, XIX (1968), 25–31. Not the education of a prince nor a study of honor, the play's main theme is Hal's "politic concealment and exhibition of seminally transmitted virtue."

Berman, Ronald. "The Nature of Guilt in the *Henry IV* Plays," *Shakespeare Studies*, I (1965), 18–28. Images of disease reflect the guilt of Henry IV, a guilt which Hal escapes by abandoning his personal being for his role as King.

Bowden, William R. "Teaching Structure in Shakespeare: *I Henry IV*, *Twelfth Night*, and *Hamlet*," *CE*, XXIII (1962), 525–531. Suggests a way of charting each scene of the play in terms of "Political (Loyal and Rebel)" and "Comic," which clearly reveals the structure of the multilinear plot of *Henry IV, Part I*.

Bowman, Thomas D. "Two Addenda to Hotspur's Tragic Behavior," *Journal of General Education*, XVI (April 1964), 68–71. III,iii dramatizes qualities of Hotspur that will later antagonize his fellow rebels; IV,iv lays groundwork for his major strategic error in V,ii ("I cannot read them now.")

Bryant, J. A. Jr. "Prince Hal and the Ephesians," *Sewanee Review*, LXVII (1959), 204–219. Relates Hal's efforts toward "redeeming time" to Ephesians 5:15–16.

Connor, Seymour. "The Role of Douglas in *Henry IV, Part One*," *TSE*, XXVII (1948), 215–221. Accounts for the change in Hal's estimation of Douglas from "vile" to "noble."

Dickinson, Hugh. "The Reformation of Prince Hal," *SQ*, XII (1961), 33–46. The education of a prince to a realization of his duty and an acceptance of its burdens is the theme of the play.

Dorius, R. J. " 'A Little More than a Little,' " *SQ*, XI (1960), 13–26. Themes and related imagery of good husbandry and extravagance link the sequence from *Richard II* through *Henry V*, and develop a dark side to Falstaff's role in the plays.

Gross, Alan G. "The Text of Hal's First Soliloquy." *English Miscellany* XVIII (1967), 49–54. Errors by the printer have caused the difficulties of interpretation.

Hapgood, Robert. "Falstaff's Vocation," *SQ*, XVI (1965), 91–98. The unifying pattern in the *Henry IV* plays of the "robber robbed," and the illumination of thieveries in high places by those in low.

Humphreys, Arthur. "Shakespeare's Political Justice in *Richard II* and *Henry IV*," *Stratford Papers on Shakespeare* 1964, ed. Berners Jackson, pp. 30–50. These plays are concerned with something beyond the gaining and retaining of power: supporting Bolingbroke's success is something morally significant and productive of ultimate national good; behind the rebels' failure is felt a moral failing auguring national disaster should the rebels prevail.

Hunter, G. K. "*Henry IV* and the Elizabethan Two-Part Play," *RES*, V (1954), 236–248. Any unity between the two parts of *Henry IV* results from a parallel presentation of incident and not from a continuity of plot or character.

Jenkins, Harold. *The Structural Problem in Shakespeare's Henry the Fourth* (1956) [repr. in Dorius, *Discussions*, noted above]. Part I is well unified as an independent entity; Parts I and II are actually two distinct versions of a single reformation.

Jorgensen, Paul A. " 'Redeeming Time' in Shakespeare's *Henry IV*," *Tennessee Studies in Literature*, V (1960), 101–109 [repr. in Jorgensen's *Redeeming Shakespeare's Words*, (1962)]. An interpretation of Hal's much-discussed soliloquy (I,ii).

Kirschbaum, Leo. "The Demotion of Falstaff," *PQ*, XLI (1962), 58–61. Qualifying the warmth and laughter of I,ii, Hal's insistence on the consequences of crime adumbrates Falstaff's imprisonment in Part II and his lonely demise in *Henry* V.

Kris, Ernst. "Prince Hal's Conflict," *Psychoanalytic Quarterly*, XVII (1948), 487–506. A psychological analysis of Hal and the King in terms of a father-son conflict.

La Branche, Anthony. " 'If Thou Wert Sensible of Courtesy': Private and Public Virtue in *Henry IV, Part One*," *SQ*, XVII (1966), 371–382. The revelation of the play as well as of *Richard II* is that a public man's *public* worth is what ultimately matters and that his private virtues must find their significance in public value.

McGuire, Richard L. "The Play-Within-the-Play in 1 *Henry IV*," *SQ*, XVIII (1967), 47–52. Neither burlesque nor purely comic, the play-within-the-play found in II,iv is an integral part of its larger frame in that Hal realizes that it is now time for the change he had earlier predicted in I,ii.

McNamara, Anne Marie. "*Henry IV*: The King as Protagonist," *SQ*, X (1959), 423–431.

McNeir, Waldo F. "Structure and Theme in the First Tavern Scene of *Henry IV, Part One*," in *Essays on Shakespeare*, ed. G. R. Smith (1965), pp. 67–83. Although II,iv is a carefully structured miniature drama in its own right, it is integral to the whole play, echoing what has gone before and foreshadowing what is to follow.

Mitchell, Charles. "The Education of a True Prince," *Tennessee Studies in Literature*, XII (1967), 13–21.

Shaw, John. "The Staging of Parody and Parallels in 1 *Henry IV*," *Shakespeare Survey*, XX (1967), 61–73. The use of gestures and stage properties as a means of underlining parallel scenes and episodes.

Simons, Richard C. "The Clown as a Father Figure," *Psychoanalytic Review*, LII,ii (1965), 75–91. Pages 85–89 deal with Falstaff.

Tomlinson, Maggie. "*Henry IV*," *Melbourne Critical Review*, No. 6 (1963), 3–15. Falstaff as the embodiment of comic spirit, who despite his grasp on reality is the supreme illusionist.

Unger, Leonard. "Deception and Self-Deception in Shakespeare's *Henry IV*," in *The Man in the Name* (1956), pp. 3–17. The psychological disorders of the main characters reflect the social disorder of the state.

Webber, Joan. "The Renewal of the King's Symbolic Role: from *Richard II* to *Henry V*," *TSE*, IV (1962), 530–538. Properly prepared by his experiences as a prince, Henry V renews the role of kingship, expressing a view of life more meaningful than Falstaff's and in language more inspiring than his father's.

Williams, Philip. "The Birth and Death of Falstaff Reconsidered," *SQ*, VIII (1957), 359–365. Supports J. I. M. Stewart's anthropological view of Falstaff.

Wilson, Elkin Calhoun. "Falstaff—Clown and Man" in *Studies in the English Renaissance Drama*, ed. Josephine W. Bennett *et al.* (1956), pp. 345–356. Accounts for Falstaff's capacity to earn both our laughter and sympathy.

Zitner, S. P. "Anon, Anon: or a Mirror for a Magistrate," *SQ*, XIX (1968), 63–70. Caught between talking with Hal of running away from his indenture and answering Poins' summons, Francis reflects Hal's own problem—"a Prince who would and would not be king."

Long-playing records of the play have recently been made by the Marlowe Society of Cambridge University, under the direction of George Rylands, and by The Shakespeare Recording Society, under the direction of Peter Wood.